EU Regulatory Responses to Crises

EU Regulatory Responses to Crises

Adaptation or Transformation?

Edited by
DIANE FROMAGE
ADRIENNE HÉRITIER
PAUL WEISMANN

OXFORD
UNIVERSITY PRESS

OXFORD
UNIVERSITY PRESS

Great Clarendon Street, Oxford, OX2 6DP,
United Kingdom

Oxford University Press is a department of the University of Oxford.
It furthers the University's objective of excellence in research, scholarship,
and education by publishing worldwide. Oxford is a registered trade mark of
Oxford University Press in the UK and in certain other countries

Published in the United States of America by Oxford University Press
198 Madison Avenue, New York, NY 10016, United States of America

British Library Cataloguing in Publication Data
Data available

Library of Congress Control Number: 2024946922

ISBN 9780198913818

DOI: 10.1093/9780198913825.001.0001

Printed and bound by
CPI Group (UK) Ltd, Croydon, CR0 4YY

MIX
Paper | Supporting
responsible forestry
FSC® C013604
FSC
www.fsc.org

The manufacturer's authorised representative in the EU for
product safety is Oxford University Press España S.A. of el
Parque Empresarial San Fernando de Henares, Avenida de
Castilla, 2 – 28830 Madrid (www.oup.es/en).

Brief Contents

Detailed Contents

Table of Cases

CASES OF THE COURT OF JUSTICE OF THE EUROPEAN UNION

Court of Justice of the European Union

General Court

NATIONAL CASES

Germany

Table of European Union Acts

DECISIONS

DIRECTIVES

REGULATIONS

RECOMMENDATIONS

RESOLUTIONS

Abbreviations

ACER	Agency for the Cooperation of Energy Regulators
ASAP	Act in Support of Ammunition Production
BEPG	broad economic policy guideline
BRRD	Bank Recovery and Resolution Directive
BSE	bovine spongiform encephalopathy
CEAS	Common European Asylum System
CEEAG	Climate, Energy and Environmental Aid Guidelines
CFSP	Common Foreign and Security Policy
CJEU	Court of Justice of the European Union
CSDP	Common Security and Defence Policy
CSR	country-specific recommendation
DG	Directorate-General
DG COMP	Directorate-General for Competition
DG IV	Directorate-General 4 of the European Commission
EAHC	Executive Agency for Health and Consumers
EASO	European Asylum Support Office
ECA	European Court of Auditors
ECB	European Central Bank
ECDC	European Centre for Disease Control
ECSC	European Coal and Steel Community
ECSDP	European Common Security and Defence Policy
EDC	European Defence Community
EDF	European Defence Fund
EDIP	European Defence Investment Programme
EDIRPA	European Defence Industry Reinforcement through common Procurement Act
EDP	excessive deficit procedure
EEAS	European External Action Service
EEC	European Economic Community
EFB	European Fiscal Board
EFSF	European Financial Stability Facility
EFSM	European Financial Stabilisation Mechanism
EHIC	European Health Insurance Card
EIA	Environmental Impact Assessment
EIOPA	European Insurance and Occupational Pensions Authority
EMA	European Medicines Agency
EMU	Economic and Monetary Union
ENTSO-E	European Network of Transmission System Operators for Electricity
ENTSO-G	European Network of Transmission System Operators for Gas
ENVI	Committee on Environment, Public Health and Food Safety
EP	European Parliament

EPC	European Political Cooperation
EPF	European Peace Facility
ESA	European Supervisory Authority
ESFS	European System of Financial Supervision
ESM	European Stability Mechanism
ESMA	European Securities and Markets Authority
ESRB	European Systemic Risk Board
ETS	Emissions Trading System
EU	European Union
EUAA	European Union Asylum Agency
EUAM	European Union Advisory Mission
EUMAM	European Union Military Assistance Mission
EURI	European Union Recovery Instrument
FSR	Foreign Subsidies Regulation
GBER	General Block Exemption Regulation
GDP	gross domestic product
GFC	Great Financial Crisis
GHRSR	Global Human Rights Sanctions Regime
HERA	Health Emergency Preparedness and Response Authority
HR	High Representative
ICPA	International Centre for the Prosecution of the Crime of Aggression
IMF	International Monetary Fund
IRA	Inflation Reduction Act
MEP	Member of the European Parliament
MIP	macroeconomic imbalance procedure
MS	Member States
NATO	North Atlantic Treaty Organization
NGEU	NextGeneration EU
OECD	Organization for Economic Co-operation and Development
OMC	open method of coordination
OMT	Outright Monetary Transactions
PEPP	Pandemic Emergency Purchase Programme
PSC	Political and Security Committee
PSPP	Public Sector Purchase Programme
QMV	qualified majority voting
RMV	reverse majority voting
RQMV	reverse qualified majority voting
RRF	Recovery and Resilience Facility
SEA	Single European Act
SGP	Stability and Growth Pact
SRB	Single Resolution Board
SRM	Single Resolution Mechanism
SRMR	Single Resolution Mechanism Regulation
SSM	Single Supervisory Mechanism
SURE	Support to mitigate Unemployment Risks in an Emergency
TCTF	Temporary Crisis and Transition Framework
TEU	Treaty on European Union
TF	temporary framework

TFEU	Treaty on the Functioning of the European Union
TPI	Transmission Protection Instrument
TSCG	Treaty on Stability, Coordination and Governance
UK	United Kingdom
UNRWA	United Nations Relief and Works Agency
US	United States
VP	Vice-President
WEU	Western European Union
WHO	World Health Organization
WMA	World Medical Association

Contributors

Jonathan Bauerschmidt, Dr iur, is Legal Adviser, Council of the European Union, Legal Service, Brussels, Belgium, UCLouvain Saint-Louis, Brussels, Belgium. https://orcid.org/0000-0003-2691-3150

Jonas Bornemann is Assistant Professor of European Law, Rijksuniversiteit Groningen, Netherlands. https://orcid.org/0000-0001-8485-3673

Michelle Cini, PhD, is Professor of European Politics, University of Bristol, Bristol, United Kingdom. https://orcid.org/0000-0003-2602-8397

Sandra Eckert, Dr, is Chair of Comparative Politics, Institute of Political Science, Friedrich-Alexander-Universität Erlangen-Nürnberg, Germany. https://orcid.org/0000-0003-2179-1924

Andreas Eriksen, PhD, is Researcher, ARENA Centre for European Studies, University of Oslo, Norway/ Associate Professor, Oslo Metropolitan University, Norway. https://orcid.org/0000-0001-7229-6902

Michelle Everson, PhD, is Professor, Faculty of Law and Business, Birkbeck College, University of London, London, United Kingdom.

Diane Fromage is Professor of European Law, Faculty of Law and Salzburg Centre of European Union Studies, University of Salzburg, Austria. https://orcid.org/0000-0001-6911-0468

Adrienne Héritier is Emerita Professor of Political Science at the Social and Political Sciences Department, European University Institute, Florence, Italy.

Ole Windahl Pedersen is Professor of Environmental Law, Department of Law, Aarhus University, Denmark. https://orcid.org/0000-0002-9980-621X

Juan Jorge Piernas López, PhD, is Senior Lecturer of Public International Law and European Union Law at the Faculty of Law, University of Murcia, Spain. https://orcid.org/0000-0002-6515-2094

Lucia Quaglia, DPhil, is Professor of Political Science, Department of Political and Social Sciences, University of Bologna, Bologna, Italy. https://orcid.org/0000-0001-8816-0583

Kolja Raube, PhD, is Associate Professor in European Governance and EU External Action, Leuven Institute for European and International Studies, KU Leuven, Leuven, Belgium. https://orcid.org/0000-0002-6545-6995

Magnus G. Schoeller is Researcher, Department of Political Science, University of Vienna, Austria. https://orcid.org/0000-0002-5826-0900

Daniel Thym, Dr LLM, is Professor of Public, European, and International Law and Managing Director of the Research Centre Immigration and Asylum Law, University of Konstanz, Germany. https://orcid.org/0000-0003-0361-6719

Paul Weismann is Associate Professor of European Law, Faculty of law and Salzburg Centre of European Union Studies, University of Salzburg, Austria. https://orcid.org/0000-0002-4414-3586

1

Introduction

The Crisis-induced Development of EU Rule-making

Diane Fromage, Adrienne Héritier**, and Paul Weismann****

That the European Union (EU) has found itself in a continuous crisis mode since the latest revision of its Treaties in late 2009 has become a truism by now.[1] However, this does not necessarily mean that the EU itself is in a state of crisis, that is, that it is in a dire situation that requires the adoption of urgent new measures. In reacting to crises such as the Great Financial Crisis (GFC), the migration crisis, and the COVID-19 pandemic, in some regards at least, the EU admittedly displayed evidence of malfunctioning. Arguably, this partial malfunctioning has demanded (and still demands) reforms, as will be set out in the subsequent chapters. It was, though, not these crises which caused the malfunctioning. Pre-existing problems simply became more visible due to the need for fast and efficient action to counter these crises.

This edited volume focuses on the EU's regulatory responses to crises. To explain its ambition, let us start with the term 'crisis'. Rooted in ancient Greek and later Latin, it originally described 'a state of affairs in which a decisive change for better or worse is imminent'; 'a turning point' where distinction, decision, choice, election, judgement, or dispute was at stake. In contrast to this neutral meaning, this term has, in today's common parlance, a primarily negative connotation and is referred to as either 'a situation or period characterized by intense difficulty, insecurity, or danger, either in the public sphere or in one's personal life' or a 'sudden emergency situation'.[2] A crisis regularly marks a caesura in the development of a person, an entity, or a part of an entity, and—as is also enshrined in its etymology (distinction, decision, choice, etc)—it calls

* Professor of European Law at the University of Salzburg.
** Emerita Professor of Political Science at the European University Institute.
*** Associate Professor of European Law at the University of Salzburg.

[1] Different terms have been used to address this phenomenon, eg 'polycrisis', 'multiple crises', or 'permanent crisis mode'; see, *ex multis*, Jonathan Zeitlin and Francesco Nicoli (eds), *The European Union Beyond the Polycrisis? Integration and Politicization in an Age of Shifting Cleavages* (Routledge 2020); Maurizio Cotta and Pierangelo Isernia (eds), *The EU through Multiple Crises Representation and Cohesion Dilemmas for a 'Sui Generis' Polity* (Routledge 2023); Annette Bongardt and Francisco Torres, 'What Way Forward for European Integration in Permanent Crisis Mode?' in Annette Bongardt and Francisco Torres (eds), *The Political Economy of Europe's Future and Identity: Integration in Crisis Mode* (EUI and UCP Press 2023) 1.

[2] These definitions are taken from the Oxford English Dictionary; for approaches focusing on the political impact and for the distinction between 'crisis' and 'turbulence', see Marianne Riddervold, Jarle Trondal and Akasemi Newsome, 'European Union Crisis: An Introduction' in Marianne Riddervold, Jarle Trondal and Akasemi Newsome (eds), *The Palgrave Handbook of EU Crises* (Palgrave Macmillan 2021) 3, 7, with many further references.

Diane Fromage, Adrienne Héritier, and Paul Weismann, *Introduction* In: *EU Regulatory Responses to Crises*. Edited by: Diane Fromage, Adrienne Héritier, and Paul Weismann, Oxford University Press. © Diane Fromage, Adrienne Héritier, and Paul Weismann 2025. DOI: 10.1093/9780198913825.003.0001

for reaction. The swiftness and effectiveness of reactions to crises depend on the dimension of the crisis at issue, the organizational complexity of the actor(s) forced to react to it, and its (or their) preparation for the crisis. Smaller crises will be resolved more quickly and more easily, whereas a successful reaction to a complex crisis will require more time and consideration.[3] Similarly, small organizational units (eg a department of a company) hit by a crisis will react more promptly (in particular, where they can rely on previous experiences or an action plan they have prepared for such cases) than larger entities (eg a state) or even a group of entities who have to coordinate themselves (eg the EU, together with its Member States).

The second expression in the title requiring some explanation is 'EU regulatory responses'. We conceive of the term 'regulatory responses' in the broadest possible way. It describes any form of rule-making (an expression used frequently throughout this book), directly or indirectly linked to one of the identified crises (see below), that is the adoption of new rules or the amendment of existing rules, irrespective of whether these are abstract (general) or concrete (individual) in scope,[4] legislative or non-legislative, legally binding or legally non-binding. We have refused to refer to the underlying acts by using the term 'crisis measures' or similar phrases, as our research interest pertains not only to crisis-related acts as such but also to the development of the forms of rule-making these crises bring about, so that rule-making may remain different to the *status quo ante* even after the crisis has been overcome. The latter phenomenon may have different reasons, for example that it seems politically unwise to abolish a measure which has proved to be successful during a crisis, or that it turns out to be impossible to re-establish a political taboo which it was deemed necessary to break in order to counter the crisis.

Also, the reference to the EU in 'EU regulatory responses' is to be understood broadly, so as to encompass not only acts of the EU *stricto sensu* but also measures taken by Member States collectively in an attempt to complement or reinforce EU measures, or to take common action where the EU, due to competence limitations, did not have the mandate to act.

The latter point brings us to one of the key characteristics of the EU—the determination of its mandate by the Member States. The rules on the functioning of the EU and

[3] It may appear that the term 'crisis' has come to be used in an inflationary manner. However, given its relatively broad definition, this reproach is to be refuted, at least in the given context; note the differentiated utterances of Claudia Scheid, '(Re)präsentation deutschsprachiger Soziologie' (2016) 17 Sozialer Sinn 165, 168 f (fn 4). In order still to allow for a qualitative and quantitative distinction between various crises, their respective scales and effects need to be specified. In the field of public international law, an excessive scholarly focus on crises as events leading to a development of public international law has been criticized with good arguments: see, in particular, Hilary Charlesworth, 'International Law: A Discipline of Crisis' (2002) 65 Modern Law Review 377. The crises referred to here are rough and antagonistic and, more generally, the creation/development of (general) rules in public international law follows long-winded and often cumbersome processes. In the EU's comparatively sophisticated rule-making machinery, reforms are made virtually on an everyday basis. Thus, we do not think that the reproach of overemphasizing the meaning of crises for the development of law is valid in the EU context.

[4] Thus, the distinction between (individual) decision-making and (general) rule-making, which is sometimes drawn in the literature, is not applied here; for a broad concept of 'rule-making', see also Carl Fredrik Bergström and Dominique Ritleng (eds), *Rulemaking by the European Commission* (OUP 2016); Martina Conticelli, Maurizia De Bellis and Giacinto della Cananea (eds), *EU Executive Governance: Agencies and Procedures* (G. Giappichelli Editore 2019).

its limitations have essentially been laid down by its Member States in the EU Treaties and in the EU Charter of Fundamental Rights (primary law). The EU may adopt rules only in accordance with primary law, even in the case of a crisis.[5] Should the EU be purveyed additional powers—for example, exceptional powers to be used to counter a crisis—Member States have to revise the Treaties first, the only (very limited) exception to this being the EU's possibility to resort to the flexibility clause contained in Article 352 of the Treaty on the Functioning of the European Union (TFEU), which foresees that

> [i]f action by the Union should prove necessary, within the framework of the policies defined in the Treaties, to attain one of the objectives set out in the Treaties, and the Treaties have not provided the necessary powers, the Council, acting unanimously on a proposal from the Commission and after obtaining the consent of the European Parliament, shall adopt the appropriate measures. (paragraph 1)

However, '[m]easures based on this Article shall not entail harmonisation of Member States' laws or regulations in cases where the Treaties exclude such harmonisation' (paragraph 3).

Since the entry into force of the Treaty of Lisbon, the likelihood, from a political perspective, of further reforms has become more and more limited, as Member States do not seem to be ready to go down this path and all of them would have to agree to it for any reform to be possible. As was mentioned above, during this period the EU (including its Member States) has been challenged by various, sometimes overlapping, examples of what—with reference to one of the definitions presented earlier—we could call 'periods characterized by intense difficulty, insecurity, or danger'.[6] While all of these periods have exerted a significant level of stress on the EU, unsurprisingly they differ from each other in numerous ways. We distinguish symmetric from asymmetric and endogenous from exogenous crises; sudden and slow crises; crises calling for financial support of Member States and/or their respective economies from other crises which require medical, logistical, or other forms of action; or crises requiring strict law enforcement for their resolution from those to be managed through fine-tuned diplomacy, etc. In this book, the focus is placed on the *GFC* (including its components, such as the banking crisis and the euro-area crisis); the *migration crisis*; the *climate crisis*; the *pandemic*; and, most recently, the *war in Ukraine* and the EU's support for it, the ensuing *energy crisis*, and a period of exceptionally high inflation in the EU. These

[5] Primary law does not provide for general simplified procedures of rule-making in the case of a crisis. It contains only single provisions for specific cases of difficulties, crisis, or emergency, eg art 122, art 144(1), or art 78(3) TFEU; for the EU's powers in a state of emergency (which a crisis may be, but does not necessarily have to result in), see Vojtěch Belling, 'Legality and Legitimacy of the EU "Emergency Governance": On the Application of the State of Emergency in the European Union' (2018) 73 Zeitschrift für öffentliches Recht [Journal of Public Law] 271.

[6] The (predecessors of the) EU had been confronted with (endogenous and exogenous) crises ever since the foundation of the three Communities in the 1950s, but the frequency of (partly overlapping) crises referred to here is unprecedented; see also Riddervold, Trondal and Newsome (n 2) 3, 4.

crises differ much in terms of their causes, the scope of their effects, and the measures taken to combat them. What they have in common, however, is the high degree of uncertainty surrounding them, in combination with the high level of pressure they exerted on the EU and its Member States to take immediate action to combat them, on the one hand, and to adopt measures to prevent similar crises in the future or at least to be prepared for them, on the other. Also, their exogenous character is a commonality. Unlike Brexit or the rule of law crisis in selected Member States—two occurrences which have strongly affected not only the respective countries but also the EU as a whole—the roots of the crises which form our focus lay (predominantly) outside the EU. At the same time, from the EU's perspective, the crises selected here concern one or a limited number of policy fields, and these guide our analysis across the various chapters of this volume. Only the climate crisis, most recently, has given rise to EU action in all kinds of policy fields, thereby developing into a truly cross-sectional concern of EU rule-making.

The EU has reacted to these challenges by launching a number of reforms in all the affected policy fields. As an expression of crisis management, most of these reform measures have in common that they were taken under a dual time pressure: there was little time for negotiating upon and eventually adopting the measures at issue and, further, there was an expectation on the part of the general public that these measures, once adopted, would lead to results in the short run. What is more, the measures were taken with the objective of tackling (specific aspects of) the respective crises effectively: that is, as comprehensively and as incisively as possible. This striving for effective responses to a specific crisis was, at times, impeded by the existing distribution of competences between the EU and its Member States, as well as by the contestation as to the required remedy among EU institutions and the Member States, and among Member States themselves.

A response to a crisis hitting all or most of the Member States can often unfold in both a timelier and a more efficient manner if the underlying measures are taken at the EU and not at the national level. This conviction—aptly expressed in the statement that 'the European Union moves faster and further when it has to'[7]—leads to an increased attractiveness of taking a measure at EU level, subject to the political agreement (of the Member States, in particular) on the content of the measure. Where the EU's competence to take a certain measure in its entirety is contested, the attractiveness of adopting this measure at the EU level may incentivize, for example, a broad interpretation of legal provisions, the creative combination of legal bases in primary law, or the adoption of non-binding EU rules ('soft law'), instead of not acting at all. Also, the creation of new EU agencies or the further empowerment of existing EU agencies has become a recurrent feature in the EU's reactions to crises. Further dimensions of this approach concern cooperation with national bodies, for example the introduction of

[7] Commission, 'Conference on the Future of Europe. Putting Vision into Concrete Action' (Communication) COM (2022) 404 final, 1.

instruction rights of EU bodies vis-à-vis national authorities, the adoption of regulations rather than directives, or the exceptional application of national law by EU bodies instead of their national pendants. This is not to say that most of these phenomena may not be witnessed in regular—that is, non-crisis—times. However, the frequency and boldness—in one word, the *intensity* with which these techniques are used—seem to increase in reaction to crises.

But it is not only the actors involved but the procedures applied or the forms of rules that have changed. The substance of existing rules (including primary law) has also been reconsidered as a result of unprecedented challenges. In this vein, we have seen, as illustrative examples, a deviation in practice from the Dublin system as regards the distribution of refugees, the EU indebting itself on a significant scale in the wake of the pandemic, and the boosting of foreign and defence policy as a result of the war in Ukraine.

Perceived as a whole, these sorts of developments, taking place in reaction to various crises, seem to have affected not only the substance of existing rules but also the relationships between the EU institutions and bodies, between the EU and its Member States, and between the Member States themselves. All of this together may have resulted in a *de facto* reform of the EU's constitution (ie primary law), which, if this qualification can be affirmed in the first place, was essentially brought about by acts ranking below the level of primary law—something which we could call an 'invisible' reform.[8]

Against this backdrop, it is the aim of this edited volume to analyse the changes, short of Treaty change, that have emerged in EU rule-making in reaction to the various crises mentioned above. A number of policy fields have been strongly affected by one or more of these crises. Furthermore, structural modifications may have been effectuated beyond single policy fields—that is to say, in a horizontal perspective of the EU's rule-making activity as a whole—due to the near-permanent crisis mode in which the EU has found itself in the past fifteen years. In other words, a comprehensive picture will be drawn of the rule-making tools the EU has been using during the various crises, taking account of their individual characteristics, and it will be examined how the legal and institutional set-up of the EU and the (strongly rule-based) relationship to its Member States, and the relationships of the Member States among themselves, have thereby been changed, both in the context of selected policy fields and on a horizontal level, encompassing the development of EU rule-making as a whole.

In order to provide a certain degree of representativeness, seven policy fields have been selected which have been hit particularly by the aforementioned crises in the past fifteen years and in which, as a reaction thereto, EU rule-making has developed in various ways. These policy fields are: *economic and monetary policy* (Chapter 2); *financial regulation and supervision* (Chapter 3); *health policy* (Chapter 4); *state aid control* (Chapter 5); *energy policy* (Chapter 6); *migration policy* (Chapter 7); and *foreign and defence policy* (Chapter 8). These policy fields are each analysed by a team of two authors (except for Chapter 8), taking a legal and a political science perspective in an interdisciplinary

[8] For this terminology, see n 10.

manner.[9] The aim is to present the measures adopted as a result of at least one crisis and assess them with a view to answering the following *research questions*:

(1) What was the state or nature of EU rule-making in the affected policy fields prior to the relevant crisis or crises?
(2) Did EU rule-making in reaction to these crises break new ground in that it was unprecedented formally or materially and, if so, how?
(3) Were EU competences extended in the respective policy fields and, if so, how has this affected the EU's inter-institutional balance?
(4) How did EU rule-making in reaction to said crises affect the relationships between the EU and its Member States, and among Member States?
(5) Can we even identify aspects of an 'invisible' transformation of the EU's constitution without Treaty revision?

The first question asks for the *status quo ante*, that is, for the practice of rule-making prior to the relevant crisis/crises. A clear picture of pre-crisis rule-making is imperative to discerning whether something, and if so what, has changed during the respective crises.

Second, on the basis of these findings, it will be analysed whether rule-making has broken new ground formally or materially, as compared with before the examined crisis. This relates to reforms which were (deemed to be) unfeasible legally and/or politically prior to the crisis, but which could eventually be adopted when the crisis arose. These reforms may have a formal (new forms of rules, new bodies, new procedures, etc) or a material (the adoption of rules with a new normative content, the reinterpretation of existing rules, etc) character. A comprehensive understanding of the character of these reforms should allow us to examine how crises may facilitate overcoming legal or political boundaries. As set out above, EU rule-making during the crises at issue here did not see (comprehensive) Treaty revision. Thus, the aforementioned reforms needed to be adopted *on the basis of* the Treaties. But even if the text of the Treaties remained the same over a certain period, their provisions may have been interpreted differently—more narrowly, or more extensively—over time.

Consequently, the third question asks whether EU competences were extended to implement the reforms at issue and, if so, how this has affected, both legally and politically, the relationship between the EU institutions and other bodies, that is, the EU's inter-institutional balance.

However, a certain interpretation and—eventually—application of Treaty provisions may not only affect the inter-institutional balance but also the relationships between the EU and the Member States, and among the Member States themselves. These relationships may be affected for various reasons, for example with respect to administrative cooperation between EU and national authorities, or due to the competence

[9] An originally envisaged chapter on environmental policy eventually, and unfortunately, could not be added to this volume.

dichotomy underlying the EU, meaning that competences are distributed between only two levels—the EU and its Member States or, with regard to the relationships of Member States *inter se*, due to the differences among Member States (eg net payers versus net receivers, members versus non-members of the euro area, etc). Thus, the fourth question asks for changes in the vertical relationship between the EU and its Member States, and in the relationships among the Member States themselves.

On the basis of the findings emanating from answering the above four research questions, eventually the fifth question will be posed. In answering this question, it will be addressed whether aspects of an 'invisible' transformation of the EU's constitution, without Treaty revision, can be identified. The concept of the invisible or silent transformation has been developed in scholarship (in different contexts) in order to describe changes of EU law which were brought about—not necessarily ad hoc but often over a more extended period of time—without an explicit amendment of the letter of the law, but, for instance, through a new interpretative approach resulting in new rules of secondary law or in a new inter-institutional practice.[10] This question is also reflected upon in the book's subtitle, '*Adaptation or Transformation?*'. Not each and every form of change represents a transformation. EU rule-making may also result in a mere adaptation to new (crises-induced) requirements. A definitory distinction can be drawn in the following way: whereas an adaptation signifies the adjustment to new circumstances, a transformation describes a fundamental change. Thus, the question is whether or not core properties of the object of the process have been changed for good. Whether a process brings about adaptation or transformation hence depends on the intensity and durability of the change.

In the final chapter (Chapter 9), a horizontal perspective is provided, again taking an interdisciplinary (legal/political science) perspective. It comprises a summary of the main findings of each previous chapter, a transversal account of what the changes in the individual policy fields have meant for EU rule-making during and after crises as a whole, and conclusions. Thereby, potential learning effects will also be addressed. On the one hand, this involves an investigation of whether a successful reaction to one crisis has been applied—possibly also in a different policy field—in the context of subsequent crises in such a way that rule-making tools which have proven effective in one crisis may also be utilized in successive crises (cross-fertilization potential). Through such positive path dependency, the EU may even have established something which we could call a *kit of EU crisis management tools*. On the other hand, learning effects may also be displayed by the EU avoiding an approach which proved unsuccessful, in one way or another, in a previous crisis.

[10] See, eg, Henry Farrell and Adrienne Héritier, 'The Invisible Transformation of Codecision: Problems of Democratic Legitimacy' (2003) 7 Swedish Institute for European Policy Studies Report 1; note also the frequently used German term '*stiller Verfassungswandel*'; see, eg, Peter Badura, 'Verfassungsänderung, Verfassungswandel, Verfassungsgewohnheitsrecht' in Josef Isensee and Paul Kirchhof (eds), *Handbuch des Staatsrechts der Bundesrepublik Deutschland*, vol VII (3rd edn, CF Müller 2009) 592, 597 f, with further references. Related concepts are 'competence creep', '*révision froid*', or '*schleichender Verfassungswandel*'.

2

Economic and Monetary Union

Incremental Adaptation under Legal and Political Constraints

Magnus G Schoeller and Paul Weismann***

2.1 Introduction

How have crises affected the Economic and Monetary Union (EMU) and, in particular, its legal foundations, institutional design, and governance? In order to answer this question, we start by outlining EMU's legal foundations, as laid down in the Treaty on the Functioning of the European Union (TFEU) (section 2.2.1), and then trace the most important measures in economic and monetary policy taken in response to crises (section 2.2.2). In a second step, we assess the political-economic consequences of these legal foundations (section 2.3). In particular, we identify a twofold asymmetry of EMU, namely a policy asymmetry (economic versus monetary policy) *and* an institutional asymmetry (fiscal constraints versus macroeconomic rules versus fiscal capacities).[1] The third step, then, serves to analyse crisis-induced developments in EMU rule-making. These developments are addressed with regard to economic and fiscal policy rules (taking three examples) (section 2.4.1), common fiscal capacities, in particular the European Stability Mechanism (ESM) and the Recovery and Resilience Facility (RRF) (section 2.4.2), and the evolving role of the European Central Bank (ECB) (section 2.4.3).[2]

Based on this analysis, we draw the political implications, arguing that past crises have led to learning effects in EMU (section 2.5). Indeed, we demonstrate how EMU's asymmetric institutional design has been partially corrected *without* major Treaty change. We therefore offer a theory-informed explanation of crisis-induced incremental change in EMU, taking place *despite* a restrictive primary law and a constraining

* Political Scientist at the Centre for European Integration Research, University of Vienna.
** Associate Professor of European Law at the University of Salzburg.

[1] In this chapter, the term 'institutions' is used in a twofold sense. On the one hand, we refer to the EU institutions (eg European Parliament, Council, Commission, etc). On the other hand, we use the term to denote rules that constrain individual behaviour in order to shape collective action (eg formal decision-making rules, such as laws or informal norms and practices).

[2] As regards the cooperation between the ECB and national central banks, art 282(1) TFEU stipulates: 'The European Central Bank, together with the national central banks, shall constitute the European System of Central Banks (ESCB). The European Central Bank, together with the national central banks of the Member States whose currency is the euro, which constitute the Eurosystem, shall conduct the monetary policy of the Union'. For the sake of readability, in this contribution we refer only to the ECB.

Magnus G Schoeller and Paul Weismann, *Economic and Monetary Union* In: *EU Regulatory Responses to Crises*.
Edited by: Diane Fromage, Adrienne Héritier, and Paul Weismann, Oxford University Press.
 DOI: 10.1093/9780198913825.003.0002

political framework. More specifically, we argue that EMU's inertia is broken up by crises 'spilling over' from other policy areas (eg finance, health). The resulting reform measures sufficed to preserve the single currency but did not correct EMU's inbuilt asymmetries. Hence, rather than being 'built through crises',[3] as a series of purposeful and efficient responses to functional incentives, we expect EMU to keep on 'failing forward',[4] as a series of originally unintended, suboptimal fixes to incomplete policy designs. In the conclusions, we reflect on these findings in light of the research questions underlying this book (section 2.6).

2.2 Legal Foundations of EMU and Anti-crisis measures Adopted in this Policy Field

2.2.1 Treaty framework

The primary law framework of EMU, originally introduced with the Treaty of Maastricht[5] in 1993, is now laid down in Part Three, Title VIII, TFEU. In terms of economic policy measures, the core provisions are Article 121 on the multilateral surveillance procedure, Article 126 on the excessive deficit procedure (EDP), Article 125—the so-called 'no-bailout clause'—and Article 122, allowing the EU to take emergency measures (including financial assistance) in support of Member States in need. Article 136 allows for the adoption of specific rules for euro-area Member States. These provisions relate to a merely coordinating competence of the EU (Article 5 TFEU).

In terms of monetary policy measures, the core provisions are Article 127 on the ECB's tasks and powers and Article 123, prohibiting monetary financing of the EU or its Member States.[6] Monetary policy for the euro-area Member States belongs to the exclusive competences of the EU (Article 3 TFEU).

Let us first discuss the dissimilar twins Article 121 and Article 126. According to Article 121(1), Member States 'shall regard their economic policies as a matter of common concern and shall coordinate them within the Council'. To this end, the Council shall formulate broad economic policy guidelines (BEPGs) to be concluded upon by the European Council, on the basis of which the Council shall address recommendations to the EU and its Member States (economic policy coordination). If the economic policies of a Member State are inconsistent with this regime, warnings and/

[3] Jean Monnet, *Memoirs* (William Collins 1978) 417.

[4] See David Howarth and Lucia Quaglia, 'Failing Forward in Economic and Monetary Union: Explaining Weak Eurozone Financial Support Mechanisms' (2021) 28 Journal of European Public Policy 1555; Erik Jones, Daniel Kelemen and Sophie Meunier, 'Failing Forward? The Euro Crisis and the Incomplete Nature of European Integration' (2016) 49 Comparative Political Studies 1010.

[5] Treaty on European Union [1992] OJ C191/1.

[6] While art 123 of the TFEU belongs to the chapter on economic policy, it also contributes to shaping the ECB's monetary policy.

or recommendations may be addressed to that Member State (multilateral surveillance procedure).

The regime set out in Article 126 allows the Commission to monitor the Member States' fiscal policies in terms of annual deficit and government debt. Protocol No 12 to the Treaties sets the reference values measured in terms of the gross domestic product, with 3 per cent (annual deficit) and 60 per cent (government debt), respectively.[7] Compliance with these reference values can be requested by means of Council recommendations. Where the Member State at issue belongs to the euro area, the Council may also impose sanctions.

In order to further underpin fiscal discipline, Article 125 sets out a no-bailout principle. It stipulates that the EU or a Member State 'shall not be liable for or assume the commitments' of a(nother) Member State or public undertakings of this (other) Member State.[8] Another relevant provision in this context is Article 136(3) TFEU, which was inserted by a simplified Treaty revision procedure, taking effect in 2013.[9] It does not empower the EU or its institutions but states that the Member States 'may establish a stability mechanism to be activated if indispensable to safeguard the stability of the euro area as a whole'. Financial assistance under this mechanism may only be granted 'subject to strict conditionality'.

Article 122 allows the Council to decide, 'in a spirit of solidarity between Member States, upon the measures appropriate to the economic situation, in particular if severe difficulties arise in the supply of certain products, notably in the area of energy' (para 1). Its paragraph 2 stipulates that where Member States are 'in difficulties or [are] seriously threatened with severe difficulties caused by natural disasters or exceptional occurrences beyond [their] control', the Council 'may grant, under certain conditions, Union financial assistance' to the Member States concerned.[10]

Article 127 prescribes the maintenance of price stability as the ECB's 'primary objective'. As part of its secondary objectives, the ECB 'shall support the general economic policies in the Union' only to the extent that this does not negatively affect this primary objective.

Article 123 prevents the ECB and the national central banks (NCBs), first, from providing '[o]verdraft facilities or any other type of credit facility' in favour of the EU, its Member States, or public undertakings, and, second, from purchasing debt instruments directly from these actors.[11]

[7] Protocol No 12 may be changed by the Council in accordance with art 126(14) TFEU.

[8] This shall be 'without prejudice to mutual financial guarantees for the joint execution of a specific project'.

[9] European Council Decision 2011/199/EU.

[10] For the sake of completeness, arts 143 and 144 TFEU ought also to be mentioned. These norms provide for the possibility of financial support in the event that a Member State outside the euro area faces difficulties as regards its balance of payments.

[11] See also Council Regulation 3603/93 specifying definitions for the application of the prohibitions referred to in what are now arts 123 and 125 TFEU.

2.2.2 Anti-crisis measures adopted by the EU or within the framework of the EU

2.2.2.1 Measures taken in the area of economic policy

In this context, we can distinguish two main groups of measures, namely those relating to the fiscal discipline of (euro-area) Member States and those on building up collective fiscal capacities in order to support all, or only specific, Member States. To the first group belong the reforms of the Stability and Growth Pact (SGP), brought about by the so-called 'six-pack' and 'two-pack' as a reaction to the Great Financial Crisis (GFC) and the ensuing euro crisis. These measures were complemented by the Treaty on Stability, Coordination and Governance (TSCG, often referred to as the 'Fiscal Compact').[12] To the second group belong the various financial assistance mechanisms, most importantly the ESM. Facing the drastic economic consequences of the COVID-19 pandemic and its containment, the EU, on the one hand, suspended the application of certain fiscal rules, and on the other—and this is another example of collective capacities—adopted the European instrument for temporary Support to mitigate Unemployment Risks in an Emergency (SURE), and the RRF, in order to supply financial support to the Member States.

The six-pack consists of five EU regulations and one EU directive which were adopted on the basis of Article 121(6) TFEU, either on its own or in conjunction with Article 136 TFEU, and on Article 126(14) subparagraph 3 TFEU, respectively. They are aimed at reinforcing and complementing the SGP. Among other things, these reforms establish a European Semester: an annual cycle of economic and fiscal policy coordination, in the course of which the EU adopts country-specific recommendations (CSRs) for each Member State. The two-pack encompasses two regulations, both based on Article 136 in conjunction with Article 121(6) TFEU. One of these strengthens economic and budgetary surveillance of euro-area Member States challenged by serious difficulties with respect to their financial stability, while the other sets up common provisions for monitoring and assessing draft budgetary plans and ensuring the correction of excessive deficits in euro-area Member States.

As an early reaction to the pandemic crisis, in March 2020 the Council suspended the fiscal rules applicable to Member States by using the general escape clause enshrined in (various provisions of) the SGP. According to the Council, this '[would] ensure the needed flexibility to take all necessary measures for supporting our health and civil protection systems and to protect our economies'.[13] The escape clause was 'deactivated' by the end of 2023.[14]

[12] Treaty on Stability, Coordination and Governance in the Economic and Monetary Union (2012).

[13] Council, Press release of 23 March 2020 <https://www.consilium.europa.eu/en/press/press-releases/2020/03/23/statement-of-eu-ministers-of-finance-on-the-stability-and-growth-pact-in-light-of-the-covid-19-crisis/> accessed 19 November 2023.

[14] See Marcello Messori, 'New EU Fiscal Rules in Light of Contract Theory: Improvements and Unsolved Problems', IEP@BU Policy Brief, January 2024 <https://iep.unibocconi.eu/sites/default/files/media/attach/PB_MESSORI%20FISCAL%20RULES_0.pdf> accessed 13 September 2024.

The above fiscal and economic policy regime has recently been reformed.[15]

The TSCG is an international treaty concluded between the Member States.[16] Its main content, the so-called debt brake (to be transposed into national law), reinforces the medium-term budgetary objective in Council Regulation 1466/97, as replaced by Regulation 2024/1263. This rule applies only to the euro-area Member States and to those Member States who have committed to this regime pursuant to Article 14(5) TSCG. Compliance with the debt brake is to be monitored by independent fiscal bodies at the Member State level.[17]

The ESM is also based on an international treaty, this time concluded only between the euro-area Member States, each of whom has financially contributed to building it up. The ESM has the capacity to financially support ailing euro-area Member States (eg in the form of loans) up to a total amount of 500 billion euros. This support is conditional upon reform measures to be taken in the beneficiary states ('conditionality'). Its compliance with EU law, and in particular with Article 125 TFEU, was questioned before the Court of Justice of the European Union (CJEU). The Court held that, due to the conditionality applied in the context of ESM loans, there had been no violation of this provision.

In the course of the pandemic, the EU adopted SURE in the form of a Council Regulation based on Article 122(1) TFEU. SURE provided loans to Member States for them to cope with a sudden rise in unemployment and short-term work, and the ensuing increase in public expenditure.

On a broader level, the EU adopted the RRF (as part of 'NextGeneration EU' or 'NGEU'), a facility of about 724 billion euros which the EU spends in the form of loans and grants to support the Member States. These financial means should allow the Member States to build up their economies after the calamities brought about by the pandemic. This expenditure on the part of the Member States ought to help the EU 'to achieve its target of climate neutrality by 2050 and sets Europe on a path of digital transition, creating jobs and spurring growth in the process'.[18] Regulation 2021/241 on the creation of the RRF is based on Article 175 TFEU, a provision on the EU's cohesion policy. Council Regulation 2020/2094, which establishes the 'European Union Recovery Instrument'—that is, the policy framework within which RFF support (and financial means allocated to pre-existing funds) shall be granted to the Member States—rests on Article 122 TFEU. This regulation also refers to Article 5 of the EU's Own

[15] <https://www.consilium.europa.eu/en/press/press-releases/2024/02/10/economic-governance-review-council-and-parliament-strike-deal-on-reform-of-fiscal-rules/> accessed 15 March 2024. See Regulation 2024/1263, Council Regulation 2024/1264, and Council Directive 2024/1265.

[16] Treaty on Stability, Coordination and Governance in the Economic and Monetary Union (2012). The TSCG was originally concluded by all Member States except for the Czech Republic and the UK. With Croatia joining the EU in 2013 and the TSCG in 2018, the Czech Republic joining the TSCG in 2019, and the UK leaving the EU in 2020, the TSCG (or at least parts thereof) is/are now effective for all Member States: <https://www.consilium.europa.eu/en/documents-publications/treaties-agreements/agreement/?id=2012008> accessed 19 November 2023.

[17] See art 3(2) TSCG; see also Recitals 10 and 17 of Regulation 473/2013.

[18] <https://ec.europa.eu/info/business-economy-euro/recovery-coronavirus/recovery-and-resilience-facility_en> accessed 19 November 2023.

Resources Decision, according to which the Commission is empowered to borrow, on behalf of the EU, funds on the capital markets of up to 750 billion euros in 2018 prices, '[f]or the sole purpose of addressing the consequences of the COVID-19 crisis through the Council Regulation [2020/2094]'.[19] The Commission and the Council justified this approach as merely a temporary deviation from budgetary principles.[20]

2.2.2.2 Measures taken in the area of monetary policy

The crises dealt with here have also been addressed by the ECB. During the euro crisis, the ECB announced its 'Outright Monetary Transactions' (OMT) programme (which has never been applied) and later performed the so-called 'Public Sector Purchase Programme' (PSPP). Both programmes, which are just prominent examples of the ECB's non-standard measures, envisaged the purchasing of state bonds of euro-area Member States on secondary markets. The ECB argued that this was a means to ensure price stability, *in concreto* an increase of the inflation rate, thereby 'safeguarding an appropriate monetary policy transmission and the singleness of the monetary policy'.[21] The dysfunctionality of the sovereign bond market was reflected in highly heterogeneous and partly unsustainable spreads across the euro area.[22] In its judgments in the cases of *Gauweiler* and *Weiss*, the CJEU supported this argument, thereby refusing, among other things, the claim that the ECB's actions qualified as economic policy, and that they went against Article 123 TFEU.

During the pandemic, the ECB again resorted to non-standard measures and launched, in particular, the 'Pandemic Emergency Purchase Programme' (PEPP).

With the inflation rate having increased dramatically after Russia's invasion of Ukraine (partly due to the resulting skyrocketing of energy prices), the ECB has gradually wound down its purchase programmes, has started to unwind its portfolio of assets (quantitative tightening), and has quickly increased the key interest rate. In order to accompany this transition period, the ECB's Transmission Protection Instrument (TPI) was launched in July 2022. According to the ECB, this government bond purchase programme may 'be activated to counter unwarranted, disorderly market dynamics that pose a serious threat to the transmission of monetary policy across the euro area'.[23]

[19] The Own Resources Decision (Council Decision 2020/2053) was ratified by all Member States in May 2021.

[20] See Bruno de Witte, 'The European Union's COVID-19 Recovery Plan: The Legal Engineering of an Economic Policy Shift' (2021) 58 Common Market Law Review 635, 664; sceptically: Päivi Leino-Sandberg and Matthias Ruffert, 'Next Generation EU and its Constitutional Ramifications: A Critical Assessment' (2022) 59 Common Market Law Review 433. In favour of the legality of the EU indebting itself on the basis of the (amended) Own Resources Decision, see Ulrich Häde, 'Art. 122 AEUV' in Christian Calliess and Matthias Ruffert (eds), *EUV/AEUV* (6th edn, CH Beck 2022) para 15.

[21] <www.ecb.europa.eu/press/pr/date/2012/html/pr120906_1.en.html> accessed 19 November 2023.

[22] See, eg Armin Steinbach, 'The Lender of Last Resort in the Eurozone' (2016) 53 Common Market Law Review 361, 370 f.

[23] <www.ecb.europa.eu/press/pr/date/2022/html/ecb.pr220721~973e6e7273.en.html> accessed 19 November 2023. The measures the ECB has taken to address the climate crisis can only be referred to here; see, eg, Chiara Zilioli and Michael Ioannidis, 'Climate Change and the Mandate of the ECB: Potential and Limits of Monetary Contribution to European Green Policies' (2022) 59 Common Market Law Review 363.

2.3 Political-economic Assessment

From a political-economic perspective, the Treaty framework described in section 2.2.1 above turned out to be a 'good-weather' framework. While the institutional design of EMU worked well during the first decade of the common currency, it reinforced instability and required institutional ad hoc fixes in times of crises (see section 2.2.2).[24] *First*, EMU's design has remained incomplete due to the asymmetric integration of strongly interdependent policies. While monetary policy in the euro area was fully integrated in the form of a single currency and an independent central bank (complete supranationalization), economic and fiscal policy was largely left in the hands of Member States, with only weak coordination and monitoring mechanisms at the European level. *Second*, EMU has been incomplete regarding the asymmetric institutional provisions to stabilize the single currency. The binding fiscal constraints at the Member State level were not matched by effective macroeconomic rules and/or fiscal capacities at the European level.

EMU's *asymmetry in terms of sectoral integration* (ie monetary versus fiscal/economic policy) is problematic from a political-economic point of view.[25] By adopting the euro, Member States give up the competences for their own currencies. This means that they issue their sovereign debt in a currency they cannot control.[26] In other words, euro-area members cannot guarantee their creditors that they will pay back their debts under any circumstances. This would not be so much of a problem if they all had the same growth model (or way of organizing their economies). However, while some countries, mainly in the north of the euro area, traditionally pursued 'export-led' growth strategies based on wage restraint and low inflation, others followed 'demand-led' growth models by stimulating internal demand and thus accepting higher inflation rates. As a consequence, the fixed exchange rate of the single currency gives the more competitive export-led economies an advantage in the markets of the other Member States. The resulting macroeconomic imbalances cannot be offset by the less competitive states, as they can no longer devalue against their trading partners.[27]

The trade surpluses of the more competitive EMU economies are boosted by the fact that the external exchange rate of the euro is that of the entire euro area, including the deficit states, and therefore does not necessarily rise with increasing exports of single surplus states. In other words, the surplus states benefit from a currency that,

[24] See Paul de Grauwe and Yuemei Ji, 'Correcting for the Eurozone Design Failures: The Role of the ECB' (2015) 37 Journal of European Integration 739; Peter A Hall, 'The Economics and Politics of the Euro Crisis' (2012) 21 German Politics 355; Howarth and Quaglia (n 4); Alison Johnston and Aidan Reagan, 'European Monetary Integration and the Incompatibility of National Varieties of Capitalism' (2016) 54 Journal of Common Market Studies 318.

[25] See, eg Nicolas Jabko, 'The Elusive Economic Governance and the Forgotten Fiscal Union' in M Matthijs and M Blyth (eds), *The Future of the Euro* (OUP 2015) 70–89; David Howarth and Amy Verdun, 'Economic and Monetary Union at Twenty: A Stocktaking of a Tumultuous Second Decade: Introduction' (2020) 42 Journal of European Integration 287.

[26] Paul de Grauwe, 'The Governance of a Fragile Eurozone' (2012) 45 Australian Economic Review 255.

[27] Hall (n 24).

measured against their individual trade balances, is undervalued. In good times, these imbalances do not appear problematic. The equivalent of the trade surplus in export-oriented countries can flow into deficit countries, where the relatively cheap loans boost domestic demand, employment, and wages. This was the case during the euro's first decade. At the same time, however, international competitiveness in deficit countries continues to decline and the macroeconomic imbalances increase further. This becomes a problem when the money flow comes to a sudden stop, as was the case in the global financial crisis following the collapse of Lehman Brothers in 2008. In addition to their own refinancing problems, deficit countries may then be forced to rescue their banks from insolvency, thus converting private debt into public debt and even creating a 'doom loop' in which the increased public debt reduces the value of government bonds held by national banks, thereby further deteriorating their creditworthiness, and so on. Given the lack of reliable fiscal safety nets in EMU, market speculation against the countries concerned may come, in addition to the issues already described.[28]

As 'printing money' and taking on even more debt are not options in euro-area Member States, the only chance left for debtor states is painful internal devaluation through austerity measures and structural reforms. But even then, the inbuilt problem of EMU remains: less competitive Member States risk entering a liquidity crisis each time the euro area is hit by an external shock, since they cannot devalue externally. In short, a common monetary policy has considerable externalities on Member States' economic and fiscal policies. If the latter policies are not sufficiently integrated as well, this leads to economic imbalances, high vulnerability to crises, and reinforced instability in times of external shocks.

In addition to its asymmetry in terms of sectoral integration, EMU faces an *asymmetry regarding its institutional provisions* meant to preserve the single currency.[29] A common currency can be seen as a collective good that risks being wrecked by the self-interested behaviour of its beneficiaries if there are no institutional rules to preserve it.[30] On the one hand, fiscal constraints at the national level must ensure that the individual Member States do not jeopardize the common currency by issuing excessive debt. On the other hand, macroeconomic rules and/or joint fiscal capacities need to ensure that, in times of crises, the reliance on fiscal constraints alone does not destabilize the entire monetary union.

A *first* set of institutions to preserve the single currency relate to *fiscal constraints*. Lacking the possibility to devalue unilaterally, deficit countries in the euro area may be tempted to close their financing gaps by taking on excessive debt (instead of implementing painful budget cuts and structural reforms). A high price stability of the

[28] See, eg de Grauwe and Ji (n 24).

[29] Like Howarth and Verdun (n 25), the present authors diagnose a dual asymmetry of EMU. However, instead of distinguishing between a sectoral asymmetry and a centre–periphery asymmetry, we distinguish between a sectoral and an *institutional* asymmetry. Still, the difference from Howarth and Verdun's conceptualization is smaller than it may seem at first glance, since the centre–periphery asymmetry largely results from EMU's institutional asymmetry.

[30] See Waltraud Schelkle, *The Political Economy of Monetary Solidarity: Understanding the Euro Experiment* (OUP 2017).

common currency and low interest rates are additional pull factors. Therefore, EMU needs effective fiscal constraints. Indeed, such rules have existed from the outset. The so-called Maastricht criteria already stipulate that, among other things, a country may only join the euro area if it runs an annual budget deficit of less than 3 per cent and its public debt does not exceed 60 per cent of its GDP. As outlined in section 2.2.1 above, Article 126 TFEU makes these two criteria binding and enforceable also after a country has joined the euro area, and the TSCG provides for an additional debt brake to be incorporated into national (constitutional) law. While there is no doubt that such fiscal constraints are useful in good times, they can become counterproductive in bad times if they are not accompanied by macroeconomic rules and/or joint fiscal capacities (for the application of the EDP in practice, see section 2.4.1.3 below). This is because such fiscal rules have a procyclical effect. When a country experiences an economic crisis, fiscal constrains not only prevent it from stabilizing its economy, but may even exacerbate the economic downturn, as fiscal restraint hampers internal demand. Moreover, when GDP shrinks, the relative reference values (sovereign deficit and debt) increase 'automatically'; that is, even without an actual increase in absolute figures.

Therefore, in addition to fiscal rules, a *second* set of institutions concerns *macroeconomic rules*. First, such rules can prevent external shocks from leading to crises in the first place. As outlined above, an external shock, such as a credit crunch, is only the trigger through which existing macroeconomic imbalances lead to refinancing problems in deficit countries. Second, rules to prevent or correct macroeconomic imbalances would take away adjustment pressure from deficit countries and thus allow them to invest in sustainable growth. Importantly, such rules relate not only to current account balances, but also other potential imbalances, such as diverging wage dynamics or private sector debt.[31] From a practical point of view, however, it may be difficult to effectively implement macroeconomic rules, such as the balancing of a current account surplus, in free-market economies. This may be one reason why, at the outset of EMU, the only macroeconomic rules were the rather toothless BEPGs. With the six-pack, a 'macroeconomic imbalance procedure' (MIP) was introduced as a response to the euro crisis. For the (non-)application of this procedure in practice, see section 2.4.1.1 below.

A *third* set of institutions to preserve a common currency concerns joint *fiscal capacities*. First, such capacities serve as a safety net if a crisis hits despite fiscal and macroeconomic precautions. By providing financial assistance to single Member States in trouble, the spread of a crisis to the entire monetary union can be prevented. In addition, central capacities can provide for budgetary leeway if fiscal rules preclude national spending to fight a crisis. A safety net also has psychological effects, and thus implies a preventive function: if markets can be sure that euro-area members will not become insolvent, due to effective central capacities, they will not speculate against them in the first place.

[31] See, eg Lucio Baccaro and Tobias Tober, 'The Role of Wages in the Eurozone' (2022) 29 Review of International Political Economy 1263.

However, at the outset of EMU, such joint capacities were not only strikingly absent, but the 'no-bailout clause' (Article 125 TFEU) even prohibited the EU or its Member States from assuming financial commitments or liabilities on behalf of a(nother) Member State. Only since the establishment of the ESM, in response to the euro-area crisis, has there been a permanent intergovernmental capacity to provide financial assistance to ensure the stability of the entire euro area. Eventually, the COVID-19 crisis led to the establishment of a supranational fiscal capacity, in the form of the RRF. Nevertheless, providing loans (instead of grants) to deficit states, as is done by the ESM, and partly by the RRF, does not compensate for EMU's inbuilt imbalances and even exacerbates the problem of over-indebtedness: while such loans provide liquidity in the short term, they only add to the existing debt pile. Moreover, financial assistance from both the ESM and the RRF is strictly limited in time and volume (see section 2.4.2 below). This distinguishes this type of financial assistance from the regular issuance of common bonds or the ECB's purchase programmes, which are theoretically unlimited. Only unlimited instruments can ultimately prevent markets from speculating against the euro or individual Member States and therefore fully guarantee their refinancing options.[32]

Given the institutional asymmetry between fiscal constraints on the one hand, and insufficient macroeconomic rules and fiscal capacities on the other, in the euro crisis, only the monetary capacities of the *ECB* could ultimately preserve the single currency.[33] However, as outlined in section 2.2.1 above, the ECB's legal mandate was not shaped to support or rescue the euro area or its Member States. On the contrary, Article 123 TFEU even prohibits monetary financing by the ECB. Therefore, the ECB needed to elaborate sophisticated programmes such as OMT, which allowed it to purchase sovereign bonds despite its narrow legal mandate. In other words, the ECB has the 'unlimited firepower' to stabilize the currency union in times of crisis, but is constrained by restrictive Treaty rules (see section 2.4.3 below).

[32] In addition to fiscal and macroeconomic institutions, provisions to break the sovereign-bank nexus (or 'doom loop') have been brought up as necessary institutions to preserve the common currency: see Schelkle (n 30); for EU measures taken in this context, see the contribution by Bauerschmidt and Quaglia in this book. Indeed, the linkage between insolvent banks that need to be bailed out by the state whose bonds they hold, with the resulting increase in public debt further deteriorating the banks' balance sheets, is a key factor that turned the global financial crisis into a sovereign debt crisis in the euro area. However, what is true for the global financial crisis does not necessarily apply to other external shocks, such as the COVID-19 pandemic or the war in Ukraine. Moreover, the sovereign-bank nexus is not inherent to the institutional design of EMU, but applies also to other currency areas. It is only because of the lack of macroeconomic rules and fiscal capacities that it is particularly threatening to the euro area.

[33] See de Grauwe and Ji (n 24); Magnus G Schoeller, 'Leadership by Default: The ECB and the Announcement of Outright Monetary Transactions' (2018) 51 Credit and Capital Markets 73.

2.4 Crisis-induced Developments in EMU Rule-making in Detail

2.4.1 Economic and fiscal policy rules

2.4.1.1 Macroeconomic/excessive imbalance procedure

As an expression of the lessons learned during the GFC and the euro crisis (see section 2.3 above), the EU legislator introduced Regulation 1176/2011 on the prevention and correction of macroeconomic imbalances (including excessive imbalances)[34] and Regulation 1174/2011 (applicable only to euro-area Member States) on enforcement measures to correct excessive macroeconomic imbalances. Thus, similarly to the SGP, the MIP has a preventive and a corrective arm.

The most remarkable part of this regime, in which the Commission and Council may also push for compliance with CSRs (see section 2.2.2.1 above),[35] is the excessive imbalance procedure. Upon the detection of an excessive imbalance, an excessive imbalance procedure can be initiated by the Council upon a Commission recommendation.[36] Member States under this procedure are required to submit a corrective action plan, upon which corrective action is monitored by the Commission and eventually assessed by the Council.[37]

So far, the Commission has detected macroeconomic imbalances—sometimes even excessive imbalances—in many cases, with a number of Member States continuously displaying (excessive) imbalances over years. As a reaction, it has intensified surveillance as part of the preventive arm.[38] However, the Commission and Council have shied away from opening excessive imbalance procedures (the corrective arm), even though the ECB has repeatedly urged them to do so.[39] As a result of this, the possibility to impose sanctions on euro-area Member States according to Regulation 1174/2011 has also not been used.[40] More generally, while the need to address macroeconomic imbalances is widely acknowledged, the set-up and implementation of the macroeconomic branch of EU economic policy has been criticized as non-transparent, incoherent, and ineffective.[41]

[34] For the definitions of 'imbalances' and 'excessive imbalances', see art 2, Regulation 1176/2011.

[35] In the past, the MIP has not increased compliance with CSRs on the part of the Member States concerned; see Agnès Bénassy-Quéré and Guntram Wolff, 'How Has the Macro-economic Imbalances Procedure Worked in Practice to Improve the Resilience of the Euro Area?' (2020, study requested by the ECON committee of the European Parliament) 31.

[36] art 7, Regulation 1176/2011.

[37] arts 8–10, Regulation 1176/2011.

[38] See Beatrice Pierluigi and David Sondermann, 'Macroeconomic Imbalances in the Euro Area: Where Do we Stand?' (2018) ECB Occasional Paper Series 1, 40.

[39] See ECB, Economic Bulletin 2/2019, 64 f and preceding issues of this Bulletin; for a broader critique of the regime and its application in practice, see European Court of Auditors, 'Audit of the Macroeconomic Imbalance Procedure (MIP)' (Special Report 2018).

[40] See Willi Koll and Andrew Watt, 'The Macroeconomic Imbalance Procedure at the Heart of EU Economic Governance Reform' (2022) 57 Intereconomics 56, 57.

[41] See Koll and Watt (n 40) 56; Sebastian Dullien and others, 'Between High Ambition and Pragmatism: Proposals for a Reform of Fiscal Rules without Treaty Change' (2022) IMK Study No 77, 17, both with further references; for the Commission's own discontent with the procedure, see COM (2020) 55 final, 13.

Regulations 1176/2011 and 1174/2011 are to be seen as an attempt to extend the scope of economic policy by means of new rules (beyond the weak macroeconomic policy guidance contained in the BEPGs). The shape of this displays a certain path dependency, in that the preventive/corrective arm of the SGP may have served as a model, and in that the threat of sanctions was (originally) also deemed an appropriate enforcement tool here.[42] From a legal perspective, it is questionable whether the primary legal basis of the two regulations (see section 2.2.2.1 above) allows for the adoption of all of their respective provisions. Notably, the reverse qualified majority voting (RQMV) in the Council, and the sanctions regime, were said to go against primary law.[43]

In conclusion, the macroeconomic imbalances regime serves as an example of crises leading to the extension of a policy field beyond its original scope, resulting in the introduction of new substantive and procedural rules. But the story does not end here. In a recent Communication, the Commission pondered reform ideas, stating that, '[w]ith respect to the surveillance of macroeconomic imbalances, the framework had been successful in raising awareness of broader risks to macroeconomic stability but did not generate sufficient policy responses'.[44] Also, the long-demanded improvement of the interlinkage of the preventive arm of the SGP and the macroeconomic imbalance regime was tackled by the legislator in a recent reform.[45] This illustrates how continuous policy learning effects and an increasing interconnection of its various components underlie EMU rule-making.

2.4.1.2 Institutional objectification, expansion, and innovation: reverse (qualified) majority voting, the lending of EU institutions, and the establishment of the European Fiscal Board

In economic and fiscal policy, politically delicate decisions are, according to primary law, regularly to be taken by the Council, with a qualified majority, upon a Commission recommendation/proposal. This dominance of the Council, *de facto* the Member States, was criticized as one important reason for the malfunctioning of this policy field. The infamous blocking of the EDP against Germany and France in the early 2000s may serve as an illustration of this.[46] The solution to this problem has been to reinforce the role of the Commission and diminish that of the Council.[47]

[42] See Francesco Costamagna and Alberto Miglio, 'Sanctions in the EMU Economic Pillar' in S Montaldo, F Costamagna and A Miglio (eds), *EU Law Enforcement: The Evolution of Sanctioning Powers* (Routledge, G. Giappichelli Editore 2021) 139, 147.

[43] See, eg Rainer Palmstorfer, *Die WWU, ihre Krise und Reform* (Verlag Österreich 2021) 170 f; Matthias Ruffert, 'The European Debt Crisis and European Union Law' (2011) 48 Common Market Law Review 1777, 1800 f; for the criticism of RQMV, see below.

[44] Commission, 'Communication on orientations for a reform of the EU economic governance framework', COM (2022) 583 final 3. The Commission added that 'the Union had been more successful in reducing current account deficits than in reducing persistent and large current account surpluses. Surveillance had remained untested in preventing the accumulation of new vulnerabilities and risks and in fostering the adequate preventive policy action. Links between various surveillance strands had not always been fully exploited.'

[45] See art 31, Regulation 2024/1263.

[46] See, eg Marco Buti and Lucio R Pench, 'Why Do Large Countries Flout the Stability Pact? And what Can Be Done about It?' (2004) 42 Journal of Common Market Studies 1025; see also Case C–27/04 *Commission v Council* [2004] ECLI:EU:C:2004:436.

[47] Already under the Treaty of Lisbon, the Commission's position in the EDP had been slightly improved by allowing it to address recommendations under art 126(5) TFEU directly to the Member States concerned.

With the six-pack, the legislator decided that the role of the Commission should be strengthened in economic and fiscal policy more generally. This was done, among other things, by introducing reverse (qualified) majority voting (R(Q)MV).[48] This tool was then reused in the two-pack, and in the TSCG.[49] Under R(Q)MV, Council decisions are deemed to be taken as the Commission's recommendation/proposal suggests, unless the Council *objects* by (qualified) majority.[50] Thus, the requirement of approval by the Council has been replaced by a requirement of mere non-objection. While the Commission is by no means a depoliticized body, it is designed to be independent from the Member States. Thus, R(Q)MV has the potential to make decision-making more objective, and hence to improve, the quality of decision-making. However, since this peculiar voting mode is not provided for anywhere in primary law, its prescription by secondary law is problematic from a legal perspective.[51] These reservations notwithstanding, R(Q)MV has now also been introduced in legislative acts outside EMU.[52] Thus, it seems that this voting mode, as a tool rendering decision-making at the EU level more objective, is here to stay.

The ESM and TSCG are important complements of EU economic and fiscal policy. In both cases, the Member States involved agreed to take a policy measure in the form of public international law because, for legal and/or political reasons, they deemed it impracticable[53] or even impossible to adopt it under EU law.[54] In order to achieve as close a proximity to the EU as possible, the Member States put EU institutions in charge of the implementation of the ESM and TSCG. This allows EU institutions to act outside the scope of EU law. In the CJEU's view, the ESM 'is to ensure the financial stability of the euro area as a whole'.[55] Against this background, it had no reservation as to the Commission's, the ECB's, and its own involvement in the application of the ESM Treaty.[56] This borrowing of EU institutions can be described as an instance of

[48] See, eg art 3(3), Regulation 1174/2011 (sanctions); art 10(3), Regulation 1176/2010 (decision establishing non-compliance); art 4(2) (imposition of an interest-bearing deposit), art 5(2) (imposition of a non-interest-bearing deposit), and art 6(2) (imposition of a fine), Regulation 1173/2011. In some cases, the legislator provided for reverse simple majority voting in the Council: art 6(2)(5) and art 10(2)(5), Regulation 1466/97, as amended by Regulation 1175/2011. Regulation 1466/97 was recently replaced by Regulation 2024/1263.

[49] art 14(1) (extension of the duration of the post-programme surveillance) and art 14(4) (corrective measures), Regulation 472/2013; art 7 TSCG.

[50] Note that, eg, the establishment of an excessive deficit under art 126(6) is still to be decided by the Council with a (regular) qualified majority.

[51] See the comprehensive account by Rainer Palmstorfer, 'The Reverse Majority Voting under the "Six Pack": A Bad Turn for the Union?' (2014) 20 European Law Journal 186; see also Ruffert (n 43) 1800 f; less sceptically: Alberto de Gregorio Merino, 'Article 136 TFEU' in R Böttner and H-J Blanke (eds), *Treaty on the Functioning of the European Union – A Commentary* (vol II, Springer 2023) paras 16 and 17.

[52] See art 23(10), Regulation 1303/2013; art 14(3), Council Regulation 1024/2013 (with regard to the ECB). RMQV was also suggested in Commission Proposal COM (2018) 324 final on a general regime on rule of law conditionality, but the Council opposed it in the negotiations on what became Regulation 2020/2092.

[53] On the question of whether enhanced cooperation could/should have been used in order to stay within the realm of EU law, see, eg Loïc Azoulai and others, 'Another Legal Monster? An EUI Debate on the Fiscal Compact Treaty' (2012) 9 EUI Working Papers 1, 3 f and 9.

[54] The main rules contained in the TSCG were originally planned to be inserted in primary law by means of a Treaty revision. However, the UK thwarted these plans through its opposition.

[55] Case C-370/12 *Thomas Pringle v Government of Ireland and Others* [2012] ECLI:EU:C:2012:756, para 164.

[56] *Pringle* (n 55) paras 164 f; for the role of the ECB, see Jonathan Bauerschmidt, 'The ECB and Economic Integration' in T Beukers, D Fromage and G Monti (eds), *The New European Central Bank* (OUP 2022) 136, 144–47, with further references. For the relevance of EU fundamental rights in this context, see Joined Cases C-8/15 P to C-10/15 P *Ledra Advertising* [2016] ECLI:EU:C:2016:701, paras 67 f.

institutional expansion. Later attempts to incorporate these regimes into Union law failed for lack of support by all Member States and for lack of prioritization by the succeeding Von der Leyen Commission.[57]

The European Fiscal Board (EFB) is a committee created by the Commission, although in a less ambitious shape than originally envisaged in the so-called Five Presidents' Report,[58] and eventually created by the Commission.[59] It is composed of a chair and four members, who should all be 'internationally renowned experts [appointed] on the basis of merit, skills, and knowledge to be assessed according to proven analytical experience and competences in the analysis of public finances and in macroeconomics'.[60] The chair and the members are appointed by the Commission upon a proposal by the President of the Commission.[61] In spite of its status as an independent body, the Board is institutionally attached to the Commission's Secretariat-General.[62] Created as an 'experiment at the supranational level',[63] originally with the intention to make the Commission's approach towards the enforcement of economic and fiscal rules more determined,[64] the Board's task now is to advise the Council and Commission on their functions in the multilateral fiscal surveillance.[65] For that purpose, it will cooperate with the independent fiscal institutions in the Member States.[66] The EFB was reformed in 2024 with the aim to strengthen the mandate and role of the EFB, 'while preserving the surveillance role conferred on the Commission by the EU Treaties'.[67]

2.4.1.3 Excessive deficit procedure

The application, in practice, of the EDP indicates remarkable deviations during different periods of time. Whereas, in the wake of the GFC, the Commission chased after

[57] As part of the so-called St Nicholas Package, the Commission, in December 2017, launched a proposal to incorporate the ESM (renamed the European Monetary Fund) and the TSCG into EU law: Commission Proposals COM (2017) 827 final and COM (2017) 824 final.

[58] See Annex 3 of the Five Presidents' Report: Commission, 'Completing Europe's Economic and Monetary Union' (2015) and note, in particular, the coordination of (and not only cooperation with) its national counterparts which was envisaged for the EFB <https://commission.europa.eu/document/download/261ad02b-070a-47a1-b52b-b242db48addf_en?filename=The%20Five%20President%27s%20Report%3A%20Completing%20Europe%27s%20Economic%20and%20Monetary%20Union>.

[59] Commission Decision 2015/1937/EU; recently repealed by Commission Decision 2024/2115.

[60] art 3(3), Commission Decision 2024/2115.

[61] See further art 3(5), Commission Decision 2024/2115.

[62] art 6, Commission Decision 2024/2115; for the Member States' and the Commission's different ideas regarding the EFB's independence, see Tobias Tesche, 'The European Fiscal Board: Supranational De Novo Body or Orchestrator?' (2021) 51 Italian Political Science Review 389, 390 f; for an assessment of the EFB's independence (in particular with regard to the Commission), see Zareh Asatryan and Friedrich Heinemann, 'The European Fiscal Board: An Experiment at the Supranational Level' in R Beetsma and X Debrun (eds), *Independent Fiscal Councils: Watchdogs or Lapdogs?* (VoxEU/CEPR Press 2018) 165, 169 f; European Parliament, 'What Role for the Advisory European Fiscal Board?' (Briefing 2022) 4, with references to opinions of the ECB and IMF.

[63] Asatryan and Heinemann (n 62) 165.

[64] See Tesche (n 62) 391 f.

[65] art 2(1), Commission Decision 2015/1937/EU.

[66] art 2(2)(d), Commission Decision 2024/2115. The independent fiscal institutions shall be established due to art 8a, Council Directive 2011/85/EU, as amended by Council Directive 2024/1265.

[67] Commission Proposal COM (2023) 240 final, 8.

nearly all Member States—euro-area Member States and Member States 'with a derogation' alike—it applied a different approach throughout the pandemic. During the GFC (as in the years before this crisis), the procedures took a couple of years on average, and ended with a Council decision abrogating the decision on the existence of an excessive deficit pursuant to Article 126(12) TFEU. No fines have been imposed on euro-area Member States for not taking action to correct their respective excessive deficits. Fines against Spain and Portugal were cancelled by the Council.[68]

During the pandemic, the Commission limited itself to issuing reports pursuant to Article 126(3) TFEU—indicating that a Member State 'does not fulfil the requirements under one or both of [the deficit] criteria'—for most of the Member States. This can be explained only in part by the Council's (transitional) suspension of the deficit criteria (see section 2.2.2.1 above). The Council based this decision on the so-called general escape clause, as introduced to the SGP by the six-pack,[69] thereby confirming the existence of a 'severe economic downturn' caused by the pandemic (and Member States' countermeasures).[70] In terms of the SGP's corrective arm, the existence of a severe economic downturn not only allows for a more flexible handling of ongoing EDP, but also renders excessive deficits 'exceptional' within the meaning of Article 126(2)(a) TFEU.[71] If the ratio remains close to the 3 per cent value and the excess is, in addition to that, 'temporary',[72] the Commission will not initiate proceedings pursuant to Article 126 TFEU.

In its 2023 report pursuant to Article 126(3) TFEU, the Commission concluded that fifteen Member States had exceeded the deficit reference value in 2022, or planned to exceed it in 2023. It considered all of these excesses exceptional, but only one of them was close to the 3 per cent value. In nine cases, it also expected them not to be temporary. Among the Member States whose debt exceeded 60 per cent of their respective GDPs, the debt reduction requirement had not been met by three Member States.[73] The Commission's overall conclusion was that, due to the 'persistently high uncertainty for the macroeconomic and budgetary outlook at this juncture', no new EDP ought to

[68] Council Implementing Decisions 2017/2350 and 2017/2351. This cancellation was based on art 6(4) (second alternative), Regulation 1173/2011, ie not due to 'exceptional economic circumstances', but due to requests by the two Member States. With its Implementing Decisions 2015/1289 and 2018/818, the Council imposed fines on Spain and Austria, respectively, on the basis of art 8(1), Regulation 1173/2011, for the manipulation of debt data. Implementing Decision 2015/1289 was unsuccessfully challenged before the Court of Justice; see Case C-521/15 *Spain v Council* [2017] ECLI:EU:C:2017:982.

[69] This clause was contained in arts 5(1), 6(3), 9(1) and 10(3), Regulation 1466/97, as regards the preventive arm of the SGP, and, with a view to its corrective arm, in arts 3(5) and 5(2), Regulation 1467/97. See now arts 25 and 26, Regulation 2024/1263, and the references to these provisions in Regulation 1467/97, as amended by Council Regulation 2024/1264.

[70] Commission Communication, COM (2020) 123 final; Council, press release 173/20 (23 March 2020).

[71] See art 2(1)(1), Regulation 1467/97 and the further specification in art 2(1)(2).

[72] See art 2(1)(2), Regulation 1467/97.

[73] Commission, 'Report prepared in accordance with Art 126(3) of the Treaty on the Functioning of the European Union', COM (2023) 631 final, 35. Remarkably, in the 2022 Report (Commission, 'Report prepared in accordance with Article 126(3) of the Treaty on the Functioning of the European Union', COM (2022) 630 final, 7 and 35), the Commission had still referred to 'the current exceptional economic conditions'.

be launched for the time being, but that in spring 2024 it would propose to the Council the opening of deficit-based EDP.[74]

Not only from an economic, but also from a legal perspective, it is justified for the Commission to take into account various economic parameters when assessing the situation in the Member States.[75] But it is remarkable that the Commission, while confirming an excess of the reference values in many cases, already at this stage of the procedure excluded the initiation of an EDP, apparently not even waiting for the opinion of the Economic and Financial Committee, as foreseen in Article 126(4) TFEU. Instead of trusting in the effectiveness of EDPs, the Commission seems to prefer concentrating on preventive measures in economic and fiscal policy. In its 'Fiscal policy guidance for 2024', it recommends that substantially or moderately indebted Member States should plausibly and continuously reduce their debt, while investing (like the remaining Member States) in the economy (with a focus on greening and digitalization) with the RRF resources allocated to them.[76]

In conclusion, we note two remarkable characteristics of the practical application of the EDP over the past fifteen years. First, no sanctions have been imposed. This means that there has been a continuous non-application of the enforcement scheme since the introduction of the EDP. Second, the Commission, unlike during the GFC, has refused to launch new EDPs during, and in the aftermath of, the pandemic, even though the deficit, and in particular the debt threshold, was exceeded in a number of Member States. This is not to say that EDPs do not have certain effects on Member States' fiscal discipline,[77] but it is clear that the Commission and, even more so, the Council, have shied away from using all the tools available under the EDP.

2.4.2 Common fiscal capacities

The idea of creating common fiscal capacities in addition to the comparatively small EU budget has seen a choppy development since the GFC. Although already favoured by some, in the 1990s, as a natural extension to economic coordination, rules on fiscal discipline, and a monetary policy strongly focusing on price stability, a number of Member States, most prominently Germany, have always been sceptical of taking steps in the direction of what is called a 'transfer union'.[78] On being confronted with the euro crisis, some concessions were made, resulting, after temporary solutions (the European

[74] See Commission, 'Fiscal policy guidance for 2024', COM (2023) 141 final, 9.

[75] See art 2(3)(1), Regulation 1467/97.

[76] See Commission, 'Fiscal policy guidance for 2024', COM (2023) 141 final, 8.

[77] See Jasper FM De Jong and Niels D Gilbert, 'Fiscal Discipline in EMU? Testing the Effectiveness of the Excessive Deficit Procedure' (2020) 61 European Journal of Political Economy 1.

[78] See, eg references in Bruno de Witte, 'The Innovative European Response to COVID-19: Decline of Differentiated Integration and Reinvention of Cohesion Policy' (2021) ECB Legal Conference 2021 (Continuity and Change – How the Challenges of Today Prepare the Ground for Tomorrow) 394, 395; David Howarth and Joachim Schild, '*Nein* to "Transfer Union": The German Brake on the Construction of a European Union Fiscal Capacity' (2021) 43 Journal of European Integration 209; Magnus Schoeller and Olof Karlsson, 'Championing the "German Model"? Germany's Consistent Preferences on the Integration of Fiscal Constraints' (2021) 43 Journal of European Integration 193.

Financial Stabilisation Mechanism (EFSM) and European Financial Stability Facility (EFSF)), in the creation of the permanent ESM, from which euro-area Member States could request financial support if they faced difficulties in financing themselves on the capital markets.

In the search for a legal basis for this, the euro-area Member States eventually came to the conclusion that, under the EMU chapter of the TFEU, no ESM could be created *as a measure of EU law*. Thus, they decided to create this mechanism in the form of an agreement among the euro-area Member States, concluded under public international law (see section 2.4.1.2 above). It was contested, among other things, whether the ESM would be in accordance with Article 125 TFEU. To be on the safe side, the Member States introduced a new paragraph 3 to Article 136 TFEU (see section 2.2.1 above). Due to delays in the ratification process, some bad timing occurred: Article 136(3) TFEU entered into force on 1 May 2013, whereas the ESM Treaty had already entered into force on 27 September 2012.

These and other legal concerns were addressed by the CJEU in the *Pringle* judgment. Given the 'strict conditionality' applicable under the ESM,[79] the Court confirmed compliance of the ESM with Article 125 TFEU (and other provisions of EU law).[80] With regard to the newly introduced Article 136(3) TFEU, it held that it had only declaratory value; that is, that its creation was not needed for the ESM to be in conformity with EU law.[81] This rendered the above-mentioned time gap legally irrelevant.

In the aftermath of *Pringle*, a debate was conducted on the reasonability and legal feasibility of a permanent fiscal capacity for the euro area (in addition to the ESM).[82] In 2018, Germany and France came up with a proposal for creating a euro-area budget within the framework of EU law. The two countries proposed the new facility—to be financed primarily by the euro-area Member States (partly, for example, by a financial transactions tax) and to be part of the EU budget—to 'foster convergence and incentivize reform implementation in particular by co-financing growth-enhancing public expenditures'. Also, its potentially 'stabilising function in the eurozone, especially as investments are prone to be shed in case of pressure on national public finances' was mentioned.[83] This explanation clearly hints at cohesion policy, which the two Member States had in mind as the legal basis of the euro-area budget. More concretely, Article 175(3) TFEU was suggested as the main such provision, possibly in conjunction with other Treaty provisions.[84] Eventually the proposal failed, mainly due to the resistance of the Netherlands and other (smaller) 'creditor' Member States.[85]

[79] See art 136(3) TFEU and the reference in Recital 2 of the ESM Treaty. For the development of 'strict conditionality' in political and legal discourse, see Marijn van der Sluis, 'The Role of Constitutional Law for the ECB: Past, Present, and Future' in T Beukers, D Fromage and G Monti (eds), *The New European Central Bank* (OUP 2022) 392, in particular 403.

[80] *Pringle* (n 55) in particular para 143.

[81] *Pringle* (n 55) in particular paras 72 f.

[82] This idea received strong support from the European Parliament; see, eg Resolution of 16 February 2017 on budgetary capacity for the euro area, P8_TA(2017)0050.

[83] <https://www.consilium.europa.eu/media/37011/proposal-on-the-architecture-of-a-eurozone-budget.pdf> accessed 19 November 2023.

[84] Remarkably, the proposal states that '[t]his instrument should not be a precedent for the EU's cohesion policy'.

[85] See Magnus Schoeller, 'Preventing the Eurozone Budget: Issue Replacement and Small State Influence in EMU' (2021) 28 Journal of European Public Policy 1727.

Following up on this debate, in July 2019 the Commission launched a more conventional proposal for a 'budgetary instrument for convergence and competitiveness' for the euro area.[86] The financial means—eventually not more than around 10 billion euros—would have come from the national budgets of the euro-area Member States. Distributional (or stabilizing) features were largely removed, so that the proposed instrument would have been a reform delivery tool rather than a budget for the euro area. The proposal was dropped in view of the pandemic and the ensuing more ambitious reform discussions.[87]

These discussions resulted in the next big step in this development, namely the creation of the RRF as the main element of NGEU. The (expected) economic and fiscal calamities brought about by anti-COVID-19 measures, which hit all Member States, gave way to agreement on the creation of a common fiscal capacity. The RRF was established as a measure of cohesion policy based on Article 175(3) TFEU,[88] the 'flexibility clause' of the TFEU's cohesion policy chapter.[89] This was achieved through a very broad interpretation of the term 'cohesion policy'.[90] Even more remarkable is how the RRF is financed. Article 5 of the new Own Resources Decision[91] stipulates that '[e]xtraordinary and temporary additional means to address the consequences of the COVID-19 crisis' shall be borrowed on capital markets by the Commission on behalf of the EU. (The issuing of bonds by the EEC in the 1970s was still based on the flexibility clause, which is now laid down in Article 352 TFEU.) As set out in section 2.2.1 above, the RRF's financial means are used within the framework of the European Union Recovery Instrument on the basis of Article 122 TFEU.[92] This choice of legal basis, which has recently been taken more and more often,[93] is not uncontested in legal scholarship.[94] From a democratic legitimacy perspective, it has been criticized that the European Parliament (EP) is only to be consulted under this provision. By strategically making the RRF Regulation, which was adopted under the ordinary legislative procedure, part of a package deal with NGEU and the new Multiannual Financial Framework, the EP

[86] COM (2019) 354 final. As legal bases, the Commission proposed art 136(1)(b) in combination with art 121(6) TFEU.
[87] See de Witte, 'European Response to COVID-19' (n 78) 396.
[88] Regulation 2021/241.
[89] de Witte, 'European Response to COVID-19' 399.
[90] See Päivi Leino and Tuomas Saarenheimo, 'Fiscal Stabilization for EMU: Managing Incompleteness' (2018) 43 European Law Review 623, 639.
[91] Council Decision 2020/2053.
[92] Council Regulation 2020/2094 establishing a European Union Recovery Instrument to support the recovery in the aftermath of the COVID-19 crisis. With regard to the legal basis, the Commission held: 'The present situation is unprecedented. It is characterized by severe difficulties caused by exceptional occurrences beyond the Member States' control. Therefore, it is appropriate to adopt under Article 122 TFEU exceptional temporary measures to support recovery and resilience across the Union' (COM (2020) 441 final, 2 f). The Regulation does not state on which of the two paras of art 122 TFEU it shall be based; indicating a tendency towards para 1, see Council, 'Opinion of the Legal Service', 9062/20, paras 119–22. The grant of financial assistance is explicitly referred to only in para 2 of art 122 TFEU.
[93] See Merijn Chamon, *The Use of Article 122 TFEU* (EP Study 2023) 25 ff.
[94] See, eg Häde, 'Art. 122' (n 20) para 9; Caroline Heber, 'Europarechtliche Grenzen für den Wiederaufbaufonds' (2021) 56 Europarecht 416, 437 f.

pressed for further involvement.[95] For example, within the framework of the recovery and resilience dialogue, it receives regular information from the Commission on the implementation of the RRF.[96]

In conclusion, the RRF is a measure of cohesion policy which is largely financed by means which the EU have borrowed on the capital markets, and which are provided to the Member States on the basis of a provision of economic policy, namely Article 122 TFEU.[97] While the interlinkage of cohesion policy and EMU is not entirely new,[98] the approach of making use of Article 175(3) TFEU in addition to Article 122 TFEU can be questioned. After all, the EFSM and SURE, as measures also providing (limited) funds to the (euro-area) Member States, were based solely on Article 122 TFEU.[99] What rather speaks in favour of also invoking Article 175 TFEU is the RRF's redistributive character. In relation to their GDPs, Greece, Romania, and Croatia benefit most strongly.[100]

In terms of the origin (debt) and scale of the financial means, the RRF is certainly an unprecedented instrument.[101] Whether it will be a further milestone on the way towards a transfer union will be seen once the EU starts paying back its debt.[102] If the instalments are paid from the income of existing own resources, the divide between net-payer and net-receiver states will resurface.[103] But even if new resources (eg new EU-wide taxes) are created, this divide may at best be reduced, depending on the shape of the new income.[104] In that sense, even though there has been contestation about the design of the RRF (and NGEU more broadly), an important part of the necessary policy decisions has been postponed.[105]

Another aspect to be discussed here is conditionality. With regard to the ESM, the strict conditionality ('austerity measures') required for financial support was one of the

[95] See Lucy Kinski and Ermela Gianna, 'The Role of the European Parliament in the Design of the Recovery and Resilience Facility: United and Influential?' (2023) 135 EU Law Live Weekend Edition (special issue, *The Way Forward in the EMU*, pt II) 15.

[96] art 26, Regulation 2021/241; for the application of this regime in practice, see Commission, 'Recovery and Resilience Facility: Two years on. A unique instrument at the heart of the EU's green and digital transformation' (Communication), COM (2023) 99 final, 7 f.

[97] art 122 TFEU was also used as a basis for SURE (see section 2.2.2.1 above), the financing of which went along similar lines (even though on a much lower scale).

[98] See Leo Flynn, 'Greater Convergence, More Resilience? Cohesion Policy and the Deepening of the Economic and Monetary Union' (2019) Maastricht University Faculty of Law Working Paper Series (Diane Fromage and Bruno de Witte (eds), 'Recent Evolutions in the Economic and Monetary Union and the European Banking Union: A Reflection') 48.

[99] See, eg Diane Fromage, 'The Future of EMU Architecture Post-COVID' (2020) 47 Legal Issues of Economic Integration 295, 310.

[100] See Lucas Schramm, Ulrich Krotz and Bruno de Witte, 'Building "Next Generation" after the Pandemic: The Implementation and Implications of the EU Covid Recovery Plan' (2022) Journal of Common Market Studies 1, 3.

[101] See also COM (2020) 445 final, 4: 'unprecedented nature of this operation and the exceptional amount of those funds'.

[102] The repayment will start in 2028 and is scheduled until 2058.

[103] For Germany's presumed contribution, see <https://wirtschaft.com/eu-wiederaufbaufonds-deutschland-wird-groesster-nettozahler> accessed 19 November 2023.

[104] Another option would be to reduce the EU's (other) expenditure. Where no other solution can be found, 'the Member States, as the Commission's last resort, shall make the resources necessary for that purpose available to the Commission' (art 9(4), Council Decision 2020/2053).

[105] See de Witte, 'European Response to COVID-19' (n 78) 397 f. A foretaste of this discussion is provided by the Commission's review of the current Multiannual Financial Framework and proposals for new financial sources at EU level, among other things to service the EU's debt in view of increasing interest rates; see Commission proposal COM (2023) 331 final for an amendment of the Council's Own Resources Decision.

main reasons why the CJEU, in the *Pringle* judgment, confirmed its compatibility with Article 125 TFEU.[106] In this context, conditionality has become an instrument for creating policy rules, by means of which the Commission and the ECB could, regardless of the division of competences between the EU and its Member States, impose reform obligations[107] on beneficiary Member States.[108] Also, under the RRF, some conditions apply. Conditionality under the two regimes differs considerably, though. Under the ESM, during the euro crisis, it was set out in much detail ('strict') and encompassed all kinds of policy measures (social reforms, liquidation of banks, tax enforcement, etc).[109] Under the RRF, the conditions are much more flexible, essentially defined by the Member States themselves, and directly connected to the financial means.[110] These conditions determine how the Member States intend to use the money to be transmitted to them, with a widely drafted focus on greening and digitalization. In their national recovery and resilience plans—upon which the Commission authorizes funding—the Member States also have to address, inter alia, economic problems identified in the European Semester.[111] This strengthens the link between cohesion policy and economic and fiscal policy under the RRF, and may contribute to further increasing the importance of CSRs and other (legally non-binding) output adopted in the context of the European Semester.[112] By making RRF financial means conditional upon consideration of CSRs, the legislator has provided for an important lever (to be operated mainly by the Commission) in pushing for compliance with these legally non-binding acts.[113] This can be read as a form of hardening of rules which could otherwise be enforced only in the course of an EDP.[114]

The ESM seems to have reconsidered its approach towards conditionality, too: during the pandemic, the ESM offered funding to euro-area Member States (Pandemic Crisis

[106] *Pringle* (n 55), in particular para 111.

[107] On the legal (non-)bindingness of the memoranda of understanding concluded in this context, see Claire Kilpatrick, 'Are the Bailouts Immune to EU Social Challenge because they Are Not EU Law?' (2014) 10 European Constitutional Law Review 393, 409 f, with further references.

[108] See, eg Michael Ioannidis, 'Europe's New Transformations: How the EU Economic Constitution Changed during the Eurozone Crisis' (2016) 53 Common Market Law Review 1237, 1267–71.

[109] For the notion of creditor domination, which was strong under the ESM, but is rather weak under the RRF, see Malte Frøslee Ibsen, 'Creditor Domination in the Eurozone: A Republican View' (2022) 20 Comparative European Politics 689.

[110] The specific rule of law conditionality, an instrument which applies to Member States' spending of EU financial means more generally, can only be mentioned briefly here: see, eg Antonia Baraggia and Matteo Bonelli, 'Linking Money to Values: The New Rule of Law Conditionality Regulation and its Constitutional Challenges' (2022) 23 German Law Journal 131; for different categories of conditionality, see ibid 150; for the broad scope of this form of conditionality, see also the contribution in this book by Eriksen and Everson on health policy (in particular, section 4.3).

[111] See art 17(3), Regulation 2021/241.

[112] See also Bart Vanhercke and Amy Verdun, 'The European Semester as Goldilocks: Macroeconomic Policy Coordination and the Recovery and Resilience Facility' (2021) 60 Journal of Common Market Studies 204; see also Commission, 'Enforcing EU law for a Europe that delivers', COM (2022) 518 final, 13 f; ambivalent with regard to (non-)compliance with social recommendations, see Francesco Corti and Patrik Vesan, 'From Austerity-conditionality towards a New Investment-led Growth Strategy: Social Europe after the Recovery and Resilience Facility' (2022) Social Policy & Administration 513.

[113] For the hardening and softening tendencies of different CSRs (irrespective of the RRF), see Sonja Bekker, 'Hardening and Softening of Country-specific Recommendations in the European Semester' (2021) 44 West European Politics 114.

[114] In the course of MIP, compliance with particular (MIP-related) CSRs could be enforced.

Support Programme).[115] The 'only requirement' was that the recipient state committed to using the credit line to support domestic financing of direct and indirect costs related to healthcare, cure, and prevention due to the pandemic.[116]

It is striking that the provision of jointly collected repayable funds to (euro-area) Member States for them to service their debts must be subject to strict conditionality in order to avoid a conflict with Article 125 TFEU, whereas for the provision of jointly borrowed, partly non-repayable funds to Member States for them to invest in their economies—which spared them from borrowing the money themselves—it is sufficient to link it to some broad policy objectives and to adherence to (broad) EU guidelines under the European Semester. 'National ownership'—a buzzword which strongly informed the discussion on the reform of EU economic governance—also characterizes the procedure in which the use of the financial means of the RRF by the individual Member States is determined.

2.4.3 The role of the ECB

Early on during the euro crisis, the ECB had been involved in tasks related to macroeconomic stabilization.[117] Under Council Regulation 407/2010 on the creation of the EFSM, the ECB had, among other things, to be consulted by the Commission when determining the conditions for 're-establishing a sound economic or financial situation in the beneficiary Member State'.[118] Also, the EFSF Framework Agreement made use of the ECB's expertise. Among other tasks, the ECB was involved, together with the Commission and the International Monetary Fund (IMF), in the negotiation of memoranda of understanding under the EFSF.[119] The ECB also played this role within the framework of the EFSF's successor, the ESM.[120] Thereby, the ECB, as part of the Troika, has influenced policy measures (macroeconomic adjustment programmes) on the level of the beneficiary states to a considerable extent.

In addition, the ECB's non-standard measures had a strong macroeconomic impetus, in particular the (announced) acquisition of state bonds on a very large scale. One of the early answers to the economic downturn caused by the pandemic came, again, from the ECB: the PEPP. Critics of the ECB invoked the economic impetus of the ECB's measures to challenge their qualification as 'monetary policy'. Substantially, it is,

[115] See Menelaos Markakis, 'The Reform of the European Stability Mechanism: Process, Substance, and the Pandemic' (2020) 47 Legal Issues of Economic Integration 359, 373 ff; Mauro Megliani, 'The ESM Pandemic Crisis Support Facility: A Changing Conditionality?' (2022) 33 European Business Law Review 227.

[116] <https://www.esm.europa.eu/sites/default/files/migration_files/20200508-pcs-term-sheet-final.pdf> accessed 19 November 2023. However, none of the eligible states applied.

[117] On this involvement prior to the euro crisis, and its intensification in the course of this crisis, see Thomas Beukers, 'The New ECB and its Relationship with the Eurozone Member States: Between Central Bank Independence and Central Bank Intervention' (2013) 50 Common Market Law Review 1579, 1583 ff.

[118] art 3(3) and (4), Council Regulation 407/2010.

[119] S 2(1)(a), EFSF Framework Agreement.

[120] While the EFSF still exists, after the establishment of the ESM it was the ESM alone which provided financial support to euro-area Member States. The EFSF and ESM share 'staff, facilities, and operations': <https://www.esm.europa.eu/about-us/history#the_programmes> accessed 19 November 2023.

in places, difficult to clearly disentangle monetary policy from economic policy. Doing 'whatever it takes to preserve the euro'[121] could be seen as more than just maintaining price stability. At the same time, it can be argued that maintaining price stability logically implies preserving the single currency.

The CJEU has drawn the distinction between monetary policy and economic policy, which is important for the question of competence,[122] based on the objective(s) of the measure at issue. Apart from that, it has also considered relevant the instruments employed to achieve the objective(s).[123] If the ECB claims maintaining price stability to be the objective of one of its measures, and if this assertion is not flawed by a manifest error of assessment, and does not go beyond the TFEU otherwise, the CJEU will allocate it to the field of monetary policy in accordance with Article 127(1) TFEU. The achievement of additional (positive) effects does not harm its status as a monetary policy measure. A monetary policy measure, the Court held with a view to the strong stabilizing effects of the OMT and PSPP, cannot be allocated to economic policy 'for the sole reason that it may have indirect effects that can also be sought in the context of economic policy'.[124] Notwithstanding a clear mandate setting price stability as the 'primary objective', the Court's moderate standard of review grants the ECB considerable room for manoeuvre.[125]

Considering the reactions of the capital markets to the ECB's non-standard measures, the positive effect on stabilizing the euro area was arguably much more visible than the effect on maintaining price stability. Between 2014 and early 2022, the inflation rate in the euro area continuously ranged between values far below 2 per cent.[126] Thus, the inflation rate of close to, but below, 2 per cent and (after the 2021 monetary policy strategy review) 2 per cent, over the medium term, was never reached during this period. After Russia's invasion of Ukraine, starting in February 2022, inflation increased dramatically. In 2022, the average inflation rate came close to 10 per cent.[127] Against this background, the ECB started to return to a conventional monetary policy, quickly increasing its key interest rate from 0 per cent in January 2022 to 4.5 per cent by September 2023, thereby making use not only of 0.25 and 0.5 per cent leaps, but also of unprecedented 0.75 percentage point leaps.[128] In order to mitigate the effects of this return to conventional monetary policy, in July 2022 the ECB approved the TPI, with a focus on public sector securities, to be activated in case of market dynamics posing a

[121] <https://www.ecb.europa.eu/press/key/date/2012/html/sp120726.en.html> accessed 19 November 2023.

[122] See section 2.2.1 above.

[123] See *Pringle* (n 55) paras 53 ff; Case C-62/14 *Peter Gauweiler and Others v Deutscher Bundestag* [2015] ECLI:EU:C:2015:400, paras 42 ff; Case C-493/17 *Weiss* [2018] ECLI:EU:C:2018:1000, paras 53 ff.

[124] *Weiss* (n 123) para 61, with references to the Cases *Pringle* (n 55) and *Gauweiler* (n 123). Another important point of criticism was the alleged violation of art 123 TFEU. But also in that regard, the Court confirmed the ECB's compliance with EU law.

[125] Takis Tridimas and Napoleon Xanthoulis, 'A Legal Analysis of the *Gauweiler* Case. Between Monetary Policy and Constitutional Conflict' (2016) Maastricht Journal of European and Comparative Law 17, 38, even speaks of 'enormous discretion'.

[126] <https://www.inflationtool.com/rates/euro/historical> accessed 19 November 2023.

[127] <https://www.global-rates.com/de/wirtschaftsstatistiken/inflation/2022.aspx> accessed 19 November 2023.

[128] Key interest rate for main refinancing operations; <https://www.ecb.europa.eu/stats/policy_and_exchange_rates/key_ecb_interest_rates/html/index.en.html> accessed 19 November 2023.

threat to the transmission of monetary policy in the euro area. In addition to this, from March 2023 onwards, the ECB has gradually reduced its asset holdings ('quantitative tightening'). Meanwhile, inflation has decreased, and so has the key interest rate.[129]

In addition to its involvement in drafting conditionality requirements, as set out above, the ECB's non-standard measures have also had an impact in this respect: in *Gauweiler*, the CJEU emphasized the 'strict and effective conditionality attached to an appropriate [EFSF/ESM] programme'[130] which the ECB required for its announced purchases under OMT. This linkage to conditionality was seen as a confirmation of the ECB's obligations under Article 127(1) in conjunction with Article 119(3) TFEU—'to comply with the guiding principle that public finances must be sound'—and with the prohibition of monetary financing.[131] The ECB's involvement in formulating the conditions it later somewhat enforced through its monetary policy was not considered problematic by the Court.[132]

With regard to PEPP,[133] the ECB stresses that all asset categories eligible under the asset purchase programmes launched from 2014 onwards (including, for example, the PSPP) are also eligible under the new programme.[134] Greek state bonds do not meet these criteria, but are nevertheless considered eligible.[135] It was argued that, with enormous public investment programmes being launched by the Member States from the early days of the COVID-19 crisis, the term 'sound budgetary policies' should be interpreted more broadly than in the years before the pandemic. Thus, the requirements for PEPP should not be considered too high.[136] In the TPI, the Commission's more relaxed approach towards economic and fiscal policy during and following the pandemic (see sections 2.4.1.3 and 2.4.2 above) has been translated into monetary policy: parts of the eligibility criteria for this programme are that a Member State is not subject to an EDP or an excessive imbalance procedure, and that it is complying with its commitments under the RRF framework.[137]

In its monetary policy strategy review from 2021, the ECB took account of their practice of non-standard measures. With their new dogma, '[f]inancial stability is a

[129] For the ECB's concern that inflation may 'remain too high for too long', see <https://www.ecb.europa.eu/press/pr/date/2023/html/ecb.mp230727~da80cfcf24.en.html> accessed 19 November 2023.

[130] OMT press release; <https://www.ecb.europa.eu/press/pr/date/2012/html/pr120906_1.en.html> accessed 19 November 2023.

[131] *Gauweiler* (n 123) paras 61 and 120; see also Jonathan Yiangou, Mícheál O'Keeffe and Gabriel Glöckler, '"Tough Love": How the ECB's Monetary Financing Prohibition Pushes Deeper Euro Area Integration' (2013) 25 European Integration 223, 234.

[132] See, sceptically, Herwig CH Hofmann, 'Controlling the Powers of the ECB: Delegation, Discretion, Reasoning and Care. What *Gauweiler, Weiss* and others Can Teach us' (2018) ADEMU Working Paper Series 1, 18 f. With regard to PSPP, the Court contented itself with the temporary nature of the programme and 'a series of safeguards designed to limit the effects of the PSPP on the impetus to pursue a sound budgetary policy' enshrined in the relevant ECB Decision 2015/774; see *Weiss* (n 123) paras 129 ff, para 137.

[133] For this, and further measures the ECB has taken in the context of the pandemic and legal and economic assessment thereof, see Klaus Tuori, *The European Central Bank and the European Macroeconomic Constitution* (CUP 2022) 239 ff.

[134] <https://www.ecb.europa.eu/mopo/implement/pepp/html/index.en.html> accessed 19 November 2023.

[135] art 3, ECB Decision 2020/440; for the suspension of rules by the ECB during the euro crisis, see Beukers (n 117) 1595.

[136] See Stefan Grund, 'Legal, Compliant and Suitable: The ECB's Pandemic Emergency Purchase Programme (PEPP)' (2020) Hertie School Policy Brief 1, 6 f with further references.

[137] <https://www.ecb.europa.eu/press/pr/date/2022/html/ecb.pr220721~973e6e7273.en.html> accessed 19 November 2023.

precondition for price stability and vice versa',[138] they justify the strong economic effects of their measures—for the past, and for the future. This new perspective ought to allow the ECB to consider financial stability 'whenever this is relevant to the pursuit of price stability'.[139]

2.5 Crisis Politics in EMU: Explaining Incremental Institutional Change

What we have written so far leaves us with a puzzle. On the one hand, EMU has clear legal and political limits. For example, EU joint fiscal capacities have not been envisaged in the Treaty framework and are opposed by so-called 'frugal' countries in (the north of) the euro area. On the other hand, we have seen crisis-induced change, albeit not enough to remedy EMU's inbuilt asymmetries.[140] In the following, we therefore seek to explain, first, why EMU governance and reform have been likely to end up in deadlock, and, second, why incremental change, often based on the 'lowest common denominator', has nevertheless taken place—and may continue to do so in the future.

To explain why EMU reform tends to stall, we draw on rational-institutionalist assumptions. Accordingly, joint policy decisions and institutional change are the product of collective action between actors who pursue their individual preferences under given institutional constraints.[141] Regarding the institutional design and governance of EMU, the most relevant actors are the Member States. Roughly speaking, their preferences can be divided into two diametrically opposed camps. So-called creditor (or surplus) countries, mainly in the north of the euro area, prefer national adjustment based on internal devaluation and structural reforms ('austerity'), whereas so-called debtor (or deficit) states in the south prefer cross-national risk-sharing, such as common fiscal capacities ('solidarity').[142] These strongly diverging preferences make agreement difficult from the outset. In addition, most important decisions on EMU reform are taken under unanimity (with the exception of issues regarding 'multilateral surveillance').[143]

Hence, considering diverging Member State preferences over outcomes, under strong institutional constraints—unanimity—the odds are not in favour of institutional

[138] <https://www.ecb.europa.eu/pub/financial-stability/fsr/focus/2021/html/ecb.fsrbox202111_08~d3131413c2.en.html> accessed 19 November 2023.

[139] <https://www.ecb.europa.eu/pub/financial-stability/fsr/focus/2021/html/ecb.fsrbox202111_08~d3131413c2.en.html> accessed 19 November 2023.

[140] Both EMU's crisis-induced macroeconomic rules (MIP) and fiscal capacities (ESM) turned out to be ineffective and/or insufficient.

[141] In this context, 'institutions' are understood as rules of behaviour that constrain individual action and thus shape collective action: see, eg Adrienne Héritier, *Explaining Institutional Change in Europe* (OUP 2007).

[142] See, eg Klaus Armingeon and Skyler Cranmer, 'Position-taking in the Euro Crisis' (2018) 25 Journal of European Public Policy 546; Jeffry Frieden and Stefanie Walter, 'Understanding the Political Economy of the Eurozone Crisis' (2017) 20 Annual Review of Political Science 371; Hall (n 24); Thomas Lehner and Fabio Wasserfallen, 'Political Conflict in the Reform of the Eurozone' (2019) 20 European Union Politics 45.

[143] Even if unanimity among Member States is *not* required, the ordinary legislative procedure, according to which Member States in the Council have to find an agreement with the EP, based on a proposal by the European Commission, poses high institutional hurdles to finding agreement in the case of diverging preferences.

change in EMU.[144] At the same time, in the event of existential crises that threaten the survival of the common currency, non-agreement is not an option either.[145] As a consequence, Member States compromise on the 'lowest common denominator' of their diverging preferences; that is, they do as little as possible but as much as is needed to preserve the common currency. In the words of Howarth and Quaglia, the results are 'sticking plaster' solutions, which 'help to stop the "bleeding", but do not address the underlying "pathology" of divergence and asymmetries in EMU'.[146] Given a limiting Treaty framework, diverging preferences over outcomes, and strong institutional constraints, Member States 'fail forward'[147] rather than completing EMU through crises. Especially after the reform of EMU in response to the euro crisis (see section 2.2.2 above), the room for manoeuvre provided by the Treaty framework seems (close to) exhausted, and there is little common political will to agree on further stabilizing measures in EMU. This can explain deadlock, but why do we still see substantial institutional change, such as the suspension and revision of the SGP or the establishment of the RRF?[148]

We argue that the deadlock in EMU is broken up, time and again, by crises 'spilling over' from other policy areas (finance, health, security, etc).[149] Since the asymmetric EMU cannot absorb such external shocks—as states cannot print their own money, each crisis might push the less competitive euro-area members into a liquidity crisis—they risk quickly resulting in economic crises. At the same time, these exogenous crises create high political pressure for action and this facilitates the unprecedented use of existing legal bases. For example, shortly after the COVID-19 pandemic started to spread through Europe, sovereign bond yields of single Member States started to rise and the ECB reacted quickly by launching PEPP to stabilize the markets in the short run. In the further course, Member States agreed to set up the RRF: a common debt instrument and fiscal capacity that had been called for before the pandemic (inter alia, under the label 'eurobonds'), but had been considered unrealistic from both a legal and a political perspective. However, not only did the looming economic crisis create unprecedented political pressure to act,[150] but the pandemic also provided for recourse to legal bases that were not (considered) available during the euro crisis, in particular Article 175 TFEU and Article 122 TFEU, as the legal foundation of RRF financial assistance.

[144] See, already, Fritz W Scharpf, 'The Joint-Decision Trap: Lessons from German Federalism and European Integration' (1988) 66 Public Administration 239.

[145] See, eg Frank Schimmelfenning, 'Liberal Intergovernmentalism and the Euro Area Crisis' (2015) 22 Journal of European Public Policy 177; Stefanie Walter, Ari Ray and Nils Redeker, *The Politics of Bad Options: Why the Eurozone's Problems Have Been So Hard to Resolve* (OUP 2020).

[146] Howarth and Quaglia (n 4) 1556.

[147] Jones, Kelemen and Meunier (n 4).

[148] Although the RRF is no genuine euro-area instrument, but applies to all Member States, it is a fiscal capacity (joint debt is issued in euros) that provides stability to EMU.

[149] In our account, the spillover of crises from other policy fields to EMU is an inductive finding based on the respective empirical observations. However, the question under which conditions a crisis spills over to EMU opens an avenue for future theory-guided research; for the effects in the named policy fields, see also the respective chapters in this book.

[150] This crisis included the threatening collapse of the single market and even the possible fragmentation of EMU, as euro-area Member States have to face economic crises without the help of their national banks as 'lenders of last resort' and the usual automatic stabilizers in their national budgets: see de Grauwe and Ji (n 24) 740–44.

A similar argument can be made for the suspension of the SGP, which was based on the general escape clause in case of a severe economic downturn.

The argument is not restricted to the COVID-19 pandemic. For example, the consequences of the war in Ukraine and the concomitant shortage in energy supply led to a prolongation of the suspension of the SGP. Based on Article 122(1) TFEU, joint fiscal capacities for energy procurement could become possible in addition to that. Moreover, the enduring political need to support Ukraine and/or invest in EU countries' own defence will require additional financial resources which can be freed up either by providing for exceptions in the SGP or by creating new common funds.

In short, from the outset, institutional change in EMU is unlikely, given a constraining institutional framework and diverging preferences among members. However, exogenous crises destabilize the asymmetric EMU and thus increase the pressure to apply or develop the incomplete rules creatively. This leads to *incremental* institutional change based legally on stretching the existing framework, and politically on lowest-common-denominator decisions.

Against the background of an incomplete legal framework and diverging preferences among Member States, the supranational institutions are pushed to the limits of their possibilities. This is true of both the ECB and the CJEU. As Member States cannot agree on a credible fiscal backstop for EMU for legal and political reasons, the ECB has to step in whenever the inherently unstable EMU faces a crisis. This became most obvious in the euro crisis, when the establishment of the ESM could not reduce the fragmentation risk in the euro area, and the ECB had to commit to purchasing government bonds on secondary markets.[151] In doing so, the ECB broke with a taboo, as the purchase of single Member States' government bonds could have been interpreted as prohibited monetary financing. However, the subsequent purchasing programmes follow the same logic. On the one hand, ECB action is more effective than decision-making among Member States, as the rule-making constraints are considerably lower.[152] Thus, the ECB can act more quickly, and does not have to content itself with lowest-common-denominator decisions. On the other hand, in acting as the euro area's lender of last resort, the ECB has to stretch its legal mandate to the limits, as the various court cases—especially before the German Federal Constitutional Court—demonstrate. From a political perspective, however, the ECB cannot act differently, as preserving the euro means preserving its own *raison d'être*.[153]

In a similar vein, the CJEU's creative rulings, notably *Pringle*, *Gauweiler*, and *Weiss*, can be read as legal justifications of political necessities. However, in light of an incomplete institutional framework, the only way between a break-up of the euro area and outright Treaty change is incremental adaptation based on creative rule interpretation.

[151] See, eg de Grauwe and Ji (n 24); Schoeller, 'Leadership by Default' (n 33).

[152] See Magnus G Schoeller, *Leadership in the Eurozone: The Role of Germany and EU Institutions* (Palgrave Macmillan 2019) 159–93.

[153] Schoeller, *Leadership in the Eurozone* (n 152).

2.6 Conclusions: EMU Rule-making in Times of Crises

We structure our conclusions according to the five guiding questions of this volume.

First, asked for the nature of rule-making prior to the relevant crises—notably the euro crisis following the GFC, and the COVID-19-induced economic crisis—we diagnosed a twofold asymmetry in EMU. In terms of policies, monetary policy in the euro area was completely supranationalized (made an exclusive EU competence), whereas economic and fiscal policy has remained largely in the hands of Member States (a merely coordinating EU competence). In terms of institutional rules, there were strict institutional constraints from the outset, but only rudimentary macroeconomic provisions and no common fiscal capacities. While this twofold asymmetry still persists, it has been mitigated as a reaction to EMU's crises. Prior to the crises, both economic policy and monetary policy were applied with a narrower ambit, both politically and legally: while EMU as a whole was dedicated to *common* guiding principles even before the GFC,[154] its economic policy focused primarily on sound public finances and a sustainable balance of payments. Likewise, the ECB was able to limit its monetary policy to maintaining price stability and sound monetary conditions, while eschewing unorthodox measures with obvious macroeconomic implications. This worked during the euro's first decade. However, the euro crisis exposed that market discipline alone cannot replace a common economic and fiscal policy, and the Member States' inability to stabilize the euro area forced the ECB to give up on its seemingly technical role and take on the political role of a lender of last resort.

Second, in answering the question of whether EU rule-making broke new ground, we found that this was the case formally and materially, but only in an incremental way. EMU reform encompassed the amendment of existing rules (SGP), but, with the introduction of the MIP and the establishment of the ESM, also tapping into the new fields of macroeconomic rules and fiscal capacities. Moreover, the reform saw the establishment of new decision-making rules (such as RQMV), the empowerment of EU institutions by regimes outside the EU legal order (such as the TSCG), the creation of new bodies (such as the EFB), and, importantly, new interpretative approaches towards existing rules. The non-application of the EDP during, and in the aftermath of, the pandemic is supposed to be a temporary phenomenon, not a reform in the strict sense, but it also contributes to the changing priorities in the field of EMU. The ECB increased the intensity and outreach of its monetary policy by announcing or applying unprecedented capital market interventions. It thus embarked on a new form of monetary policy with obvious economic implications, for example by making the acquisition of sovereign bonds of euro-area Member States conditional upon their compliance with set economic policy requirements. Hence, the ECB broke new ground and became the euro area's 'lender of last resort', thus filling the gap left by the lack of an (unlimited) fiscal capacity.

[154] See art 4(3) of the Treaty Establishing the European Community (TEC), now art 119(3) TFEU.

As a consequence, these incremental reforms brought about a paradigm change in EMU. In reaction to the euro crisis, shifts from market funding towards financial assistance, and from market discipline towards public control (conditionality), could be discerned.[155] During the EU-wide COVID-19 crisis, a recalibration took place. The financial assistance originally provided by the (euro-area) Member States was now granted by the EU, and the economic policy conditionality originally imposed by EU institutions (the Troika) now displayed a larger degree of 'national ownership'.

The *third* guiding question, which asked whether EU competences were extended and whether this affected the EU's inter-institutional balance, can also be answered in the affirmative. The developments described above went hand in hand with an extension of EU competences, but not (primarily) in the sense that the EU impinged upon areas which fell within the competences of the Member States. Rather, both the EU and its Member States engaged in activities which, in a (by then) conventional understanding of pertinent EU law, would have been prohibited. The ECB, by interpreting its mandate more broadly than before, stepped in during the euro crisis and achieved what the (euro-area) Member States had unsuccessfully approached as their objective—the stabilization of the euro area. Through its various purchasing programmes, the ECB extended its competences and gained in power vis-à-vis the Member States. The second 'winner' from EMU crisis management is certainly the Commission, which strengthened its role in the implementation of EMU's spending policies at the expense of the Council. This becomes obvious from the introduction of R(Q)MV, or the Commission's enhanced role in the RRF as compared with the ESM, for example. In particular, the Commission can now enforce policy goals (as, for example, spelled out in the CSR) through the conditionality of the RRF, which applies to all Member States, and not just to those under an EDP. Moreover, the increasing importance of economic policy competences (in particular, Article 122 TFEU) brought the marginalization of the EP to the fore, although the latter still punched above its (legal) weight in crisis-induced EMU reforms.[156]

The *fourth* guiding question asked how E(M)U rule-making in reaction to the crises affected the relationship between the EU and its Member States, as well as the relationships among the Member States themselves. The unprecedented strictness vis-à-vis euro-area Member States that came with euro-crisis management, as well as the conditionality related to the assistance programmes, turned out to be toxic for both the vertical relationship between the EU and its Member States and the horizontal relationship between so-called 'creditor' and 'debtor' states. Not only did the creditor states in the north of the euro area have preferences that were diametrically opposed to those of the southern debtor states ('austerity' versus 'solidarity'), but, through the ESM, 'creditor countries' like Germany suddenly obtained a say in the economic and fiscal policy of 'debtor countries' like Greece. This exposed problems of democratic legitimacy and

[155] See Ioannidis (n 108).

[156] See Magnus G Schoeller and Adrienne Héritier, 'Driving Informal Institutional Change: The European Parliament and the Reform of the Economic and Monetary Union' (2019) 41 Journal of European Integration 277; Adrienne Héritier and others, *European Parliament Ascendant: Parliamentary Strategies of Self-Empowerment in the EU* (Palgrave Macmillan 2019) ch 7.

triggered antagonistic attitudes. Likewise, the politicized roles of the Commission and the ECB in the so-called Troika, which monitored and enforced the agreed conditionality measures, were perceived as democratically not legitimized. These problems were largely rectified in the management of the COVID-19-induced crisis, when the ESM was *de facto* ousted by the RRF, and Member States obtained significantly more ownership of conditionality.

Fifth, on the question of an 'invisible' transformation of the EU's constitution, EMU is a relatively young policy field of the EU, and some of its core provisions in primary law were brought to life only during the crises discussed here. Thus, we can neither look back to a long history of political practice nor to an extensive body of case law which has evolved over time. This makes the assessment of constitutional transformation particularly difficult. Overall, the constitutional framework of EMU, as laid down in primary law, has been reinterpreted, adapted, and complemented in many ways—notably without its formal amendment.[157] Thus, to the extent it affected primary law, all of this change was 'invisible'.

A most remarkable consequence was the reductive interpretation of the no-bailout principle (as framed, in particular, in Articles 125 and 122, and in Article 123 TFEU), both by the EU and its Member States, with the eventual backing of the CJEU. This interpretation gave Member States, the EU legislator, and the ECB an increased flexibility, and paved the way for further progressive reforms, notably the establishment of the RRF. This instrument (further) mitigated the no-bailout principle by abolishing the 'strict conditionality' still applicable in the context of the ESM. What is more, the EU's indebting itself on a considerable scale to endow the RRF is unprecedented and, from a constitutional perspective, highly contested. Also, the ECB's additional role as macroeconomic stabilizer has a constitutional impact, meaning that it shapes the ECB's mandate beyond what is ingrained in the Treaties.[158] Also important and subject to legal debate, but vested with much less transformative potential, appear other reforms, such as the introduction of R(Q)MV, the lending of EU institutions to (euro-area) Member States' regimes established under public international law, and the reinforcement of fiscal discipline during the euro crisis.

These transformative elements will be developed further, as the ongoing war in Ukraine has not only led to energy shortages and a 'return of inflation', but also requires substantial financial resources to support and rebuild Ukraine. In the EMU context, this could mean either creating fiscal space at the national level—for example, by exempting expenditure on energy, defence, and support for Ukraine from EMU's fiscal rules—or setting up common fiscal capacities at the European level.

[157] For Treaty reform proposals, see Stefan Griller and Elisabeth Lentsch, 'Why the EU's Constitutional Deadlock is Hampering EMU Reforms, and How This Could Be Resolved' (2021) 28 Journal of European Public Policy 914, with further references.

[158] This new shape of the ECB has been described as a 'new ECB' or an evolution 'from a central bank of stability to a central bank of crisis': Beukers (n 117); T Beukers, D Fromage and G Monti (eds), *The New European Central Bank* (OUP 2022); Tuori (n 133) 275; Massimo Rostagno and others, *Monetary Policy in Times of Crisis: A Tale of Two Decades of the European Central Bank* (OUP 2021) 1: 'Two Decades, Two Regimes'.

3

Financial Regulation and Supervision

Crisis as Catalyst for Institutional and Policy Reforms

*Jonathan Bauerschmidt** *and Lucia Quaglia***

3.1 Introduction

The Great Financial Crisis (GFC), which started in 2008 and was followed by the sovereign debt crisis in the euro area from 2009 onwards (for ease of reading, in this chapter, we refer to the GFC as meaning both of these crises), fundamentally transformed the regulatory landscape for banks and capital markets in the European Union (EU). On the one hand, these consecutive crises brought to the fore the risks of financial instability, produced, inter alia, by an excessive reliance on poor-quality bank loans, excessive leverage by banks, and their reliance on short-term funding.[1] When the governments of the Member States stepped in to bail out banks, this triggered a vicious circle of dependence between banks and sovereigns,[2] threatening financial stability in the EU. On the other hand, these financial crises amplified the fragmentation of financial markets, especially banking, in Europe, by increasing the so-called domestic bias, meaning that banks collected deposits and made loans primarily in their home countries.[3]

The word crisis has its origins in the Greek κρίσις (*krisis*) and refers to an existential situation where it is necessary to choose, judge, and decide. Yet, crises also provide 'windows of opportunities' because they can bring about major institutional and policy changes, rearranging the existing institutional and policy framework.[4] For the project of European integration, crises have always been a threat and an opportunity, and the GFC is no exception. This crisis highlighted fault lines and shortcomings concerning financial regulation and supervision in the EU, as well as in the architecture of

* Dr iur, Member of the Legal Service, Council of the European Union and Visiting Professor at Université Catholique de Louvain. The views expressed by the author are strictly personal and do not engage the institution for which he works.

** Professor of Political Science at University of Bologna.

[1] Adam Tooze, *Crashed* (Allen Lane 2018); Dirk Schoenmaker, *Governance of International Banking: The Financial Trilemma* (OUP 2013).

[2] The so-called 'doom loop' is explained in section 3.2 below; Silvia Merler and Jean Pisani-Ferry, 'Hazardous Tango: Sovereign-Bank Interdependence and Financial Stability in the Euro Area' (2012) 16 Banque de France Financial Stability Review 201.

[3] Daniel Gros, 'The Single European Market in Banking in Decline – ECB to the Rescue?' in Thomas Beck (ed), *Banking Union for Europe—Risks and Challenges* (CEPR 2012) 49–54.

[4] See the illuminating article by Reinhart Koselleck, 'Crisis' (2006) 67 Journal of the History of Ideas 357.

Jonathan Bauerschmidt and Lucia Quaglia, *Financial Regulation and Supervision* In: *EU Regulatory Responses to Crises*.
Edited by: Diane Fromage, Adrienne Héritier, and Paul Weismann, Oxford University Press.
 DOI: 10.1093/9780198913825.003.0003

Economic and Monetary Union (EMU),[5] threatening the very existence of the single currency. Yet, this crisis also proved to be a catalyst for change, through the adoption of unprecedented measures in order to propel European integration forward, testing the flexibility of the constitutional framework of the EU.

The EU responded to the GFC by adopting several institutional and policy reforms, discussed in this chapter.[6] First, the EU established a European System of Financial Supervision (ESFS). Despite far-reaching pre-crisis harmonization of financial regulation in the EU, supervision itself had remained at national level, leading to divergence in the application of EU rules. Moreover, national supervisors did not sufficiently take into account the interconnectedness of the financial sector, the cross-border effects of their actions, and the building up of systemic risk. To address these shortcomings, the EU created the European Systemic Risk Board and three sectoral European Supervisory Authorities (ESAs).

Second, the EU created the banking union, with a view to breaking the vicious circle of dependence between banks and sovereigns. In the banking union, the competences for banking supervision and resolution were partly transferred to the supranational level.

Third, the EU proposed the creation of a capital markets union, to unlock new sources of funding, be less reliant on banks, reduce financial market fragmentation, and increase cross-border capital flows. On the whole, the EU replaced many soft laws with hard laws in the form of legally binding EU legislation and made greater use of regulations rather than directives. At the same time, the ESAs and the European Central Bank (ECB) issued a considerable amount of soft law. Thus, there was a proliferation of both 'harder' soft law and 'softer' hard law in the EU after the crisis, for example more detailed and elaborate soft law provisions and more flexible provision in hard law instruments.

This chapter is structured as follows. The second section (3.2) argues that while undertaking post-crisis reforms, the EU had to deal with two main challenges: to reconcile the competing interests and different priorities of Member States, and to combine the depoliticization of certain financial issues with a sufficient level of accountability. The third (3.3), fourth (3.4), and fifth (3.5) sections examine, respectively, the ESFS, the banking union, and the capital markets union. The final section (3.6) identifies some common themes concerning the EU's responses to financial crises and draws some conclusions about the flexibility and rigidity of the constitutional architecture. Some caveats about the scope of this chapter are needed. Although, post-crisis, the EU issued new legislation concerning previously unregulated or lightly regulated financial services, such as hedge funds, derivatives, insurance, and, more recently, crypto assets,

[5] David Howarth and Lucia Quaglia, 'The Political Economy of the Euro Area's Sovereign Debt Crisis: Introduction' (2015) 22 Review of International Political Economy 457. See also Chapter 2 of this volume.

[6] For an overview, see Charlotte Burns, Judith Clifton and Lucia Quaglia, 'Explaining Policy Change in the EU: Financial Reform after the Crisis' (2017) 25 Journal of European Public Policy 728; Niamh Moloney, Eilis Ferran and Jennifer Payne (eds), *The Oxford Handbook of Financial Regulation* (OUP 2015).

etc,[7] we do not discuss these specific pieces of legislation, nor do we discuss rule implementation and the application of rules in practice to concrete cases.

3.2 Reforming Finance and Confronting Challenges

The GFC triggered important institutional and policy changes in the EU. To begin with, in 2009, the committees of national supervisors in banking, securities markets, and insurance (the so-called Level 3 Lamfalussy committees) were transformed into ESAs, namely the European Banking Authority, the European Securities and Markets Authority, and the European Insurance and Occupational Pension Authority. These EU agencies, which have legal personality, have increased budgets and enhanced powers as compared with committees, and were charged with the tasks of coordinating the application of supervisory standards and promoting stronger cooperation between national supervisors.[8] Furthermore, the European Systemic Risk Board (ESRB) was established to monitor macro-prudential risks in the EU, although it was given very limited powers (mostly the power to issue recommendations) to prevent the building up of systemic risk.

The second main institutional change triggered by the sovereign debt crisis was the establishment of the banking union, whereby the ECB became responsible for banking supervision in the euro area, in cooperation with national banking supervisors, and a new EU agency, the Single Resolution Board, was set up to deal with banking resolution in the euro area.[9] The establishment of these new EU-level bodies also affected cooperation with national competent authorities. The third institutional change was the launch of the project of capital markets union, which was intended to create deeper and more integrated capital markets across the Member States and expand the non-bank part of Europe's financial system.[10]

As far as rule-making is concerned, post-crisis the EU replaced many soft rules. For instance, the code of conduct for credit rating agencies, and pre-crisis self-regulation by industry—for example, for hedge funds and derivatives—was replaced by hard law, meaning legally binding EU legislation.[11] Furthermore, the EU made greater use of

[7] For a discussion of EU post-crisis regulation across a variety of financial services, see Lucia Quaglia, 'The "Old" and "New" Politics of Financial Services Regulation in the European Union' (2012) 17 New Political Economy 515; Daniel Mügge (ed), *Europe and the Governance of Global Finance* (OUP 2014); Lucia Quaglia, *The European Union and Global Financial Regulation* (OUP 2014).

[8] Alexandra Hennessy, 'Redesigning Financial Supervision in the European Union, 2009–13' (2014) 21 Journal of European Public Policy 151; Niamh Moloney, *The Age of ESMA: Governing EU Financial Markets* (Hart Publishing 2018).

[9] David Howarth and Lucia Quaglia, *The Political Economy of European Banking Union* (OUP 2016); Rachel Epstein and Martin Rhodes, 'The Political Dynamics Behind Europe's New Banking Union' (2016) 39 West European Politics 415; Gabriel Glöckler, Johannes Lindner and Marion Salines, 'Explaining the Sudden Creation of a Banking Supervisor for the Euro Area' (2016) 24 Journal of European Public Policy 1135.

[10] Niamh Moloney, 'Capital Markets Union: "Ever Closer Union" for the EU Financial System?' (2016) 41 European Law Review 307; Lucia Quaglia, David Howarth and Moritz Liebe, 'The Political Economy of European Capital Markets Union' (2016) 54 Journal of Common Market Studies Annual Review 185.

[11] Stefano Pagliari, 'Who Governs Finance? The Shifting Public–Private Divide in the Regulation of Derivatives, Rating Agencies and Hedge Funds' (2012) 18 European Law Journal 44.

regulations, which must be directly applied in their entirety across the EU, rather than directives, which require domestic transposition and often leave room for national discretion (which may also lead to discrepancies across Member States). For instance, the Prospectus Regulation replaced the former Prospectus Directive, issued in 2003. Moreover, the ESAs and the main components of the banking union, namely the Single Supervisory Mechanism (SSM) and the Single Resolution Mechanism (SRM), were established by making use of regulations. At the same time, the ESAs and the ECB issued a considerable amount of soft law. As for the content of post-crisis EU rules for financial services, they tended to be less principle-based and more stringent than prior to the crisis. For instance, bank capital requirements were increased and so were the amount of bank deposit guarantee schemes. Moreover, the perimeter of EU financial regulation was extended to previously unregulated or lightly regulated entities (for example, hedge funds, credit rating agencies) and activities (for example, derivatives; parts of the shadow banking system, such as money market funds; securitization).[12]

While undertaking the post-crisis reforms just outlined, the EU had to deal with two main challenges: to reconcile the competing interests and different priorities of Member States, and to combine the depoliticization of certain financial issues with a sufficient level of accountability.

3.2.1 Competing interests and different priorities of Member States

To begin with, in general, Member States were hesitant to delegate further competences to the EU level or to share, at that level, competences that previously were only national (notably, bank resolution). Moreover, Member States had competing interests or different priorities with reference to the banking union and the capital markets union. With reference to the banking union, one coalition of Member States was led by Germany and included policymakers from Austria, Finland, and the Netherlands. These countries shared similar interests: they had sound fiscal positions and mostly healthy banks, and were likely to be net contributors to any mechanism for financial support in the banking union. The German authorities were particularly concerned about 'moral hazard'—that is to say, not to provide incentives for 'risky' behaviour of sovereigns and banks—and 'legacies problems' deriving from past 'supervisory forbearance'.[13] Policymakers in these countries were, therefore, eager to minimize the elements of the banking union that could result in fiscal transfers from fiscally and financially stable Member States to ailing Member States.

The other coalition of Member States was led by France and included policymakers from Italy, Spain, and other countries in the euro-area periphery. These countries shared similar interests: they each had weaker fiscal positions and several ailing banks,

[12] Quaglia, 'The "Old" and "New" Politics' (n 7); Pagliari, 'Who Governs Finance?' (n 11).

[13] David Schaffer, 'A Banking Union of Ideas? The Impact of Ordoliberalism and the Vicious Circle on the EU Banking Union' (2016) 54 Journal of Common Market Studies 961; Shawn Donnelly, *Power Politics, Banking Union and EMU: Adjusting Europe to Germany* (Routledge 2018).

and were at risk of contagion from the crisis. It should be noted that France was in a better fiscal position and had fewer ailing banks, compared with other members of this coalition. Yet, France was at risk of contagion once the crisis extended to Spain and Italy in 2011–12.[14] The banking union began to take shape when France moved away from the Franco-German alliance, which had led the initial response to the sovereign debt crisis, and moved closer to the positions of the Member States in the euro-area periphery. Policymakers in this coalition were eager to secure financial support mechanisms for ailing banks and sovereigns. In return, they were willing to accept the supranationalization of banking supervision.[15]

As for capital markets union, it was enthusiastically supported by the UK and the Member States that had the most well-developed and diversified financial sectors, including Ireland, the Netherlands, Sweden, and Luxembourg. These Member States supported the market liberalization agenda in capital markets union and were well-positioned to attract business from Member States that had less competitive capital markets. For the opposite reason, the Member States with less competitive capital markets expressed reservations about capital markets union, as they feared that business would move towards deeper and more dynamic capital markets in the EU.[16] By contrast, the most competitive parts of the financial industry—the main transnational players, such as large banks engaged in securitization, insurance companies, and the international financial centres in the EU, first and foremost the City of London—supported capital markets union.[17]

3.2.2 Depoliticization and accountability

The second challenge for the EU in reforming its rule-making after the GFC concerned the politicization of finance, which can be seen from two perspectives. First, a considerable body of work in political science points out that, in the wake of financial crises, finance and financial regulation gained high public salience because public opinion and politicians realized that regulatory failures in this sector can have far-reaching implications for the economy, the state, and taxpayers' money.[18] Hence, financial regulation becomes politicized in the short term, as it is no longer dealt with by a rather insulated 'policy community' of 'financial experts'. However, in the medium term, as the memories of a crisis fade away, financial regulation returns to being a matter of limited salience for politicians and the broader public, till the next crisis. This trend

[14] Donnelly (n 13).

[15] Zdenek Kudrna, 'Financial Market Regulation: Crisis-induced Supranationalization' (2016) 38 Journal of European Integration 251.

[16] Lucia Quaglia and David Howarth, 'Policy Narratives on Capital Markets Union' (2018) 25 Journal of European Public Policy 990.

[17] Benjamin Braun, Daniela Gabor and Martine Hubner, 'Governing through Financial Markets: Towards a Critical Political Economy of Capital Markets Union' (2018) 2 Competition and Change 101.

[18] Pepper Culpepper, *Quiet Politics and Business Power: Corporate Control in Europe and Japan* (CUP 2010); Stefano Pagliari, 'Public Salience and International Financial Regulation. Explaining the International Regulation of OTC Derivatives, Rating Agencies, and Hedge Funds' (PhD dissertation, University of Waterloo 2013).

generates 'regulatory cycles', whereby more stringent regulation is adopted in the wake of crises and is subsequently watered down over time. For instance, shortly after the GFC, the EU adopted rather stringent rules on financial securitization, but those rules were made less stringent as time went by. As explained in the Introduction above, these rules are, however, outside the scope of this chapter.[19]

The second perspective concerning the politicization of finance, in particular in banking, means that there are rather strong ties between a state (and its authorities) and its domestic banks. As Rachel Epstein notes, 'states and banks have traditionally maintained close ties. At various points in time, states have used banks to manage their economies and soak up government debt, while banks enjoyed regulatory forbearance, restricted competition, and implicit or explicit guarantees from their home markets'.[20] The rather 'cosy' ties between states and domestic banks can lead to political interference in the banking business, as well as supervisory forbearance, whereby supervisors tend to be lenient in the application of rules to the financial institutions they oversee, for instance granting concessions to troubled banks, or underestimating their financial difficulties.[21] Moreover, political interference is likely to occur in dealing with ailing banks because bank failures attract public attention and the key question becomes 'who pays'[22] (ie who should bear the cost) for bank failures (for example, bank shareholders, debt owners, depositors, taxpayers?). Dealing with ailing banks has distributional implications not only within countries, but also across countries, because, as the Governor of the Bank of England, Mervyn King, pointed out, large banks are 'international in life, but national in death'.[23]

At the outset of the GFC, the politically acrimonious and economically inefficient rescue of a large cross-border bank, Fortis, demonstrated that even amongst countries with a well-established track record of economic cooperation, such as the Benelux countries, cross-border bank resolution could be problematic.[24] At the EU level, at the beginning of the GFC, all matters related to banking supervision and possible banking resolution were highly political. Hence, the heads of state or government in the European Council expressed their views numerous times on how the vicious circle between banks and sovereigns might be broken.[25] In addition, the finance ministers of the Eurogroup were heavily involved, as were national parliaments.

A striking example is the banking crisis in Cyprus: when turmoil broke out in March 2013, the eurozone ministers negotiated a 10 billion euros rescue package with the Cypriot government, on 16 March 2013. The terms of this agreement, which affected

[19] Lucia Quaglia, 'It Takes Two to Tango: The European Union and the International Governance of Securitisation' (2021) 59 Journal of Common Market Studies 1364; Pagliari, 'Who Governs Finance?' (n 11); Quaglia, 'The "Old" and "New" Politics' (n 7).

[20] Rachel Epstein, *Banking on Markets: The Transformation of Bank-State Ties in Europe and Beyond* (OUP 2017).

[21] Nicolas Véron, 'Banking Nationalism and the European Crisis' (Bruegel Policy Paper, 19 October 2013).

[22] David Mayes, 'Who Pays for Bank Insolvency?' (2004) 23 Journal of International Money and Finance 515.

[23] Steve Schifferes, 'Can Banking Regulation Go Global?' (*BBC*, 18 March 2009).

[24] Zdenek Kudrna, 'Cross-border Resolution of Failed Banks in the European Union after the Crisis: Business as Usual' (2012) 50 Journal of Common Market Studies 283.

[25] All relevant European Council conclusions on banking union can be found under <https://www.consilium.europa.eu/media/21548/20141020-banking_union_-_relevant_ec_conclusions.pdf> accessed 15 January 2024.

both local savers and wealthy foreign depositors, were rejected by the parliament in Nicosia a few days later because they did not differentiate between smaller protected deposits and larger unprotected deposits. The resulting uncertainty and political deadlock were overcome in long negotiations. In a statement of 25 March 2013, the Eurogroup outlined the measures envisaged by the Cypriot authorities in order to restore the viability of the financial sector.[26] Crucially, this statement confirmed that the measures would safeguard all deposits below 100,000 euros, in accordance with EU rules on covered deposits.[27] Only with this firm commitment to protect covered deposits did the Cypriot parliament pass the relevant national legislation.[28] This example shows how important it is during high political negotiations not to lose sight of very important technical details.

As the GFC unfolded, the vicious circle between ailing banks and struggling sovereigns came to the fore, whereby fragile national banks held growing amounts of sovereign debt, while the sustainability of a number of national public debt loads was increasingly being questioned.[29] The banks–sovereign 'doom loop' highlighted the need to depoliticize banking by disentangling the banks–sovereigns ties and supranationalizing banking supervision and resolution. This is what the banking union was designed to do by setting in place procedures for banking supervision and resolution. More generally, the proliferation of agencies (the ESAs, the Single Resolution Board (SRB)) and institutionalization within the ECB (the SSM and the ESRB) were intended to contribute to the depoliticization of these matters, which were to be discussed in technocratic fora, outside the political limelight. Yet, politics always comes in, albeit in a more structured way, as will be shown in sections 3.3 and 3.4 below.

The challenge of depoliticizing banking supervision and resolution went hand in hand with the EU's need to ensure sufficient accountability. There have been many attempts to find a common definition of the slippery term 'accountability'.[30] As a political concept, it overlaps greatly with the concept of responsibility and the duty to justify oneself and to give reasons for a certain behaviour.[31] Accountability is both retrospective for past behaviour and prospective for future intended behaviour and entails procedural and substantive dimensions. Thus, accountability can be understood as a relationship between an actor and a forum in which the actor has an obligation to explain and justify their behaviour, the forum can pose questions and pass judgment,

[26] Eurogroup Statement on Cyprus of 25 March 2013: <https://www.consilium.europa.eu/uedocs/cms_Data/docs/pressdata/en/ecofin/136487.pdf> accessed 15 January 2024. See, on the legal qualification of that statement, Joined Cases C-597/18 P, C-598/18 P, C-603/18 P, and C-604/18 P *Council v Chrysostomides* EU:C:2020:1028.

[27] See, in particular, Directive 94/19/EC of the European Parliament and of the Council of 30 May 1994 on deposit-guarantee schemes [1994] OJ L135/5.

[28] See Jan Strupczewski and Annika Breidthardt, 'Last-minute Cyprus Deal to Close Bank, Force Losses' (*Reuters*, 25 March 2013).

[29] Daniel Gros, 'Banking Union with a Sovereign Virus' (2003) 48 Intereconomics 93.

[30] Mark Bovens, *The Quest for Responsibility* (CUP 1998) 45 ff.; Richard Mulgan, 'Accountability: An Ever-expanding Concept?' (2000) 78 Public Administration 555, 557 ff.

[31] See the classical treatment by Benjamin Constant, *La Résponsibilité des Ministers* (H. Nicolle 1815) and, more recently, Pierre Rosanvallon, *Le Bon Gouvernement* (Èditions du Seuil 2015) 253 ff.; Paul Ricoeur, 'Le Concept de responsabilité' (1994) Esprit 28, 30 ff.

and the actor may face consequences.[32] This also shows the strong link between accountability and legitimacy, which is particularly important for the EU's governance system.[33]

To create the legal framework to overcome the crisis and establish the accountability mechanisms, it should be noted that most of the measures were adopted by the Union legislator either following the ordinary legislative procedure by the European Parliament (EP) and the Council (based on Article 114 TFEU, in most cases) or following special legislative procedures by the Council after consulting the EP and the ECB (based on Article 127(6) TFEU). This allowed for the tapping into of the full sources of democratic legitimacy in accordance with the Treaties. And it was only in one instance that the representatives of the governments of Member States stepped outside the Treaties to adopt an intergovernmental agreement to complement a supranational measure.[34] The involvement of the Union legislator allowed for deliberation and decision-making on the main legal reforms and the empowerment of various executive bodies, ranging from the Commission and the ECB all the way to newly established agencies, to implement those reforms. This depoliticization of implementation was accompanied by new mechanisms for holding the executive to account, as can be shown for the ECB and the ESAs.[35]

On the one hand, the ECB is accountable to the EP and the Council for the implementation of supervisory policy. This not only requires the ECB to submit annual reports but the chair of the Supervisory Board is also required to participate in discussions with members of the EP.[36] Moreover, the accountability arrangements are further fleshed out in an inter-institutional agreement between the ECB and the Parliament.[37] In addition, the ECB is also accountable to national parliaments, and the chair of the Supervisory Board may be invited to the national parliaments to participate in an exchange of views.[38] It is, therefore, not surprising that the independence of the ECB regarding monetary policy goes much further than its independence regarding banking supervision.[39] This new system of accountability is well-aligned with the executive role of the ECB in supervision: in contrast to monetary policy, which the ECB (together with national central banks) conceives and implements on its own to achieve price stability, the rules for supervisory policy are set by the Union legislature (with some

[32] See, in this sense, Arthur Benz, Carol Harlow and Yannis Papadopoulos, 'Introduction to a Special Issue on Accountability' (2007) 13 European Law Journal 443 ff.; Mark Bovens, Deirdre Curtin and Paul 't Hart, *The Real World of EU Accountability* (OUP 2010) 32 ff.; Mark Bovens, Robert E Goodin and Thomas Schillemans, *Oxford Handbook of Public Accountability* (OUP 2014) 5 ff.

[33] Anthony Arnull and Daniel Wincott, *Accountability and Legitimacy in the European Union* (OUP 2000).

[34] See section 3.4.2 below.

[35] Established, respectively, by the EBA Regulation (EU) 1093/2010, EIOPA Regulation (EU) 1094/2010, and ESMA Regulation (EU) 1095/2010 [2010] OJ L331/12.

[36] See art 20 of the SSM Regulation (EU) 1024/2013.

[37] Interinstitutional Agreement between the EP and the ECB on the practical modalities of the exercise of democratic accountability within the framework of the SSM (2013/694/EU) [2013] OJ L320/1.

[38] See art 21 of the SSM Regulation (EU) 1024/2013.

[39] Chiara Zilioli, 'The Independence of the ECB and its New Banking Supervisory Competences' in Dominique Ritleng (ed), *Independence and Legitimacy in the Institutional System of the EU* (OUP 2016) 125, 165 ff.

options and discretions left to national authorities) and the ECB has to implement this supervisory policy.[40]

On the other hand, the ESAs only had a general provision on accountability vis-à-vis the EP and the Council when they were established in 2010.[41] However, this changed significantly during the revision of their founding regulations, in 2019.[42] The revised provision on accountability requires the ESAs to transmit annual activity reports to the Parliament and the Council and reply to any questions of the Union legislator with five weeks of their receipt.[43] In addition, the Parliament's Economic and Monetary Affairs Committee now holds annual hearings where the chairs of the authorities need to answer the questions of parliamentarians. Since some of the topics discussed may entail confidential information, the hearings may also take place behind closed doors, and all the participants are required to respect the obligations stemming from professional secrecy.[44] More declaratory in nature is the obligation of the ESAs to cooperate fully with any committee of inquiry established by the Parliament in accordance with Article 226 TFEU. This revised system of accountability reflects the growing responsibilities of the ESAs, while acknowledging that these responsibilities are of an implementing nature.[45] The accountability mechanisms evolved on the basis of previous precedents. However, they do not follow a general blueprint, but are, rather, the result of case-by-case negotiations between the two Union legislators.

3.3 The European System of Financial Supervision (ESFS)

One of the main responses of the EU to the GFC was the establishment of the ESFS, which is a network[46] of public authorities and committees whose main objective is to ensure the appropriate application of the rules governing the financial sector, thereby ensuring financial stability.[47] A network can be understood as a combination of nodes whose relationship is governed less by hierarchical subordination than by cooperative exchange.[48] The ESFS drew on the influential de Larosière report of 2009, which

[40] Jonathan Bauerschmidt, 'Financial Stability as the Objective of the Banking Union' (2020) 17 European Company and Financial Law Review 155, 172.

[41] See the identical arts 3 of the EBA Regulation (EU) 1093/2010, EIOPA Regulation (EU) 1094/2010, and ESMA Regulation (EU) 1095/2010 [2010] OJ L331/12.

[42] Regulation (EU) 2019/2175 [2019] OJ L334/1.

[43] See the new Art 3(3) and (7) introduced by Regulation (EU) 2019/2175.

[44] See the new Art 3(4) and (8) introduced by Regulation (EU) 2019/2175.

[45] See, for an assessment, Jonathan Bauerschmidt, 'Article 3 Regulation 1095/2010' in Christoph Seibt, Petra Buck-Heeb and Rafael Harnos (eds), *Wertpapierhandelsrecht* (12th edn, CH Beck 2024) paras 36 ff.

[46] Eilís Ferran and Kern Alexander, 'Can Soft Law Bodies Be Effective? The Special Case of the European Systemic Risk Board' (2010) 35 European Law Review 751, 763. See also an in-depth analysis by Manuel Patrick Schwind, *Netzwerke im Europäischen Verwaltungsrecht* (Mohr Siebeck 2017) 273 ff.

[47] See art 2(1) of the EBA Regulation (EU) 1093/2010.

[48] See, on the concept of network, in legal scholarship in particular, François Ost and Michel van de Kerchove, *De La Pyramide au Réseau?* (Université Saint-Louis 2002) 267 ff.; Karl-Heinz Ladeur, 'Ein Recht der Netzwerke für die Weltgesellschaft oder Konstitutionalisierung der Völkergemeinschaft?' (2011) 49 Archiv des Völkerrechts 246, 252 ff.; Anne-Marie Slaughter, *A New World Order* (PUP 2004) 36 ff.

recommended stronger macro-prudential and micro-prudential supervision at EU level.[49] The ESFS comprises the ESRB and three ESAs.

3.3.1 The European Systemic Risk Board (ESRB)

One of the major gaps highlighted by the 2008 GFC was the lack of macro-prudential supervision, in addition to micro-prudential supervision, to prevent the building up of systemic risk. In the EU, the ESRB[50] was established to monitor developments in the financial system and to avert and contain systemic risks to financial stability.[51] To accomplish this task, the ESRB has a noteworthy organizational structure and acts in the form of soft law. Similarly to the ESAs (discussed next), the ESRB is based on Article 114 TFEU,[52] but unlike the former it has no legal personality and no enforcement powers vis-à-vis third parties. The central body is the Governing Board, which comprises national central bankers and representatives of the supervisory authorities, the President and Vice-President of the ECB, a member of the Commission, and the chairpersons of the ESAs.[53] The Board is assisted and controlled by the steering committee and advised by a scientific committee and a technical committee.[54] The ESRB is chaired by the President of the ECB, which also ensures close proximity with the monetary policy analyses and decisions of the Eurosystem. In addition, the ECB provides the secretariat, for which additional tasks to support financial stability in the internal market have been transferred to the ECB through a specific authorization under Article 127(6) TFEU.[55]

The ESRB may take actions in the form of warnings and recommendations pursuant to Article 16 of the ESRB Regulation, if significant risks to the stability of the financial system are identified. Thus, the ESRB acts through soft law laid down in instruments that do not have legally binding force as such, but which may, nevertheless, produce certain (indirect) legal effects in Union law.[56]

Warnings and recommendations shall, at the discretion of the ESRB, be addressed to the Union, the Member States, the ESAs, or national supervisors, and may be specific or more general. While both warnings and recommendations are strictly confidential,

[49] 'Report of the High-level Group on Financial Supervision in the EU', chaired by Jacques de Larosière, 25 February 2009 <http://ec.europa.eu/economy_finance/publications/pages/publication14527_en.pdf> accessed 15 January 2024, points 173 ff on macro-prudential supervision and points 183 ff on micro-prudential supervision.

[50] Regulation (EU) 1092/2010 on European Union macro-prudential oversight of the financial system and establishing a European Systemic Risk Board [2010] OJ L331/1.

[51] art 3(1), 1st sentence, and Recitals 10 and 11 of Regulation (EU) 1092/2010.

[52] See, regarding the legal basis, Ferran and Alexander (n 46) 768 ff.

[53] art 6 of Regulation (EU) 1092/2010 distinguishes between members with and without voting rights and foresees the participation of the chairs of the Advisory Scientific Committee, Advisory Technical Committee, and Economic and Financial Committee.

[54] arts 4–13 of Regulation (EU) 1092/2010.

[55] Regulation (EU) 1096/2010 conferring specific tasks upon the European Central Bank concerning the functioning of the European Systemic Risk Board [2010] OJ L331/162.

[56] Linda Senden, *Soft Law in European Community Law* (Hart 2004) 113; Karel Wellens and Glenn Borchardt, 'Soft Law in European Community Law' (1989) 14 European Law Review 267, 285; Peter-Christian Müller-Graff, 'Das Soft Law der europäischen Organisationen' (2012) Europarecht 18, 22.

they can be published in accordance with Article 18 of the ESRB Regulation by a decision of the board of directors acting with a two-thirds majority.[57] Whereas warnings are non-binding knowledge statements of the ESRB, Article 17 of the ESRB Regulation provides for a noteworthy 'act or explain' mechanism for recommendations: the addressee of the recommendation must inform the ESRB (and the Council) of the implementation measures taken or justify its inaction. As the ESRB Regulation does not require certain kinds of reasons, any legal and factual obstacle may, in principle, justify inaction. In fact, even a deviating risk assessment by the addressee may be suitable to justify inaction, but will then require a significantly increased justification.[58] Thus, neither warnings nor recommendations are legally binding, but are intended to be actually perceived as such and, if necessary, obeyed. Therefore, warnings and recommendations fall into the wide range of soft law instruments in the field of financial market regulation, which, although not legally binding, have proved to be quite effective—this is an example of 'hard' soft law.[59]

3.3.2 The European Supervisory Authorities (ESAs)

The European Banking Authority (EBA), European Securities and Markets Authority (ESMA), and European Insurance and Occupational Pensions Authority (EIOPA) were all created on the basis of the competence to regulate the internal market in Article 114 TFEU. In the absence of specific Treaty provisions, the conferral of powers to agencies under Union law relies on the case law of the Court of Justice. Thus, for the first time, in 1958, the Court stated, in the *Meroni* case, that the delegation of wide discretionary powers to another body violated the institutional balance between the supranational institutions.[60] The ensuing case law was collectively referred to as the *Meroni* doctrine,[61] and dealt with the questions of how autonomously an agency can act and what kind of oversight by Union institutions created in primary law is necessary.

At the height of the GFC, the *Meroni* doctrine was tested before the Court, which had to decide in the *ESMA* case whether, on the basis of Article 114 TFEU, a European agency may be created and be conferred powers of intervention vis-à-vis individual entities. Pursuant to the relevant regulation, ESMA may, in exceptional circumstances, prohibit short selling on the European financial markets, which is particularly the case

[57] art 10(3) of Regulation (EU) 1092/2010. Similarly, recommendations have to be adopted with a two-thirds majority, whereas unpublished warnings can be adopted by simple majority.

[58] Ferran and Alexander (n 46) 774 ff; Ann-Kathrin Kaufhold, 'Der Europäische Ausschuss für Systemrisiken im Finanzsystem als Ausprägung einer neuen Aufsichtsform' (2013) 46 Die Verwaltung 21, 45 ff; Christoph Ohler, 'Finanzmarktregulierung und -aufsicht' in Matthias Ruffert (ed), *Enzyklopädie Europarecht V* (2nd edn, Nomos 2020) paras 133 ff.

[59] Overview by Ferran and Alexander (n 46) 760 ff.

[60] Case 9/56 *Meroni* EU:C:1958:7, p 152.

[61] Case C-98/80 *Romano* EU:C:1981:104; Joined Cases C-154/04 and C-155/04 *Alliance for Natural Health* EU:C:2005:449; C-217/04 *United Kingdom v Parliament and Council (ENISA)* EU:C:2006:279. See in general, on agencies, Edoardo Chiti, 'European Agencies' Rulemaking: Powers, Procedures and Assessment' (2013) 19 European Law Journal 93.

when there are serious threats to the integrity of financial markets or the stability of the financial system.[62]

While Advocate General Jääskinen was sceptical of transferring such a power, based on Article 114 TFEU,[63] echoing criticism previously expressed by scholars,[64] the Court did not follow. Since the Union legislator enjoys broad discretion to choose the most appropriate technique for harmonization, they may deem it necessary to create an EU agency responsible for contributing to the implementation of a process of harmonization.[65] Moreover, according to the Court, the legislature may also empower such a body to issue binding decisions for specific market participants, in order to address serious threats to the orderly functioning and integrity of the financial markets or the stability of the financial system.[66] With this judgment, the Court significantly developed its case law by specifying that clearly defined powers of intervention without wide discretion may be delegated to Union agencies. This clarification has largely been welcomed by scholars.[67]

Beyond intervention powers, the three ESAs (ie EBA, ESMA, and EIOPA) are also involved in a quickly growing body of soft law. They are the main authors of four important types of soft law.[68]

First, the ESAs are empowered to draft so-called regulatory technical standards and implementing technical standards. These drafts can be considered as soft law, as they are mere recommendations to the Commission to adopt delegated acts under Article 290 TFEU for regulatory technical standards, or implementing acts under Article 291(2) TFEU for implementing technical standards.[69] These drafts fulfil an important pre-law function until they are adopted as hard law by the Commission.

Second, the ESAs may adopt guidelines and recommendations addressed to national supervisory authorities or financial institutions. These instruments aim to establish consistent, efficient, and effective supervisory practices. The competent authorities are obliged to make every effort to comply with these guidelines and recommendations and must comply or explain their non-compliance. Similarly, market participants are obliged to report, in a clear and detailed way, whether they comply with a given guideline or recommendation.[70] The Court of Justice has clarified that neither guidelines

[62] art 28 of Regulation (EU) No 236/2012 on short selling and certain aspects of credit default swaps [2012] OJ L86/1.

[63] AG Jääskinen, C-270/12 *United Kingdom v Parliament and Council (ESMA)* EU:C:2013:562, paras 51 ff. He proposed using the competence of Art 352 TFEU.

[64] Jörn Axel Kämmerer, 'Das neue Europäische Finanzaufsichtssystem (ESFS)' (2011) Neue Zeitschrift für Verwaltungsrecht 1281, 1283; Niamh Moloney, 'EU Financial Market Regulation after the Global Financial Crisis' (2010) 47 Common Market Law Review 1317, 1340 ff.

[65] Case C-270/12 *United Kingdom v Parliament and Council (ESMA)* EU:C:2014:18, paras 102–04, with reference to Case C-217/04 *United Kingdom v Parliament and Council (ENISA)* EU:C:2006:279, para 44.

[66] *Parliament and Council (ESMA)* (n 65) para 108.

[67] Carl Fredrik Bergström, 'Shaping the New System for Delegation of Powers to EU Agencies' (2015) 52 Common Market Law Review 219, 241; Christian Calliess, 'Artikel 13 EUV' in Christian Calliess and Matthias Ruffert (eds), *EUV/AEUV Kommentar* (6th edn, CH Beck 2022) para 52; Martin Nettesheim, 'Artikel 13 EUV' in Eberhard Grabitz, Meinhard Hilf and Martin Nettesheim (eds), *Das Recht der EU* (79th supp, CH Beck 2023) para 50.

[68] Niamh Moloney, 'The European Union in International Financial Governance' (2017) 3 RSF Journal of the Social Sciences 138, 143 ff.

[69] See the procedure in arts 10–15 of the ESMA Regulation (EU) No 1095/2010.

[70] See art 16 of the ESMA Regulation (EU) No 1095/2010.

nor recommendations can be regarded as producing binding legal effects for national authorities or financial institutions.[71] Therefore, these soft law instruments cannot be the subject of actions for annulment under Article 263 TFEU. However, since national authorities may follow these soft law instruments and since national courts need to take them into consideration, guidelines and recommendations may be reviewed by the Court of Justice in preliminary reference procedures under Article 267 TFEU.[72]

Third, the ESAs may also provide opinions to the EP, the Council, or the Commission, upon their request or on the ESAs' own initiative, on all issues related to the ESAs' area of competence. Introduced during the ESAs reform in 2019,[73] this gives the ESAs a remarkable advisory role in the EU legislative process, not unlike the Economic and Social Committee or the Committee of the Regions.

Fourth, the ESAs may publish questions and answers relating to the practical implementation of EU financial law provisions. Questions may not only be submitted by competent authorities but also any natural or legal person may inquire about these provisions. The answers by the ESAs are non-binding and are published on their website. This has led to a remarkable body of interpretative help, leading to increased regulatory convergence.[74]

In conclusion, the ESFS, comprising the ESRB and the three ESAs, is an innovative response establishing the administrative structure to provide macro- and micro-prudential supervision. This not only allows expertise to be pooled for supervision at EU level but also denationalizes and depoliticizes these tasks. Moreover, these novel administrative structures also act through innovative means, making broad use of soft law to ensure compliance and coherence in supervision.

3.4 The Banking Union

The banking union, as originally conceived, was to be based on three main pillars concerning supervision, resolution, and a deposit guarantee scheme, which would be a fund designed to reimburse depositors up to a certain amount in case of bank failures. The first and second pillars—that is, the SSM and the SRM—are discussed next. Action on the third would-be pillar of the banking union, a common European deposit guarantee scheme, has been dormant for some time—not least because of German reluctance on this initiative[75]—after showing some promising signs of advancing.[76]

[71] Case C-911/19 *FBF* EU:C:2021:599, paras 36–49.

[72] ibid, paras 68–75.

[73] See art 16a of the ESMA Regulation (EU) No 1095/2010 as amended by Regulation (EU) 2019/2175.

[74] See for ESMA <https://www.esma.europa.eu/rules-databases-library/questions-and-answers> accessed 15 January 2024.

[75] Donnelly (n 13); Howarth and Quaglia, *The Political Economy of European Banking Union* (n 9); Bauerschmidt, 'Financial Stability as the Objective of the Banking Union' (n 40) 178 ff.

[76] See article by the then German finance minister, Olaf Scholz, 'Germany Will Consider EU-wide Bank Deposit Reinsurance', *Financial Times* (London, 5 November 2019).

3.4.1 The Single Supervisory Mechanism (SSM) and the ECB

The first pillar of the banking union is the SSM. The SSM Regulation (EU) 1024/2013[77] confers on the ECB the task of supervising systemically important banks. The aim is to contribute to the safety and soundness of credit institutions and the stability of the financial system in the Union, in accordance with Article 1 of the SSM Regulation.

The SSM Regulation is based on Article 127(6) TFEU, which allows the Council, acting by unanimity, after consulting the EP, to confer 'specific tasks upon the European Central Bank concerning policies related to the prudential supervision of credit institutions and other financial institutions'. Such a conferral on a Union institution rather than a newly established agency avoids the difficult task of rendering the conferral compatible with the *Meroni* doctrine. However, the suitability of this legal basis was contested, especially in German-language contributions, which argued that this provision only allowed a narrow transfer of 'special tasks' or '*besondere Aufgaben*' related to banking supervision. They argued that the full transfer of banking supervision powers was not possible and, according to this view, the ECB may only have a supporting role.[78]

On closer examination, there are good reasons why the SSM Regulation was correctly adopted on the basis of Article 127(6) TFEU. When looking at the wording, this provision allows the conferral of 'specific tasks', which requires those tasks to be delimited and separable from other tasks. While the German version speaks of '*besondere Aufgaben*', which translates as 'special tasks', and suggests a narrower reading, the provision has to be interpreted in the light of all official languages and by reference to the purpose and general scheme of the rules of which it forms part.[79] In this vein, the French text uses the term '*missions spécifiques*', the Italian text '*compiti specifici*', the Spanish text '*tareas específicas*', and the Polish text '*szczególne zadania*', which therefore seem to require delimited tasks rather than only subordinated or purely supportive tasks.

Against this background, the SSM Regulation is limited *ratione loci* to the euro Member States and those Member States which have established close cooperation pursuant to Article 7. Moreover, *ratione personae* the scope of application generally refers to the largest and most systemically relevant banks, and *ratione materiae* not all financial supervision powers are transferred to the ECB. Rather, questions of consumer protection, the fight against money laundering, and the supervision of third-country credit institutions remain at national level. Finally, a comparison of Article 127(5) and 127(6) TFEU supports the possibility of conferring specific supervisory powers on the ECB. Whereas the former provision allows the European System of Central Banks to contribute to supervisory policy and support (national) supervisors without any further

[77] Regulation (EU) 1024/2013 conferring specific tasks on the European Central Bank concerning policies relating to the prudential supervision of credit institutions [2013] OJ L287/63.

[78] Matthias Herdegen, 'Europäische Bankenunion' (2012) Wertpapiermitteilungen 1889, 1891 ff.; Ann-Kathrin Kaufhold, *Systemaufsicht* (Mohr Siebeck 2016) 285 ff.; Benedikt Wolfers and Thomas Voland, 'Europäische Zentralbank und Bankenaufsicht' (2014) Zeitschrift für Bank- und Kapitalmarktrecht 177, 178 ff.

[79] Case 29/69 *Stauder v Stadt Ulm* EU:C:1969:57, para 3; Case C-511/08 *Heinrich Heine* EU:C:2010:189, para 51; Case C-488/11 *Asbeek Brusse* EU:C:2013:341, para 26.

legislation, the latter provision requires a special legislative procedure. This formed part of a compromise during the negotiations of the Treaty of Maastricht, which left the question of prudential supervision at EU level open to political deliberations, subject to a unanimous decision of the Council. Therefore, the Union legislator could rightfully empower the ECB to assume supervisory tasks through the SSM Regulation, based on Article 127(6) TFEU.[80]

In the meantime, this view has been confirmed by the Court of Justice, which never took issue with the legal basis of the SSM Regulation, and underlined that the ECB has the exclusive competence to supervise all banks in the euro area, while national supervisory authorities only assist the ECB regarding less significant banks.[81] Conversely, the German Constitutional Court held, in its *Banking Union* case, that the SSM Regulation does not exceed the competences conferred on the EU, while emphasizing that national supervisory authorities retain their competences, especially for less significant banks.[82] Thus, although the two courts have a different understanding as regards the exact scope of Article 127(6) TFEU, especially for less significant banks, the German Constitutional Court avoided an open conflict by not questioning the SSM Regulation as such.

This raises the follow-up question of whether monetary policy is sufficiently separated from the tasks of banking supervision. This is by no means a purely theoretical problem. Rather, the ECB may be tempted to lower its interest rates or loosen the conditions for its purchases in order to facilitate access to liquidity for banks, thereby undermining banking supervision through monetary policy. Conversely, the ECB relies on a functioning banking system that serves as a transfer mechanism for its monetary policy. Banking supervision may, thus, spill over into monetary policy.[83]

An adequate separation of monetary and supervisory functions is based on the distinction between price stability and financial stability. Under Articles 127(1) and 282(2) TFEU, the primary objective of monetary policy is to ensure price stability. By contrast, the SSM Regulation, based on Article 127(6) TFEU, pursues the objective of financial stability. This is accompanied by an important distinction in the separation of competences: while monetary policy in the euro area pursuant to Article 3(1)(c) TFEU constitutes an exclusive competence, the SSM Regulation[84] and the rules to be applied

[80] That the SSM Regulation can be adopted on the basis of Art 127(6) TFEU is also shown by Kern Alexander, 'European Banking Union: A Legal and Institutional Analysis of the SSM and the SRM' (2015) 40 European Law Review 154, 168; Alberto de Gregorio Merino, 'Institutional Report' in Gyula Bándi and others (eds), *FIDE Report on European Banking Union* (Kluwer 2016) 168 ff.; Klaus Lackhoff, *Single Supervisory Mechanism* (CH Beck 2017) 16 ff.; Gianni Lo Schiavo, *The Role of Financial Stability in EU Law and Policy* (Kluwer 2017) 207 ff.; Josef Ruthig, 'Die EZB in der europäischen Bankenunion' (2014) 178 Zeitschrift für das gesamte Handels- und Wirtschaftsrecht 443, 451 ff.; Martin Selmayr, 'Artikel 127 AEUV' in Hans von der Groeben, Jürgen Schwarze and Armin Hatje (eds), *Europäisches Unionsrecht* (7th edn, CH Beck 2015) paras 51 ff.

[81] See Case C-450/17 P *Landeskreditbank Baden-Württemberg v ECB* EU:C:2019:372, paras 36–41.

[82] BVerfG 2 BvR 1685/14 and 2 BvR 2631/14, DE:BVerfG:2019:rs20190730.2bvr168514, paras 171–82.

[83] On the tension between monetary and supervisory policy, see Cornelia Manger-Nestler and Robert Böttner, 'Ménage à trois? – Zur gewandelten Rolle der EZB im Spannungsfeld zwischen Geldpolitik, Finanzaufsicht und Fiskalpolitik' (2014) Europarecht 621, 630 ff; Kern Alexander, 'The European Central Bank and Banking Supervision' (2016) European Company and Financial Law Review 467, 488 ff.

[84] It is not called into question by the findings in Case T-122/15 *Landeskreditbank Baden-Württemberg v ECB* EU:T:2017:337, paras 54, 63, and 72 (confirmed on appeal in Case C-450/17 P EU:C:2019:372, para 49) that Art 4(1) of the SSM Regulation confers an 'exclusive competence' on the ECB, as the exclusivity relates to the tasks

by the ECB in the Capital Requirements Regulations[85] and the Capital Requirements Directives[86] fall into the area of shared competence.[87] The different objectives of stability (ie price stability and financial stability) have a direct impact on the separation of functions. To this end, the SSM Regulation foresees a strict separation of supervisory and monetary functions. According to Article 25(1) SSM Regulation, the ECB may, when exercising supervisory tasks, only pursue the objective of this regulation and, in particular, the objective of financial stability. In addition, supervisory tasks must be exercised separately from monetary policy, according to Article 25(2) SSM Regulation.

In order to categorize a specific measure in an individual case, regard must be had to the objective and the effect of that measure. First, it must be determined whether the measure pursues the objective of financial stability or price stability.[88] For this, the content and justification of the measure must be evaluated. Second, a supervisory measure must be assessed as to whether it interferes with, or is determined by, monetary policy. Whether there is an interference with monetary policy can be assessed by means of the case law of the Court of Justice. While these cases concern the delineation between economic and monetary policy, the underlying reasoning can also be applied for the delineation between supervisory and monetary policy. In *Pringle*, the Court held that an indirect effect on price stability was not sufficient to classify a measure as monetary policy.[89] However, this also means that direct effects on price stability affect monetary policy, and that such supervisory measures are prohibited. Whether or not a supervisory measure is determined by monetary policy can be examined by having recourse to the *Gauweiler* and *Weiss* cases. According to the Court, indirect effects on the stability of the euro area are not sufficient to treat a monetary policy measure as being equivalent to an economic policy measure.[90] However, it can also be deduced that monetary policy measures with a direct effect on financial stability go beyond the monetary mandate and improperly determine supervisory measures.

The separation between monetary and supervisory functions and the distinction between individual measures by means of price stability and financial stability are supported by institutional arrangements in the ECB. Article 26 of the SSM Regulation establishes the Supervisory Board as an internal body of the ECB which plans and executes supervision.[91] It consists of a chairman, a deputy, four other representatives of the ECB, and representatives of national supervisory authorities of participating Member

enumerated in this provision and applies to the banks under direct ECB supervision but not to the entire field of prudential supervision.

[85] Regulation (EU) 575/2013 on prudential requirements for credit institutions [2013] OJ L176/1, significantly amended by Regulation (EU) 2019/876 [2019] OJ L150/1.

[86] Directive 2013/36/EU on access to the activity of credit institutions and the prudential supervision of credit institutions [2013] OJ L176/338, significantly amended by Directive (EU) 2019/878 [2019] OJ L150/253.

[87] See Art 4(2)(a) TFEU regarding the internal market, and Nettesheim (n 67) para 6, on shared competence as a 'catch-all' category for those instances where the category of competence is not laid down in the Treaties.

[88] See, on the scope of review, Case C-370/12 *Pringle* EU:C:2012:756, paras 53 and 55; Case C-62/14 *Gauweiler* EU:C:2015:400, para 46; Case C-493/17 *Weiss* EU:C:2018:1000, para 53.

[89] *Pringle* (n 88) para 56.

[90] *Gauweiler* (n 88) para 52; *Weiss* (n 88) para 61.

[91] Lackhoff (n 80) 60 ff.

States. While the Supervisory Board plans and executes banking supervision, binding decisions need to be taken by the ECB's Governing Council, in accordance with Article 129 TFEU. Thus, the Supervisory Board proposes complete draft decisions, which are deemed adopted unless the Governing Council objects within a period of not more than ten working days. The Governing Council may object to the draft decision and, in particular, invoke monetary policy concerns. To settle disagreements on the separation of functions, Article 25(5) of the SSM Regulation creates a mediation panel. This should not only avoid conflicts of interest but also ensure that each function is exercised in accordance with the applicable objectives, as Recital 65 explains. The ECB has also adopted further internal measures[92] to ensure the separation of functions, including IT systems and information exchange.[93] That this separation works well is proven not least by the fact that the mediation panel has, so far, never been called upon to intervene.

In conclusion, a particular measure by the ECB of hardening softer law should be mentioned. The prudential rules contained in the Capital Requirements Regulations and Directives contain a range of options and discretions left to competent authorities. In the context of the SSM, the ECB decided to exercise these options and discretions by way of regulations,[94] which are accompanied by a soft law guide explaining the choices made.[95] This shows how softer hard law (options and discretions) is hardened not only by hard law regulations but also by soft guidance, and is an example of the complexities surrounding financial regulation.[96]

3.4.2 The Single Resolution Mechanism (SRM) and the Bank Recovery and Resolution Directive (BRRD)

Banking resolution—to be precise, the SRM—is the second pillar of the banking union. It is, however, less supranational than the SSM.[97] Ailing banks can be liquidated following insolvency proceedings, or they can be subject to resolution. Whereas insolvency is dealt with by courts retrospectively in order to fulfil the claims of creditors, banking resolution is carried out by the executive branch prospectively in order to ensure financial stability. The Bank Recovery and Resolution Directive 2014/59/EU[98] harmonized national resolution law and procedures, while the SRM Regulation

[92] Decision ECB/2014/39 of 17 September 2014 on the implementation of separation between the monetary policy and supervision functions.

[93] Lackhoff (n 80) 79 ff.

[94] Regulation (EU) 2016/445 on the exercise of options and discretions available in Union law [2016] L 78/60, amended by Regulation (EU) 2022/504 [2022] OJ L102/11.

[95] ECB Guide on options and discretions available in Union law (latest version of March 2022) <https://www.bankingsupervision.europa.eu/ecb/pub/pdf/ssm.supervisory_guides2022_ond.en.pdf> accessed 15 January 2024.

[96] See, in more detail, on the ECB's soft law instruments on supervision, Daniel Segoin, 'The Accountability of the ECB as a Subsidiary or Secondary Macroprudential Supervisor' (forthcoming).

[97] David Howarth and Lucia Quaglia, 'The Steep Road to Banking Union: Constructing the Single Resolution Mechanism' (2014) 50 Journal of Common Market Studies Annual Review 125.

[98] Directive 2014/59/EU establishing a framework for the recovery and resolution of credit institutions and investment firms [2014] OJ L173/190.

806/2014[99] established a new Union agency (the Single Resolution Board), which, in principle, finances itself autonomously from bank contributions to the Single Resolution Fund (SRF).

Both the BRRD and the SRM Regulation are based on Article 114 TFEU, which allows the EU to adopt measures 'which have as their object the establishment and functioning of the internal market'. In order to justify recourse to this legal basis, the BRRD states in Recital 3 that the failure of a cross-border bank is likely to affect the stability of the financial markets in the Member States. Similarly, the SRM Regulation refers in Recitals 2, 10, and 12 to financial stability as an essential condition for the establishment and functioning of the internal market. Whereas the BRRD needs to be transposed by Member States and resolution procedures are mainly national, subject to increased coordination in cross-border cases, the SRM Regulation introduces a centralized approach for resolution. To this end, it builds upon the main elements of the BRRD, including the distinction between the preparatory phase with resolution planning (Articles 8–12 SRM Regulation), the early intervention phase (Article 13 SRM Regulation), and the resolution phase (Articles 14–29 SRM Regulation). In addition, the newly established SRB wields considerable, yet clearly circumscribed, powers to resolve banks.

The decision-making for resolving a bank was key during legislative deliberations. Whereas the initial proposal foresaw an *ex ante* control of the SRB by the Commission through the adoption of the resolution decision,[100] the resolution procedure adopted by the Union legislature foresees an *ex post* control of the SRB by the Commission and possibly the Council. This aimed to give the SRB greater influence while ensuring compliance with the *Meroni* doctrine, which prohibits delegating a 'discretionary power implying a wide margin of discretion which may, according to the use which is made of it, make possible the execution of actual economic policy'.[101] And since the resolution of a bank includes not only technical assessments but also the weighing of different policy objectives, the SRB may not decide autonomously to resolve a bank. Thus, the resulting resolution procedure is complex, involving not only the SRB but also the ECB, the Commission, and the Council as Union institutions.

In the initial assessment phase, it is assessed whether a bank is failing or is likely to fail, whether there are alternative private measures to resolution, and whether resolution is in the public interest.[102] Subsequently, the SRB adopts a resolution scheme, which only enters into force 'if no objection has been expressed by the Council or by the Commission within a period of 24 hours'.[103] Thus, the Commission either endorses

[99] Regulation (EU) 806/2014 establishing uniform rules and a uniform procedure for the resolution of credit institutions and certain investment firms in the framework of a Single Resolution Mechanism and a Single Resolution Fund [2014] OJ L225/1.

[100] See arts 14, 16(6), and 16(7) of the Proposal for a Regulation establishing uniform rules and a uniform procedure for the resolution of credit institutions and certain investment firms in the framework of a Single Resolution Mechanism and a Single Bank Resolution Fund, COM (2013) 520 final.

[101] *Meroni* (n 60) p 152. See also section 3.3.2 above.

[102] art 18(1)–(5), SRM Regulation.

[103] art 18(7), 5th subparagraph, SRM Regulation.

or objects to the resolution scheme with regard to the discretionary aspects. However, where such an objection concerns the fulfilment of the public interest criterion or a material modification of the financial means provided by the SRF, the Council needs to be seised by the Commission. In the event that there are modifications or objections to the resolution scheme by the Union institutions, the SRB has to modify the resolution scheme within eight hours.[104] The reason for this complex decision-making procedure is to ensure compliance with the *Meroni* doctrine.[105] Since the Union legislator expressly reserved the decision on the discretionary aspects to Union institutions, the SRB has not received any autonomous powers, as was most recently confirmed by the General Court.[106]

Another novelty of the SRM is its Single Resolution Fund, which is fully owned by the Single Resolution Board. This fund is financed through a system of parafiscal contributions levied from banks. Articles 70 and 71 of the SRM Regulation foresee so-called *ex ante* and *ex post* contributions. Over the course of a build-up period of eight years, the fund should raise at least 1 per cent of the amount of covered deposits held by banks (on the basis of 2011 data this would have amounted to 55 billion euros, but in the meantime has become much higher). Moreover, if expenses are necessary for banking resolution, *ex post* contributions can be levied under Article 71 SRM Regulation. However, these contributions could be illegal if, under Article 114(2) TFEU, they are regarded as fiscal provisions.[107] In particular, this prohibition is intended to prevent circumvention of the specific Union competences for indirect (Article 113 TFEU) and direct taxation (Article 115 TFEU).[108] Both types of taxation may be harmonized by the Union only through a special legislative procedure with unanimity in the Council, while Article 114 TFEU provides for the ordinary legislative procedure by a qualified majority in the Council and a decision by the EP.

Some authors argue that taxes, in the meaning of Article 114(2) TFEU, also include parafiscal contributions. It is underlined that supranational levies may affect the national budget revenues and thus the Member States' ability to operate nationally. Therefore, the term 'fiscal provisions' ('*dispositions fiscales*' or '*Bestimmungen über Steuern*') in Article 114(2) TFEU should be interpreted broadly so as to prevent the EU from adopting rules with fiscal content against the will of a Member State.[109]

[104] art 18(7), 7th subparagraph, SRM Regulation.

[105] See Recital 24, SRM Regulation.

[106] Case T–510/17 *Del Valle Ruiz v Commission and SRB* EU:T:2022:312, paras 204–19; Case T–628/17 *Aeris Invest v Commission and SRB* EU:T:2022:315, paras 121–34. Both judgments are currently under appeals which, however, do not concern the *Meroni* aspects.

[107] This question is currently being raised by a number of applicants challenging their *ex ante* contributions before the General Court (see, eg, T–413/18 and T–481/19 *Portigon*; T–405/21 *Dexia*). BVerfG 2 BvR 1685/14 and 2 BvR 2631/14, ECLI:DE:BVerfG:2019:rs20190730.2bvr168514, paras 293–308 on the banking union did not consider the contributions to the SRF to be violating the German constitution, since the transfer is set out in the Intergovernmental Agreement of 21 May 2014 (n 121).

[108] Case C–338/01 *Commission v Council* EU:C:2004:253, paras 60–64; Case C–533/03 *Commission v Council* EU:C:2006:64, paras 45–47.

[109] See, in general, Christoph Ohler, *Die fiskalische Integration in der Europäischen Gemeinschaft* (Nomos 1997) 206 ff.; and, regarding the SRM Regulation, Christian Calliess and Christopher Schoenfleisch, 'Die Bankenunion, der ESM und die Rekapitalisierung von Banken' (2015) JuristenZeitung 113, 120.

This view, however, is not convincing when having regard to the wording, genesis, systematics, and telos of the provision. In the case law, the CJEU first points out that the Treaties do not contain a clear indication of the interpretation of the term 'fiscal provisions'. 'It is, however, necessary to point out that, by reason of their general character, those words cover not only all areas of taxation, without drawing any distinction between the types of duties or taxes concerned, but also all aspects of taxation, whether material rules or procedural rules.'[110] In addition to the rate of tax, this also includes the basis of assessment and the detailed rules for levying the various duties.[111] In a recent ruling, the Court stated that Article 114(2) TFEU seeks to exclude Chapter 2 within Title VII of the TFEU, entitled 'Tax provisions'.[112] This already gives a clear indication that the rules on paying contributions to the Single Resolution Fund are not fiscal provisions, since they are neither an internal taxation on domestic products in the meaning of Articles 110–12 TFEU nor a form of indirect taxation in the sense of Article 113 TFEU. This finding is also supported by historical, systematic, and teleological arguments.

With regard to the genesis of Article 114(2) TFEU in the Single European Act,[113] it must be pointed out that a supranational concept of taxation existed at that time and can be used systematically, even today. Under the Protocol on Privileges and Immunities (Protocol No 7), the Union is exempt from any direct tax. In the case law, the concept of taxes includes three elements: firstly, taxes must be levied on the basis of law; secondly, in accordance with the principle of universality (ie not binding revenue to a specific purpose), taxes are accrued to the general budget; and, thirdly, taxes have no direct and compelling connection to any benefits received.[114] This case law has subsequently been confirmed[115] and excludes, in particular, special charges which are earmarked for a specific purpose.[116] In this vein, the Court of Justice held recently that the contributions to the Single Resolution Fund follow an 'insurance-based logic' obliging the financial sector to provide adequate resources encouraging each institution concerned to pursue less risky methods of operation.[117] In return for their contribution, each institution gets the potential benefit of receiving money from the Single Resolution Fund if the public interest in Article 18 of the SRM Regulation is fulfilled and the additional conditions for the use of the Fund in Article 76 of the SRM Regulation are also fulfilled. Moreover, the institutions also receive a systemic benefit in return, since the Single Resolution

[110] Case C-338/01 *Commission v Council* EU:C:2004:253, para 63. See also Case C-533/03 *Commission v Council* EU:C:2006:64, para 47.

[111] Case C-338/01 *Commission v Council* EU:C:2004:253, para 65.

[112] Case C-83/21 *Airbnb Ireland* EU:C:2022:1018, paras 25 and 29.

[113] See Claus-Dieter Ehlermann, 'The Internal Market Following the Single European Act' (1987) 24 Common Market Law Review 361, 370.

[114] Case 32/67 *Van Leeuwen v Gemeente Rotterdam* EU:C:1968:8, p 48; Case 23/68 *Klomp v Inspectie der belastingen* EU:C:1969:6, p 20.

[115] See Case C-191/94 *AGF Belgium* EU:C:1996:144; Case C-199/05 *European Community v Belgian State* EU:C:2006:678, as well as the opinions of the Advocates General in these cases on the interpretation of Art 3 of today's Protocol (No 7) on the Privileges and Immunities of the European Union.

[116] See, in detail, Philipp Kreibohm, *Der Begriff der Steuer im Europäischen Gemeinschaftsrecht* (Nomos 2003) 172 ff.

[117] Joined Cases C-584/20 P and C-621/20 P *Commission v Landesbank Baden-Württemberg* EU:C:2021:601, para 113.

Fund plays a key role in ensuring financial stability. All banks benefit equally from this systemic benefit even if they are not subject to resolution.

Assuming, finally, that the purpose of Article 114(2) TFEU is to protect the revenues of national budgets and thus the proper functioning of the Member States,[118] there is no problem with the legal basis. At national level, there are no comparable taxes levied from banks in order to contribute to banking recovery and resolution. Therefore, there cannot be any interference with existing national tax regulations. In line with considerable voices in the literature,[119] it can therefore be concluded that parafiscal (special) levies, such as the bank contributions of the SRM Regulation, can be established in the context of approximation of laws, and that these do not constitute 'fiscal provisions' in the meaning of Article 114(2) TFEU. These contributions are not entered in the general budget without earmarking but are available only to the SRB for the resolution of ailing banks. Article 67(2) of the SRM Regulation also prevents the Union budget or national budgets from being held liable for expenses or losses of the Single Resolution Fund. Therefore, the contributions may only be used to achieve the objectives set out in the SRM Regulation, in particular financial stability, and are unlike taxes earmarked for a specific purpose.[120]

In conclusion, the novel way of financing the SRM through banking contributions is compatible with the Treaties. Nevertheless, the Member States whose currency is the euro, and those Member States which have established close cooperation with the ECB for supervision purposes, have agreed to conclude an intergovernmental agreement on the transfer and mutualization of contributions to the Single Resolution Fund.[121] This intergovernmental agreement not only lays down how the contributions raised at national level in accordance with the BRRD and the SRM Regulation are transferred to the Fund but also sets out an allocation mechanism during the transitional build-up period of eight years. The existence of the intergovernmental agreement was important for the German Constitutional Court in finding that the SRM Regulation was compatible with the German Constitution.[122] Hence, although the intergovernmental agreement was not legally necessary, since the Union legislator could impose contributions on banks, it allowed the German Constitutional Court to avoid an open conflict and thus served its purpose in the establishment of the banking union.

[118] See n 111.

[119] Eberhard Grabitz, 'Handlungsspielräume der EG-Mitgliedstaaten zur Verbesserung des Umweltschutzes' in Rüdiger Breuer and others (eds), *Umweltrecht und Technikrecht* (Werner 1989) 85 and 119; de Gregorio Merino (n 80) 207 ff.; Meinhard Hilf, 'Umweltabgaben als Gegenstand von Gemeinschaftsrecht und -politik' (1992) Neue Zeitschrift für Verwaltungsrecht 105, 107; Kreibohm (n 116) 193.

[120] On the compatibility of the SRM Regulation with the system of own resources in art 311 TFEU, see Jonathan Bauerschmidt, 'Der Einheitliche Bankenabwicklungsmechanismus' in Jonathan Bauerschmidt and others (eds), *Konstitutionalisierung in Zeiten globaler Krisen* (Nomos 2015) 347, 365 ff.

[121] Intergovernmental Agreement (IGA) on the transfer and mutualisation of contributions to the Single Resolution Fund of 21 May 2014, Council document ST 8457/14.

[122] See BVerfG 2 BvR 1685/14 and 2 BvR 2631/14, ECLI:DE:BVerfG:2019:rs20190730.2bvr168514; paras 293–308 did not consider the contributions to the SRF to be violating the German constitution since the transfer is set out in the IGA (n 121).

3.5 The Capital Markets Union

While the establishment of the banking union set out to break the vicious circle between sovereigns and banks, the capital markets union sought to unlock new sources of financing that were less dependent on banks. The capital markets union project was originally launched by then President of the European Commission, Jean-Claude Juncker, in 2014.[123] The aim of the capital markets union was to create a single market for capital across the EU by providing businesses—especially small and medium-sized enterprises (SMEs)—with a greater choice of funding, offering new opportunities for savers and investors, and facilitating cross-border investments. A fully functioning and integrated market for capital would allow the EU's economy to grow and make it more competitive.[124] The Commission set out its ambitions in two successive action plans, in 2015[125] and 2020.[126] Thus, rather than being a short-term stimulus, the capital markets union was designed as a structural and long-term transformation of how financial intermediation works in the EU. Some legislative measures, discussed next, particularly stand out.

3.5.1 Securitisation Regulation and Covered Bonds Directive

The first piece of EU legislation concerned securitization, the financial practice which allows various types of contractual debt, including mortgage loans, to be pooled, and their related cash flows to be sold to third parties as securities. This practice was a key driver of the GFC because it encouraged the use of complex financial instruments whose risks were poorly understood. However, if the risks are managed properly, securitization can increase the availability of credit and reduce the cost of funding. Therefore, the EU passed a new Securitisation Regulation (EU) 2017/2402, creating a framework for simple, transparent, and standardized securitization.[127] Based on Article 114 TFEU, the Securitisation Regulation sets out requirements related to simplicity, transparency, and standardization of securities, and tasks ESMA with maintaining a register of all these securities in the EU.[128] Labelling some securities as 'simple, transparent and standardised' aims to build confidence among market participants by reducing some of the complexities. Today, ESMA lists a range of these securities,[129] indicating that this more secure financial practice has brought new liquidity to markets.

[123] For an overview see n 10 above, in particular Quaglia, Howarth and Liebe.

[124] For more details, see Commission, 'What is the Capital Markets Union?' <https://finance.ec.europa.eu/capital-markets-union-and-financial-markets/capital-markets-union/what-capital-markets-union_en> accessed 15 January 2024.

[125] Commission, 'Action Plan on building a capital markets union of 30 September 2015' COM (2015) 468 final.

[126] Commission, 'A capital markets union for people and businesses – new action plan of 24 September 2020' COM (2020) 590 final.

[127] Regulation (EU) 2017/2402 laying down a general framework for securitisation [2017] OJ L347/35.

[128] arts 18–27, Securitisation Regulation.

[129] See <https://registers.esma.europa.eu/publication/searchRegister?core=esma_registers_stsre> accessed 15 January 2024.

The second piece of the capital markets union legislation concerned covered bonds. Covered bonds are particular debt securities issued by a bank, which are collateralized against cover assets to which investors have direct recourse as preferred creditors. Unlike asset-backed securities created during securitization, covered bonds allow the investor to have recourse against both the issuer and the cover asset, sometimes called 'dual recourse'. Covered bonds had an important impact on the GFC but also played an important role for financial recovery. In order to encourage the use of covered bonds as a particularly safe investment, the EU legislator passed the Covered Bonds Directive (EU) 2019/2162,[130] based on Article 114 TFEU and setting out substantive as well as supervisory requirements for covered bonds. In addition, this directive also created the labels 'European Covered Bond' and 'European Covered Bond (Premium)' for certain bonds. These labels indicate that all the requirements of the Covered Bonds Directive have been met and make it easier for investors to assess the quality of their investments.

3.5.2 Prospectus Regulation

The third piece of the capital markets union legislation concerned the legal framework for prospectuses, setting out the disclosure requirements when securities are offered to the public or admitted to trading on a regulated market. The Prospectus Directive, from 2003, needed revision and was transformed into a regulation.[131] This allowed the establishment of rules which were directly applicable in all Member States and avoided the lengthy transposition process for directives. At the same time, the EU legislature does not have to establish rules for all areas of a regulation. In fact, it can also task Member States with enacting all the necessary legal and administrative provisions for the effective implementation of a regulation.[132] This regulatory technique leads to provisions that, like directives, require the adoption of national law to become binding. For instance, in the capital markets union, this regulatory technique has been used to oblige Member States to designate national authorities and give them certain powers vis-à-vis market participants. This is particularly important for the enforcement and imposition of sanctions based on EU law, which, despite some harmonization, still remains to large extents the responsibility of Member States.[133]

This national responsibility was also acknowledged recently by the Court, which had to adjudicate a case on prospectus law and the Member State's obligation to ensure that civil liability applies to those persons responsible for the information in a prospectus.

[130] Directive (EU) 2019/2162 on the issue of covered bonds and covered bond public supervision [2019] OJ L328/29.

[131] Regulation (EU) 2017/1129 on the prospectus to be published when securities are offered to the public or admitted to trading on a regulated market [2017] OJ L168/12.

[132] See Case 31/78 *Bussone* EU:C:1978:217, paras 28–33; Case 230/78 *Eridania* EU:C:1979:216, para 34; Case C-606/10 *ANAFE* EU:C:2012:348, para 72; Case C-146/13 *Spain v Parliament and Council* EU:C:2015:298, para 105. See Richard Král, 'National Normative Implementation of EC Regulations' (2008) 33 European Law Review 243.

[133] See Commission Communication of 8 December 2010, 'Reinforcing sanctioning regimes in the financial services sector' COM (2010) 716 final.

In this case, the Court held that that Member States have 'a broad discretion' when laying down the rules for bringing an action for damages. Hence, Member States may be allowed, or even required, to take into account the expertise of the investor when laying down civil liability rules.[134] This broad discretion of Member States is an emanation of their institutional and procedural autonomy. It is, however, not unlimited, as it must be applied in compliance with the principles of equivalence and effectiveness, in order to preserve the effectiveness of the applicable provisions of EU law. The principle of equivalence requires that national procedural provisions governing situations subject to EU law must be no less favourable than those governing similar domestic actions, while the principle of effectiveness requires that such provisions must not make it impossible or excessively difficult to exercise rights conferred by EU law.[135] While rendered for the old Prospectus Directive, this judgment is fully applicable to the new Prospectus Regulation, which maintained the directive-like provision requiring Member States to ensure civil liability.[136]

In conclusion, the capital markets union provides an umbrella for numerous political initiatives to unlock new sources of financing that are less dependent on banks. Therefore, the individual legislative measures are not as coherently aligned as the measures which led to the establishment of the ESFS or the banking union. Yet, by setting the objective of tapping into new sources of financing while ensuring a high level of market stability, practices such as securitization and covered bonds, which had an important impact on the GFC, could also play an important role for financial recovery. In addition, the Prospectus Regulation, in particular, shows that even where the Union legislator chooses to adopt rules which are directly applicable in all Member States, this proliferation of hard law may contain surprisingly soft provisions.

3.6 Conclusion

The GFC has proven to be an important catalyst for change in the area of financial regulation and supervision. This crisis laid open the fault lines and shortcomings of the regulatory architecture at EU level, to which the EU legislator responded by putting forward a series of measures comprising the ESFS, the banking union, and the capital markets union. Despite competing interests and different policy priorities between various Member States, policymakers worked through their differences to find politically acceptable solutions. At the same time, these measures tested the flexibility and rigidity of the constitutional architecture in at least three respects.

First, the responses to the GFC led to subconstitutional engineering to create novel administrative structures. Rather than revising the Treaties, the Union legislator decided to create a range of new agencies in secondary law to supervise banking and

[134] Case C-910/19 *Bankia SA/UMAS* EU:C:2021:433, paras 42 and 44.

[135] ibid, paras 45 and 46, with reference to previous case law.

[136] art 11(2), Prospectus Regulation.

financial market activities through the ESAs. Moreover, within existing Union institutions, new structures could also be established without revising the Treaties: the ECB received new supervisory powers and a newly created internal body, the Supervisory Board, was tasked to propose complete draft decisions to the ECB's main decision-making body, the Governing Council. These administrative arrangements serve to separate the ECB's Treaty tasks for monetary policy from their newly acquired supervisory tasks. Similar subconstitutional engineering took place when the SRB received powers to plan banking resolution, which will enter into force if no objection is expressed by the Commission or the Council. These novel administrative structures draw on technical expertise and depoliticize certain tasks while being respectful of the institutional balance established by the Treaties.

Second, the GFC also shifted the public–private divide in the EU. An over-reliance on the invisible hand of the market led to situations where only the iron glove of the sovereigns was able to re-establish financial stability. However, this fundamental shift towards public intervention not only created problems for public households but also proved unpopular, as taxpayers' money was used to bail out private banks. In order to rebalance the division between public intervention and private responsibility, the Union legislator created a novel system of contributions whereby the banking sector has to autonomously finance a fund which serves the sole purpose of providing liquidity in the event of a banking resolution, thus protecting taxpayers' money. Other examples of the shifting public–private divide are the legislative measures in the capital markets union, whereby some of the financial instruments which contributed to the building up of the GFC, such as securitization, became more tightly regulated in order to make use of their potential to provide private funding beyond banks.

Third, the responses to the GFC also led to a remarkable proliferation of harder soft law, as well as softer hard law. This can be attributed to at least three major causes: the complexity of financial markets, the divergence of views of lawmakers and regulators, and the constitutional limitations for the newly established agencies to adopt abstract and general rules. Although recourse to soft law may seem less than optimal, the growing body of ever-more detailed and pervasive guidelines, recommendations, and other forms or soft law has proven to be rather effective in ensuring compliance and coherence in financial supervision. Conversely, by using softer hard law, the Union legislator can accommodate national particularities, especially as regards sanctioning and enforcement mechanisms, while harmonizing the minimum requirements. This ties in with a greater trend of the Union legislator to adopt regulations rather than directives, since the former do not need to be transposed into national law, sparing national legislatures the burden of often lengthy transposition procedures. Especially where regulations contain softer, directive-like provisions, they combine the advantages of the directly applicable regulation with the flexibility of the directive for specific cases.

Looking back, the responses to the GFC bode rather well for other crises the EU has to tackle. They show the resolve and ingenuity of policymakers to tackle the challenges of a crisis and overcome their differences. This may not always lead to straightforward solutions and the negotiations may require many compromises. However, the existing constitutional framework has proven to give the rigidity for policymakers to use existing procedures to adopt the necessary responses to the crisis. At the same time, this framework also provided the flexibilities to accommodate new solutions, including the establishment of powerful agencies and their financing through contributions from the banking sector. While this may appear, to some, like an 'invisible' transformation of the EU's constitutional framework, the findings in this chapter rather suggest that the responses adopted have tapped into previously unused potential in the EU Treaties. Thus, the EU Treaties served a crucial constitutional function by providing rigidity and flexibility at the same time. Taken together, all the responses in the area of financial regulation and supervision show how a crisis can act as catalyst for change without changing the existing constitutional framework. Hence, in response to the GFC, the EU could and did prove that it is more than the sum of its parts.

4

Health Policy

A Cautionary Tale of Constitutional Slippage and Polity Building between Crisis and Nation Building

*Andreas Eriksen** *and Michelle Everson***

4.1 Overview

Briefed with the task of detailing the development of rule-making in the area of European Union (EU) health policy since the Lisbon Treaty, this chapter is faced with a conundrum: as is commonplace in EU terms,[1] rule-making for health in Europe has comprehensively sprung its formal Treaty confines. Competence creep, however, is both an inevitable part of an integration process which has long impacted on the social and political contexts of European life far beyond the narrow market sphere and an understandable response to a series of crises which have demanded a joint European response, the most pressing of which has been the COVID-19 pandemic. The expansion in competences is also one which should perhaps be welcomed, as long as it represents the overdue victory of social (political) over market values.[2]

Above all, the EU response to the COVID-19 crisis has been met with a wave of optimism within the social sciences: the autonomous EU financing of the 'NextGenerationEU' (NGEU) recovery plan (via the Own Resources Decision), containing a European Union Recovery Instrument (EURI), a Recovery and Resilience Facility (RRF), and a suspension of the conditionality placed upon budgetary measures within the European Semester,[3] is regarded as a major advance upon what are argued to be the failed and alienating politics of the EU response to financial and sovereign debt crises.[4] In this analysis, a corrective political momentum, generated in large part by a new Franco-German alliance against full imposition of austerity policies, lays the basis for a future of European solidarity: an effort to ensure 'social fairness' by addressing 'inequalities of opportunities as well as of outcome'.[5] European citizens,

* Researcher at ARENA Centre for European Studies and Associate Professor at Oslo Metropolitan University.
** Professor of Law at Birkbeck College, University of London.

[1] Vincent Delhomme and Tamara Hervey, 'The European Union's Response to the Covid-19 Crisis and (the Legitimacy of) the Union's Legal Order' (2022) 41 Yearbook of European Law 48.

[2] Delhomme and Hervey (n 1) 48.

[3] As Delhomme and Hervey note (n 1, 54–55), NGEU is 'a complex legal construction', modifying budgetary requirements under the Growth and Stability Pact, which relies on two legal bases, Arts 122 and 175 TFEU, both purporting to facilitate 'solidarity' between Member States in times of crisis.

[4] Vivien Schmidt, 'Economic Crisis Management in the EU: From Past Eurozone Mistakes to Future Promise beyond the COVID-19 Pandemic' in A Wetter Ryde (ed), *EU Crisis Management* (SIEPS Report 2022) 19–39.

[5] Schmidt (n 4).

Andreas Eriksen and Michelle Everson, *Health Policy* In: *EU Regulatory Responses to Crises*. Edited by: Diane Fromage, Adrienne Héritier, and Paul Weismann, Oxford University Press. © Andreas Eriksen and Michelle Everson 2025.
DOI: 10.1093/9780198913825.003.0004

it seems, can now look to a bright future, where the EU is a source not only of market opportunity, but also of social solidarity. The mood in legal circles is equally upbeat. Recognizing the unfortunate European tendency whereby crisis responses generally involve 'changes taking place outside Union legal structures, with the law sometimes "playing catch up" in later Treaty amendments', 'the Union's Covid-19 crisis response' is nevertheless asserted to be 'new' and 'at least *purportedly*' taking 'place within existing legal constraints'.[6] The limited solidarities demanded of the Member States in crisis situations by Articles 122 (1) and (2) are paired with Article 175 to lay the basis for NGEU to overcome the European 'economic constitutional settlement'; 'a Union based on a legally encoded dominance of the "economic" over "health" interests' ... 'is replaced by Union law based on *creative interpretations* of formal competences, designed to meet the needs of human health as well as Unionwide economic recovery'.[7]

Nevertheless, optimism must also be tinged with a degree of concern—suspicion, even. Jürgen Habermas has recently reminded us of the degree to which his concept of democracy—the public sphere of rational communication—has been undermined by the social inequalities created by our dominant modes of economic interchange.[8] It is to this exact degree that we might welcome competence creep and creative interpretations of formal competences which lay the basis for EU legitimacy in reassertion of health above economic interests. And yet, Habermas' point has far deeper conceptual roots, and therein lies the conundrum—the paradox addressed by this chapter. Overcoming social inequalities will not suffice to re-establish democratic sentiment within the public sphere; efforts to salvage social equality, especially if couched in the technical obscurantism of legal informalities and technocratic delivery, cannot but further undermine democratic will formulation, lacking the simple transparency to be fully debated and evaluated within the communicative public sphere.[9] And it is in this regard—the enhancement of the legitimacy of the EU order—that the accelerated development of the European polity during the COVID-19 crisis, for all of its newness, or 'purported' basis within existing legal provision, can also be argued to represent a continuity whereby the politics of ever-closer European integration unfolds in institutional informality. This is an uncomfortable stretching of the normative provisions of the European Treaties, which might, in certain lights, be characterized not simply as a positive evolution within the European polity but also as a challenge to a founding, democracy-enhancing European rule of law.[10]

Health and health policy within the EU play their own very distinct part within the COVID-19 response beyond the generalist economic parameters of NGEU, as well as within a more usual or habitual stretching of a European rule of law. For example, the

[6] Delhomme and Hervey (n 1) 54 (emphasis added).

[7] Delhomme and Hervey (n 1) 54 (emphasis added).

[8] Jürgen Habermas, *Ein neuer Strukturwandel der Öffentlichkeit und die deliberative Politik* (Suhrkamp Verlag 2022).

[9] Habermas (n 8) 109.

[10] Most importantly, to the explicit precept that the EU is not concerned with redistribution between Member States (most powerfully expressed in Art 125 TFEU).

Commission's EU4Health programme 2021–2027,[11] snappily entitled 'a vision for a healthier European Union', ostensibly a joint EU–MS response to the COVID-19 crisis, nevertheless also includes the desire to support the Member States in enhancing access to healthcare as a part of a programme designed to 'pave the way to a European Health Union'.[12] In so doing, it not only steps, in its stated aspirations, far beyond the limitations of its founding Treaty basis[13]— albeit in largely rhetorical mode—but also reveals itself as one more step in a long-standing process of competence creep whereby the various crises of the last two decades[14] have only confirmed Member State concerns, re-asserted in the Lisbon Treaty (Article 168(7)TFEU), that very particular steps must be taken in order to limit the incursion of the EU into national health systems.

At the same time, it is clear that the integration of health policy and health systems within Europe is a simple inevitability, albeit that crisis plays an accelerating role. Taking on board widespread and accepted distinctions between public health and (individual) healthcare policies, and between proactive health protection (or promotion) and the organization of, and access to, healthcare services,[15] all issues of health and healthcare are nevertheless found at the very core of the political economy. They are impacted upon by a myriad of tangential economic and social policies, and are simultaneously a part of the redistributive and security functions of the state. Seen in this light, the area of health and healthcare has presented a historical conundrum within European integration processes. The area is inevitably impacted upon by more general EU programmes and competences, above all completion of the single market and the legislative competence laid down in Article 114 TFEU, as well as the entrepreneurial function of the Court of Justice (CJEU) in relation both to market rights and human rights, including the right to health laid down in Article 35 of the Charter of Fundamental Rights of the European Union.[16] Nevertheless, we must exercise caution towards a significant portion of academic health literature that welcomes creative interpretation of formal competences and is sanguine—confident, even—that the hardening of soft powers within formal or executive European competences such as the

[11] Regulation (EU) 2021/522 of the European Parliament and of the Council of 24 March 2021 establishing a Programme for the Union's action in the field of health ('EU4Health Programme') for the period 2021–2027, and repealing Regulation (EU) No 282/2014 (Text with EEA relevance), PE/69/2020/REV/1, with a legal basis in Article 168 TFEU (OJ L107, 26.3.2021, pp 1–29).

[12] European Commission, 'European Health Union: Protecting our health together' <https://commission.europa.eu/strategy-and-policy/priorities-2019-2024/promoting-our-european-way-life/european-health-union_en> accessed 18 January 2024.

[13] As we explain below, Art 168 does not provide for harmonization of health systems; quite the contrary.

[14] Beginning with the BSE crisis (Michelle Everson and Ellen Vos, 'EU Agencies and the Politicized Administration' in Johannes Pollak and Peter Slominski (eds), *The Role of EU Agencies in the Eurozone and Migration Crisis* (Palgrave 2021) 21–51), proceeding with judicial activism within the internal market and the actions of national and European health policy entrepreneurs seeking to benchmark and coordinate national practices within the open method of coordination (OMC), as well as a hardening of health-based OMC practices within the European Semester (see Pierre Bocquillon, Eleanor Brooks and Tomas Maltby, 'Speak Softly and Carry a Big Stick: Hardening Soft Governance in EU Energy and Health Policies' (2020) 22 Journal of Environmental Policy and Planning 843).

[15] Anniek de Ruijter, *EU Health Law and Policy: The Expansion of EU Power in Public Health and Health Care* (OUP 2019).

[16] Charter of Fundamental Rights of the European Union, OJ C 326, 26.10.2012, pp 391–407; Eleanor Brooks, 'Crossing Borders: A Critical Review of the Role of the European Court of Justice in EU Health Policy' (2012) 105 Health Policy 33.

European Semester can be viewed in a positive light, or as a part of an opportunity to encourage the betterment of healthcare provision throughout the continent. The 'web of European [health] competences', we read,[17] obviates the need for Treaty revision, and for a clear (redistributive) EU competence on health and healthcare.

Rather, whereas some see this process as an expression of their faith in the ability of 'experimentalist' processes of democracy to make good the democratic gap at the outer limits of the regulatory state,[18] and yet others assert that the establishment of a joint European approach to redistribution within a healthcare market would be all of a part with the eventual recognition that healthcare shortages cannot be overcome within a marketization paradigm, this chapter doubts the sustainability within the area of healthcare of integration paradigms founded in 'integration by stealth'[19] or 'covert integration'.[20] The core problem here is that health and healthcare are not simply a part of the national political economy but, by exact virtue of that position, are also core elements within the 'moral economy' of the Member States, or within national debates on the moral values which guide the redistribution of social risks. As such, the provision of health and healthcare within the EU lies at the heart of our contemporary juxtaposition of schemes of justice founded in 'inclusion' with schemes of justice founded in the solidarity of risk-sharing.[21] In other words, although the EU possesses its own firmly normativized values of inclusion (see assertion of the ban on discrimination on the grounds of nationality), the formal structures of the Treaties are generally hostile to sustained risk-pooling between Member States, beyond the limited confines of 'emergency law'.[22]

Working against this background, this chapter explains how the ambition of creating a European Health Union might require an explicit moral renegotiation of the terms of integration—from non-discrimination to redistribution. The field of health cannot be Europeanized as a regulatory win-win deal; it instead requires engagement with solidarity, risk-pooling, and further issues of the moral political economy that currently lack firm grounding in European Treaties. The chapter simultaneously questions how instruments ostensibly developed for market supervision can have legitimacy as tools for social reform. Where formal competences no longer reflect actual practice, we reassess current practices from a rule of law perspective. Certainly, it is possible to conceive of current EU integration and rule-making within a framework of 'redistributive

[17] Kai P Purnhagen and others, 'More Competences than You Knew? The Web of Health Competence for European Union Action in Response to the COVID-19 Outbreak' (2020) 11 European Journal of Risk Regulation 297.

[18] Anniek de Ruijter, 'Institutional Build-up of EU Health Actors, EU Health Law and Policy' in de Ruijter, *The Expansion of EU Power* (n 15).

[19] Giandomenico Majone, *Dilemmas of European Integration: The Ambiguities and Pitfalls of Integration by Stealth* (OUP 2005).

[20] Adrienne Héritier, 'Covert Integration in the European Union' in Jeremy Richardson and Sonia Mazey (eds), *European Union Power and Policy-making* (Routledge 2015) 351–69.

[21] Alexander Somek, 'From Workers to Migrants, from Distributive Justice to Inclusion: Exploring the Changing Social Democratic Imagination' (2012) 18 European Law Journal 711.

[22] Bruno de Witte, 'The European Union's Covid-19 Recovery Plan: The Legal Engineering of an Economic Policy Shift' (2021) 58 Common Market Law Review 635. Granted, de Witte argues powerfully that emergency law can form the basis for enduring European solidarity.

technocracy'. Nevertheless, the simple focus on epistemic rather than institutional authority is an insufficient basis for critical evaluation. As an alternative, we propose to rethink how the classical rule of law virtues—clarity, predictability, and justiciability—can ground a template for health governance that is both epistemically attractive and democratically justifiable. The chapter straddles the fields of legal sociology and political theory. Methodologically, it pursues an empirical reconstruction of the aims and commitments that govern the Union's health field, through document analysis and literature review. This reconstruction is then complemented with a normative analysis from a rule of law perspective.

4.2 A Norm of Suspicion Suspended?

As our overview above makes clear, the COVID-19 crisis at least appears to have had a major impact on the aims of the rule-making deployed within European health policy, with new initiatives being fashioned within the existing but 'creatively' reinterpreted structures of EU law, in order to form a substantively new approach to human health in Europe. Health has an importance beyond the market. Nevertheless, this act of creative reinterpretation can and will be argued to be part of a continuity within the form of EU rule-making, wherein Member States have always been concerned about an EU competence creep in the matter of health, which is largely inevitable within the parameters and demands of the European market, the emerging European polity (autonomous policy entrepreneurs), and successive crises of cross-border regulation, but which similarly threatens the composition of national health core provisions and the core moral economy of the Member States. In these terms, it is therefore possible to speak of the Member States' historical attitudes to the establishment of an EU health policy in terms of the casting of the primary Treaty norm on which the EU competence is based, Article 168 TFEU, as a 'norm of suspicion' or an expression of formalized disquiet. Our question within this chapter is, accordingly, whether this norm of suspicion has been suspended following the pandemic crisis.

Article 168 TFEU, which assumed its current form in the Lisbon Treaty, would seem highly incongruous in most legal settings, be they national or international in character. Above all, the disjunction between paragraphs one and seven of the EU 'competence' for health laid down in Article 168 is even more odd when the Lisbon Treaty is regarded as a constitutional-type framework for the governance of the EU. On the one hand, the Union declares its integral interest in the concept of health and its determination to 'mainstream' health in all of its policies and activities;[23] on the other, however, it simultaneously normativizes, or gives 'constitutional character' to, a basic paradox whereby the Member States of the EU seek explicitly to restrict EU health competences, just as they widen them:

[23] Tamara Hervey and Anniek de Ruijter, 'The Dynamic Potential of European Union Health Law' (2020) 11 European Journal of Risk Regulation 726.

> 1. A high level of human health protection shall be ensured in the definition and implementation of all Union policies and activities.
>
> Union action, which shall complement national policies, shall be directed towards improving public health, preventing physical and mental illness and diseases, and obviating sources of danger to physical and mental health. Such action shall cover the fight against the major health scourges, by promoting research into their causes, their transmission and their prevention, as well as health information and education, and monitoring, early warning of and combating serious cross-border threats to health.
>
> The Union shall complement the Member States' action in reducing drugs-related health damage, including information and prevention.
>
> **********
>
> 7. Union action shall respect the responsibilities of the Member States for the definition of their health policy and for the organisation and delivery of health services and medical care. The responsibilities of the Member States shall include the management of health services and medical care and the allocation of the resources assigned to them.[24]

The underlying problem, however—the root cause of constitutional confusion—is one of the place of health within the political economy and the place of the political economy within the integration process; or the difficult act of coordinating, let alone harmonizing, the complex web of moral principles, social policies, political contingencies, and legal frameworks which are specific to each of the Member States and, in particular, their healthcare systems, with concomitant respect for a growing set of formal European competences, as well as informal imperatives to act at European level, especially in response to crises.

[24] The remaining sections of the Article are as follows: (2) The Union shall encourage cooperation between the Member States in the areas referred to in this Article and, if necessary, lend support to their action. It shall in particular encourage cooperation between the Member States to improve the complementarity of their health services in cross-border areas. Member States shall, in liaison with the Commission, coordinate among themselves their policies and programmes in the areas referred to in paragraph 1. The Commission may, in close contact with the Member States, take any useful initiative to promote such coordination, in particular initiatives aiming at the establishment of guidelines and indicators, the organisation of exchange of best practice, and the preparation of the necessary elements for periodic monitoring and evaluation. The European Parliament shall be kept fully informed. (3) The Union and the Member States shall foster cooperation with third countries and the competent international organisations in the sphere of public health. (4) By way of derogation from Article 2(5) and Article 6(a) and in accordance with Article 4(2)(k) the European Parliament and the Council, acting in accordance with the ordinary legislative procedure and after consulting the Economic and Social Committee and the Committee of the Regions, shall contribute to the achievement of the objectives referred to in this Article through adopting in order to meet common safety concerns: (a) measures setting high standards of quality and safety of organs and substances of human origin, blood and blood derivatives; these measures shall not prevent any Member State from maintaining or introducing more stringent protective measures; (b) measures in the veterinary and phytosanitary fields which have as their direct objective the protection of public health; (c) measures setting high standards of quality and safety for medicinal products and devices for medical use. (5) The European Parliament and the Council, acting in accordance with the ordinary legislative procedure and after consulting the Economic and Social Committee and the Committee of the Regions, may also adopt incentive measures designed to protect and improve human health and in particular to combat the major cross-border health scourges, measures concerning monitoring, early warning of and combating serious cross-border threats to health, and measures which have as their direct objective the protection of public health regarding tobacco and the abuse of alcohol, excluding any harmonisation of the laws and regulations of the Member States. (6) The Council, on a proposal from the Commission, may also adopt recommendations for the purposes set out in this Article.

Despite the existence of widespread and accepted distinctions between public health and (individual) healthcare policies, and between proactive health protection or promotion and the organization of, and access to, healthcare services,[25] all issues of health and healthcare are nevertheless found at the very core of the political economy. The 'obvious' solution whereby the EU would concentrate, in accordance with Article 168(1) TFEU, upon the promotion of public health, and especially so as it relates to the combating of health dangers arising within the free trade context (see the mad cow disease or BSE crisis), while the Member States would retain exclusive competences for the redistributive issue of access to healthcare systems, is a chimera. It is difficult, if not impossible, to make any enduring distinction between the marketized regulatory politics of Pareto efficiency and the moral process of the sharing or pooling of risks. Each seemingly distinct form of health policy is undoubtedly a political act of risk management—of planning for risk—and is, accordingly, inexorably impacted upon by a myriad of tangential economic and social policies. At the same time, however, health risk management, be it a matter of health protection or health provision, is simultaneously a part of the redistributive and/or security functions of the state. Accordingly, it is in this regard that we also can talk of human health as part of a 'moral economy', wherein it is impacted upon, not simply by economic or political factors, but by deeper considerations, such as notions of solidarity and redistribution, which were historically the preserve of the nation state.

Seen in this light, health and healthcare have presented a historical conundrum within processes of European integration. As noted, the area is impacted not only by more general EU programmes and competences but also by the entrepreneurial function of the CJEU, both in relation to market rights and human rights.[26] We could no longer conceive, for example, of the existence of a European citizen without access to cross-border health services, or of an EU that allows a crisis in public health—such as the BSE crisis—either to spread unchecked throughout the continent or irrevocably close the borders of the single market to cross-border trade. At the same time, however, processes of spillover and competence creep at the European level cannot but eat away at a 'core' competence of the Member States impacting upon welfare and national security, or, per the German Constitutional Court in its *Lisbon* judgment,[27] at a constitutive element within the national polity over which national parliamentary forces must retain control. The constitutional stakes are high, and contradictory—the urge towards 'managed health integration', especially in crises as well as the coordination of and even the pooling of risk, is overwhelming, but so, too, is the need to retain enough of the core constitutional identity of the Member States, or the competence-competence of the constitutionalized states which themselves constitute the Union.

Hence, the norm of constitutional suspicion which makes its appearance in Article 168(7): the inevitable tension which has arisen within integration processes—the ad

[25] de Ruijter, *EU Health Law and Policy* (n 15).
[26] Brooks (n 16).
[27] BVerfGE 123, 267 – Lisbon Decision (Lissabon-Urteil).

hoc evolution of a European presence within areas of health and healthcare policy which seem to lie beyond what are sometimes argued to be the 'non-redistributive' contours of a simple regulatory state[28]—is explanation enough for the strangely circumscribed EU competence for health. As Hervey and de Ruijter note,[29] the original establishment of a distinct EU competence for health, in the Maastricht Treaty (Article 129 EC), was marked by the same paradox: the clear need for an EU competence in relation to, say, the management of public health crises (for example, BSE), and a clear concern on the part of some Member States that a positive, circumscribed statement of EU competence would not be sufficient to prevent slippage in EU action on healthcare, especially with regard to the highly sensitive area of provision of, and access to, healthcare.

Subsequent history cannot but confirm the concern of those Member States that the long trend of competence creep in the area of health would only continue, even after the Lisbon rationalization of EU institutions and rule-making. Strikingly, the EU4Health programme 2021–2027, the 'vision for a healthier European Union'[30] post-COVID-19 crisis, seeks to support the Member States in enhancing access to healthcare as a part of the programme designed to 'pave the way to a European Health Union'. It is a clear and inspirational call to a new form of European solidarity competence. Health crises, more particularly the pandemic, clearly play their part in this shift.[31] They are not alone, however, and the inspirational move to a solidaristic European Health Union is also a child of judicial activism, building on the seminal 1990s cases of *Kohll* and *Decker*,[32] as well as of policy entrepreneurs, seeking to benchmark and coordinate national practices within the open method of coordination (OMC), provided for in Article 168(2) TFEU.[33] Individual actors, be they judicial actors committed to realizing the human face of the internal market in the right to access healthcare across borders, or social actors charged with filling in the gaps in EU social competences through informal exchange of best practice, have pursued their own visions of an integrated European health competence, challenging or unravelling the established place of health policy within the national political economies.[34]

[28] See Michelle Everson, 'Independent Agencies: Hierarchy Beaters?' 1 European Law Journal 180, investigating Giandomenico Majone's concept of the regulatory state; but also critical—the regulatory state, after all, is primarily concerned with a distribution of risk.

[29] Hervey and de Ruijter (n 23), referring to the Maastricht Treaty, Treaty on European Union, OJ C 191, 29.7.1992, pp 1–112.

[30] Regulation (EU) 2021/522 (n 11) pp 1–29.

[31] Sharon Baute and Anniek de Ruijter, 'EU Health Solidarity in Times of Crisis: Explaining Public Preferences towards EU Risk Pooling for Medicines' (2022) 29 Journal of European Public Policy 1183.

[32] Case C–158/96 *Kohll v Union des Caisses de Maladie* [1998] ECR I-1931; Case C–120/95 *Decker v Caisse des Maladie des Employes Prives* [1998] ECR I-1831. See, for subsequent guidelines on the application of the principle of free access to cross-border provision, C–368/98 *Vanbraekel v Alliance National des Mutualites Chretiennes (ANMC)* [2001]; C–157/99 *Geraets-Smits v Stichting Ziekenfonds VGZ*; *Peerbooms v Stichting CZ Groep Zorgverzekeringen* [2001]; *Mueller-Faure v Onderlinge Waarborgmaatschappij OZ Zorgverzekeringen UA*; C–385/99 *VanRiet v Onderlinge Waarborgmaatschappij ZAO Zorgverzekeringen* [2003]; and C–372/04 *Watts v Bedford Primary Care Trust and Secretary of State for Health* [2006].

[33] Anniek de Ruijter, 'EU "Public Health" and "Health-care" Law and Policy' in de Ruijter, *The Expansion of EU Power* (n 15).

[34] An interesting example of the Commission's coordination of networks of policy entrepreneurs in the health field is the Health Policy Platform, which can be found at https://webgate.ec.europa.eu/hpf/.

Equally, however, institutional actors and structures for the pursuit of health policy continue to grow in importance. This is occurring within explicitly political institutions, such as the European Parliament (EP)'s Committee on Environment, Public Health and Food Safety (ENVI). But it is also a feature within the EU's governance structures, for example the High Level Health Group, now subsumed within the Council, that was established as a soft governance mechanism within the 2007 Health Strategy, and which continues to operate by making use of techniques of soft coordination (benchmarking etc) developed within the OMC instrument.[35] Equally, however, and perhaps most importantly, especially in health crises, the expansion of the EU's health competence is also very much visible within the explicitly technocratic structures of EU governance, both within the remaining structures of comitology or myriad committees which mostly, though not exclusively, have Directorate-General SANTÉ as their focus,[36] and within the more general process of agencification that has seen European agencies step up to act within the distinctly grey area between formal competence and technical need, and thus to increase their influence upon the dense web of EU policy-making, especially in response to the various crises with which the EU has been confronted in the last two decades.[37]

At one level, the process of agencification appears to have reached its limits within the COVID-19 crisis. Many expected the new Health Emergency Preparedness and Response Authority (HERA) to be a semi-autonomous agency in the classic EU mould.[38] And yet HERA, with a budget of around 1 billion euros per annum, has been founded as a new Directorate-General within the European Commission.[39] It has a stated aim 'to strengthen Europe's ability to prevent, detect, and rapidly respond to cross-border health emergencies, by ensuring the development, manufacturing, procurement, and equitable distribution of key medical countermeasures',[40] an ambition to rival the global influence and reach of the World Health Organization (WHO), and a staffing and equipment capacity to achieve that aim. HERA itself represents a massive increase in the EU's practical capacity, not only to avoid a repeat of the damage done to the single market by poor coordination in the early days of COVID-19, but also to pursue an autonomous EU health policy. It is perhaps this significance that explains the presence of HERA within the more explicit political reach of the Commission; it is,

[35] de Ruijter, 'EU "Public Health" and "Health-care" Law and Policy' (n 33).

[36] 'Making a list of all health committees and groups that exist is a completely impossible task. Half of them are sleeping but have never really been abandoned', de Ruijter cites a Member State's representative to the Council group on health as saying, in de Ruijter, 'Institutional Build-up' (n 18) 92. Note also that some committees are political/interest committees. Others are technical/expert in nature.

[37] Michelle Everson and Ellen Vos, 'European Union Agencies' in Marianne Riddervold, Jarle Trondal and Akasemi Newsom (eds), *The Palgrave Handbook of EU Crises* (Palgrave 2021) 315–37.

[38] Olivier J Wouters and others, 'The Launch of the EU Health Emergency Preparedness and Response Authority (HERA): Improving Global Pandemic Preparedness?' (2023) 133 Health Policy 104844.

[39] Commission Decision of 16 September 2021 establishing the Health Emergency Preparedness and Response Authority [2021] OJ C3931/3.

[40] European Commission, 'Communication from the Commission to the European Parliament, the European Council, the Council, the European Economic and Social Committee and the Committee of The Regions. Introducing HERA, the European Health Emergency preparedness and Response Authority, the next step towards completing the European Health Union' COM (2021) 526 final: https://ec.europa.eu/health/system/files/2021-09/hera_2021_comm_en_0.pdf.

equally, a significance that cannot detract from the concomitant post-crisis increase in the health functions and competences of existing European agencies.

Above all, mirroring the foundation of the EU Food Safety Agency in response to the BSE crisis, increases in competence have been achieved, or are envisaged, for EU agencies concerned with health protection, but also healthcare. Thus, just as the European Centre for Disease Control (ECDC) was itself created following a crisis, namely the 2003 severe acute respiratory syndrome (SARS) outbreak, the Commission is now in the process of preparing a new regulation to enhance its abilities to respond to future cross-border pandemics.[41] Equally, and perhaps more far-reaching, given its role in the day-to-day authorization of medicines for more 'mundane' healthcare, the role of the European Medicines Agency (EMA) has been strengthened with regard to crisis preparedness and management.[42]

Although it is a central theme of this chapter that more general trends of EU competence accrual in European integration processes should never be ignored, it is this latter, crisis-based expansion in EU policy- and rule-making capacity that is most striking, and perhaps most troublesome within this analysis, but not simply with regard to the COVID-19 crisis. During the pandemic, the stirrings of explicit political solidarity between the Member States, even if retarded in its development, began to become visible. Above all, the 'rescEU' instrument, a public procurement process based on Article 222 TFEU, providing for solidarity in crises, created the possibility for the centralized EU procurement of emergency goods; an instrument which was deployed, however belatedly, for the purposes of joint procurement of COVID-19 vaccines, regardless of the various political, social, and even formal legal factors (for example, Article 125 TFEU) which militate against the pooling of risk among, and thus cross-subsidization between, Member States.[43] Beyond such visible expressions of risk-pooling and cross-subsidization, however, risk-pooling has been, and is, a part of the technical-political exercise of competence by European agencies. Be it an exercise of operational powers by the ECDC, established in 2004 with powers of surveillance and response with regard to the spread of infectious diseases, an exercise of management powers by the Executive Agency for Health and Consumers (EAHC) in its oversight of EU health programmes, or an exercise of quasi-regulatory powers by the EMA in its approval/non-approval of pharmaceuticals, including COVID-19 vaccines for use throughout Europe, European agencies concerned with health necessarily operate at the very edges of the non-redistributive regulatory state,[44] above all in crisis where, for

[41] Delhomme and Hervey (n 1) 57–58.

[42] Regulation (EU) 2022/123 of the European Parliament and of the Council of 25 January 2022 on a reinforced role for the European Medicines Agency in crisis preparedness and management for medicinal products and medical devices [2022] OJ L20/1. Both regulations are based on art 114 TFEU.

[43] See Commission Implementing Decision (EU) 2020/414 of 19 March 2020 amending Implementing Decision (EU) 2019/570 as regards medical stockpiling, building on earlier capacities to tackle SARS; see also Regulation (EU) 2021/836 of the European Parliament and of the Council of 20 May 2021 amending Decision No 1313/2013/EU on a Union Civil Protection Mechanism (Text with EEA relevance), for underlying regulation. See, for comment, Baute and de Ruijter (n 31).

[44] Giandomenica Majone, *Regulating Europe* (Routledge 1996).

example, approval of vaccines within joint procurement schemes impacts heavily upon the pooled resources of the Member States.

While our primary question is whether the norm of suspicion—the paradoxical constitutionalization of the desire both to enable and to restrain the development of EU health policy—has become, following crisis, a norm of 'constitutional toleration', the danger here, in response to technocratic accrual of powers, is one at least of a perception of 'integration by stealth'.[45] The problem remains one of a lack of clear competence of European agencies to engage in formal rule-making, even where they have no choice but to act under conditions of crisis, a process of 'covert integration' (Héritier 2015) that is inevitably a challenge to necessary democratic process and the rule of law, and an undermining of the nation-state functions that are constitutive of the solidarity that underlies risk-pooling and redistribution.[46]

As we have noted, the post-COVID-19 environment, especially with regard to the suspension of budgetary conditionality within the European Semester, has given rise to a wave of optimism about the end to the 'legally encoded dominance of the "economic" over "health interests" '.[47] Nevertheless, this belated optimism does perhaps also obscure the institutional dangers posed to constitutive national solidarities by the EU system, and above all its response to sovereign debt crisis in the language of 'conditionality'. For our purposes, the establishment of the European Semester was particularly important with regard to the hardening of soft EU health powers (the OMC) by means of the inclusion of OMC-based health policy within it.[48] As noted by Crespy, the consequences of the post-sovereign debt crisis schema, whereby assessment of Member State expenditure on health provision and health systems becomes a means to ensure their fiscal compliance with the European Stability and Growth Pact and related rules,[49] not only has the potential to extend the punitive regime imposed by the Troika on the healthcare systems of debtor nations during the financial crisis to all EU states,[50] but has also increased pressures of marketization on welfare systems throughout the eurozone.[51] Much of the intervening health literature was, nevertheless, sanguine—confident, even—that this hardening of soft powers, or the aspiration to converge national health systems, within formal or executive European competences, as well as, for example, the potential undermining of the protective special provision of Member States' health and healthcare policies as 'services of general economic interest' (SGEIs),[52] can be viewed in a positive light, as a part of an

[45] Majone, *Dilemmas of European Integration* (n 19).
[46] Héritier (n 20); Everson and Vos, 'European Union Agencies' (n 37).
[47] Delhomme and Hervey (n 1) 54.
[48] Bocquillon, Brooks and Maltby (n 14).
[49] See the Fiscal Compact established by the Treaty on Stability, Growth and Co-ordination (2012). Document 42012A0302(01) in EUR-Lex, not published in the Official Journal.
[50] See Amandine Crespy, *Welfare Markets in Europe: The Democratic Challenge of European Integration* (Palgrave 2016) for the dramatic impacts of memoranda of understanding on the Greek and Dutch health systems.
[51] Crespy, *Welfare Markets in Europe* (n 50).
[52] Specifically, with regard to the application of state aid law to Member State support for healthcare services, see Andrea Biondi and Oana Ştefan, 'EU Health Union and State Aid Policy: With Great(er) Power Comes Great Responsibility' (2020) 11 European Journal of Risk Regulation 894.

opportunity to encourage the betterment of healthcare provision throughout the continent, as policy entrepreneurs pursue their benchmarking and rationalization agendas.

Has this optimism perhaps also borne its own fruit in a 'post-conditionality' age, where resilience and recovery might now be construed as requiring the establishment of a positive steering capacity for health?[53] Many authors were always clear that the benign nature of this 'web of European competences'[54] held true even within the more formal structures of EU budgetary regimes which could result in Commission compliance measures, should Member State activities threaten the stability of the euro. This, it was and is still argued that interlocking competences—the hardening of informal response mechanisms—obviates the need for Treaty revision, and reduces the requirement for a clear (redistributive) EU competence on health and healthcare, and for a rationalization and democratization of the institutions of European health oversight. For some, this is an expression of their faith in the ability of 'experimentalist' processes of democracy to make good the democratic gap at the outer limits of the regulatory state;[55] for others, it is a belief that shock therapy at the EU level, for example the end of state aid exemptions for national healthcare provision, and the establishment of a joint European approach to redistribution within a healthcare market, would be commensurate with the eventual recognition that healthcare shortages cannot be overcome within a marketization paradigm.[56] The acceptance of the extension of the European health competence would seem to be rooted in progressive rather than authoritarian or market-based approaches to European integration. As such, these readings are also indicative of a caesura in the political economy; of a crisis-driven acceptance throughout the broader sweep of European and national debate that the era of unbridled growth-based marketization is coming to an end, and that a restatement of redistributive paradigms is needed. Nevertheless, the aim of this chapter is not simply to doubt the assertion that 'political will' alone is needed to establish a legitimately comprehensive European health policy within the existing web of competences established by the Lisbon Treaty and its predecessors. Rather, this contribution seeks also to unravel and assess, in the context of health, the proper nature of a redistributive function within the EU and its constitutive basis, as well as its proper relationship with technocratic and expert decision-making, or the distinct but interrelated structures of social and market-based (efficient) management.

[53] Delhomme and Hervey (n 1).
[54] Purnhagen and others (n 17).
[55] Anniek de Ruijter, 'The Silent Revolution in EU Health Law and Policy' in de Ruijter, *The Expansion of EU Power* (n 15).
[56] Biondi and Stefan (n 52).

4.3 From Non-discrimination to Solidarity: Markets, Governance, and the Pooling of Risk

In den insgesamt wachsenden kapitalistischen Gesellschaften unserer, wie sich heute herausstellte, nicht besonders stabilen Demokratien entsteht dieses überraschende Widerstandspotential und lässt das politische System von innen zerbröseln, wenn auf der Basis wachsender sozialer Ungleichheiten der Zerfall der politischen Öffentlichkeit nur weit genug fortgeschritten ist.[57]

As noted above, Jürgen Habermas is pessimistic about the future for democracy. He has recently addressed the particular dangers posed to his vision of the deliberatively democratic closing of the constitutional circle between the self-serving instincts of the rights-bearing individual and the imperatives of solidarity within a political community by the recent trend to 'populism'. For Habermas, degradation of political discourse through manipulation of conspiracy theories and the denial and destruction of truth by power-driven demagogues is a headline problem. Nevertheless, degradation of political discourse and the constitution—the weakening of the ability to translate facticity into validity—is not simply a matter of the crass undermining of the facts of public discourse. Instead, the mediating constitution, or rule of law, is threatened both as increasing inequalities within market societies emerge as an alienating condition, ripe for demagogic exploitation, and as political discourse, or its technocratic substitute, grows too complex for an increasingly alienated polity to follow. In other words, the rule of law, public trust, and democracy are undermined as constitutionalized political discourse is overwhelmed by technocracy, and by informal decision-making, which is far too complex to translate into an explicitly firm argument for common decision-making, which can prove costly to the individual in service of the collective (deliberative basis for solidarity).

The Habermasian assertion that the common good in constitutional regulation of individual right and collective action is in unprecedented danger within our mature and maturing democracies has two points of relevance for this analysis. First, the development of a comprehensive European solidarity competence for health might be considered an imperative for the maintenance of political community and the rule of law within the EU. Certainly, the current 'web of competences' for European health policy-making is not without its own clear founding values, above all the value of 'non-discrimination' or inclusion within the building of the European market.[58] Nevertheless, non-discrimination or inclusion may be a necessary, but it is not a sufficient condition for cross-border polity-building, making common the notion of supranational opportunity but leaving the cost in the decentralized hands of the Member States, potentially also to be borne by disadvantaged Europeans to whom the opportunities of integration all too often appear to be available only to a privileged and

[57] Habermas (n 8) 109.
[58] Somek (n 21).

mobile few.[59] The health of the European polity and rule of law is fully dependent upon the evolution of a redistributive health value within the Constitution of the Union, but not just in response to crises, such as the pandemic, or in mechanisms such as NGEU. Instead, reformed values of solidarity and community are needed far beyond the strictly confined terms of joint purchasing procedures within Article 222 TFEU; far beyond the enduring hostility of the current European Treaty to cross-subsidization and redistribution (for example, Article 125 TFEU). In other words, the question remains whether creative interpretations of formal EU competences—the cumulative pairing of Articles 122(1) and (2) with Article 175 TFEU[60]—are sufficient to underpin solidarity-forming deliberation within the EU.

To this exact extent, expansion of the EU competence in health to include the aspiration to support the Member States in enhancing access to healthcare (EU4Health programme 2021–2027), in seemingly happy disregard for the limitations of Article 168 TFEU, cannot but be welcomed: arguably, the emphasis on market-building and the rights of the cross-border European has always distracted from the need to secure, and even enhance, the solidarity-based rights of the European citizen under our national welfare and health settlements. By the same Habermasian token, however, Vivien Schmidt's appreciation of 'social fairness' in response to pandemic crisis—the establishment of redistributive value through the effort to address 'inequalities of opportunities as well as of outcome'[61]—should be addressed, but cannot simply be satisfied with the rolling out of the EU's health competence, either in the obscure technocratic parameters of supposedly depoliticized EU agencification[62] or in the tolerance of still-opaque processes of 'experimentalist deliberation' within OMC processes designed to close the competence gap within more general integration mechanisms. Neither can it be met within the pandemic crisis-driven adjustment, or partial suspension, of conditionality criteria within the European Semester,[63] established as a response to financial and sovereign debt crisis. Granted, the latter processes can also be characterized as a part of the effort to adjust facticity to normativity within Europe,[64] to make good missing and redistributive competences against existing market-oriented and institutional trends. Nevertheless, in this analysis, adaptive institutional complexity, for all that it seeks to establish social justice, just as surely also frustrates legitimizing political deliberation.

Both of these problems are acknowledged by Schmidt in her comments on developments within the European Semester following the pandemic crisis. Noting that

[59] See Neil Fligstein, *Euroclash: The EU, European Identity, and the Future of Europe* (OUP 2008): the perception of privilege may only be that—a perception—yet perception is enough to create alienation or to lay a basis upon which a demagogic claim to alienation may be made.

[60] Delhomme and Hervey (n 1) 54.

[61] Schmidt (n 4).

[62] Everson and Vos, 'EU Agencies and the Politicized Administration' (n 14); Delhomme and Hervey (n 1).

[63] See section 4.1 and n 50 above.

[64] For the battle to adjust facticity to validity, especially in the sphere of conditionality, see Michelle Everson and Christian Joerges, 'Facticity as Validity: The Misplaced Revolutionary Praxis of European Law' in Emilios Christodoulidis, Ruth Dukes and Marko Goldoni (eds), *Research Handbook on Critical Legal Theory* (Edward Elgar 2019) 407–27; for the development of conditionality (in reaction to the pandemic), see also Chapter 2 of the current volume.

contemporary 'bottom-up exercises by Member State governments' are necessarily still subject to Commission 'oversight via conditionality'—that is, a Commission that 'makes recommendations for reform—such as determining whether certain pre-agreed "milestones" in terms of economic reform are met before disbursing the next tranche of funding'—Schmidt asserts that 'this "conditionality" is a far cry from what it was during the early phase of the Eurozone crisis ... when structural reform largely meant cutting welfare states and deregulating labour markets.' For Schmidt, conditionality is now 'focused [instead] on attacking national economic vulnerabilities and administrative hindrances, as well as social "fairness", by addressing inequalities of opportunities as well as of outcome'. And yet, the reinvention of the once market-oriented and technocratic Commission as an important social actor and supporter of socially oriented policy entrepreneurs within the Member States is indelibly marked and undermined by the early years of operation of the Treaty on Stability, Coordination and Governance in the Economic and Monetary Union (2012) (the 'Fiscal Compact'):

> because EU actors in the first five crisis years largely reinterpreted the rules by stealth, legitimacy remained in question. Fundamental flaws persisted, with suboptimal rules hampering economic growth and feeding populism, as citizens punished mainstream parties while anti-system parties prospered. Even though most EU actors had begun to acknowledge their reinterpretations by 2015, and growth had begun to return across the EU, the damage had been done.[65]

In other words, the legitimacy of EU rule is undermined *both* by the legacy of the long-term pursuit of market efficiencies and by the stealthy, creative, or technocratic effort to repurpose governance exactly in order to re-establish 'fairness' in the gap between European market and national social competences. The conundrum is a bitter one, but also, as we have seen, no stranger within the area of health policy. Anniek de Ruijter reminds us of the primary reason why a limited EU health competence was bound to expand in EU market competences to challenge national prerogatives with regard to access to healthcare: 'Mr Kohll's legal case was, seemingly, an unremarkable one.'[66] And yet, the unremarkable efforts of a father to secure speedy dental care for his Luxembourger daughter across the border in Germany unleashed a series of remarkable events involving a judgment of the CJEU whereby the refusal of the Luxembourg health authorities to pay for the cross-border dental services was first to fall victim to Article 49 TFEU, constitutionalizing the principle of the free movement of services within the European market, and then to be impacted by EU legislative action under Articles 114 and 168 TFEU to regulate the acquisition by European citizens of cross-border rights to health care (EHIC cards).[67] The expansion of European health policy

[65] Schmidt (n 4) 21.

[66] de Ruijter, 'EU "Public Health" and "Health-care" Law and Policy' (n 33) *Kohll*, loc cit n 15, 1.

[67] Directive 2011/24/EU of the European Parliament and of the Council of 9 March 2011 on the application of patients' rights in cross-border healthcare (OJ L88/45).

beyond the confines of Article 168 TFEU is also a simple and inevitable result of the creation of a European market.

Granted, the development of the EU health competence is far from being devoid of social value or being wholly market-related. And yet, the very particular values which underlie European market-building present their own problems within a European polity. Above all, within the EU setting, the power of the principle of non-discrimination, applied consistently by the CJEU in order to unleash the cross-border market-building capacities of the European (economic) citizen, is simultaneously an expression of the shift in popular (social democratic) values away from bounded community and towards inclusion, and perhaps a necessary realignment of the more usual (national) solidarity community in order to address and ease the real-life circumstances and needs of a host of 'others', above all non-national others, not recognized within the history, culture, or imagined ties of our individual polities of redistribution. Nevertheless, for all of this necessary universalization of theories of justice, Alexander Somek is subsequently correct in his questioning of the contradiction within the European market—of its inability to establish equally visible ties of recognition and solidarity for Europeans in stasis; that is, for EU citizens who do not move:

> The shift from distributive justice to inclusion reflects either a loss of confidence in society's ability to affect its most elementary moral fabric (the 'basic structure' in Rawlsian parlance) or a growing scepticism as to the reasonableness of any attempt to alter it. In the case of social democratic sensibilities, this shift is not by accident linked to a reconsideration of the group that is deemed to be both disadvantaged and capable of playing the role of a transformative social force.[68]

Progressive political forces cannot but question their own restrictive delineation, or 'closure' of justice communities. But, at the same time, 'a resolution of the conflict between distributive justice and inclusion needs to demonstrate which of the two moral ideals is better capable of addressing the core social predicament of modern capitalism',[69] which is the increase of inequality within the polity, as well as its political alienation.

Seen in this light, the cheerful acceptance of the growing web of EU competences in the field of health must be doubted, at least to the degree that marketization, linked with the actions of polity entrepreneurs, is seen as a positive where national healthcare policies, as SGEIs, are challenged by the application of state aid law,[70] or by promotion of the primacy of certain EU rules over others, for example the right to conduct business under Article 16 of the European Fundamental Rights Charter above a right to health under Article 35.[71] Even where they aim to create a common European mode

[68] Somek (n 21) 721.
[69] Somek (n 21) 721.
[70] Biondi and Stefan (n 52).
[71] See Michelle Everson and Rui Correia Gonçalves, 'Article 16 of the European Charter of Fundamental Rights: Defining the European Economic Constitution' in Steve Peers and others (eds), *The European Charter of Fundamental Rights: A Commentary* (2nd edn, Bloomsbury/Hart Publishing 2022) 463–88, detailing how the

of redistribution, rationalization agendas, including application of market strategies to national healthcare systems, may have the potential to improve healthcare provision. Yet, their application within a market idiom must also surely be bitterly contested within the complex technical arena of coordination of the solidarity health insurance schemes of (largely tax-based funded) national welfare states with the redistributive social insurance schemes of the 'Bismarckian' social models of other Member States,[72] which also, troublingly for marketization approaches, demand regulatory adjustment of interlinking private market models.[73]

Cheerful acceptance of a web of competences, however, must be doubted not simply for the limits to market models, but also for the equal obsolescence of the Prodi model of (informal) European governance established in tandem with the (formal) structures of the Lisbon Treaty. Set against the failure of the ratification process of the Treaty establishing a Constitution for Europe, and predating only briefly the compensating signature of the Lisbon Treaty, the 'formalized' adoption of a notion of (necessarily informal) governance within European politics, as announced by Romano Prodi within his famous 2001 White Paper,[74] presenting ideas for a democratically reformed 'European governance', seemed an act full of promise and innovation, especially as regards the autonomous administrative/executive function. For years, the Union had played host to extra-legal developments and institutional innovations that had widened the discrepancies between the EU's activities and its formal legal structures. Above all, the move away from a then more informal system of 'comitology'[75] to the institutionalization of an ever-expanding EU executive competence within bodies such as autonomous European agencies may have been highly desirable, having its roots within various regulatory crises. However, bolstered by the New Public Management philosophies that dominated at national as well as European level throughout the 1990s,[76] it was similarly clear by the turn of the millennium that the ad hoc establishment of a fourth branch of government at EU level had sprung the formal structures of the EU. Above all, the agency phenomenon, operating outside the structures of the Treaties, had induced a shift away from the Community method of indirect administration, whereby most EU policies were implemented by Member States, to a more direct administrative form, whereby implementation was often carried out at the EU level, contributing to a still-ongoing trend of the supranationalization of executive power within the EU.

CJEU has constantly been called upon to balance a right to health against a right to freedom of business. Although, and importantly so, art 35 (right to health) and the notion of services of general economic interest have, to date, largely prevailed over commercial interests.

[72] Andre den Exter and Keith J Syrett, 'Access to Healthcare in Europe' in David Orentlicher and Tamara Hervey (eds), *Oxford Book of Comparative Healthcare* (OUP 2020) 242–72.

[73] Michelle Everson, 'The Federal Supervisory Authority for Insurance' in Majone, *Regulating Europe* (n 44).

[74] European Commission, 'European Governance – A White Paper' COM(2001) 428 final (2001/C 287/01).

[75] Now highly formalized under arts 290 and 291 TFEU.

[76] Morten Egeberg and Jarle Trondal, 'Agencification of the European Union Administration: Connecting the Dots', TARN Working Paper no 1/2016.

The problem for the Prodi Commission was thus not so much the emergence of executive, expert-led governance institutions outside established EU structures: such institutions were indispensable to the functioning of the Union. Instead, Europe was now faced with a crisis of validity, or a crisis of *ex post* legitimation, to which the notion of governance seemed a potent solution. As Philippe Schmitter convincingly argues,[77] the 'oversell and vagueness' of the concept notwithstanding, governance usefully designates 'a distinctive method/mechanism for resolving conflicts and solving problems that reflects some profound characteristics of the exercise of authority that are emerging in almost all contemporary societies and economies'. It is a virtue of the concept that it captures actor configurations and problem-solving activities which have emerged as responses to functional exigencies. Modern governance depends on, and similarly builds on, expert knowledge and the management capacities of enterprises and organizations. It cannot confine itself to conventional law production within a binary code of legal and illegal practices. It cannot be organized hierarchically. While governance is a concept that also helps us to discover and explain tensions between function and form, the Commission's Working Programme, drawing on the expertise and experiences of actors both within and outwith the Commission, was a platform for constructive debate. And yet governance is also a troublesome concept. Writing way back in 1980, Claus Offe asserted the dangers posed by 'organisations which are unknown to democratic theory ... operating behind the façade of parliamentary democracy' and responsible for 'both political conflict and the resolution of policy issues'.[78] Accepting Offe's premise that institutions inevitably develop behind and beyond conventional democratic processes, in pragmatic order that we might adjust our schemes of legitimation to this simple truth, is one (important) step. Nevertheless, the question of what form of legitimation might be found for governance remains an open one, and perhaps inevitably so: 'governance' rather than 'government and administration' captures modern political action, its emphasis upon the social knowledge and the management capacities of enterprises and organizations, its eschewal of command and control policy-making and policy implementation, and its response to real social problems, and to bottlenecks within the political system and its administrative machinery. This is the desired outcome, but it is also the problem; the point at which 'is' and 'ought' part company and the search for a sustaining legitimation is revealed as a simple chimera. In the final analysis, governance is an analytical and not a normative tool.

As we have seen, the story of health by stealth—where the *de facto* competences mushroom and policy agendas expand in the absence of Treaty revisions—is intertwined with recurrent crisis management, court-led integration, and marketization. This is not a story of merely paving the way to increased regulatory efficiency. Rather,

[77] Philippe Schmitter, 'What is There to Legitimize in the European Union... and how Might This Be Accomplished?' in Christian Joerges, Yves Mény and JHH Weiler (eds), 'Symposium: Mountain or Molehill? A Critical Appraisal of the Commission White Paper on Governance' (Jean Monnet Working Paper 6/2001) 8–9.

[78] Claus Offe, 'The Separation of Form and Content in Liberal Democratic Politics' (1980) 3 Studies in Political Economy 5, 8.

it comprises a set of deeply controversial moves towards increased pooling of risk and commitments to solidarity.

On the one hand, this falls into familiar categories of 'competence creep' and 'failing forward'. On the other hand, we lack a framework assessing this in normative terms. While 'creep' sounds suspicious and 'forward' has the air of improvement, the applicable standards remain obscure or implicit. For example, it has been claimed that '[m]aintaining support for the expansion of EU health policy while it moves into much more contested and complex political terrain, in the midst of recovery from a global pandemic, is the challenge now facing the EU's health actors.'[79] Few would deny that 'support' is needed, but whose support and on what terms?

Hence, an important task for analysis is to introduce more explicit normative categories for assessing what counts as improvement. We propose to analyse this field from a rule of law perspective. In the upcoming sections, we argue that the concept of 'liquid authority' provides a useful analytical lens for capturing key dynamics that matter to the rule of law. In the literature that theorizes global governance, liquid authority is 'characterized by a higher level of dynamism and typically driven by informality and institutional multiplicity'.[80] In the sections below, the meaning of these three features—dynamism, informality, and institutional multiplicity—will be illustrated with cases of EU health governance. However, while these concepts may prove descriptively adequate, our ambition is to contrast them with normative EU commitments—clarity, predictability, and justiciability—in order to spell out the applicability of rule of law standards.

In the upcoming sections, our path towards assessing the normative landscape of EU health governance will continue to use the COVID-19 crisis as the primary entry point. Reiteration of some facts and happenings of the COVID-19 crisis is a natural gateway, for two reasons. First, it has a salient connection with the EU's rule of law conditionality legislation.[81] Second, it exemplifies tendencies that have marked the post-Lisbon years; that is, for each feature of governance that we identify in the COVID-19 crisis, we can easily find it foreshadowed in the preceding decade or so.

4.4 Crisis as Blueprint?

For some analysts, the COVID-19 crisis has proven to be a magnifying glass under which potentially legitimacy-enhancing features of complex modes of governance have been brought into focus. For example, it has been claimed that 'the experiences and successes (or failures) of NGEU (Next Generation EU) might serve as a blueprint

[79] Eleanor Brooks and Robert Geyer, 'The Development of EU Health Policy and the Covid-19 Pandemic: Trends and Implications' (2020) 42 Journal of European Integration 1057, 1073.
[80] Nico Krisch, 'Liquid Authority in Global Governance' (2017) 9 International Theory 237, 237.
[81] Rule of Law Conditionality Regulation (2020/2092): OJ L 433I, 22.12.2020, pp 1–10.

for further and more permanent EU funding schemes.'[82] In the same vein, Schmidt sees COVID-related EU action as an opportunity for change that should not be missed: 'Legitimacy, which was so much at risk during the Eurozone crisis, seems to have improved as a result of this new EU-level solidarity—but will it last?'[83] In particular, she argues that the European Semester is the 'perfect vehicle' for ensuring the success of such funding schemes, as long as the flexibility regarding budget deficits and public debt rules necessitated by the crisis is reconceived as a feature not a bug: 'Rather than simply readjusting the rules and numbers, however, they should be permanently suspended, to be replaced, perhaps, by a set of "fiscal standards" to assess sustainability in context.'[84]

Naturally, in times of crises, it is easy to appreciate the virtues of 'creative legal engineering' and the need for flexibility. But before the creative legal engineers are given more permanent reign, it is worth sorting out what the developments mean from a more traditional rule of law perspective. As we will see, the basic governance features of the COVID-19 crisis are not particularly new in the field of health, but they are seldom analysed systematically for their constitutional effects.

In fact, the COVID-19 crisis has proved to be a natural occasion to clarify the relevant rule of law constraints on legitimacy, given that it coincided with the approval of the rule of law conditionality legislation mentioned above. The funding of the crisis measures required some agreement on what the operative conception of rule of law entails. On the face of it, that kind of agreement seems utopian. Centuries of philosophical disagreement have basically established little consensus beyond the fact that the rule of law provides 'protection and recourse against the arbitrary exercise of power through the distinctive instrumentalities of the law'.[85] Beyond this abstract idea, the rule of law has stubbornly remained an 'essentially contested concept'.[86]

Unsurprisingly, the notion that the rule of law is an essentially contested concept is echoed in Hungary's and Poland's cases against the Regulation before the CJEU. Hungary argued that the wording of the Regulation was 'vague, ambiguous, unlimited and incapable of uniform interpretation and application'.[87] Similarly, Poland claimed that, '[w]hile it is true that international organisations, in particular the Council of Europe, have drawn up certain criteria for assessing whether those principles have been observed, the specific embodiment of those principles is confined, in EU law, to mentioning the aims which they pursue.'[88]

The complaints did not convince the Court, which held that the operative conception of the rule of law was sufficiently defined and circumscribed to protect legal

[82] Lucas Schramm, Ulrich Krotz and Bruno de Witte, 'Building "Next Generation" after the Pandemic: The Implementation and Implications of the EU Covid Recovery Plan' (2022) 60 Journal of Common Market Studies 114.

[83] Schmidt (n 4) 31.

[84] Schmidt (n 4) 32.

[85] Gerald Postema, *Law's Rule* (OUP 2022) 23.

[86] Jeremy Waldron, 'Is the Rule of Law an Essentially Contested Concept (in Florida)?' (2002) 21 Law and Philosophy 137.

[87] Case C-156/21 *Hung v Eur Parl & Council* [2022] ECLI:EU:C:2022:97.

[88] Case C-157/21 *Pol v Eur Parl & Council* [2022] ECLI:EU:C:2022:98.

certainty and legitimate EU objectives. What matters for our purposes is not the substance and legality of this particular regulation, however, but how it highlights the EU's general commitment to the rule of law and how this, in turn, calls for more attention to the conditions of legitimacy for its mode of governance in the health field. Following the Treaty of Lisbon, the commitment is now codified into Article 2 TEU, and in the Commission's interpretation of the Court's case law, the commitment entails, among other things, the following principles:

(a) the principle of legality, which in substantial terms includes a transparent, accountable, democratic and pluralistic process for enacting laws;
(b) legal certainty, which requires amongst other things that rules are clear and predictable and cannot be changed retrospectively;
(c) prohibition of arbitrariness of the executive powers. The principle of the rule of law regulates the exercise of public powers and makes sure that every State intervention has a legal basis and is constrained by law.[89]

Although these principles are formulated to include a range of concerns, in the following we will restrict the discussion to the concerns of clarity, predictability, and justiciability. These appear to be basic and primary concepts involved here, but what do they imply in terms of assessing the actual EU health governance?

On the one hand, the overarching commitment to these principles does, obviously, not encourage normalization of the legal acrobatics involved in stretching the EU's competences to their limit to secure a recovery plan.[90] On the other hand, the principles do not specify a cookbook approach to good governance. Rather, they leave legislators with a set of broad considerations that must be preserved in one way or another. It is, therefore, an open question whether, for example, Schmidt's proposal of exchanging exact rules with flexible standards in the European Semester is compatible with a basic commitment to the rule of law.

This is a matter of interpretation not simply because it involves specifying contested or vague value questions, but also because whether some mode of governance is legitimate in one institution or policy area depends on what is going on in the surrounding institutional landscape. In the sanguine slogan of deliberative systems theory, 'two wrongs can make a right'.[91] The reasonable idea behind this slogan is that political systems can embody institutional complementarity, where the virtues and vices of one institution mesh with overall distribution of institutional qualities. This is otherwise called the 'ecological' aspect of legitimacy assessments: 'It is often not possible to determine the legitimacy of an institution in isolation; instead, its legitimacy may be a

[89] European Commission, Annexes to the Commission Communication on a new EU Framework to strengthen the Rule of Law, Annex I: The Rule of Law as a foundational principle of the Union, COM(2014) 158 final, 11 March 2014.

[90] For analysis in terms of 'stretching', see, eg de Witte (n 22); Delhomme and Hervey (n 1) 57.

[91] Jane Mansbridge and others, 'A Systemic Approach to Deliberative Democracy' in John Parkinson and Janse Mansbridge (eds), *Deliberative Systems: Deliberative Democracy at the Large Scale* (CUP 2012) 3.

function of how it fits into a network of institutions.'[92] What, then, are relevant features of the ecology of EU health governance?

4.5 The Union's Liquid Mode of Governance

The EU's involvement in health-related issues is deep, complex, and evolving. However, given that we are at a crossroads where some analysts and policymakers are hoping that the COVID-19 crisis will provide structure and direction to the further evolution of this field, it is worth reiterating the extent to which the modes of governance that prevailed during the crisis were already foreshadowed in the post-Lisbon years. A first step towards mapping this landscape is to appreciate the extent to which the EU conforms to the kind of 'liquid authority' we introduced above, and which is characterized by the features of dynamism, informality, and institutional multiplicity.[93] These three features are easy to spot in the existing analyses of EU health-related policy.

4.5.1 Dynamism

The notion of 'dynamism' is key to the mode of governance called 'experimentalism'.[94] The core idea behind experimentalist governance is that epistemically demanding and inherently uncertain policy fields require solutions that are less hierarchical and institutionally rigid than traditional constitutional perspectives prescribe. Institutions should be more attuned to processes of learning and creative adaptation. In experimentalist governance, the currency of legitimacy is evidence-based deliberation.

Proponents, therefore, highlight instances where the authority of institutional hierarchies is overturned by arguments and facts. The increasingly broad and socially oriented scope of the OMC, as it manifests itself in the reports and recommendations that are now linked to the European Semester, is commended for its ability to trigger processes of reflexive uptake of evidence.[95] As a complement to the orientation towards evidence-based policy-making, proponents of experimentalism call for new modes of accountability. The goal is to move beyond traditional principal–agent relations where the agent is answerable to a predefined mandate on pain of sanctions. The preferred alternative is 'forward-looking accountability' that consists in defending decisions according to standards acceptable to epistemic peers.[96]

This experimentalist dynamism came to the fore in the EU's handling of the pandemic. Increased flexibility in implementation of the European Structural and

[92] Allen Buchanan, *The Heart of Human Rights* (OUP 2013) 198.
[93] Krisch (n 80).
[94] Charles F Sabel and Jonathan Zeitlin (eds), *Experimentalist Governance in the European Union: Towards a New Architecture* (OUP 2010).
[95] Jonathan Zeitlin and Bart Vanhercke, 'Socializing the European Semester: EU Social and Economic Policy Co-ordination in Crisis and Beyond' (2018) 25 Journal of European Public Policy 149.
[96] Sabel and Zeitlin (n 94) 13.

Investment Funds was an early measure.[97] This involved more freedom for Member States to reallocate resources, fewer administrative burdens, and more discretion in the calculation of the final payment at the end of the programming period. More significantly, the fiscal rules of the Stability and Growth Pact were suspended and Member States were encouraged to spend massively.[98] On the surface, this dynamism was a break with a more rigid regime where fiscal austerity trumped other desiderata, such as public health. However, those who have studied the evolution of the European Semester and the country-specific recommendations over time have observed that economically oriented frameworks have gradually been socialized to take more account of health.[99] There are 'termites' in the European institutional system, using a variety of tools for weakening the weight of economic goals and broadening the scope of social indicators.[100]

This means that formal governance architectures will not reflect actual dynamics, in line with the thesis of liquid authority. While proponents of experimentalist governance are largely satisfied with recurrent breakdowns of formal frameworks into flexible and dynamic arrangements, some analysts see these as a pathological sign that adequate constitutional mechanisms are lacking: 'Without a radical change in the underlying political economy of the EU, it is hard to see how this pattern of policy cycling, of new architectures and industrious termites, will change.'[101] These authors do not specify what the needed 'radical change' consists in, but presumably the lack of a clear mandate to pursue health objectives in any substantive fashion is part of the problem, because it creates the need for termite tactics. In more explicit terms, Bruno de Witte argues that the COVID-19 crisis is an occasion for Member States to give up their 'stranglehold' on European budgets and allow the Union to 'breathe more freely'.[102]

With regard to the EU's commitment to the rule of law, as expounded above, the values of clarity, predictability, and justiciability are not promoted by termite tactics that undermine formal frameworks. Nevertheless, a measure of dynamism and ongoing deliberation is a necessary feature of intelligent governance in uncertain and epistemically demanding policy fields. The problem is probably not dynamism in and of itself; rather, it is the discrepancy between the formal framework and the actual practice that is troubling.[103] Dynamism is not institutionalized in a sufficiently clear and justiciable manner. Moreover, as we will argue next, dynamism takes a particularly troubling form when it is coupled with an unstable mix of formal and informal arrangements.

[97] Regulation (EU) 2020/558 of the European Parliament and of the Council of 23 April 2020 amending Regulations (EU) No 1301/2013 and (EU) No 1303/2013 as regards specific measures to provide exceptional flexibility for the use of the European Structural and Investments Funds in response to the COVID-19 outbreak: OJ L 130, 24.4.2020, pp 1–6.

[98] Activation of the general escape clause of the Stability and Growth Pact (COM (2020) 123).

[99] Zeitlin and Vanhercke (n 95).

[100] Scott L Greer, Anniek de Ruijter and Eleanor Brooks, 'The COVID-19 Pandemic: Failing Forward in Public Health' in Marianne Riddervold, Jarle Trondal and Akasemi Newsom (eds) (n 37) 747–64.

[101] Scott L Greer and Eleanor Brooks, 'Termites of Solidarity in the House of Austerity: Undermining Fiscal Governance in the European Union' (2021) 46 Journal of Health Politics, Policy and Law 71, 87.

[102] de Witte (n 22) 681.

[103] See Delhomme and Hervey (n 1) 59.

4.5.2 Informality

The magnifying glass effect of the COVID-19 crisis was particularly strong concerning the informal features of EU health governance. As analysts recount the range of mechanisms and forums available for a European crisis response, they find a governance structure that relies on fluid efficiency rather than on formalized process: 'The informal dimensions of this structure were bigger than they looked on paper and rooted it more deeply in member state politics than an outside observer might have thought.'[104]

The playbook of steering clear of formal hurdles had been rehearsed by the relevant institutions numerous times before. For example, on paper, the Health Security Committee of experts from Member State administrations has a rather restricted set of coordination tasks. But as water finds the path of least resistance, policymakers know that coordinating through this committee is easier and quicker than Treaty revisions, even where there is a lack of formal competences. Hence, the Health Security Committee 'extended beyond its legal mandate into areas where member states wanted coordination.'[105]

From an instrumental policy-making perspective, the advantage of informality is not only flexibility and speed in the face of crises, but also that it creates more discretion in the application of soft governance tools. While the conditionalities of the 'socialized' European Semester have not been systematically backed by sanctions, and have been marked by low compliance, the COVID-19 crisis linked the Semester and the RRF and thereby made the 'recommendations' into something more like authoritative instructions.

That is at least one interpretation. It is, in fact, unclear how the various conditionalities tied to funding are supposed to work: 'Without any clear methodology spelled out, a lot seems left to the Commission's interpretation and bilateral negotiations ongoing in bureaucratic arenas remote from democratic politics.'[106] This is confirmed in a later report by the European Court of Auditors (ECA), which highlights that the amounts paid do not reflect costs for achieving milestones and achievements in a request, but rather on the fallout of *negotiations*.[107] In general, the ECA notes that overly vague or broad milestones and targets have been accepted, and that the result is hardly a uniform method: 'In practice, for the six sampled Member States we note a significant heterogeneity in disbursement profiles in terms of both the proportion of total funding in each instalment and the number of milestones and targets to be achieved for each instalment.'[108] In other words, there appears to be ample room for improvement in terms of the rule of law virtues clarity, predictability, and justiciability.

[104] Greer and others, 'The COVID-19 Pandemic' (n 100) 754.
[105] Greer and others, 'The COVID-19 Pandemic' (n 100) 753.
[106] Amandine Crespy, 'Can Scharpf Be Proved Wrong? Modelling the EU into a Competitive Social Market Economy for the Next Generation' (2020) 26 European Law Journal 319, 328.
[107] European Court of Auditors, 'Special Report on the Commission's Assessment of National Recovery and Resilience Plans 2021/22'.
[108] ECA 2021/22 (n 107) 32.

Democratic experimentalists are optimistic, nevertheless. They speak of a set of stakeholders ready to seize the opportunity to shape national recovery and resilience plans, and of a receptive Commission.[109] Consider this assessment of the process of shaping RRF conditionality:

> At the time of writing, summer 2021, as the EU has reached close to 70 per cent first dose vaccination rate and the International Monetary Fund (IMF) (2021) is forecasting a strong recovery, following a deep recession, it may be that the Semester practices may be returned to sooner than initially expected. This seemingly surprising result confirms that the governance processes of the Semester continue to offer opportunities and resources for strategic agency by contending groups of actors, also with a view to reshaping pre-existing power balances.[110]

The assessment builds on an account of how 'social actors' are ready to 'jump in at the first opportunity', and of how the Commission has become more 'receptive to social issues'.[111] Moreover, it is highlighted that 'the language in the Regulation is flexible and enables a mix of speed and ability to tailor to different national circumstances: not all member states have equally institutionalized roles for social partners and other stakeholders'.[112] All in all, the process appears to be characterized by the Commission's broad discretionary powers in both shaping and enforcing the RRF Regulation. Praising the Semester as an arena for 'reshaping pre-existing power balances' may appear justified when the preferred social actors have the ear of the Commission, but what are the safeguards in times when the Commission proves less receptive to the social agenda? It is worth recalling that the RRF is a temporary instrument, and that flexibility in using 'carrots' may translate into flexibility in using 'sticks'. Moreover, the escape clause of the Stability and Growth Pact is also just a temporary 'deviation',[113] meaning that the Commission could return with powers to monitor and assess budget plans, but now paired with an extended practice of discretionary authority.

This is not to negate the virtues of informality. Informality may have democratic credentials when it lowers entry costs to the political game and provides a broader epistemic base. But the coupling of informality to the kind of dynamism described above creates troubling interaction effects, in terms of making the process of policy-making unclear and unpredictable. In turn, this harms justiciability in a way that Martin Shapiro noted long ago: rule-making amounts to a 'big, soft pillow that is very hard to punch legally. No one ever quite broke the law or ever quite obeyed it because nothing

[109] Bart Vanhercke and Amy Verdun, 'The European Semester as Goldilocks: Macroeconomic Policy Coordination and the Recovery and Resilience Facility' (2022) 60 Journal of Common Market Studies 204.

[110] Vanhercke and Verdun (n 109) 217.

[111] Vanhercke and Verdun (n 109) 217.

[112] Vanhercke and Verdun (n 109) 216. The reference is to Regulation (EU) 2021/241 of the European Parliament and of the Council of 12 February 2021 establishing the Recovery and Resilience Facility: OJ L 57, 18.2.2021, pp 17–75.

[113] Communication from the Commission to the Council on the activation of the general escape clause of the Stability and Growth Pact, COM(2020) 123.

is the law.'[114] Flexible attunement to arguments and evidence is a virtue in times of crisis and uncertainty, but the lessons learnt through this attunement may be lost if they are not safeguarded by more robust institutional mechanisms.

Robust institutional mechanisms are not about rigidity and stagnation. From a rule of law perspective, what matters is the right kind of stability;[115] that is, legal frameworks should enable institutions of governance to adjust to changing circumstances, but this adjustment should be possible through established procedures rather than ad hoc engineering that leads to the atrophy of the values of clarity, predictability, and justiciability. The need to think more systematically about the role for the rule of law in EU health governance is made even clearer when we add the third component of liquid authority, namely institutional multiplicity.

4.5.3 Institutional multiplicity

The hashing out of the content of the NGEU and the Multiannual Financial Framework during the COVID-19 crisis was an opportunity to observe how different Union institutions tend to interfere with each other's work. According to the formal balance of powers, the European Council is supposed to develop an overarching framework for political action, leaving detailed matters of budget and execution to the Commission. In reality, it delivered a Conclusions document that expanded well into the territory of other institutions: 'What do we make of this in the light of the little sentence in Article 15 TEU that the European Council "shall not exercise legislative functions"? In those 65 pages, the European Council did something that looks very much like legislative drafting.'[116] Moreover, the essential points were determined before the EP could have its say, although the EP had co-decision powers on some aspects of the package.

To recall once again: this is wholly symptomatic of how the field of health had developed ahead of the COVID-19 crisis. Anniek de Ruijter explains how health competences have proven difficult to contain in any systematic fashion, both regarding the Union as a whole and regarding its internal divisions.[117] First, Member State attempts to limit EU competences through Treaty revisions have, paradoxically, led to health emerging more clearly as a free-standing objective that can be pursued through a variety of mechanisms, as opposed to an indirect constraint on other legislation.[118] This is in line with earlier neofunctionalist accounts of health as a paradigm of 'uninvited Europeanization.'[119] Second, however, EU health governance also draws heavily on scientific expertise through its agencies and committees. These experts have stronger

[114] Martin Shapiro, '"Deliberative," "Independent" Technocracy v. Democratic Politics: Will the Globe Echo the EU?' (2005) 68 Law and Contemporary Problems 341, 351.
[115] Postema (n 85) 152.
[116] de Witte (n 22) 672.
[117] de Ruijter, *EU Health Law and Policy* (n 15).
[118] de Ruijter, 'EU "Public health" and "Health-care" Law and Policy' (n 33) 74, 78.
[119] Scott L Greer, 'Uninvited Europeanization: Neofunctionalism and the EU in Health Policy' (2006) 13 Journal of European Public Policy 134.

incentives to pursue substantive policy goals than to worry about the constitutional dangers of competence creep:

> These experts may be more interested in engaging on a particular health policy topic than being concerned with institutional divisions and legislative powers. However, what they may take home, or contribute to at EU level—be that in the context of an agency, a committee or an expert group—could still entail an authoritative allocation of value, facilitated by their participation in EU policy mechanisms.[120]

This nicely illustrates the liquid character of EU health governance. Experts can participate in one forum endowed with mere informational or advisory competence, but rules and standards then tend to 'cascade' through regulatory regimes in unpredictable and often untraceable ways.[121] In addition, however, this institutional multiplicity cannot be properly understood without considering the role of more global regulatory or expert networks. Standards developed by expert groups in the WHO or World Medical Association (WMA) can go from advisory to mandatory through adoption in EU directives, and then be variously reinterpreted in Member State laws, and then again in regulatory compliance documents: 'the number of points of transposition may have been so great or so dispersed in time and/or space that those transposing, using and interpreting it may not be aware of [the rule's] original source'.[122]

In terms of authoritative allocation of value (to use de Ruijter's phrase), a key example is the presence of international fiscal models and surveillance instruments. The fiscal governance architecture that emerged after the eurozone crisis gave the International Monetary Fund (IMF) increased surveillance capacity, which means that its views on prudent healthcare spending have become more relevant for the Commission and other EU institutions of fiscal surveillance.[123] Moreover, fiscal surveillance instruments long used by the IMF and the Organization for Economic Co-operation and Development (OECD), such as 'cyclically-adjusted budget balance', have become key tools in EU surveillance.[124]

The institutional multiplicity gestured at here is interwoven with the dynamism and informality sketched above. It would clearly be an exaggeration to claim that the result is total flux and complete absence of solid and stable authority relations. Procedures, institutional divisions, and formal mandates are part of the EU's approach to health. Nevertheless, the liquid features that accompany solid governance structures are not minor details. Rather, they illuminate how competences are stretched,

[120] de Ruijter, 'EU "Public Health" and "Health-care" Law and Policy' (n 33) 119.

[121] Julia Black, '"Says Who?" Liquid Authority and Interpretive Control in Transnational Regulatory Regimes' (2017) 9 International Theory 286.

[122] Black (n 121) 290.

[123] Scott L Greer, Holly Jarman and Rita Baeten, 'The New Political Economy of Health Care in the European Union: The Impact of Fiscal Governance' (2016) 46 International Journal of Health Services 262, 271.

[124] Phillip Heimberger, Jakob Huber and Jakob Kapeller, 'The Power of Economic Models: The Case of the EU's Fiscal Regulation Framework' (2020) 18 Socio-Economic Review 337, 347; Martin Larch and Alessandro Turrini, 'The Cyclically-adjusted Budget Balance in EU Fiscal Policymaking: A Love at First Sight Turned into a Mature Relationship' (2009) DG ECFIN Economic Paper No 374, 109.

instrumentalized, reinterpreted, and even circumvented. They therefore deserve closer attention from a rule of law perspective.

This raises the question of how much tweaking or upgrading the traditional perspective requires in order to be both realistic and still normatively attractive. Analysts of liquid authority are prone to hypothesize radical changes in legitimacy discourses, where formality gives way to quality:

> Sources such as expertise, moral principle, or problem-solving capacity are likely to move to the foreground when formal, delegated powers are unavailable. We may thus hypothesize that legitimacy discourses around liquid authority are likely to emphasize the quality of decision makers, rather than procedural, democratic foundations, more strongly than those around solid authority.[125]

There are reasons to see this framing as neither empirically plausible nor normatively attractive. First, this prediction underestimates the scope and depth of disagreement in all matters that involve political action, not least in the field of health competences. Notions such as 'expertise, moral principle, or problem-solving capacity' make little political sense without some procedural arrangements for determining relevant expertise, interpreting moral principles, or defining problems. The very idea that we can have constructive legitimacy discourses decoupled from formal arrangements is an illusion. Second, liquid authority is not some mystically emerging natural phenomenon. It emerges through institutional opportunities that are allowed to exist. The question is not primarily how legitimacy discourses should change to fit the new institutional reality, but rather how the institutional reality should change to fit a reasonable legitimacy discourse.

And it is exactly at this point, in the midst of paradigm change and a return to a belief in the necessity for, and efficacy of, interventionist steering programmes (of redistribution)—at a moment when we consider that human health may take precedence over market forces[126]— that we must also remember how costly healthcare provision can be for the individual. We must admit openly of the redistributive frameworks which underpin whichever solidarity or welfare settlement is created or evolves within the EU, and of the need for the anchoring of that framework (moral economy of healthcare) in a visible and explicit European public discourse, underpinned by, and constitutive of, European rule of law.

4.6 Conclusion

Crises have natural tendency to legitimate a 'whatever-it-takes' attitude to political action, and it is trite to merely ask for a return to legality and procedural accuracy once

[125] Krisch (n 80) 252.
[126] Delhomme and Hervey (n 1).

the dust settles. The aim of this chapter has been different. The field of health illustrates that analyses in terms of 'stealthy' or 'covert' integration should be considered precursors to a more fundamental discussion about the EU as a redistributive political agent. While Article 125 TFEU—'the no-bailout clause'—upholds firm divisions of liabilities, it is becoming increasingly unclear who is bailing out who in any given circumstance and what the normative implications are. Others in this anthology discuss the financial intertwinements in more detail, but the case of health adds a distinct moral and political tenor to the notion of joint liabilities and commitments. Threats to health, either regarding prevention of risk or provision of care, go straight to the basic concerns of security and respect that legitimate any social compact. This is not a novel revelation, yet the COVID-19 crisis exposed more fully the need for institutions that openly and explicitly acknowledge the considerations of justice and solidarity that inform political response in this regard.

Hence, in taking a rule of law perspective on this issue, we are not urging the reigning in of solidaristic impulses or the taming of the project of socializing Europe. On the contrary, our claim is that 'covert integration' and 'termite tactics' need replacing by institutionally robust integration and democratic tactics; that is, instead of taking the lesson of the pandemic to be the virtues of informality, dynamism, and institutional multiplicity, it should be that the moral and political causes enabled by such liquid modes of governance need to be secured through more solid institutional and legal structures. And while functionalist accounts hold that the COVID-19 crisis represents another case of 'failing forward', there is a need to complement the language of 'deeper' or 'complete' integration with a language that tracks conditions of just and fair integration.

The fact of political controversy and opposition to morally and institutionally robust integration is no objection to the claim as such. From a theoretical perspective, the problem is not that change is hard or unlikely, but rather that the difficulties of change are apt to cloud normative principles. When we get to the core of things, there are only two options: either retreat to a mere efficiency-based union based on win-win regulation or embrace the political project for what it has become and institutionalize the remaining discussions in a democratically respectable fashion. Even if the feasibility of the latter option appears doubtful, the former option is radically and conceptually doubtful. Importantly, the in-between solution of inflating executive authority through technical framings of political decision-making is not only inherently unstable; it is a betrayal of the EU's own rule of law principles.

5

State Aid Control

Rule Making and Rule Change in Response to Crises

Juan Jorge Piernas López[*] *and Michelle Cini*[**]

5.1 Introduction

European Union (EU) state aid control is a distinctive category of competition law and policy which regulates (limits and facilitates) EU Member States' ability to provide financial support for firms operating within their borders. The state aid regime serves to protect the internal market from subsidy races, while also guiding Member States to direct their aid so that it falls into line with, and supports, EU policy objectives. While aid was prohibited in the 1951 European Coal and Steel Community (ECSC) Treaty[1], in Article 4(c), the state aid rules as they exist today were introduced in 1957, under Articles 92–94 of the European Economic Community (EEC) Treaty[2]. Although they have since been subject only to relatively minor changes, they have been bolstered and interpreted by the European Commission, through a corpus of mainly soft law instruments such as guidelines and communications, by Commission decisions, by a small number of regulations, and through the EU Courts by means of their case law. While Article 107 of the Treaty on the Functioning of the European Union (TFEU)[3] rests on a prohibition of state aid (Article 107(1)), exceptions to that general rule are spelt out in Article 107(2) and Article 107(3), the latter giving the Commission (with the administrative and legal work undertaken by the Directorate-General for Competition (DG Competition or DG COMP)) considerable discretion.

The Members of the European Commission, and the Commission officials whose job it is to apply the state aid rules, have had to respond to various crises that have affected the EU. In many of these crises, undertakings and citizens have turned to their governments for enhanced assistance and protection, in recognition that EU support could not compare with national aid. While the state aid rules should, in principle, be flexible

* Senior Lecturer of Public International Law and European Union Law at the University of Murcia.
** Professor of European Politics at the University of Bristol.

[1] Treaty establishing the European Coal and Steel Community (ECSC Treaty), also known as the Treaty of Paris, 18 April 1951, United Nations, Treaty Series, vol. 261, p 140 https://op.europa.eu/en/publication-detail/-/publication/353a22f9-8e69-4dd9-b1cf-db402253e897 accessed 17 October 2024.

[2] Treaty establishing the European Economic Community (EEC), also known as the Treaty of Rome, 25 March 1957, United Nations, Treaty Series, vol. 298, p.3 , https://eur-lex.europa.eu/legal-content/EN/TXT/?uri=celex%3A11957E%2FTXTaccessed 17 October 2024 [in the original French]

[3] Treaty on the Functioning of the European Union (TFEU), OJ C 326/49, 26.10.2012.

Juan Jorge Piernas López and Michelle Cini, *State Aid Control* In: *EU Regulatory Responses to Crises*. Edited by: Diane Fromage, Adrienne Héritier, and Paul Weismann, Oxford University Press. © Juan Jorge Piernas López and Michelle Cini 2025.
DOI: 10.1093/9780198913825.003.0005

enough to respond to such demands during times of crisis, this has not always been the case. In the early years of the European Community (EC), state aid control was not that much of a priority. Indeed, the ECSC Treaty's unconditional prohibition of national aid was totally disregarded by Member States,[4] in part due to its strictness. Similarly, during the 1973 oil crisis, there was a significant increase in state aid, accompanied by a noticeable evasion of the state aid rules, which the Commission proved unable to enforce.[5] Since 2008, the EU has witnessed multiple crises, to the extent that crisis seems to have become the 'new normal' for the EU. In this chapter we ask, therefore, whether the EU in general, and the Commission in particular, have found an alternative way of operationalizing the state aid rules during times of crisis. More specifically, we are interested in how EU institutions have responded to crises by introducing new rules and engaging in new forms of rule-making. This chapter addresses these questions by focusing on the key crises that have affected the state aid regime since 2008. Specifically, it covers the Great Financial Crisis (GFC) of 2008–12, the COVID-19 crisis of 2020–22, and the most recent iteration of the Ukraine crisis, from early 2022 onwards. Other crises, such as those linked to migration/Schengen and Brexit, have had much less impact on EU state aid policy. The chapter concludes by arguing that the legacy of the EU response to recent crises in this field is mixed. On the one hand, the use of rarely applied provisions and the swift adoption of soft law in the form of temporary frameworks have allowed for a coordinated response, and therefore avoided subsidy races while providing legal certainty. On the other hand, the flexibility of the Commission's responses risks the social, territorial, and economic cohesion of the internal market, and has led to allegations of discrimination made before the EU Courts. Finally, it is submitted that the crisis responses in this area have led to an increased demand for the federalization of financial instruments—for EU aid instead of national aid—of which the Recovery and Resilience Facility (RRF), part of the NextGeneration EU (NGEU) temporary recovery instrument, is the best example.

The rest of the chapter is divided into three sections. The first section (5.2) addresses the EU's response to crises in the state aid field. In the case of the GFC, we shed light on the scheme for banks, whereas in our coverage of subsequent crises we place more emphasis on the real economy, as this is where the most important developments have occurred. This section focuses primarily on changes to rule-making, with a particular focus on the legal bases and the procedures applied, and with regard to the increasing importance of soft law. The next section (5.3) then considers changes to the rules themselves. The penultimate section (5.4) addresses legal and policy effects alongside

[4] Claus-Dieter Ehlermann, 'State Aid Control in the European Union: Success or Failure?' (1994) 18 Fordham International Law Journal 1216.

[5] On the increase in state aids as a reaction to the 1973 crisis, see Manfred Caspari, 'The Aid Rules of the EEC Treaty and their Application' in Jürgen Schwarze (ed), *Discretionary Powers of the Member States in the Field of Economic Policies and Their Limits under the EEC Treaty* (Nomos Verlagsgesellschaft 1988) 48. For the evasion of Community rules on state aids by the Member States, see, eg Fiona Cownie, 'State Aids in the Eighties' (1986) 11 European Law Review 247, 248; O. Wulff, 'National Economic Policy: An Obstacle to the European Community?' in Schwarze (ibid) 9, 16; Jan Steenbergen, 'Trade Regulation since the Tokyo Round' in Edmond LM Volker (ed), *Protectionism and the European Community* (Kluwer 1987) 187, 194–95.

broader legacy issues. The conclusion (5.5) then pulls together the key contribution and argument of this chapter.

5.2 The Main Elements of the EU's Response to Crises in the State Aid Field: Changes to Rule-making

When the GFC first hit Europe in 2007–08, the state aid regime offered a ready-made set of EU-level regulatory instruments to deal with the economic turmoil. This enabled the EU to impose restructuring obligations on systemically important banks in need of support. However, even at that time, it was unclear whether these rules were fit for purpose in crisis situations, and whether Member States would respect them, given the enormous pressure they were under to support their financial institutions. This not only raised the prospect of evasion by Member States, but also, controversially, of the possible use of Article 108(2) TFEU, which allows the EU Council, by unanimity, to override the state aid regime and declare certain aids compatible with the Treaty. The use of this provision would have undermined the Commission's central role in state aid enforcement, setting an important precedent for future Council intervention in the policy. In the event, Article 108(2) was not used, even if, at the start of the COVID-19 crisis, this issue became pertinent again when certain states, most prominently Austria, argued for a total suspension of the rules.[6]

The difficulty for the Commission was that, when the GFC broke out, the EU had no specific regulation on the financial sector, and no sector-specific rules on granting aid to financial institutions. The Commission's state aid policy was thus put to a tough test. Failing that test would not only have severely impacted the financial sector and the economies of the Member States but would also have called into question the entire system of state aid control and the role of the Commission within it.[7]

It should be kept in mind that, at that time, only Member States and their sub-state authorities could lawfully grant financial support to undertakings to cope with the effects of a systemic crisis. In other words, notwithstanding the relatively small amounts available indirectly under the EU structural funds, the EU had no aid to offer undertakings directly that could have helped them adjust to crisis situations. Consequently, Member States might legitimately consider that it was for them, and them alone, to intervene through financial means to palliate the effects of a significant crisis. In this scenario, the task of the European Commission was a difficult one: it had to apply the state aid rules, including the general prohibition of state aid enshrined in Article 107(1) TFEU, to control the Member States' crisis interventions, while failing to offer them a meaningful alternative to deal with the crisis. As of 2021, however, the setting-up of the Recovery and Resilience Facility (RRF) as the cornerstone of the NGEU temporary

[6] 'Austria Wants EU Suspension of Rules on State Aid' (*Reuters*, 20 April 2020) https://www.reuters.com/article/us-health-coronavirus-eu-austria-idUSKBN2220ZT accessed 11 January 2023.

[7] Małgorzata Agnieszka Cyndecka, 'State Aid and the Financial Sector: The Crisis and Beyond' in Leigh Hancher and Juan Jorge Piernas López (eds), *Research Handbook on EU State Aid Law* (Edward Elgar 2021) 135.

recovery instrument seemed to signal a shift in this status quo, with the EU institutions now able to use the EU's financial means to direct funds both to achieve EU objectives and to respond, if only temporarily, to major crises.

The Commission began by applying the general state aid rescue and restructuring guidelines in early decisions related to the GFC.[8] As these guidelines were designed to set out conditions under which state aid for rescuing and restructuring *non-financial* undertakings in difficulty may be compatible with the internal market under Article 107(3)(c) TFEU, they proved ill-suited to the crisis conditions at hand. The Commission was quickly inundated with hundreds of notifications and soon realized that this situation was unsustainable. A specific, temporary, and more flexible approach was necessary. This new approach, geared to the crisis context, would also avoid 'contaminating' the regular or orthodox state aid regime with an exceedingly expansive reading of the rules.

The European Commission was well-positioned to take this approach as, compared with previous crises, by the late 2000s, state aid control, and particularly its enforcement by the Commission, was significantly stronger than it had ever been before. Great strides had been taken in strengthening the policy since the late 1980s, when state aid became more of a priority for the Commission department responsible (Directorate-General 4 (DG IV), subsequently renamed the DG for Competition (DG COMP)), than it had been in earlier decades. This process had begun during Peter Sutherland's term as competition commissioner when, in 1985, a special task force had been set up to review all aid granted in the EC. This mapping of aid led to a re-evaluation of the policy under Sutherland's successor, Sir Leon Brittan, with an eye to making aid more targeted and transparent, while reducing its overall quantity in the system. On these foundations, a revitalized policy was constructed.[9] The Commission was keen to do whatever it took to save the policy, while also offering an effective response to the most serious of crises. In effect, this meant the construction, albeit only informally, of a state aid crisis regime.

5.2.1 Treaty base

The response of the Commission to the GFC had to be both exceptional and flexible. At the heart of its approach sat the unprecedented application of Article 107(3)(b) TFEU (Article 87(3)(b) TEC at that time). Its use was described as the 'nuclear option' of European state aid law by senior Commission officials.[10] This legal basis allowed the

[8] Commission, 'Communication from the Commission – Guidelines on state aid for rescuing and restructuring non-financial undertakings in difficulty' OJ C249, 31.07.2014, 1 https://eur-lex.europa.eu/legal-content/EN/TXT/?uri=OJ:C:2014:249:TOC accessed 30 October 2023.

[9] Michelle Cini and Lee McGowan, *Competition Policy in the European Union* (Palgrave Macmillan 2009) 177–78.

[10] See, in this regard, the speech by Herbert Ungerer, Deputy Director-General with special responsibility for State Aids, European Commission, Directorate-General Competition, 'After the State Aid Action Plan: The EU's New State Aid Framework' (The EU State Aid Summit – State Aid Policy, Procedure and Enforcement through the

European Commission to adopt decisions declaring state aid measures compatible with the internal market, 'to remedy a serious disturbance in the economy of a Member State'. It had been applied only rarely in the past, such as in the early 1990s in the context of a Greek privatization scheme.[11] The restrictive approach towards this provision was supported by the case law of the European courts, which had consistently held that, as a derogation, Article 107(3)(b) TFEU must be interpreted narrowly, and that 'the disturbance [referred to in this provision] must affect *the whole of the economy of the Member State concerned* and not merely one of its regions or parts of its territory'.[12] As an example, the collapse of the former socialist economy of the German Democratic Republic, in the course of German reunification, was *not* classified by the European Commission as a serious disturbance in the economy of Germany, an interpretation that was confirmed by the European courts.[13]

In this regard, the Commission had, prior to the 2008 GFC, often ruled that Article 107(3)(b) TFEU could not be applied when aid was intended to help a single financial institution (so-called 'individual aid'), in line with the general restrictive approach towards this provision,[14] and even in 2007, a year before the collapse of Lehman Brothers, the Commission rejected the application of Article 107(3)(b) TFEU to a guarantee offered by Austria to a financial institution.[15]

It was in this context, in the first days of the GFC, that the commissioner for competition, Neelie Kroes, announced that the Commission would not 'shy away if need be from applying the special provisions of Article 107(3)(b) of the Treaty regarding aid granted to address a serious disturbance of the economy of a Member State'.[16] On the day after this announcement, the EU Member States welcomed 'the Commission's continued commitment to act quickly and apply flexibility in state aid decisions, within the framework of the single market and state aid regime', as well as the Commission's commitment to issue guidance on compatibility so that recapitalization and guarantee schemes could be 'rapidly assessed'. [17]

Similarly, in 2010, the European Parliament concluded, with reference to the measures adopted by the Commission in 2008, that 'state aid policies taken in relation to

Economic Crisis and Beyond, 23–24 June 2009) 13 https://ec.europa.eu/competition/speeches/text/sp2009_11_en.pdf accessed 30 October 2023.

[11] See, in this regard, Cyndecka (n 7) 137 and fn 31. See also Phedon Nicolaides, 'The Evolving Interpretation of Article 107(3)(b)' (2022) 21 European State Aid Law Quarterly 31.

[12] Case C-57/00 P *Freistaat Sachsen and Others v Commission* [2003] EU:C:2003:510, para 98 (emphasis added).

[13] ibid 99.

[14] See, in this regard, Massimo Francesco Orzan, 'Rules on Economic and Financial Crisis (Article 107(3)(b))' in Herwig CH Hofmann and Claire Micheau (eds), *State Aid Law of the European Union* (OUP 2016) 266.

[15] ibid 266–67; Commission Decision of 27 June 2007 State aid C 50/2006 (ex NN 68/ 2006, CP 102/2006) implemented by Austria for BAWAG-PSK, OJ L83, 26.03.2008, 7–34.

[16] Neelie Kroes, 'Address before the Monetary Affairs Committee, European Parliament: Dealing with the Current Financial Crisis' (European Commission, 6 October 2008) http://europa.eu/rapid/pressReleasesAction.do?reference=SPEECH/08/498 accessed 1 December 2022.

[17] Council, 'Council Conclusions – Ecofin Council of 7 October 2008, Immediate Responses to Financial Turmoil' (Luxembourg, 7 October 2008, 13930/08 (Presse 284)) https://www.consilium.europa.eu/uedocs/cms_Data/docs/pressdata/en/misc/103202.pdf accessed 30 October 2023.

financial institutions and the economic recovery process were helpful to stabilise the financial market and to tackle the effects of the credit crunch on the real economy [and] that the system of competition rules has weathered the storm so far'.[18] Notwithstanding this, the Parliament also expressed concerns about the possible distortions of competition caused by state aid granted to the financial market.[19] Parliament was right to raise these concerns. The application of Article 107(3)(b) TFEU led to the approval of virtually all aid schemes targeting financial institutions that were notified by Member States in relation to the GFC, as long as the notifications accepted a rescue and restructuring logic and a future phase-out of financial support.[20]

At the start of the COVID-19 crisis, the Commission again resorted to Article 107(3)(b) TFEU, judging it to be the most suitable legal basis for dealing with this new crisis. This time, it did so more promptly and with more confidence, resulting from the experience gained during the GFC. In contrast to the GFC, however, financial institutions were not the main beneficiaries of this aid; rather, aid was targeted at the real economy. At the start of the pandemic, the Commission underlined in a press release that Member States could grant support to remedy a serious disturbance to their economy under Article 107(3)(b) TFEU in the event of particularly severe economic situations 'such as the one currently faced by Italy'.[21] In this regard, around thirty decisions were adopted ex Article 107(3)(b) TFEU to palliate the effects of the pandemic.[22] The reaction to the COVID-19 pandemic from a state aid viewpoint has, of course, some specificities, not least in terms of the sectors receiving aid (for example, health, transport, and agriculture). This explains why the Commission's first decision related to COVID-19 was in fact adopted under Article 107(2)(b) TFEU (aid to make good the damage caused by natural disasters or exceptional occurrences—COVID-19 being defined as an 'exceptional occurrence').[23] But while Article 107(2)(b) TFEU was a suitable legal basis to compensate for the immediate damages brought about by the pandemic, such as the cancellation of events, it was clearly insufficient to deal with the severe economic consequences of the pandemic in the medium and long term. That said, approximately 100 COVID-19-related decisions were taken by the Commission between early 2020 and July 2022 on the basis of this treaty provision.[24] By contrast,

[18] European Parliament, 'Resolution of 9 March 2010 on the Report on Competition Policy 2008 (2009/2173(INI))', points 18 and 24 https://eur-lex.europa.eu/LexUriServ/LexUriServ.do?uri=OJ:C:2010:349E:0016:0024:EN:PDF accessed 30 October 2023.

[19] ibid, points 19, 23 and 25.

[20] As underlined by Nicolaides, between 2008 and 2011 the Commission only prohibited state aid in one case. See Nicolaides, 'The Evolving Interpretation of Article 107(3)(b)' (n 11) 31.

[21] Commission, 'State Aid: Commission Approves €12 million Danish Scheme to Compensate Damages Caused by Cancellations of Large Public Events Due to COVID-19 Outbreak' (Press release, 12 March 2020) https://ec.europa.eu/commission/presscorner/detail/en/ip_20_454 accessed 27 October 2023.

[22] Commission, 'Coronavirus Outbreak – List of Member State Measures Approved under Articles 107(2)(b), 107(3)(b) and 107(3)(c) TFEU and under the State Aid Temporary Framework' (Brussels, 5 May 2023) https://competition-policy.ec.europa.eu/system/files/2023-05/State_aid_decisions_TF_and_107_2b_107_3b_107_3c.pdf accessed 27 October 2023.

[23] Commission, 'State Aids SA. 56685 (2020/N) – DK – Compensation scheme for cancellation of events related to COVID-19' C (2020)1698 final (Brussels, 12 March 2020) https://ec.europa.eu/competition/state_aid/cases1/202011/285054_2139535_70_2.pdf accessed 27 October 2023.

[24] Commission, 'Coronavirus Outbreak' (n 22).

while Article 107(3)(c) TFEU could also be used by the Commission to incentivize the granting of public support to the health sector, 'as well as enhancing preparedness to respond to any further threats stemming from the virus',[25] only four pandemic-related decisions (albeit amounting to just under 3.6 billion euros in approved aid) were taken under this provision between January 2020 and July 2022.[26]

After the Russian invasion of Ukraine in late February 2022, the Commission again responded by activating Article 107(3)(b) TFEU. The Commission built on the interpretation of this provision developed during the GFC and the COVID-19 crisis and accepted its application both to aid schemes and to individual aid. The use of Article 107(3)(b) TFEU was justified by the Commission as the Russian aggression and EU and international sanctions and countermeasures were causing disruption to trade flows and supply chains, leading to price increases (especially in energy, but also in raw materials and primary goods). This constituted a serious disturbance in the economy of all Member States: 'On that basis, the Commission considers that it is appropriate to lay down the criteria for the assessment of state aid measures that Member States may take to remedy that serious disturbance.'[27] As in earlier cases, the aid must only last for a limited period, be necessary, appropriate and proportionate, and be designed to mitigate the effects of the crisis on undertakings. The cumulation of aid was permitted if it was in line with the newly drafted Ukraine crisis framework or if it fell under the state aid regime's *de minimis*[28] or General Block Exemption Regulation[29], the then still applicable COVID-19 framework, or Article 107(2)(b) TFEU.

5.2.2 Soft law instruments

The state aid response to the GFC involved the use of soft law. This came to form an important element of what the Commission called its crisis response toolbox.[30] The use of soft law as a state aid instrument by the European Commission was nothing new, as state aid policy had largely been developed, since its inception, through policy frameworks, communications, and other guidelines.[31] This was a method used by the

[25] Commission, 'State Aid' (n 21).

[26] Commission, 'Coronavirus Outbreak (n 22).

[27] Commission, 'Communication from the Commission – Temporary Crisis Framework for State Aid measures to support the aggression against Ukraine by Russia', 2022/C 131 I/01, 24 March 2022.

[28] Commission Regulation (EU) no 140/2013 of 18 December 2013 on the application of Articles 107 and 108 of the Treaty on the Functioning of the European Union to *de minimis* aid, OJ L 352/1, 24.12.2013 [subsequently replaced by Commission Regulation (EU) 2023/2831 of 13 December 2023 on the application of Articles 107 and 108 of the Treaty on the Functioning of the European Union to de minimis aid OJ L, 2023/2831, 15.12.2023.

[29] Commission Regulation (EU) no 651/2024 of 17 June 2014 declaring certain categories of aid compatible with the internal Market in application of Articles 107 and 108 of the Treaty ("General Block Exemption Regulation"), OJ L 187/1 26.6.2014.

[30] Commission, 'Communication from the Commission to the European Parliament, the Council, the European Economic and Social Committee and the Committee of the Regions, A competition policy fit for new challenges' COM (2021) 713 final/1, 2, 18 November 2021 https://ec.europa.eu/transparency/documents-register/detail?ref=COM(2021)713&lang=en accessed 27 October 2023.

[31] Michelle Cini, 'The Soft Law Approach: Commission Rule-making in the EU State Aid Regime' (2001) 8 Journal of European Public Policy 192.

Commission to fill the gap left by the absence of legal instruments, particularly procedural instruments, which Member States refused to adopt for many years. In particular, the Council had twice refused, in 1966 and 1972, a Commission proposal to adopt a procedural regulation for the application of the state aid rules. Moreover, soft law had been used to interpret Article 107 TFEU exemptions both for horizontal and sectoral aid. For example, the regional aid guidelines 'set out the criteria for identifying the areas that fulfil the conditions of compatibility under Article 107(3)(a) and (c)'.[32]

However, using soft law to address crisis situations was new, and the form that the soft law took, the now familiar 'temporary framework' model, was also different. This model was based on Article 107(3)(b) TFEU and was used to complement other forms of crisis communication. In the case of the GFC, the Commission adopted at least seven soft law instruments,[33] starting with the 2008 Banking Communication, outlining the principles under which it would assess aid granted under Article 107(3)(b) TFEU within the context of the GFC. The Commission's policy on state aid during this period evolved from a very lax approach, motivated by the high economic and political tension of the early days of the crisis, during which all decisions were approved, particularly in the aftermath of the collapse of Lehman Brothers, towards a stricter approach as the financial and economic context became more stable. The Commission's method of progressively increasing the toughness of state aid control was based on the publication of soft law instruments stating how it intended to approach the compatibility of aid for banks in different periods of the crisis.[34]

Doleys has helpfully identified three phases in the GFC, starting with the 'crisis response' period. He argued that this was followed by a 'crisis management' phase that covered the period from late 2008 to early 2009, addressing 'events surrounding the

[32] Commission, 'Communication from the Commission Guidelines on regional state aid' [2021] OJ C153/1, 29.04.2021 https://eur-lex.europa.eu/legal-content/EN/TXT/?uri=OJ:C:2021:153:TOC accessed 30 October 2023.

[33] Commission, 'Communication on the application of state aid rules to measures taken in relation to financial institutions in the context of the current global financial crisis ("2008 Banking Communication")' [2008] OJ C270/8, 25.10.2008 https://eur-lex.europa.eu/legal-content/EN/TXT/?uri=OJ:C:2008:270:TOC accessed 30 October 2023; Commission, 'Communication on the recapitalisation of financial institutions in the current financial crisis: limitation of aid to the minimum necessary and safeguards against undue distortions of competition' ("Recapitalisation Communication")' [2009] OJ C10/2, 15.01.2009 https://eur-lex.europa.eu/legal-content/EN/TXT/?uri=OJ:C:2009:010:TOC accessed 30 October 2023; Commission, 'Communication on the treatment of impaired assets in the Community financial sector ("Impaired Assets Communication")' [2009] OJ C72/1, 26.03.2009, https://eur-lex.europa.eu/legal-content/EN/TXT/?uri=OJ:C:2009:072:TOC accessed 30 October 2023; Commission, 'Communication on the return to viability and the assessment of restructuring measures in the financial sector in the current crisis under the state aid rules ("Restructuring Communication")' [2009] OJ C195/9, 19.08.2009, https://eur-lex.europa.eu/legal-content/EN/TXT/?uri=OJ:C:2009:195:TOC accessed 30 October 2023; Commission, 'Communication on the application of state aid rules to support measures in favour of financial institutions in the context of the financial crisis ("First Prolongation Communication")' [2010] OJ C329/7 https://eur-lex.europa.eu/LexUriServ/LexUriServ.do?uri=OJ:C:2013:216:0001:0015:EN:PDF accessed 17 October 2024; Commission, 'Communication on the application of state aid rules to support measures in favour of financial institutions in the context of the financial crisis ("Second Prolongation Communication")' [2011] OJ C356/7, 06.12.2011 https://eur-lex.europa.eu/legal-content/EN/TXT/?uri=OJ:C:2011:356:TOC accessed 30 October 2023; Commission, 'Communication on the application of state aid rules to support measures in favour of banks in the context of the financial crisis ("New Banking Communication") [2013] OJ C216/1, 30.07.2013 https://eur-lex.europa.eu/legal-content/EN/TXT/?uri=OJ:C:2013:216:TOC accessed 30 October 2023.

[34] See, in this regard, eg Thomas J Doleys, 'Managing State Aid in Times of Crisis: The Role of the European Commission' (Paper prepared for presentation at the ECPR Fifth Pan-European Conference on EU Politics, 23–26 June 2010, University of Oporto and University of Fernando Pessoa, Porto, Portugal).

publication of the Commission's Restructuring and Impaired Assets Communications'. The 'crisis resolution' phase, which began in early 2009, then encompassed 'the Commission's Restructuring Communication and ongoing efforts by the industry to exit the crisis'.[35] He and others also noted the evolutionary character of the policy and its increasing strictness and turn towards industrial policy-like measures. During the latter period, and particularly after the 2013 Banking Communication, which adapted the earlier 2008 version, the Commission made burden-sharing with shareholders a condition of state aid approval. This was unsuccessfully contested before the national courts.[36]

Sitting alongside the Banking Communication was the temporary framework (TF), which allowed the grant of state aid to non-financial institutions, and thus to the 'real economy'. This was another soft law instrument. The TF was designed to limit the risk of subsidy races among EU Member States. It comprised what were referred to as 'temporary additional measures', pointing to the fact that the existing state aid rules could also be adapted for use as crisis instruments. The TF covered a range of aid measures deviating temporarily from the orthodox rules, including aid in the form of subsidized interest rates, aid for the production of green products, and risk capital measures. The use of this instrument was made possible because of the flexibility with which the aid rules were drafted, allowing the Commission to assert that these steps were little more than a reinterpretation of the rules—a justification also relevant to other non-crisis forms of soft law.

The context of the COVID-19 crisis was very different from that of the GFC, as it did not involve responding directly to a banking crisis, but to an all-encompassing exogenous crisis. Yet the use of soft law was rereconfirmed, as of 2020. This again took the form of a temporary framework focusing on the impact of the crisis on the real economy. The framework was proclaimed a special legal framework and was adopted on 20 March 2020.[37] It was amended six times over the course of the pandemic.[38] Each time, the rules were clarified and new exemptions were included, increasing the flexibility of the instrument. This differed from the approach taken in the GFC, where the TF became more restrictive over time. The difference between these approaches reflects the different characters of the crises. The adoption of the COVID-19 TF was

[35] See Doleys (n 34) 7. See also, for a similar periodization, Alastair Sutton, Karl Lannoo and Chris Napoli, 'Bank State Aid in the Financial Crisis: Fragmentation or Level Playing Field?', CEPS Task Force Report, 29 October 2010 https://www.ceps.eu/download/publication/?id=6832&pdf=Task%20Force%20Report%20on%20Bank%20State%20Aid.pdf accessed 17 October 2024; See Neelie Kroes, 'Competition Law in an Economic Crisis', Opening address at the 13th Annual Competition Conference of the International Bar Association, Fiesole, Italy, 11 September 2009 (SPEECH/09/385), https://ec.europa.eu/commission/presscorner/detail/en/speech_09_385 accessed 17 October 2024, where she called on banks to change some of the business practices that led to the crisis.

[36] See the preliminary ruling in Case C–526/14 *Tadej Kotnik* [2016] EU: C: 2016: 570.

[37] Commission, 'Communication of 19 March 2020 – Temporary Framework for state aid measures to support the economy in the current COVID-19 outbreak' C 2020:0911; TOC OJ C0911, 20.03.2020, https://eur-lex.europa.eu/legal-content/EN/TXT/?uri=OJ:C:2020:091I:TOC accessed 30 October 2023.

[38] On 3 April 2020, OJ C112, 04.04.2020, pp 1–9; 8 May 2020, OJ C164, 13.05.2020, pp 3–15; 29 June 2020, OJ C218, 02.07.2020, pp 3–8; 13 October 2020, OJ C340, 13.10.2020, pp 1–10; 1 February 2021 OJ C34, 01.02.2021, pp 6–15; and 24 November 2021 OJ C473, 24.11.2021, pp 1–15.

convenient for reasons of urgency, transparency, and legal certainty. It was also fitting for the state aid discipline again to enact an extraordinary and temporary framework rather than to resort to the direct application of the existing rules on a case-by-case basis. This path allowed for a flexible interpretation of the rules, but only for a limited time and under certain conditions, applicable to all Member States. In this regard, as has been noted, the TF did not modify the existing legal framework or introduce directly applicable rules; it 'only' stated the criteria under which the Commission considered acceptable the adoption of state aid measures by Member States to counter the effects of the pandemic.[39] The fact that the Commission adopted several amendments to the TF has been positively assessed as a sign of the Commission's ability to adapt to changing circumstances. In other words, 'the continuous adjustments to the TF can be considered a key feature of the approach taken by the Commission, which may evoke what Yane Svetiev has called the "experimentalist governance" of competition law in uncertain contexts'.[40]

The TF template, subsequently labelled the temporary *crisis* framework, was used again in the Ukraine crisis. The aim, as of March 2022, was to address disruptions to supply chains caused directly or indirectly by Russia's invasion of Ukraine. It followed a structure similar to the crisis frameworks that came before it. The main differences were substantive in that they focused on the energy and agriculture sectors and expressed particular concern for the way that aid might impinge on the EU's sanctions regime. The principles were much the same, however, with reference to the ambition of the framework to allow aid that was 'targeted and appropriate' but at the same time avoid subsidy races.[41] The framework was revised on two occasions, on 20 July and 28 October 2022, with the latter version in place until the end of 2023. More recently, this framework was replaced by the Temporary Crisis and Transition Framework (TCTF), published in March 2023.[42] The TCTF amended and prolonged, in part, the previous Temporary Crisis Framework until 31 December 2025, and introduced new measures to accelerate investments in key sectors for the transition towards a net-zero economy. The TCTF was presented together with an amendment to the General Block Exemption Regulation (GBER), as a package aiming to speed up investment and financing for clean tech production.[43]

[39] See Commission, 'Temporary Framework – COVID-19' (n 37) para 10.

[40] Delia Ferri, 'State Aid Control in Times of Crisis: The COVID-19 Pandemic' in Juan Jorge Piernas López, Leigh Hancher and Luca Rubini (eds), *The Future of EU State Aid Law and Policy: Consolidation and Expansion* (EU Law Live Press 2022).

[41] Commission, 'Temporary Framework – Ukraine' (n 27).

[42] Commission, 'Communication from the Commission – Temporary Crisis and Transition Framework for State Aid measures to support the economy following the aggression against Ukraine by Russia' 2023/C 101/03, OJ C101, 17.03.2023, pp 3–46 https://eur-lex.europa.eu/legal-content/EN/TXT/?uri=OJ:C:2023:101:TOC accessed 30 October 2023.

[43] See Commission, 'State Aid: Commission Adopted Temporary Crisis and Transition Framework to Further Support Transition to Net Zero Economy' (Press release, 9 March 2023) https://ec.europa.eu/commission/presscorner/detail/en/ip_23_1563 accessed 27 October 2023.

5.2.3 Procedural change

During the GFC, the Commission adopted a specific crisis procedure, or 'general simplification package',[44] to deal with the significant number of decisions concerning aid to financial institutions that had to be adopted under high economic and political pressure, sometimes within twenty-four hours. These changes were said to be dependent on clear and complete notifications by Member States. This crisis procedure enabled, inter alia, the commissioner for competition to adopt certain decisions outside the College of Commissioners and made the language requirements more flexible. At the same time, this approach also entailed limitations concerning legal certainty and the observance of rights of interested parties.[45] In this regard, the European Court of Auditors (ECA) later found that the exceptional procedures followed to deal with state aid during the GFC were not fully transparent, and not always in line with the internal state aid manual of procedures and the State Aid Best Practices Code, particularly in view of the lengthy and informal pre-notification contacts that took place.[46]

The TFs on the COVID-19 and Ukraine crises also aimed to speed up the adoption of Commission decisions. As some commentators put it, in relation to the COVID-19 crisis: 'the Temporary Framework acts as a kind of "procedural shortcut" by which the Commission can limit its analysis in relation to the compatibility of the aid by showing adherence to the criteria in the Temporary Framework'.[47] These 'procedural facilitations' included a commitment by the Commission 'to decide on state aid notifications relating to Covid-19 within days of receiving a complete state aid notification; ... a dedicated contact point to assist Member States with any queries they have; [and that] when notifying schemes, Member States [will be] asked to sign a waiver authorising the Commission to adopt and notify its decisions in English'.[48]

5.3 Analysis of the Main Elements of the EU's Response to Crises in the State Aid Field: Rule Changes

The EU state aid crisis regimes took as their starting point the orthodox or regular state aid rules. Formally, the Commission did not adopt *new* rules in the state aid field; it just applied the *existing* rules, and particularly Article 107(3)(b) TFEU, in a flexible

[44] Commission, 'Communication from the Commission – Temporary Framework for state aid measures to support access to finance in the current financial and economic crisis (2009/c 83/01), OJ C 83/1, 7.4.2009, https://eur-lex.europa.eu/LexUriServ/LexUriServ.do?uri=OJ:C:2009:083:0001:0015:EN:PDF accessed 17 October 2024.

[45] See Philipp Werner and Martina Maier, 'Procedure in Crisis? Overview and Assessment of the Commission's State Aid Procedure during the Current Crisis' (2009) 8 European State Aid Law Quarterly 177.

[46] Dimitrios Kyriazis, 'State Aid Control in Times of Crisis: The Financial Crisis, the Missteps and the Way Forward' in Juan Jorge Piernas López, Leigh Hancher and Luca Rubini (n 40).

[47] Paula Riedel, Thomas Wilson and Shane Cranley, 'Learnings from the Commission's Initial State Aid Response to the COVID-19 Outbreak' (2020) 19 European State Aid Law Quarterly 119.

[48] Ashurst, 'The Impact of COVID-19: Navigating EU State Aid (Competition Law Update, 22 October 2020)', https://www.ashurst.com/-/media/ashurst/documents/news-and-insights/legal-updates/2020/jun/the-impact-of-covid-19---navigating-eu-state-aid.pdf accessed 18 October 2024.

and temporary manner. In this regard, the 2008 Banking Communication, the first soft law instrument adopted to deal with the GFC, underlined that Article 107(3)(b) TFEU necessitated 'a restrictive interpretation of what can be considered a serious disturbance of a Member State's economy'.[49] The Commission added that, '[i]t needs to be emphasised … that the use of Article 87(3)(b) [previously Article 92(3)(b) and now 107(3)(b) TFEU] cannot be envisaged as a matter of principle in crisis situations in other individual sectors in the absence of a comparable risk that they have an immediate impact on the economy of a Member State as a whole.'[50]

The COVID-19[51] and Ukraine TFs[52] also restated this view, adding that this provision only applied where the whole economy of a Member State, *or 'an important part'* thereof, was in jeopardy. However, the judicial formula to which the Commission refers in order to back these statements in the TFs does not include a reference to an 'important part' of the economy but only to the economy as a whole. Indeed, the formula originally coined by the General Court in the *Freistaat Sachsen* case, in 1999,[53] and subsequently quoted by both the General Court and the Court of Justice, and by the Commission in the 2008 Temporary Framework,[54] highlights, in our view, that the whole of the economy of a certain Member State, and not merely a part thereof, even if an important one, must be affected in order to apply this provision. The foregoing is legally relevant, as the Commission appears to have accepted, in some cases, the justification of a serious disturbance in the economy under Article 107(3)(b) in cases where the disturbance affected only a certain region and not the whole national economy, as the case law on that provision requires.[55]

The ECA, in a special report covering primarily the years 2013 to 2018, but also the period around the GFC, also criticized the Commission's application of the concept of a 'serious disturbance' in a Member State's economy, for not being well-defined.[56] The ECA acknowledged that the Commission's rules for the control of state aid to the financial sector were 'generally well drafted and clear'; yet it disapproved of 'the

[49] European Commission, '2008 Banking Communication' (n 33) 8.

[50] ibid, point 11.

[51] Commission, 'Temporary Framework – COVID-19' (n 37), point 17.

[52] Commission, 'Temporary Crisis Framework – Ukraine' (n 27), point 48. See also Commission, 'Temporary Crisis and Transition Framework – Ukraine' (n 42), point 54.

[53] Joined Cases T-132/96 and T-143/96 *Freistaat Sachsen* [1999] EU:T:1999:326, para 167: 'It follows from the context and general scheme of that provision that the disturbance in question must affect the whole of the economy of the Member State concerned, and not merely that of one of its regions or parts of its territory.' See also, in this regard, Nicolaides, 'The Evolving Interpretation of Article 107(3)(b)' (n 11) 34: 'However, it appears that no judgment has referred to "important part" of the economy.'

[54] Commission, 'Communication from the Commission – Temporary Community framework for state aid measures to support access to finance in the current financial and economic crisis', OJ C16, 22.01.2009, pp 1–9, point 4.1 https://eur-lex.europa.eu/legal-content/EN/TXT/?uri=OJ:C:2009:016:TOCaccessed 30 October 2023: 'In this context, the Court of First Instance of the European Communities has ruled that the disturbance must affect the whole of the economy of the Member State concerned, and not merely that of one of its regions or parts of its territory. This, moreover, is in line with the need to interpret strictly any derogating provision such as Article 87(3)(b) of the Treaty.'

[55] See Kyriazis (n 46) 195, with reference to the Commission Decision no. SA.52917 – Italy on Liquidity Support to Banca Carige, Cassa di Risparmio di Genova e Imperia OJ C7, 10.01.2020.

[56] European Court of Auditors, 'Control of State aid to Financial Institutions in the EU: In Need of a Fitness Check', Special Report 21/2020 https://www.eca.europa.eu/en/publications?did=54624 accessed 30 October 2023.

lack of explicit criteria for the determination of serious disturbance', which granted the Commission 'a great margin of appreciation'.[57] Moreover, it also questioned the Commission's analysis of whether a threat to financial stability was present in each particular state aid decision, as well as DG COMP's assessment of the impact of each proposed state aid measure on competition. While the ECA's remarks were made in relation to the Commission's reaction to the GFC, some of them are relevant in other contexts, particularly regarding the lack of criteria on the notion of 'serious disturbance', which also applies to the COVID-19 and Ukraine crises.

The recurrent application of Article 107(3)(b) TFEU since the GFC, including during the COVID-19 crisis, has also led to some clarifications by the EU courts on the interpretation of this provision. To this extent, the General Court has clarified that Article 107(3)(b) applies both to aid schemes and to individual aid,[58] overcoming the initial resistance to applying this provision in individual cases. More worryingly, the General Court has concluded, in recent cases, that Article 107(3)(b) does not require an assessment of the impact of aid on trade and competition, and thus that the Commission is not required to carry out any balancing test.[59] We believe that this finding is at odds with the role of the compatibility analysis of state aid under the Treaties; that is, the Commission's prerogative to assess whether planned state aid measures can be granted in light of their overall positive effects, mainly for certain economic activities or for certain economic areas, and their tolerable impact on competition in the internal market. The above-mentioned finding is also at odds, in our view, with the legislative history of Article 107(3)(b) TFEU, and with the previous case law of the Court of Justice,[60] as recently argued also by Advocate General Pitruzzella.[61] With the help of the General Court, therefore, the TFs seem to have altered the substance of the state aid rules, albeit only under certain conditions. It is not clear whether this change will be limited to the duration of the crises.

In terms of rule change in the context of the frameworks, we focus on both the thresholds below which state aid is permitted and the scope of the guidelines. The most distinctive measure in the 2008 TF was the possibility of granting aid not exceeding 500,000 euros per undertaking. This contrasted with the norm of 200,000 euros, over three years, in the regular state aid rules. By contrast, the COVID-19 TF allowed for the granting of 800,000 euros per undertaking. This applied to measures such as state guarantees for loans taken by undertakings from banks, and subsidized public loans to undertakings. In addition, the Commission clarified that the aid measures covered by the TF could be cumulated with aid under *de minimis* regulations. Consequently, permissible COVID-19-related state aid could potentially stretch to 1 million euros per undertaking.

[57] ibid, paras 43 and 72.

[58] ibid and particularly Case T-388/20 *Ryanair v European Commission* [2021] EU:T:2021:196, para 32.

[59] See also, in this regard, Nicolaides, 'The Evolving Interpretation of Article 107(3)(b)' (n 11) 39–42.

[60] Juan Jorge Piernas López, 'The COVID-19 State Aid Judgments of the General Court ... Every Man for Himself? Cases T-238/20 and T-259/20 *Ryanair v Commission*' (2021) 2 European State Aid Law Quarterly 261–65.

[61] Opinion of AG Pitruzzella, Case C-209/21 P *Ryanair v. Commission* EU:C:2023:223, paras 83–88.

Under the Ukraine Temporary Crisis Framework, Member States were initially able to grant up to 400,000 euros per undertaking affected by the crisis, in most sectors (for agriculture, fisheries, and aquaculture sectors, the amounts were lower). Member States were also allowed to provide subsidized state guarantees to ensure that banks continued to provide loans to all undertakings affected by the crisis, and public and private loans with subsidized interest rates. The Framework also took into account the significant repercussions of the Ukraine crisis on the energy sector, allowing Member States to grant aid to compensate for high energy prices. As introduced by Commissioner Vestager: 'The new framework will enable Member States to (i) grant limited amounts of aid to companies affected by the current crisis or by the related sanctions and countersanctions; (ii) ensure that sufficient liquidity remains available to businesses; and (iii) compensate companies for the additional costs incurred due to exceptionally high gas and electricity prices.'[62]

On 20 July 2022, the Commission adopted its first amendment to the Ukraine Framework.[63] The amendment included an increase in the maximum amount of assistance up to 500,000 euros per undertaking, and measures to support the rollout of renewable energy as well as the decarbonization of industries, in line with the REPowerEU objectives. REPowerEU, launched in April 2022, sets out the Commission's plan to reduce reliance on Russian fossil fuels. Subsequently, the Commission amended the TF for a second time, in order, inter alia, to 'exponentially'[64] increase the maximum amount of state aid that an undertaking could receive under the TF from (the already increased) 500,000 euros to 2 million euros.[65] When it was subsequently replaced by the TCTF, in March 2023, the 2 million euro threshold was retained.

5.4 State Aid Crisis Rule-making and Rule Change: Effects and Legacy

At the time of writing, in late 2023, the COVID-19 pandemic has only recently (at least in so far as the state aid rules are concerned) concluded, and the Ukraine crisis is still in full flow with no end in sight. As such, it may be somewhat premature to review the legacy issues of these crises. This is much easier to do for the GFC and, as such, we can use the GFC to reflect on the possible legacies of later crises. The legacy is mixed, as explained below.

[62] See Commission, 'State Aid: Commission Adopts Temporary Crisis Framework to Support the Economy in Context of Russia's Invasion of Ukraine' (Press release, 23 March 2023) https://ec.europa.eu/commission/presscorner/detail/en/statement_22_1949 accessed 30 October 2023.

[63] Commission, 'Communication from the Commission Amendment to the Temporary Crisis Framework for State Aid measures to support the economy following the aggression against Ukraine by Russia' 2022/C 280/01 C/2022/5342 OJ C280, 21.07.2022, pp 1–13.

[64] White and Case, 'Crisis State Aid: The Commission Adopts Important Expansion to its Temporary Crisis Framework' (3 November 2022) https://www.whitecase.com/insight-alert/crisis-state-aid-commission-adopts-important-expansion-its-temporary-crisis-framework accessed 30 October 2023.

[65] Commission, 'Temporary Framework – Ukraine' (n 27), point 55.

Firstly, the EU response to recent crises has had some very positive effects. In particular, the rapid coordination and centralization of crisis management by the European Commission, in the main, avoided a distortive subsidy race among Member States while providing legal certainty to stakeholders. According to the Commission, it also yielded economic gains. As summarized by the deputy director for state aid in relation to the pandemic:

> The Commission estimates that the contraction in GDP in 2020 has been reduced by around 4.5 percentage points due to the fiscal response, which of course was to a large extent framed by the state aid rules. The combination of state aid and other measures, such as those taken in the context of EU Next Generation and the RRF [Recovery and Resilience Fund], helped preserve jobs, reducing the increase in unemployment by 1%.[66]

In addition, the European Commission has been able to consolidate its position as the state aid crisis manager for the EU and demonstrate that the state aid regime is both resilient and flexible.

However, for each of the crises considered in this chapter, there have already been concerns raised that the impact of crisis rule changes may be of longer duration, particularly where the focus lies not so much with changes to the instruments of rule-making but with the legal and policy effects on the internal market of ostensibly temporary rules. For the GFC, these concerns are reflected in the above-mentioned ECA report, which highlights the persistence of the 2013 Banking Communication as a crisis measure that never went away.[67] In the COVID-19 case, although all 27 Member States were lawfully able to grant state aid foreseen by the TF to undertakings 'established' in their territory to the fullest extent, not all Member States were able to afford the same amount of public spending. In other words, some Member States with 'deep pockets' were able to provide (much) more public support to their undertakings than others, thereby distorting the level playing field: and even more so if undertakings 'active' in Member States without deep pockets were excluded from the aid. This is important when we consider that COVID-19 expenditure across the EU amounted to approximately 3.9 per cent of GDP.[68] The scope for competition distortions in the internal market derived from uneven public interventions is striking, even if the same argument could be made in relation to all block-exempted state aid under the regular state aid regime. However, the magnitude of permitted crisis aid matters. The unprecedented leeway for the granting of state aid under the COVID-19 framework ('the most

[66] Ben Smulders, 'A Temporary Framework for Every Crisis: Covid and Ukraine: Keynote speech, EStALI Conference 22–23 September 2022, Brussels' (2022) 3 European State Aid Law Quarterly 348–51.

[67] ECA (n 56).

[68] Commission, 'Report from the Commission to the European Parliament, the Council, the European Economic and Social Committee and the Committee of Regions: Report on Competition Policy 2020', Brussels 07.07.21, COM (2021) 373 final 6 https://eur-lex.europa.eu/legal-content/EN/TXT/PDF/?uri=CELEX:52021DC0373 accessed 30 October 2023.

flexible state aid rules yet')[69] exacerbated the risk of competition distortions, and of an asymmetric recovery.[70]

In this regard, the Commission Executive Vice-President responsible for competition law, Margrethe Vestager, was concerned enough to investigate this issue through the collection of data on actual expenditure, by means of four surveys covering expenditure up to the end of 2021. This approach recognized that there is normally a gap between the aid permitted and what is actually allocated and spent. The challenge was in calculating the latter: the actual expenditure. Vestager concluded that focusing only on the aid schemes approved by the Commission gave a false impression of the distortion, though that is not to say that the problem completely disappeared. In terms of aid approved, '[o]f the around 3 trillion euros in [COVID-19 related] aid approved to-date, more than half was approved in Germany',[71] a phenomenon that could also be observed during the 2008 GFC.[72] Vestager also noted that, from the aid actually paid out (rather than schemes approved), 'France has disbursed the largest amount of aid, at just above a third of the total, followed by Germany at 28%. Spain makes up about one fifth and Italy about 8%.' In any event, she concluded, 'the fact remains that the four largest Member States make up over 90% of total state aid disbursed in the EU between March and end of June [2020]'.[73]

Similarly, a report prepared for the European Parliament in mid-2020 concluded that '[t]here is a serious risk that excessive state aid support by some Member States will jeopardise free and fair competition in the EU single market'.[74] The report also noted that the procedures for monitoring the state aid granted were vague, and that:

> it is far from certain that these procedures will be sufficient to allow for correct monitoring and eventually for appropriate actions in case of violations. This caveat is applicable to state aid policy in general but matters even more during the COVID-19 crisis as the monitoring has not been organised yet. Given the number of state aid cases, this monitoring process will be a tremendous job. Both the European Commission and the Member States would benefit from clear and well-known procedures.[75]

[69] See the reference to the Commission's statement, which could also be found on Twitter: 'To mitigate economic shocks and save businesses, we have set the most flexible state aid rules yet, allowing EU countries to provide direct support for hard hit companies' (6 April 2020) in Adina Claici, Laurent Eymard and Shahin Vallée, 'European Union: Economists' Perspective on State Aid' (*Global Competition Review*, 24 June 2022).

[70] See also, in this regard, Lena Hornkohl and Jens van 't Klooster, 'With Exclusive Competence Comes Great Responsibility' (*Verfassungblog*, 29 April 2020), https://verfassungsblog.de/with-exclusive-competence-comes-great-responsibility/ accessed 17 October 2024.

[71] Margrethe Vestager, 'Speech on State Aid' (Berliner Gesprächskreis zum Europäischen Beihilfenrecht, 30 October 2020).

[72] See Kyriazis (n 46): 'It is a common "secret" that during the very generous approval of national measures at the beginning of the implementation of the Temporary Framework, more than 50% of all coronavirus state aid was granted by a single Member State, i.e. Germany.'

[73] Vestager, 'Speech on State Aid' (n 71). See also Antoine Matthieu Collin, Valerie Boddin and Koen van de Casteele, 'The Use of COVID-19 Related State Aid Measures by EU Member States' (*Competition State Aid Brief*, Issue 1/2021 (March 2021)).

[74] European Parliament, 'Impact of state aid on competition and competitiveness during the COVID-19 pandemic: an early assessment' (17 December 2020), PE 658.214 23 https://www.europarl.europa.eu/thinktank/en/document/IPOL_STU(2020)658214 accessed 30 October 2023.

[75] ibid 18.

The European Commission was, therefore, aware of the risks associated with the flexible approach adopted, and designed some palliative measures in response. For example, the COVID-19 TF included some safeguards to limit the negative consequences of the state aid granted under its provisions, particularly to prevent relocations between Member States due to the public support of, or the grant of aid to, companies that were already in difficulties prior to the outbreak of the pandemic. It remains to be seen whether these palliatives and safeguards, together with other initiatives adopted under the NGEU initiative, will suffice to neutralize the distortions of competition resulting from the above-mentioned public interventions.[76] However, the European Commission, including Vice-President Vestager and Deputy Director-General for State Aid Smulders, have recently maintained that the response to the COVID-19 crisis put in place by Member States was 'correlated to the loss suffered'.[77] In particular, as explained by Smulders, '[l]ooking at the relation between the amounts of COVID-19 state aid granted in 2020 and 2021 and the cumulated real GDP loss in 2020 and 2021, we note that the state aid measures actually implemented by Member States are, on average, correlated with the economic damage suffered during the crisis.'[78] That said, the data still shows the larger economies, most notably France and Germany, benefiting disproportionately from the COVID-19 state aid crisis regime.

Concerns about cohesion have been exacerbated by the interpretation given by the Commission and the General Court to the principle of equal treatment and non-discrimination, which has been raised in COVID-19-related decisions regarding support for flagship airlines, such as the Portuguese airline TAP, where either Article 107(3)(b) or Article 107(2)(b) TFEU was used to justify aid.[79] The cases proved controversial when a competitor, Ryanair, appealed before the General Court claiming, inter alia, a violation of the principle of non-discrimination.[80] To date, Ryanair has initiated twenty-six proceedings against several Member States. The aid schemes in question required aid beneficiaries to have their principal place of business or establishment in the territory of the granting Member State. Of the first ten cases to be ruled on, the General Court upheld the Commission's decisions in seven.[81] In three cases, the actions were successful on procedural grounds, though exceptionally the General Court decided to maintain the effects of the three annulled decisions until the Commission could redraft new decisions.[82]

[76] Carole Maczkovics, 'How Flexible Should State Aid Control Be in Times of Crisis?' (2020) 19 European State Aid Law Quarterly 271–83.

[77] Giuseppina Cannas and others, 'Looking Back at the State Aid COVID Temporary Framework: The Take-up of Measures in the EU' (*Competition State Aid Brief*, Issue 3/2022 (October 2022)) 1. See also, in this regard, Margrethe Vestager, 'State Aid for the Really Big Challenges: Keynote Speech, EStALI Conference 22–23 September 2022, Brussels' (2022) 3 European State Aid Law Quarterly 345–47; Smulders (n 66).

[78] See Smulders (n 66) 350.

[79] See *Portugal Aid to TAP* (SA.57369 (2020/N) COVID 19)

[80] Action brought on 22 July 2020, *Ryanair v Commission* (T-465/20).

[81] Piernas López (n 60) https://doi.org/10.21552/estal/2021/2/9 258–69.

[82] Piernas López (n 60). Art 264 TFEU reads as follows: 'If the action is well founded, the Court of Justice of the European Union shall declare the act concerned to be void. However, the Court shall, if it considers this necessary, state which of the effects of the act which it has declared void shall be considered as definitive.'

The Court of Justice will have the opportunity to analyse the repercussions of these decisions for the cohesion of the internal market, the validity of the fundamental freedoms (ie freedom of establishment), and the observance of the non-discrimination principle,[83] although a recent judgment concerning Ryanair confirms the General Court's approach on the principle of non-discrimination.[84] In any event, the answer to this question is liable to have significant consequences for the way in which EU Member States may respond to future crises through state aid. For instance, as noted recently by Buendía, Member States might be tempted to grant less state aid if the aid is open to all undertakings active in the EU, but they might also be tempted in that case to grant more individual aid (as opposed to setting up aid schemes), in which the issue of discrimination is more difficult to identify.[85] Finally, the consequences of the interpretation given by the Commission and the General Court to the principle of equal treatment in the context of crises, so far endorsed by the Court of Justice, has to be analysed together with the Commission's decision, upheld by the General Court, not to require the application of the 'balancing test' when applying Article 107(3)(b) TFEU, which, as mentioned, is not justified, in our view, and may exacerbate the risks for cohesion and of distortion of competition.

Beyond these legal issues, there has been some concern that crisis frameworks have set aside classical policy objectives of state aid measures, such as environmental protection or regional aid, in order to aid undertakings in difficulty.[86] This is not to say that these former issues disappeared from the Commission's agenda during crises. This was certainly not the case during the COVID-19 crisis, for example, not least because Commission President von der Leyen's agenda (most noted for its high-profile Green Deal and digital and industrial strategies) required DG COMP to act to ensure that Commission policy was mainstreamed across all state aid instruments. The state aid fitness check which occurred over 2019 and early 2020 also highlighted both the strengths of the regular state aid regime and areas for improvement and reform, though some initiatives were delayed because of the pandemic.[87] In this regard, the Commission reported that, in 2020, Member States' expenditure for non-crisis objectives remained within the ranges existing pre-pandemic, 'thus showing that COVID-19 aid was successfully channeled and did not crowd out public financing of important projects that supported non-crisis-related EU objectives'.[88] However, the crisis did slow down the revision of certain rules, most notably six sets of guidelines that were due for revision at

[83] See pending cases C-209/21 P *Ryanair v Commission* and C-210/21 P *Ryanair v Commission*.

[84] C-320/21 P *Ryanair v Commission* EU:C:2023:712.

[85] José Luis Buendía Sierra, 'Quo Vadis Compatibility?' in Piernas López, Hancher and Rubini (n 35) 71–72. See also, for an interesting discussion on this issue, Nicolaides, The Limits of 'Proportionate' Discrimination (2021) 20 European State Aid Law Quarterly 385.

[86] See, eg Irene Agnolucci, 'Will COVID-19 Make or Break EU State Aid Control? An Analysis of Commission Decisions Authorising Pandemic State Aid Measures' (2022) 13 Journal of Competition Law and Practice 3–16.

[87] Commission, 'Commission staff working document. Executive summary of the Fitness Check of the 2012 state aid modernisation package, railway guidelines and short-term export credit insurance' SWD(2020) 0258 final, 30.10.2020 https://eur-lex.europa.eu/legal-content/EN/TXT/PDF/?uri=CELEX:52020SC0258 accessed 30 October 2023.

[88] See Cannas and others (n 77) 1.

the end of December 2020, which were instead extended by one year,[89] and two regulations (*de minimis* and GBER) that were due for amendment,[90] though this delay was largely the product of the administrative burden resulting from the early influx of notifications, particularly in the first half of 2020.

Although this focus on policy effects is important, there are several ways in which crisis rules and rule-making may have longer-term implications for state aid control. One key question to ask is whether changes that emerged as a response to crises disappeared after the end of those crises. In the case of the GFC, a key area for investigation is aid to the financial sector, where the crisis led to the introduction of new banking rules. Indeed, from 2012, the EU set in motion plans to create a banking union. This was not something planned in EU circles prior to the GFC.

Interestingly, the 2013 Banking Communication, based on an earlier 2008 version which was set up as a crisis measure, has not been repealed but has coexisted since 2016 with the newly adopted banking union rules, including the Bank Recovery and Resolution Directive (BRRD)[91] and the Regulation establishing the Single Resolution Mechanism (SRMR).[92] The Communication has been criticized by the ECA on the grounds that the crisis framework was intended to be temporary. Indeed, at the time of writing, a decade has elapsed since the adoption of the 2013 Banking Communication.[93] As mentioned earlier, it was in this context that 'the ECA took the decision to launch [an] audit due to the realisation that the EU's banking sector remained a big beneficiary of state aid more than 10 years after the eruption of the financial crisis'.[94] Ultimately, the ECA found that the Commission possessed all the necessary powers for effective

[89] Commission, 'Communication from the Commission concerning the prolongation and the amendments of the Guidelines on Regional State Aid for 2014–2020'; Commission, 'Guidelines on State Aid to Promote Risk Finance Investments'; Commission, 'Guidelines on State Aid for Environmental Protection and Energy 2014–2020'; Commission, 'Guidelines on state aid for rescuing and restructuring non-financial undertakings in difficulty'; Commission, 'Communication on the Criteria for the Analysis of the Compatibility with the internal market of State Aid to Promote the Execution of Important Projects of Common European Interest'; Commission, 'Communication from the Commission to the Member States on the application of Articles 107 and 108 of the Treaty on the Functioning of the European Union to short-term export credit insurance', C2020/4355, OJ C224, 08.7.2020, pp 2–4 https://eur-lex.europa.eu/legal-content/EN/TXT/?uri=uriserv:OJ.C_.2020.224.01.0002.01.ENG&toc=OJ:C:2020:224:FULL, accessed 30 October 2023.

[90] Commission Regulation (EU) 2020/972 of 2 July 2020 amending Regulation (EU) No 1407/2013 as regards its prolongation and amending Regulation (EU) No 651/2014 as regards its prolongation and relevant adjustments C/2020/4349, OJ L215, 07.07.2020, pp 3–6, https://eur-lex.europa.eu/legal-content/EN/TXT/?uri=OJ:L:2020:215:TOC accessed 30 October 2023.

[91] Directive 2014/59/EU of the European Parliament and of the Council of 15 May 2014 establishing a framework for the recovery and resolution of credit institutions and investment firms and amending Council Directive 82/891/EEC https://eur-lex.europa.eu/legal-content/EN/TXT/PDF/?uri=CELEX:32014L0059 accessed 30 October 2023; see also Directives 2001/24/EC, 2002/47/EC, 2004/25/EC, 2005/56/EC, 2007/36/EC, 2011/35/EU, 2012/30/EU and 2013/36/EU, and Regulations (EU) No 1093/2010 and (EU) No 648/2012, of the European Parliament and of the Council, OJ L173, 12.06.2014, pp 190–348.

[92] Regulation (EU) No 806/2014 of the European Parliament and of the Council of 15 July 2014 establishing uniform rules and a uniform procedure for the resolution of credit institutions and certain investment firms in the framework of a Single Resolution Mechanism and a Single Resolution Fund and amending Regulation (EU) No 1093/2010, OJ L225, 30.07.2014, pp 1–90 https://eur-lex.europa.eu/legal-content/EN/TXT/?uri=OJ:L:2014:225:TOC accessed 30 October 2023.

[93] ECA (n 56). The ECA report analysed, first, whether the Commission had appropriate tools and resources to carry out its control of state aid, and, second, whether it had enforced the control of state aid to ensure that aid is exceptional and limited to the minimum necessary.

[94] See Kyriazis (n 46).

state aid control and an appropriate procedural framework to deal with the banking crisis, but criticized the lack of revisions to the Banking Communication, particularly considering the newly adopted EU banking regulations. It is too early to say whether similar effects will be seen in the years after COVID-19 and the Ukraine crisis, though an *ex post* evaluation of the COVID-19 framework was foreseen as early as November 2021,[95] and the Commission published two policy briefs in 2022 on measures adopted under the TF, concluding, inter alia, that the level playing field in the internal market had been preserved.[96] Similarly, the 2022 state aid scoreboard, published in April 2023, concluded that:

> The picture that emerges shows that the temporary state aid measures adopted in the COVID-19 crisis were proportionate and necessary, matching the economic damage suffered during the crisis. Moreover, there is no evidence of Member States that would have granted an excessively larger amount compared to the others.[97]

However, other recent accounts are more critical, notably in relation to the lack of lasting effect on the health sector of the measures adopted under the COVID-19 TF. Giosa, for example, has condemned some instances of misuse of the TF, noting that 'sometimes the Temporary Framework has offered a "smokescreen" for aid which purported to relate to tackling the COVID-19 pandemic, but which actually did not'.[98]

More recently, the TCTF has increased the concerns related to the 'not-so-temporary' effects of temporary frameworks.[99] The TCTF, adopted in a context of geopolitical developments favouring the granting of subsidies to foster green measures, particularly in the United States, exacerbates this risk. As it has been held, 'whilst there is no doubt that the climate crisis is of an urgent nature, it does not have a temporary character'.[100] The *sui generis* use of a temporary framework for such a broad objective may entail other negative consequences. Notably, Member States may use it to bypass the stricter environmental and climate requirements enshrined in the relevant Commission guidelines, namely the 2022 Guidelines on State Aid for Climate, Environmental Protection and Energy (CEEAG), as some commentators have already noted.[101] In this regard, environmental organizations had warned before the publication of the TCTF that the new

[95] Commission, 'Communication from the Commission to the European Parliament, the Council, the European Economic and Social Committee and the Committee of the Regions. A competition policy fit for new challenges' COM(2021) 713 final/1, 18.11.2021, 4 https://ec.europa.eu/transparency/documents-register/detail?ref=COM(2021)713&lang=en accessed 30 October 2023.

[96] See Collin, Boddin and van de Casteele (n 73); Cannas and others (n 77) 1–6.

[97] Commission, DG Competition, Policy and Strategy, state aid case support and policy, 'State Aid Scoreboard 2022' (24 April 2023) 44, available at https://competition-policy.ec.europa.eu/system/files/2023-06/state_aid_scoreboard_note_2022.pdf

[98] Penelope Giosa, 'Assessing the Use of the State Aid Covid Temporary Framework with regard to the Healthcare and Media Sector' (2023) 14 Journal of European Competition Law and Practice 289.

[99] Valentine Lemonnier, The EU Green Deal Industrial Plan: Did the EU Just Avert a Revolution in State Aid Law? (2023) 22 European State Aid Law Quarterly 123 124.

[100] ibid 130.

[101] Leigh Hancher, 'Energy & State Aid: An Overview of EU and National Case Law'(*e-Competitions Energy & state aid*, Art No 110194, 19 January 2023) 6. Available online (under subscription) at https://www.concurrences.com/en/bulletin/special-issues/energy-state-aid/energy-state-aid-an-overview-of-eu-and-national-case-law

instrument lacked green conditionalities, that it entailed a risk of inconsistencies with CEEAG, and that there had been a lack of public consultation and transparency on its substance.[102]

It is worth mentioning, too, that the expertise gained during the GFC and the COVID-19 crisis has had a recent legislative translation in the Foreign Subsidies Regulation (FSR),[103] which entered into force in January 2023. In particular, the Regulation has identified several possible remedies or redressive measures that build on the experience gained by the Commission in both of these crises. As the impact assessment noted, the approach taken 'is in line with state aid control, for example, with the remedial measures under the Rescue and Restructuring Guidelines, in the financial sectoral guidelines or under the Covid-19 Temporary Framework'.[104] Beyond policy legacies, crisis responses may also engender an inter-institutional legacy. Indeed, responses in the state aid field have strengthened the position of the Commission. For example, while the EU Council could have stepped in, on the basis of Article 108 TFEU, to override the Commission in the early stages of the COVID-19 crisis, the Council was ultimately reassured by the manner in which the Commission responded to the crisis. Thus, to some degree we could say that the Commission benefited from crisis, or at the very least consolidated its position. There is no evidence that the Council, as an institution, gained any capacity in state aid law-making or enforcement, though we might assume that the Commission's approach was a consequence of the Commission having to operate, to some degree, within the shadow of the Council. Meanwhile, the European Parliament maintained its somewhat detached involvement in matters of state aid control.

5.5 Conclusion

The Treaty of Rome established a system of state aid control based on the prior notification of aid plans to the European Commission and the latter's exclusive competence over the assessment of the compatibility of state aid with the internal market. That system, laid down in Articles 107 and 108 TFEU, has remained formally unchanged to this day, even after the GFC and the COVID-19 and Ukraine crises. The Grand Chamber of the Court of Justice recently summarized the system as follows:

[102] See the Open Letter by ClientEarth CEE, Bankwatch Network, CAN-E – Climate Action Network Europe, HEAL – Health and Environment Alliance, and E3G (1 March 2023) https://www.clientearth.org/media/ko4bcmks/open-letter-on-the-draft-state-aid-temporary-crisis-and-transition-framework-need-for-a-stricter-environmental-approach-more-consistency-and-increased-transparency.pdf accessed 30 October 2023.

[103] Regulation (EU) 2022/2560 of the European Parliament and of the Council of 14 December 2022 on foreign subsidies distorting the internal Market, OJ L 330, 23.12.2022, pp 1-45.

[104] Commission, 'Commission Staff Working Document Impact Assessment Accompanying the Proposal for a Regulation of the European Parliament and of the Council on foreign subsidies distorting the internal market' (SWD/2021/99 final), p 48. See, for this point, Morris Schonberg, 'The EU Foreign Subsidies Regulation: Substantive Assessment Issues and Open Questions' (2022) 21, issue 2, European State Aid Law Quarterly 151.

> Article 108(3) TFEU establishes a prior control of plans to grant new aid. The aim of that system of prior control is therefore that only compatible aid may be implemented. In order to achieve that aim, the implementation of planned aid is to be deferred until doubt as to its compatibility is resolved by the Commission's final decision.[105]

The nature of rule-making in this area prior to recent systemic crises was, therefore, characterized by the predominant role of the European Commission, under the control of the Court of Justice, and the relatively limited role of other institutions, particularly the Council and the Parliament. However, the granting of state aid, especially in times of crisis, is very sensitive and Article 108(2) TFEU recognizes this by allowing the EU Council, by unanimity, to declare certain aids compatible with the Treaty.

In this context, when recent crises hit the EU, rule-making in this area broke new ground, not by formally modifying EU primary law or adopting EU secondary law, but by resorting to a practically never-used provision, Article 107(3)(b) TFEU, and by adopting new soft law instruments—so-called temporary frameworks—that were unprecedented both formally and substantially, despite the prevalence of soft law in the pre-crisis state aid regime. The crisis response in this field, therefore, led to the activation of existing powers, albeit in ways that were unprecedented, and which would have been considered legal/political taboos even a few years earlier. Examples included the application of Article 107(3)(b) TFEU to individual aid (as well as aid schemes), even in cases where the whole economy may not have been in jeopardy, and the approval of grants of aid of up to 2 million euros per undertaking, while the maximum that can be granted in normal times under the *de minimis* Regulation is 200,000 euros for an undertaking over a three-year period.[106] The Commission's crisis responses also led to litigation based on the alleged violation of important principles of EU constitutional law, particularly the principle of equal treatment and non-discrimination, which the EU courts have had to interpret in an unprecedented manner in its relation to the Treaty rules on state aid.

Consequently, while EU competences were not formally extended, the EU institutions, and particularly the Commission, were able to provide coordinated responses to several crises in the absence of specific rules at the relevant times on the subject matter of those crises, namely banking, health, and energy. Conversely, the reactions to the crises in these policy areas have helped pave the way for EU common rules in those areas, notably in the field of banking but also to a lesser extent (so far) in the health and energy fields, and even in other areas, such as the FSR, which incorporates some of the remedies developed during the GFC and the COVID-19 crisis.

As to the relationship between the EU and its Member States, and the relationships among Member States, the picture is complex. On the one hand, the EU—that is, the Commission—resisted attempts to suspend the EU state aid rules and managed to

[105] C-75/18 *Vodafone Magyarország* EU:C:2020:139, para 19.

[106] Commission Regulation (EU) No 1407/2013 of 18 December 2013 on the application of Articles 107 and 108 of the Treaty on the Functioning of the European Union to de minimis aid, OJ L352, 24.12.2013, pp 1–8.

provide a coordinated response that has avoided an open subsidy race and the risks that unilateral responses would have created (as seen in the case of the 2008 Irish guarantee at the beginning of the GFC). On the other hand, the reinforced position of the EU institutions, and particularly of the Commission, is mitigated by the fact that the crisis frameworks have been very generous and flexible, allowing, at the onset of crises, the approval of all measures proposed by the Member States (for example, between 2008 and 2011 in the case of the GFC). This flexible approach has also entailed risks for cohesion in the internal market and therefore for relationships between Member States that can afford more state aid and those that cannot. Some of the risks associated with the TFs, also for procedural rights and transparency, have been underlined in reports published by the European Parliament and the ECA.

Finally, the intense coordination of the crisis responses at EU level since the 2008 GFC may have accelerated an 'invisible' transformation, which was perceptible before, towards the use of (national) state aid to achieve EU objectives, and more recently towards the adoption of EU (as opposed to national) financial instruments to cope with crises. In other words, part of the legacy of the response of the EU institutions to recent crises in this field is a reinforced trend towards *EU aid* and not (only) *state aid*, the RRF being the best example. In this regard, the Commission has recently held, in relation to the Ukraine crisis, that '[t]he Temporary Crisis Framework was adopted on 23 March 2022 and first amended on 20 July 2022, *to complement* the Winter Preparedness Package and *in line with* the REPowerEU Plan objectives.'[107] Similarly, some authors have recently inquired whether 'EU federalist Covid-19 aid to EU airlines' could be more advantageous than the existing framework based on *state aid*.[108] We believe, to conclude, that it would indeed be positive to have a more centralized response to future crises in a spirit of cohesion and solidarity, and that the recent case law of the Court of Justice, in Grand Chamber formation, reinforces this trend by highlighting that 'the Union budget is one of the principal instruments for giving practical effect, in the Union's policies and activities, to the principle of solidarity'.[109] For state aid control, this could ultimately entail a dramatic shift in its relevance and purpose which could end up as the most far-reaching legacy of recent crises.

[107] See the Commission's press release: 'State aid: Commission prolongs and amends Temporary Crisis Framework, 28 October 2022, Brussels, https://ec.europa.eu/commission/presscorner/detail/en/IP_22_6468, accessed 17 October 2024. Emphasis added.

[108] Luis Martín-Domingo and Juan Carlos Martín, 'The Effect of COVID-Related EU State Aid on the Level Playing Field for Airlines' (2022) 14(4) 2368 *Sustainability* 1–14.

[109] C–156/21 *Hungary v Parliament and Council* EU:C:2022:97, para 129; and C–157/21 *Poland v Parliament and Council*, EU:C:2022:98, para 147. See also Opinion of AG Campos Sánchez-Bordona, in Case C–156/21 *Hungary v Parliament and Council*, EU:C:2021:974, para 96: 'The European Union has a budget that provides it with the means necessary to attain its objectives and carry through its policies. Without prejudice to other revenue, the budget is financed from own resources (Article 311 TFEU) in accordance with provisions laid down in a decision of the Council. The budget is the instrument of EU law which, each year, translates the principle of solidarity into financial terms and it is of constitutional importance.' The AG referred in this regard to the following article co-authored by the President of the Court of Justice: Koen Lenaerts and Stanislas Adam, 'La solidarité, valeur commune aux États membres et principe fédératif de l'Union européenne' (2021) 57 Cahiers de droit européen 307–417.

6

Energy Policy

Integration by Stealth and Crisis-driven Change

Sandra Eckert and Ole Windahl Pedersen***

6.1 Introduction

While the history of European integration of energy policy dates back to the Treaties establishing the European Coal and Steel Community (ECSC) in 1952 and the European Economic Community (EEC) and European Atomic Energy Community (Euratom) in 1958, it was only in 2009, with the Lisbon Treaty, that a supranational competence in this policy field was formally recognized in primary law.[1] Over several decades, energy policy, with the exception of nuclear energy policy, developed in the absence of a policy-specific Treaty basis, and only after 2009, when the Treaty of Lisbon entered into force, could integration take place with reference to an energy chapter in the Treaties. That said, the Treaty basis soon proved insufficient in view of the actual need for change when several crises affected the field of energy policy and law. These crises include the climate crisis, the energy (supply) crisis, the COVID-19 crisis, and the war in Ukraine.

This chapter revisits key features of energy policy integration prior to Lisbon, presents the policy framework introduced with the Lisbon Treaty, and analyses the type of change that has occurred post-Lisbon. In doing so, we engage with the question of whether the recent episode of crisis-driven integration is better understood as a process of path dependency or, instead, as a process of innovative and path-breaking change.

6.2 Energy Policy before and after the Treaty of Lisbon

Energy policy is a highly relevant policy field to study in the context of this volume, which discusses changes in European Union (EU) rule-making short of Treaty change. For over five decades prior to the Treaty of Lisbon, a European energy policy emerged and developed in the absence of a dedicated Treaty basis, whereas the recent phase of

* Chair of Comparative Politics at Friedrich-Alexander-Universität Erlangen-Nürnberg.
** Professor of Environmental Law at Aarhus Universitet.

[1] Sandra Eckert, 'The Governance of Markets, Sustainability and Supply. Toward a European Energy Policy' (2016) 12 Journal of Contemporary European Research 502–517; Michèle Knodt and Marc Ringel, 'European Union Energy Policy: A Discourse Perspective' in Michèle Knodt and Jörg Kemmerzell (eds), *Handbook of Energy Governance in Europe* (Springer 2022) 121–142.

Sandra Eckert and Ole Windahl Pedersen, *Energy Policy* In: *EU Regulatory Responses to Crises*. Edited by: Diane Fromage, Adrienne Héritier, and Paul Weismann, Oxford University Press.
DOI: 10.1093/9780198913825.003.0006

integration with an express Treaty basis has been relatively short. Consequently, there is much to learn from the initial long phase of integration by stealth.[2] In this section, we therefore first provide an overview of the pre-Lisbon phase, followed by an introduction to the policy framework established with the Treaty of Lisbon and, finally, a discussion of recent advances in a context of polycrisis.

6.2.1 A long story of integration by stealth

The initial phase of European integration was characterized by a strong focus on energy issues.[3] While the Treaties establishing the ECSC, in 1952, and Euratom, in 1958, put energy-related issues front and centre, a relatively long phase of stagnation followed until market integration was commenced in the late 1980s.[4] The ECSC Treaty, terminated in 2002, created a common market in coal and steel, combining a political and economic rationale in the post-war period, yet without envisaging energy market integration, which at the time was considered incompatible with the peculiarities of the electricity and gas sectors.[5] The Euratom Treaty, still in force today, established some selective supranational competence. At the same time, it left considerable leeway to the Member States, who were themselves keen to safeguard their autonomy on strategic issues.[6] Several energy-related initiatives launched in the following two decades ran short of garnering political support.[7] In view of energy supply issues, the European Commission urged Member States to cooperate on related issues as early as 1958,[8] and by 1964 Member States had declared that they were willing to cooperate on energy policy and integrate energy markets; however, no action followed.[9] Similarly, the oil crisis in the 1970s did not trigger cooperation at supranational level, but was largely tackled bilaterally or at the international level.[10] Meanwhile, action inside the Community was characterized by limited intergovernmental cooperation, with the adoption of the energy strategies agreed in 1974 and 1986.[11] As a result, energy policy was considered one of the weakest areas of European integration well into the 1990s.[12]

[2] Giandomenico Majone, *Integration by Stealth* (OUP 2005).
[3] Janne H Matláry, *Energy Policy in the European Union* (Macmillan 1997) 14–19.
[4] Eckert, 'The Governance of Markets, Sustainability and Supply' (n 1) 507–08.
[5] The Intergovernmental Committee established by the Messina Conference, 'Rapport des chefs de délégation aux ministres des affaires étrangères' (1956) 126–33.
[6] Pamela Barnes, 'Security of Energy Supply in the New Europe: A Role for the European Atomic Energy Community in the European Union's Neighbourhood Policy?' (2008) 4 Journal of Contemporary European Research 107, 111.
[7] Robert Black, 'Plus ca change, plus c'est le même chose: Nine Governments in Search of a Common Energy Policy' in Helen Wallace, William Wallace and Carole Webb (eds), *Policy-Making in the European Communities* (John Wiley & Sons 1977) 80–91.
[8] EEC, 'First General Report on the Activities of the Community' (1958) 48–49.
[9] Johannes Pollack, Samuel R Schubert and Peter Slominski, *Die Energiepolitik der EU* (Facultas 2010) 71.
[10] Black (n 7) 188–91.
[11] Council Resolution of 17 September 1974 concerning a new energy policy strategy for the Community [1974] OJ C153/1; Council Resolution of 16 September 1986 concerning new energy policy goals of the Community for 1995 and the convergence of the policy of the member states [1986] OJ C241/1.
[12] Stephen George, 'Energy' in Stephen George (ed), *Politics and Policy in the European Community* (OUP 1991) 55; Stephen Padgett, 'The Single European Energy Market: The Politics of Realization' (1992) 30 Journal of Common Market Studies 53.

Supranational agenda-setting proved more promising once the Single European Act,[13] in force since 1987, laid down the goal of market integration and established a European competence in environmental policy, both avenues for energy-related measures based on primary law. In the following years, the European Commission issued several initiatives, for example the 1988 strategy paper 'The Internal Energy Market',[14] the 1989 legislative proposals on the transmission of gas [15] and electricity,[16] and the 1990 communication on 'Energy and Environment'.[17] Moreover, European competence in the area of Trans-European Networks (TENs), laid down in the Maastricht Treaty, in force since 1993, facilitated infrastructure-related energy projects. Market integration both in the electricity sector (, and in gas , was finally launched towards the end of the 1990s.[18] These directives allowed for considerable divergence at national level with regard to issues such as ownership of, and access to, energy infrastructure, and the institutional set-up of energy regulation. Using its prerogatives in environmental policy, the European Commission proposed various energy-related measures to tackle sustainability issues, and by 2001 a non-binding target for the share of renewable energy had been set at the European level (Directive 2001/77/EC). A further step in market integration was taken in 2003 with the adoption of a second legislative energy package including directives on electricity (2003/54/EC) and gas (2003/55/EC), this time with more prescriptive requirements regarding access to infrastructure andthe introduction of independent regulatory agencies. The Commission also sought to move ahead with its sustainability agenda, with its Roadmap on Renewable Energy and the Communication '20 20 by 2020' ,[19] which focused on achieving an increase in renewables, energy efficiency, and emission reduction.

6.2.2 A Treaty-based policy framework

The Treaty of Lisbon, which was adopted in 2007 and entered into force in 2009, established a shared competence between the EU and the Member States in the field of energy policy (Article 4 ofthe Treaty on the Functioning ofthe European Union (TFEU)). According to this energy policy framework, the ordinary legislative procedure applies, yet with some notable exceptions: tax issues are excluded and supranational law shall

[13] Single European Act OJ L 169, 29.6.1987, pp 1–28.

[14] The Internal Energy Market (Commission Working Document) COM (88) 238 of 2 May 1988.

[15] Towards Completion of the Internal Market for Natural Gas COM (89) 334 of 6 September 1989.

[16] Proposal for a Council Directive on the transit of electricity through transmission grids COM (89) 336 of 20 July 1989.

[17] Communication from the Commission to the Council on energy and the environment. COM (89) 369 of 8 February 1990.

[18] Directive 96/92/EC of the European Parliament and of the Council of 19 December 1996 concerning common rules for the internal market in electricity OJ L 27, 30.1.1997, pp 20–29 and Directive 98/30/EC of the European Parliament and of the Council of 22 June 1998 concerning common rules for the internal market in natural gas OJ L 204, 21.7.1998, pp 1–12.

[19] Communication from the Commission to the Council and the European Parliament, Renewable Energy Road Map Renewable energies in the 21st century: building a more sustainable future, COM (2006) 848 final of 10 January 2007.

not interfere with national choices concerning the energy mix (Article 194 TFEU). A significant driver behind the formal recognition of EU energy policy in the Lisbon Treaty was the energy supply crisis triggered by Russia in 2006.[20] Furthermore, a so-called 'solidarity clause' placed in the chapter on economic policy (Article 122(1) TFEU) was introduced to tackle security of supply issues, facilitating a basis for co-operation between Member States in cases of energy shortages. As a result, European policymakers no longer have to rely on prerogatives on market integration, environmental policy, or competition law in order to adopt energy policy measures, as they were accustomed to in the past.[21]

Subsequently, the EU energy *acquis* was further consolidated in the areas of both market integration and sustainability. A third energy package governing electricity and gas,[22] as well as a new directive on renewables that imposed binding targets on Member States, were adopted in 2009.[23] The energy package created a new Agency for the Cooperation of Energy Regulators (ACER) which, however, remained highly dependent on the cooperation of national regulators.[24] A more distinctive shift of competence occurred with regard to the involvement of private actors,[25] where the third energy package attributed a formal mandate to transmission system operators (TSOs), notably in the area of drafting network codes, with the creation of European Networks for Transmission System Operators for both electricity and gas (ENTSO-E and ENTSO-G).

While the rules on energy policy introduced in the Lisbon Treaty endorsed the existing energy *acquis* at the level of primary law and facilitated further policy measures,[26] they did not tip the balance between supranational and Member State powers. Instead, they safeguarded national competencies in key areas such as the energy mix and external supply. Compared to the Treaty revision, however, several crises that have occurred throughout the new millennium may have been more consequential and conducive to change—an issue to be discussed in the next section.

[20] Laura Rodríguez-Fernández, Ana B. Fernández Carvajal and Luis M. Ruiz-Gómez, 'Evolution of European Union's Energy Security in Gas Supply during Russia–Ukraine Gas Crises (2006–2009)' (2020) 30 Energy Strategy Reviews 1, 2; Carl-Fredrik Bergström, 'EU Rulemaking in Response to Crisis: the Emergence of the Principle of Energy Solidarity and its Use' (2023) 6 Nordic Journal of European Law 100.

[21] Mehdi P Amineh and Wina HJ Crijns-Graus, 'Rethinking EU Energy Security considering Past Trends and Future Prospects' (2014) 13 Perspectives on Global Development and Technology 757.

[22] Directive 2009/72/EC of the European Parliament and of the Council of 13 July 2009 concerning common rules for the internal market in electricity and repealing Directive 2003/54/EC, OJ L 211, 14.8.2009, pp 55–93 and Directive 2009/73/EC of the European Parliament and of the Council of 13 July 2009 concerning common rules for the internal market in natural gas and repealing Directive 2003/55/EC, OJ L 211, 14.8.2009, pp 94–136.

[23] Directive 2009/28/EC of the European Parliament and of the Council of 23 April 2009 on the promotion of the use of energy from renewable sources and amending and subsequently repealing Directives 2001/77/EC and 2003/30/EC, OJ L 140, 5.6.2009, pp 16–62.

[24] Regulation (EC) No 713/2009 of the European Parliament and of the Council of 13 July 2009 establishing an Agency for the Cooperation of Energy Regulators, OJ L 211, 14.8.2009, pp 1–14.

[25] Sandra Eckert and Burkard Eberlein, 'Private Authority in Tackling Cross-border Issues. The Hidden Path of Integrating European Energy Markets' (2020) 42 Journal of European Integration 59.

[26] Burkard Eberlein, 'Inching towards a Common Energy Policy: Entrepreneurship, Incrementalism, and Windows of Opportunity' in Jeremy Richardson (ed), *Constructing a Policy-Making State? Policy Dynamics in the EU* (OUP 2013) 147–169.

6.2.3 Recent advances in energy policy in a context of polycrisis

Recent advances in energy policy have emerged in a context of polycrisis. In the context of energy policy specifically, three crises stand out. The first of these is the energy supply crisis provoked by Russia since 2006, and exacerbated by Russia's annexation of Crimea and the war in Ukraine.[27] The second is the climate crisis, which has moved sustainability issues of energy policy, including energy efficiency, the increased use of renewables, decarbonization, and emission reduction, to the top of the European agenda. Finally, the COVID-19 crisis has accelerated the rollout of the European Green Deal,[28] and the halt in oil production it caused[29] has further revealed the EU's vulnerability in terms of energy security.

While the issue of energy security had already gained salience as a consequence of the 2004 and 2007 EU enlargements,[30] it was the shortage of gas supply that occurred in 2006 that urged policymakers to take action.[31] Russia's annexation of Crimea in March 2014 brought energy security issues to the fore[32] and contributed to the energy union initiative launched in 2015[33] by Commission President Jean-Claude Juncker at the beginning of his 2014–19 term. Its adoption proved difficult due to diverging positions: Eastern European Member States prioritized security of supply; Scandinavian and Western European Member States prioritized sustainability. This stalemate prevented the EU Member States from agreeing upon either binding national renewable energy or energy efficiency targets to be achieved by 2030.[34] Moreover, the EU imposed sanctions against Russia from 2014 onwards, followed by a novel surge of sanctions after Russia's invasion of Ukraine in 2022, which included an embargo on Russian coal and subsequently also a partial oil embargo.[35] The war might have had significant

[27] Rodríguez-Fernández, Fernández Carvajal and Ruiz-Gómez (n 20); Pedro Camacho and Carla Fernandes, 'The European Union and Security of Supply' in Carla Fernandes and Teresa Rodrigues (eds), *The Future of Energy: Prospective Scenarios on EU–Russia Relations* (Nova 2019); Maria R Freire, 'Russia Energy Relations: Geopoliticisation and the EU Perspective' in Fernandes and Rodrigues (eds) (ibid); Aleksei Grivach, 'Russia–EU Energy Security Issues and Prospects: View from Moscow' in Fernandes and Rodrigues (eds) (ibid); Francesco Sassi, 'The Geopolitics of the EU–Russia Gas Trade: Reviewing Power in International Gas Markets' in Farhad Taghizadeh-Hesary and Dayong Zhang (eds), *The Handbook of Energy Policy* (Springer 2023) 33–67.

[28] Sandra Eckert, 'The European Green Deal and the EU's Regulatory Power in Times of Crisis' (2021) 59 Journal of Common Market Studies 81.

[29] Peterson K Ozili and Ercan Ozen, 'Global Energy Crisis' in Kiran Sood and others (eds), *The Impact of Climate Change and Sustainability Standards on the Insurance Market* (Wiley 2023) 439–454.

[30] David Buchan, 'Energy Policy. Sharp Challenges and Rising Ambitions' in Helen Wallace and others (eds), *Policy-Making in the European Union* (OUP 2020) 321–342.

[31] Rodríguez-Fernández, Fernández Carvajal and Ruiz-Gómez (n 20) 436, 439; Tomas Maltby, 'European Union Energy Policy Integration: A Case of European Commission Policy Entrepreneurship and Increasing Supranationalism' (2013) 55 Energy Policy 435.

[32] Kacper Szulecki and Kirsten Westphal, 'Taking Security Seriously in EU Energy Governance: Crimean Shock and the Energy Union' in Kacper Szulecki (ed), *Energy Security in Europe: Divergent Perceptions and Policy Challenges* (Springer 2018) 177–202.

[33] Jean-Arnold Vinois, 'The Road to Energy Union' in Svein S Andersen, Andreas Goldthau and Nick Sitter (eds), *Energy Union: Europe's New Liberal Mercantilism?* (Palgrave 2017) 27–50.

[34] Michèle Knodt, 'Instruments and Modes of Governance in EU Climate and Energy Policy: From Energy Union to the European Green Deal' in Tim Rayner and others (eds), *Handbook on European Union Climate Change Policy and Politics* (Edward Elgar 2023) 206.

[35] Discussed by Ingmar von Homeyer, Sebastian Oberthür and Claire Dupont, 'Implementing the European Green Deal during the Evolving Energy Crisis' (2022) 60 Journal of Common Market Studies 125, 130.

ramifications for the EU's future energy policy, as it amplified an energy crisis that could have weakened the East–West divide among Member States in the EU's climate policy due to the unifying element of an external threat. However, von Homeyer and others find that while the invasion initially appeared to result in political support for a more ambitious approach, this trend did not persist.[36] Similarly, the EU's sanctions would prove to have a limited impact on the energy sector: while the Russian invasion of Ukraine and the EU's response triggered a substantial exodus of EU businesses doing business in Russia,[37] there was only partial exit in the energy sector.[38]

The transition towards a more sustainable energy system has been high on the EU's political agenda over the past two decades, and the EU's Treaty-based competences in environmental policy facilitated the emergence of energy policy as a European competence from the outset of European integration. Widespread societal mobilization on climate change in recent years has heightened the pressure on policymakers at both national and European levels to take action. The European Parliament and European Commission responded to these pressures by putting climate change mitigation and adaptation at the top of their political agendas: the European Parliament declared a 'climate emergency' in November 2019 and called for further action, and in December 2019 the European Commission with its new president, Ursula von der Leyen, put forward its Green Deal agenda.[39] The Green Deal proposal puts renewed emphasis on the existing target of climate neutrality by increasing the emission reduction target for 2030 to 50 per cent.[40] Moreover, decarbonization of the energy system is seen as 'critical to reach climate objectives'.[41] The package envisages a revision of the renewable energy directive that aims to increase the 32 per cent target to at least 40 per cent renewable energy sources in the EU's overall energy mix by 2030. Finally, the REPowerEU plan, adopted in May 2022, aims to phase out Russian fossil fuel imports and diversify energy supply while accelerating the clean energy transition.[42] In the literature, the Green Deal measures have been met with criticism regarding both scope and governance. Knodt criticizes the lack of hard governance as the 'Fit for 55' package 'does nothing to adjust the Governance Regulation to harden the soft governance in energy efficiency or even further develop the harder soft governance in renewable energies'.[43] Similarly, von Homeyer and others argue that while the climate law and the 'Fit for 55' package 'entail a significant upgrade of the EU's climate policy framework', these upgrades are not sufficient 'compared to the scale of the climate challenge'.[44]

[36] ibid.
[37] As documented by a research team taking stock of business disinvolvement at Yale University: Jeffrey Sonnenfeld and others, 'Business Retreats and Sanctions Are Crippling the Russian Economy. Measures of Current Economic Activity and Economic Outlook Point to Devastating Impact on Russia' (2022) <https://ssrn.com/abstract=4167193> accessed 16 March 2024.
[38] Sandra Eckert, 'Business Power and the Geoeconomic Turn in the Single European Market' (forthcoming) Journal of Common Market Studies 1.
[39] European Commission, 'The European Green Deal' COM (2019) 640 final.
[40] ibid 4.
[41] ibid 6.
[42] Discussed by von Homeyer, Oberthür and Dupont (n 35) 130.
[43] Knodt (n 34) 211.
[44] von Homeyer, Oberthür and Dupont (n 35) 127.

6.3 The Energy Policy Toolbox and Institutional Set-up

As discussed in the Introduction to this volume, European policymakers employ various measures in order to bring about policy change short of Treaty revision. For energy policy, this was not a new development post-Lisbon, but rather the default situation throughout the lengthy process of policy integration up until Lisbon. We will thus not restrict our discussion to this last phase, but rather question whether the kind of toolbox employed has changed during the last, crisis-driven stage as compared with before. We find that while, in the past, policymaking combined 'borrowed' Treaty competencies by using a combination of soft governance, agency governance, network governance, and private governance, a new and more recent trend is the use of geoeconomic policy tools. We differentiate between governance modes according to the degree of hierarchy involved and the type of actor constellation.[45] Agency governance involves hierarchical steering by a public institution, namely a national or European agency. The term 'private governance' is used in a broad sense to cover all kinds of private actor involvement throughout the process of policy-making, including self-regulation by industry.[46] Network governance relates to instances of non-hierarchical coordination among public and/or private actors. Finally, soft governance is characterized by non-hierarchical coordination leading to outcomes that are not binding. It is 'soft' in that it does not involve sanctions but relies on mechanisms of reputation and learning. In the European context, it is usually initiated and monitored by the European Commission, combined with a process of voluntary coordination between the Member States.

6.3.1 Borrowing policy competencies and soft governance

Energy policy integration through the 'backdoor'[47] has had a long trajectory whereby the European Commission has used market integration, competition law and environmental prerogatives set out in the Treaties to set the energy policy agenda. Examples from the second energy package include Regulation 1228/2003 on conditions for access to the network for cross-border exchanges in electricity[48] and the second Electricity Directive 2003/54/EC[49] (both now repealed), both of which were adopted under the general competences with respect to the establishing of the internal market. More recent examples emerge specifically in the context where the

[45] See also Tanja A Börzel, 'European Governance – Negotiation and Competition in the Shadow of Hierarchy' (2010) 48 Journal of Common Market Studies 191; applied to the energy sector by Eckert, 'The Governance of Markets, Sustainability and Supply' (n 1).

[46] Adrienne Héritier and Sandra Eckert, 'New Modes of Governance in the Shadow of Hierarchy: Self-Regulation by Industry in Europe' (2008) 28 Journal of Public Policy 113.

[47] Amineh and Crijns-Graus (n 21).

[48] Regulation (EC) No 1228/2003 of the European Parliament and of the Council of 26 June 2003 on conditions for access to the network for cross-border exchanges in electricity, OJ L 176, 15/07/2003, pp 1–10.

[49] Directive 2003/54/EC of the European Parliament and of the Council of 26 June 2003 concerning common rules for the internal market in electricity and repealing Directive 96/92/EC, OJ L 176, 15.7.2003, pp 37–56.

competences in the energy chapter overlap with those found in the environmental chapter and scope emerges for adopting measures under both. For example, the flagship European Emissions Trading System (ETS) Directive was based on the environment competences in Article 192 TFEU, whereas the initiatives relating to renewable energy and efficiency (eg Directive 2018/2002 amending Directive 2012/27/EU on energy efficiency) were based on the energy competence in Article 194 TFEU.

Soft governance is another solution frequently used not only to compensate for the lack of supranational competencies and to facilitate policy coordination but also to prepare the ground for more far-reaching European measures. Various energy-related initiatives followed the logic of soft governance, such as the coordination efforts as part of the Europe 2020[50] and Energy 20 20 by 2020 strategies .[51] In essence, soft governance helped to bridge multiple policy areas and levels of governance in the past.[52] Post-Lisbon, the energy union that was introduced, both with a view to reducing energy dependence and in reaction to Russia's annexation of Crimea in March 2014, strongly relies on 'soft governance with harder elements',[53] especially in the area of the energy transition. In particular, the Regulation on the Governance of the Energy Union (Regulation 2018/1999), adopted in 2018,[54] has 'hardened'[55] soft governance in the energy field, notably by introducing more specific and stringent requirements for Member States. While the energy union still relies substantially on Member State input through the development of national energy and climate plans (NECPs) as part of long-term planning, the Regulation introduces a process of regular evaluation in order to assess whether these plans are ambitious enough and in line with the targets of the 2030 framework. Importantly, the recommendations by the Commission based on this Regulation are then seen as 'necessary changes to the NECPs'[56] in the event of shortcomings; that is, there is a mandatory element in the governance architecture relying on soft modes of coordination.

6.3.2 Regulatory networks, agencies, and private governance

Energy governance relies heavily on network governance, both public and private, to this day, whereas supranational centralization has been limited in scope. ACER, the

[50] Communication from the Commission, A strategy for smart, sustainable and inclusive growth, COM(2010) 2020 final of 3 March 2020.

[51] Communication from the Commission to the European Parliament, the Council, the European Economic and Social Committee and the Committee of the Regions - 20 20 by 2020 - Europe's climate change opportunity, COM (2008) 30 final of 23 January 2008.

[52] Eckert, 'The Governance of Markets, Sustainability and Supply' (n 1).

[53] Knodt and Ringel (n 1).

[54] Regulation (EU) 2018/1999 of the European Parliament and of the Council of 11 December 2018 on the Governance of the Energy Union and Climate Action, OJ L 328, 21.12.2018, pp 1–77.

[55] Michèle Knodt, Marc Ringel and Rainer Müller, '"Harder" Soft Governance in the European Energy Union' (2020) 22 Journal of Environmental Policy and Planning 787.

[56] ibid.

agency for the cooperation of energy regulators created by the third legislative energy package (Regulation 713/2009), draws substantially on the resources and input of national regulatory authorities.[57] This has been no different after the legislative package adopted in 2019 introduced incremental rather than innovative change.[58]

The shift towards agency governance has been limited for both legal and political reasons. First, legally, because the European Commission faces constitutional obstacles in delegating executive powers: a limitation widely discussed with reference to the so-called '*Meroni* doctrine' established by a CJEU ruling in 1958,[59] even if the relative strength of the doctrine has been gradually eroded. Second, politically, because of the Commission's general reluctance to establish a powerful agency which would compete with its own powers. And third, also politically, because Member States are opposed to shifting regulatory competencies towards the European level, thus disempowering their own agencies.[60]

Another characteristic element of energy governance is the role of private governance, which occurred mainly due to the lack of centralized governance capacity of public actors. The private actors—with the caveat that some are publicly owned—particularly relevant for energy governance are transmission system operators (TSOs). In Europe, TSOs are organized in a dedicated association of European transmission system operators (ETSOs), created in 1999, and draw on a legacy of voluntary cross-border cooperation that has given them significant private authority on technical and infrastructure-related matters.[61] While it established a comparatively weak EU-level agency due to a lack of political agreement, the third energy package gave a formal mandate to TSOs to be part of the regulatory process with the creation of European Networks for Transmission System Operators for both electricity and gas (ENTSO-E and ENTSO-G). This shift was particularly strong in the area of electricity, where ENTSO-E prepares the network codes for electricity. These grid operators are key actors in the implementation of the internal energy market, if not actually co-regulators.[62]

[57] Eckert, 'The Governance of Markets, Sustainability and Supply' (n 1) 511.

[58] Sandra Eckert, 'European Administrative Networks, Private Networks and Agencies: Coexisting, Cooperating or Competing?' (2022) 29 Journal of European Public Policy 1610; Sandra Eckert, 'Supranational Authorities and Private Actors as Drivers of Single Market Integration? The State of the Union in Electricity and Banking' (2022) 44 Journal of European Integration 19.

[59] Merijn Chamon, 'EU Agencies: between Meroni and Romano or the Devil and the Deep Blue Sea' (2011) 48 Common Market Law Review 1055; Giandomenico Majone, 'Independent Agencies and the Delegation Problem: Theoretical and Normative Dimensions' in Bernard Steuenberg and Frans van Vught (eds), *Political Institutions and Public Policy* (Kluwer Academic Publishers 1997) 139–156; Ellen Vos, 'Reforming the European Commission: What Role to Play for EU Agencies?' (2000) 37 Common Market Law Review 1113.

[60] David Coen and Mark Thatcher, 'Network Governance and Multi-level Delegation: European Networks of Regulatory Agencies' (2008) 28 Journal of Public Policy 49.

[61] Eckert and Eberlein (n 25); Sandra Eckert, *Corporate Power and Regulation: Consumers and the Environment in the European Union* (Palgrave 2019).

[62] Eckert, *Corporate Power and Regulation* (n 61); Emmanuelle Mathieu, *Regulatory Delegation in the European Union: Networks, Committees and Agencies* (Palgrave 2016).

6.3.3 A move towards geoeconomic policy measures

The EU emerged as a geoeconomic player with its response to Russia's invasion of Ukraine, but also when it took measures in reaction to the changed geopolitical context when big economic powers, such as China and the United States, moved away from the liberal international order by adopting policy measures that challenged free trade and the open economy. In a nutshell, geoeconomics measures can be defined as political interventions that seek to proactively shape economic relations of interdependence,[63] strive for power maximization, and focus on relative rather than absolute gains.[64] These measures can take the form of 'sticks' as well as 'carrots'.[65] The former seek to reduce another state's wealth and power, for instance by imposing sanctions or blocking foreign investment, while the latter aim to enlarge one state's sphere of influence by making other states more dependent on them, for instance by means of investments or trade partnerships.

This shift towards geoeconomics has materialized in energy policy in various ways. The most obvious example is the economic sanctions imposed on Russia since February 2022, often discussed as an instance of 'weaponized'[66] use of the EU's economic policy tools. As documented by the so-called Yale list that takes stock of business disinvolvement from Russia,[67] European energy companies have either fully or partially exited the Russian market,[68] pursuing the EU's general strategy to massively reduce energy dependency on Russia. The energy-specific crisis response proposed by the European Commission in March 2022 is another indicator of a significant shift away from its typical toolbox.[69] Rather than suggesting formal regulatory measures, most measures involve financial compensation at the level of retail as well as wholesale markets through income support, price caps, reduction of taxation, and the adoption of a temporary state aid framework.

Similarly, the framework to accelerate the deployment of renewable energy is remarkable in that it temporarily suspends key principles of European environmental

[63] Henrique Choer Moraes and Mikael Wigell, 'The Emergence of Strategic Capitalism. Geoeconomics, Corporate Statecraft and the Repurposing of the Global Economy' (2020) FIIA Working Paper 117, 6 <https://ssrn.com/abstract=3707290> accessed 16 March 2024.

[64] ibid 8; Edward N Luttwak, 'From Geopolitics to Geo-Economics. Logic of Conflict, Grammar of Commerce' (1990) 20 The National Interest 17.

[65] Mikael Wigell and Antto Vihma, 'Geopolitics versus Geoeconomics: The Case of Russia's Geostrategy and its Effects on the EU' (2016) 92 International Affairs 605, 608.

[66] Henry Farrell and Abraham L Newman, 'Weaponized Interdependence: How Global Economic Networks Shape State Coercion' (2019) 44 International Security 42.

[67] Sonnenfeld and others (n 37).

[68] Eckert, 'Business Power and the Geoeconomic Turn in the Single European Market' (n 38).

[69] Communication from the Commission to the European Parliament, the European Council, the Council, the European Economic and Social Committee and the Committee of the Regions security of supply and affordable energy prices: options for immediate measures and preparing for next winter, COM (2022) 138 final of 23 March 2022.

policy—[70]notably those laid down in the EU Birds and Habitats Directives (see section 6.4.2 below)—in order to speed up the energy transition, with a double geoeconomic objective of reducing dependence on external supply and creating a comparative advantage in the context of international competition. The fact that the constitutional basis of the Regulation was found in Article 122(1) TFEU is significant for two separate yet related reasons. It highlights not only the urgency of the matter, and thereby the ability to adopt a response when faced with a crisis, but also the relative permanence of relying on this option going forward; that is, having never been utilized as a constitutional basis in the context of energy before, Article 122(1) has subsequently been relied upon frequently. Another example is the EU's response to the US Inflation Reduction Act (IRA), which seeks to keep investment in the EU through the adoption of a temporary crisis and transition framework for state aid, adopted in March 2023 .[71] It provides more flexibility for national subsidies, seeks to speed up the process of state aid approval, extends the scope of block exemptions, facilitates subsidies for renewable energy technologies without long-winded EU notification process, allows Member States to implement tax breaks for companies in strategic sectors, and, importantly, establishes a new state aid category—anti-relocation investment aid which allows Member States to match foreign subsidies with a view to maintaining businesses *in situ*. The willingness to use the constitutional basis found in Article 107(2)(b) TFEU, which allows for state aid to remedy a serious disturbance in the economy of a Member State, underscores the willingness of the Commission to dispense with core rules of the EU *acquis* in times of crisis. In the case of state aid, this is arguably even more significant than in the context of environmental provisions, given the centrality and historical significance of the general prohibition of state aid in Article 107 TFEU. It is in this light that the limitations and conditions attached to the granting of aid ought to be understood. The limitations and conditions restrict not only the amount of aid afforded per undertaking but also the period over which it is granted.[72]

6.4 Energy Policy Crisis Responses—Path Dependency or Innovative Change?

Based on this discussion of the evolution of energy governance and the toolbox used, we will now revisit our initial research question of whether we have witnessed path dependency or innovative change in the post-Lisbon era in the field of energy policy.

[70] Council Regulation (EU) 2022/2577 of 22 December 2022 laying down a framework to accelerate the deployment of renewable energy OJ L 335, 29.12.2022, pp 36–44.

[71] Communication from the Commission Temporary Crisis and Transition Framework for State Aid measures to support the economy following the aggression against Ukraine by Russia 2023/C 101/03, OJ C 101, 17.3.2023, pp 3–46.

[72] ibid, at 2.2.

6.4.1 More of the same—elements of path dependency

European energy policy has evolved at a relatively slow pace given the initial focus on energy of both the ECSC and Euratom, and has, from the outset, sought to address a variety of policy goals, including security of energy supply. The idea of an internal energy market, initially conceived of by economic elites,[73] came to be accepted as the policy paradigm of European energy policy[74] in the context of the Community's Single European Market agenda in the 1980s. Concerns with regard to the security of supply varied over time, due to both the international context and internal factors. Europe's dependence on external gas supplies, for instance, came to the fore with the EU's Eastern enlargement.[75] As a result, the security of supply issue became so dominant in policy discourse that a 'securitization' of energy issues has been witnessed.[76] A more recent shift in priorities occurred with respect to sustainability issues in the context of Europe's leadership aspiration on climate policy issues.[77] In a nutshell, EU energy policy seeks to square the circle of policy goals relating to market integration, security of supply, and sustainability, thus aiming to bridge various policy initiatives in order to achieve synergies. In order to move forward in view of multiple challenges, European energy policy has frequently combined the formulation of broad overarching commitments with the implementation of specific, often technocratic, changes.

This familiar pattern, recognizable from the EU's history of regulating environmental and other policy challenges in general, has also materialized in the recent phase of polycrisis. On this reading, the EU's responses take the combined form of a series of changes made across a range of existing legal regimes while adding new rules to an already bewildering regulatory landscape. The regulatory acts and legal initiatives adopted by the EU, whether in response to the climate emergency or to the energy crisis following the Russian invasion of Ukraine, are linked and entangled, and often overlap with one another. The reasons for this are obvious if one considers the clear co-benefits arising from the promotion of renewable energy. Any such initiatives (eg Council Regulation 2022/2577) will simultaneously promote energy security and diversity of supply while also delivering clear environmental benefits, aiding the EU in meeting its climate change objectives. In other words, a policy synergy emerges as responses adopted in one policy area are likely to contribute towards meeting objectives in another area. As a result, what follows does not necessarily present a clear-cut demarcation between different crises. However, as will become clear in section 6.5.1,

[73] Matláry (n 3) 19.

[74] Francis McGowan, 'Can the European Union's Market Liberalism Ensure Energy Security in a Time of "Economic Nationalism"?' (2008) 4 Journal of Contemporary European Research 90; Richard Youngs, 'Foreign Policy and Energy Security: Markets, Pipelines and Politics' in Vicki L Birchfield and John S Duffield (eds), *Toward a Common European Union Energy Policy: Problems, Progress, and Prospects* (Palgrave 2011) 41–60.

[75] Maltby (n 31).

[76] Michal Natorski and Anna Herranz Surrallés, 'Securitizing Moves to Nowhere? The Framing of the European Union's Energy Policy' (2008) 4 Journal of Contemporary European Research 71.

[77] Sebastian Oberthür and Claire Dupont, 'The European Union's International Climate Leadership: Towards a Grand Climate Strategy?' (2021) 28 Journal of European Public Policy 1095.

the emerging policy synergy is somewhat superficial, as a key characteristic of some of the regulatory responses adopted in the area of energy policy in response to the Russian invasion of Ukraine stand out because they aim to suspend important parts of the environmental *acquis*.

This points to important trade-offs in the realization of the EU's energy agenda.[78] More generally, the EU's 'market liberalism' has been found to conflict with 'economic nationalism', especially where security of supply issues have become increasingly important.[79] In this context, securitization strategies have been used by both EU and Member State actors to argue in favour of *and* against a further shift of governance capacity to the European level.[80] While, in the past, the 'green Europeanization' of energy policy overall has been more successful in terms of policy output when compared with security of supply issues, environmental issues are ultimately addressed in the internal market context.[81] There has, furthermore, been a shift towards a narrow focus on climate change goals, which arguably impinges on the realization of a wider sustainability agenda.[82] At the same time, climate policy integration has been judged to be insufficient in areas such as renewables and gas pipelines, to reach long-term climate policy objectives.[83]

6.4.2 Rebalancing policy goals—elements of innovative change

We see elements of innovative change where European policymakers have made clear policy choices that involve a rebalancing of goals and a departure from the ambition to foster synergies between market integration, security of supply, and sustainability. An illustrative example of this change is the so-called Emergency Regulation ,[84] which lays down a temporary framework to accelerate the development of renewable resources. The significance of this Regulation is underlined by the fact that, to our knowledge, this is one of the few examples where the emergency power provided for in Article 122(1) TFEU has ever been used.[85] The Regulation emphasizes the importance of renewable energy production by designating the 'planning, construction and operation' of renewable energy sources as being 'in the overriding public interest'. This, in itself, might seem an obvious point to make. But the real significance of designating renewable energy projects as being of 'overriding public interest' derives from its application in the

[78] Buchan (n 30).
[79] McGowan (n 74).
[80] Natorski and Herranz Surrallés (n 76).
[81] Israel Solorio, 'Bridging the Gap between Environmental Policy Integration and the EU's Energy Policy: Mapping out the "Green Europeanisation" of Energy Governance' (2011) 7 Journal of Contemporary European Research 396, 405.
[82] ibid.
[83] Claire Dupont and Sebastian Oberthür, 'Insufficient Climate Policy Integration in EU Energy Policy: The Importance of the Long-term Perspective' (2012) 8 Journal of Contemporary European Research 228.
[84] Council Regulation (EU) 2022/2577 of 22 December 2022 laying down a framework to accelerate the deployment of renewable energy, OJ L 335, 29.12.2022, pp 36–44.
[85] Leo Flynn, 'Article 122 TFEU' in Manuel Kellerbauer, Marcus Klamert and Jonathan Tomkin (eds), *The EU Treaties and the Charter of Fundamental Rights: A Commentary* (OUP 2019) 1282–1284.

context of the Habitats and Birds Directives and the Water Framework Directive.[86] In short, the preference given to renewable energy projects means that where renewable energy plants or installations negatively impact on special areas of conservation or where such projects result in the destruction or killing of wild birds, their nests, or eggs, these impacts are justified and the projects will override any legal protection given to protected areas and species. Moreover, the Emergency Regulation provides scope for measures derogating from habitats and species obligations that ordinarily restrict Member State actions (Article 6(4) Habitats Directive and Article 9(1)(a) Birds Directive). Similarly, environmental impacts from renewable energy installations which result in water bodies not achieving 'good status', as required under the Water Framework Directive, are permissible.

The Emergency Regulation also makes a number of significant changes to the decision-making procedures for solar energy equipment below 50kW capacity. As far as solar installations on buildings go, these are entirely exempted from environmental impact assessments otherwise required by the Environmental Impact Assessment (EIA) Directive.[87] What is more, the application process for such an installation must not exceed one month. When an authority does not respond to an application within that time limit, the project can be assumed to have been approved. Changes are also made with respect to approval processes for the upgrading of existing renewable energy facilities, so that the approval process cannot take longer than six months and environmental impact assessment requirements are narrowed to include only the increase in capacity. The speed-up of the application process for the approval of the installation of heat pumps is also included, which means the process can take no longer than three months.

Although the Emergency Regulation applies for only eighteen months, and is subject to review (Article 9), it signifies a clear direction for the future. Permanence of some of its key features are built into the new Renewable Energy Directive .[88] Changes include giving a higher priority to the collective obligation to ensure that the share of energy from renewable sources is at least 45 per cent by 2030, as opposed to 40 per cent (Article 1(2)). Such headline targets, significant as they are, are accompanied by a range of changes that are potentially even more substantial. The first of these is the adoption of a new tool of so-called 'go-to areas'/renewable acceleration areas, which are defined as locations 'particularly suitable for the installation of plants for the production of energy from renewable sources' (Article 1(1)(c)).

[86] Council Directive 92/43/EEC of 21 May 1992 on the conservation of natural habitats and of wild fauna and flora, [1992] OJ L20 and Directive 2009/147/EC of the European Parliament and of the Council of 30 November 2009 on the conservation of wild birds, [2009] OJ L20/7.

[87] Directive 2011/92/EU of the European Parliament and of the Council of 13 December 2011 on the assessment of the effects of certain public and private projects on the environment (codification), OJ L 26, 28.1.2012, pp 1–21.

[88] Directive (EU) 2023/2413 of the European Parliament and of the Council of 18 October 2023 amending Directive (EU) 2018/2001, Regulation (EU) 2018/1999 and Directive 98/70/EC as regards the promotion of energy from renewable sources, and repealing Council Directive (EU) 2015/652, OJ L, 2023/2413, 31.10.2023.

Member States are to adopt plans for the designation of locations as 'go-to'/renewable accelerating areas, and must do so within two years. The real significance, however, lies not so much in the creation of a new typology of locations but in the detailed rules of management which the Directive sets forward with respect to the administration of these 'go-to' areas. Specifically, the proposed changes anticipate a swift one-year decision of approval for projects located in these 'go-to' areas (with a maximum of six months for projects with a smaller energy output and a two-year application process deadline for renewable projects developed outside 'go-to' areas). This includes 'administrative permits to build, repower and operate plants for the production of energy from renewable sources, co-located energy storage facilities, as well as assets necessary for their connection to the grid'. In short, not only the energy structure itself but a variety of auxiliary facilities are included in this process. In addition, Member States must create specific one-stop shop points of contact for the applicant to engage with, creating a degree of administrative coherence which is often lacking in Member States' administrative regimes, covering spatial planning and land use (at various levels of administration), environmental issues, and energy and grid management issues.

Importantly, projects developed in the newly designated 'go-to' locations will be exempted from the environmental impact assessment requirements found in the EIA Directive. This is significant mainly because the EIA Directive is one of the core EU environmental law instruments and dates back to the first important wave of environmental legislation adopted by the EU prior to the adoption of the Single European Act, which famously introduced the environment as a specific policy area. Moreover, the relative importance of the EIA Directive has arguably increased over the years, as a result of the EU courts interpreting the Directive in ways that gave rise to a series of individual rights for Union citizens.[89] These developments notwithstanding, the Directive has over time caused frustration and has at times been perceived as a hindrance to strategic developments, including in the context of energy infrastructure. The attempt to streamline decision-making procedures for specific projects of particular interest is therefore not new. Exempting potentially large projects, depending on their locality, however, represents a significant change of priority. It must, of course, be borne in mind that 'go-to' areas are expected to be locations where the deployment of renewables will not have a significant environmental impact (eg not in Natura 2000 sites).[90] Moreover, the actual designation of 'go-to' locations is subject to an environmental impact assessment (and habitats assessments where applicable) prior to adoption, even if the individual projects are not subject to impact assessments. Arguably, it is specifically in, or close to, areas where projects may have a significant impact on designated habitats or species that the EIA Directive and the impact assessment under Article 6 of the Habitats Directive have exerted the strongest pressure. Significantly, the Emergency Regulation

[89] eg The Queen on the application of Delena Wells v Secretary of State for Transport, Local Government and the Regions, Judgment of the Court (Fifth Chamber), 7 January 2004 and World Wildlife Fund (WWF) and Others v Autonome Provinz Bozen and Others, Judgment of the Court (Sixth Chamber) of 16 September 1999.

[90] As made up by Special Areas of Conservation and Special Protection Areas designated under the Habitats Directive and the Birds Directive.

creates a presumption in favour of development of renewables by designating these as of being of 'overriding public interest'. This is of particular importance in the context of balancing competing public interests under (eg the Habitats Directive).

A range of other important initiatives worth highlighting, although they will not be explored in depth here, include the Renewed Resilience of the Critical Entities Directive (Resilience Directive) ,[91] which came into force in January 2023, requiring Member States to identify critical entities and essential services and subject these to regular risk assessments. Similarly, many of the above-discussed initiatives are contextualized by a series of other developments and decisions, including the G7 price cap on Russian oil, enacted in late 2022[92] The sanctions adopted against Russia, with their impact on energy relations in particular, constitute a 'weaponization'[93] of economic policy instruments and bring to the fore evidence of the geoeconomic turn of the single market.[94]

6.5 Conclusions

In conclusion, the changes to EU energy policy, both proposed and already adopted, highlight a series of thematic developments. These themes can be organized around the headings of speed and simplification (6.5.1) and the rebalancing of priorities (6.5.2).

6.5.1 Speed and simplification

An obvious theme emerging from the changes in energy policy introduced by EU institutions is that of speed. This applies on two levels: speed with respect to adopting legislation and speed with respect to domestic approval processes. For our purposes, the latter is the most relevant. Significantly, the instruments discussed above will demand significant changes to administrative approval procedures in Member States. This arguably presents a significant departure from traditional means of energy and environmental regulation in the EU. Traditionally, much of this regulation affords Member States a significant degree of leeway in relation to the precise application and approval methods at the Member State level. In addition to the requirement that certain types of project applications are now to be decided within set time limits (asking a lot of Member States), the proposed changes also include specific requirements as to

[91] Directive (EU) 2022/2557 of the European Parliament and of the Council of 14 December 2022 on the resilience of critical entities and repealing Council Directive 2008/114/EC, OJ L 333, 27.12.2022, pp 164–198.

[92] Council Decision (CFSP) 2022/2369 of 3 December 2022 amending Decision 2014/512/CFSP concerning restrictive measures in view of Russia's actions destabilising the situation in Ukraine, OJ L 311I, 3.12.2022, pp 8–12.

[93] Farrell and Newman (n 66).

[94] Anna Herranz Surrallés, Chad Damro and Sandra Eckert, 'The Geoeconomic Turn of the Single European Market? Conceptual Challenges and Empirical Trends' (forthcoming) Journal of Common Market Studies.

what technical aspects of a project—for example, grid connection facilities etc—are to be included in the approval process. Although the key feature of these changes is that the specified projects must be approved swiftly, this emphasis on speed is implicitly accompanied by a significant degree of micromanagement of the content of specific project applications and approval processes. As such, there is an increased willingness to regulate processes which have traditionally left a margin of discretion to each Member State. Related to the emphasis on speed is also the willingness to—at least temporarily—significantly simplify Member States' decision and approval procedures by exempting a subset of important projects and developments from environmental impact assessments. Similarly, designating specific 'go-to' areas in which the process for approval is effectively streamlined and heavily steered makes for significantly simpler decision-making.

6.5.2 Rebalancing of priorities

Importantly, however, it is not just through an emphasis on procedure that the EU seeks to respond to the energy crisis. Member State decision and approval processes are also substantively shaped by renewable energy projects being designated of 'overriding importance'. Not only does this create a presumption in favour of renewable energy developments even where these give rise to environmental impacts but it also removes a significant degree of political autonomy at the domestic and local level, as the balancing exercise of weighing different competing pressures and values against each other has been done in advance. In practice, the proposed changes amount to a suspension of important parts of the environmental *acquis*. This is significant in light of the precautionary emphasis often afforded to some of the key rules in the environmental *acquis*, in particular the Habitats Directive, by the EU courts. There is also a profound shift taking place. This shift manifests itself in the clear willingness of the Commission and the Council to set aside key components of the EU legal order as these relate to state aid and environmental protection. Even if the stated intention is for this development to be temporary, restricted in scope, and subject to reporting requirements, and even if it takes place with the express approval of Member States, this may nevertheless result in a rebalancing of key constitutional objects. In the area of environmental law, for example, the 'overriding preference' afforded to specific renewable energy developments significantly reins in, albeit temporarily, the decades-long jurisprudence of the EU courts in giving purpose to key provisions in the environmental *acquis*. This is significant in light of the driving role that the EU courts have played in developing the dynamic application of these rules.

There is also a new form of further integration at play, in the form of integrating energy policy into environmental law and policy. The regulatory frameworks that are being formally amended in order to speed up renewable energy development were initially put in place in an attempt to deal with climate change. Similarly, central provisions in key environmental law instruments, such as the Habitats, Birds, and Water Framework Directives are 'suspended' when they have to compete with renewable energy developments. In so doing, important environmental provisions are made subordinate for the purpose of promoting specific energy objectives. Evidently, there are weighty reasons for doing so, and renewable energy developments may well have already been given more weight in Member States' individual decisions. This, however, is the first time that the EU's 'upper hand' has been enshrined on a legislative level.

7

Migration Policy

Between Crisis Preparedness, Ad Hoc Solutions, and Administrative Capacity-building

Daniel Thym and Jonas Bornemann***

7.1 Crisis Governance in EU Migration Law and Policy

European Union (EU) migration policy has lived through a series of drastic crises. Debates at political level are not short of superlatives in this regard. The events that gained prominence as the 'migration crisis' of late summer 2015, for instance, were described as 'the largest refugee crisis since the end of World War II'[1], second only to the 'largest displacement on European soil since the Second World War', after the Russian full-scale invasion of Ukraine.[2] Moreover, the names and places associated with these crises—the island of Lampedusa, hotspots such as Moria, and the 'jungle' of Calais—have become epitomes of a deeply rooted, fundamental state of crisis in EU migration law and policy. Owing to the prominence and severity of these events, migration will be one of the first policy fields that springs to mind when discussing the EU's regulatory crisis response.[3]

Underlying causes, structures, and responses differ in several respects from those discussed in other chapters of this book. The idiosyncratic character of EU migration governance follows notably from the fact that forced migration may culminate in the 'mass influx' of many people, thus prompting hardships on the ground and putting stress on the asylum systems of the destination countries. At the same time, the emergence and perpetuation of a sense of crisis may be said to result from the insufficient ability of the EU to create structures that prevent such situations from occurring.[4] Even where measures at EU level anticipate the possibility of a crisis, the law in the books need not necessarily translate into law in practice. In the field of migration, national

* Professor of Public, European, and International Law and Managing Director of the Research Centre Immigration and Asylum Law at the University of Konstanz, Germany.
** Assistant Professor of European Law at Rijksuniversiteit Groningen.

[1] Commission and High Representative, 'Joint Communication, Addressing the Refugee Crisis in Europe: The Role of EU External Action', 9 September 2015, JOIN (2015) 40 final, 2.

[2] Commission, 'Communication, Temporary protection for those fleeing Russia's war of aggression against Ukraine: one year on', 8 March 2023, COM (2023) 140 final, 1.

[3] Migration policy will be defined broadly for the purposes of this investigation, encompassing aspects of legal migration, return, asylum, visas, border controls, and integration of third-country nationals.

[4] See Marco Scipioni, 'Failing Forward in EU Migration Policy?' (2018) 25 Journal of European Public Policy 1357.

Daniel Thym and Jonas Bornemann, *Migration Policy* In: *EU Regulatory Responses to Crises*. Edited by: Diane Fromage, Adrienne Héritier, and Paul Weismann, Oxford University Press. © Daniel Thym and Jonas Bornemann 2025.
DOI: 10.1093/9780198913825.003.0007

actors increasingly utilize their disregard of binding EU law to win support among national electorates.[5] These strategies of open defiance may lead to fundamental rights violations, including pushbacks to unsafe third states or inhumane treatment in reception facilities.

Despite the prevalence of crisis discourse, there are different analytical ways as to how crises could be conceptualized.[6] To start with, crises may be viewed as a descriptive category to qualify a situation as extraordinary in nature and detrimental to the social system at large. Other perspectives stress that crises do not exist as a matter of fact but of value judgement. In this sense, any crisis is a socially constructed category that tends to lend itself to a justification for measures that would otherwise be unacceptable.[7] Going one step further, there can be different perceptions as to why a specific situation may qualify as a migration crisis: does it relate to humanitarian hardship? Or does the crisis hypothesis concern the (in)abilities of public actors to exercise control over migration? Depending on the perspective adopted, views will vary notably.

Our investigation will explore the 'crisis' phenomenon through the lens of the regulatory design of EU migration law. It focuses on avenues in the legal framework that permit actors to respond to emergencies or events with potentially severe implications. Moreover, the analysis will examine how these powers have been used in practice. In this regard, it will highlight that recent crises did not give rise to major formal adjustments to EU migration law, but instead inspired key actors to rely on expansive interpretations of the existing legal framework and spurred changes in the governance and enforcement of EU migration policy. This conclusion applies notably to reactions following the migration crisis during 2015/16, as well as to the COVID-19 pandemic and the war in Ukraine.

Comments will start with an investigation of the legal framework with regard to powers to respond to crises (section 7.2). On that basis, the argument will be put forward that recent crises have given rise to an increasing use of informal and non-binding instruments instead of legal amendments (section 7.3). Attention will be drawn to changes in the governance and enforcement infrastructure in response to crises (section 7.4).

7.2 Crisis Preparedness in EU Migration Law

Conventional wisdom holds that, in fair weather, one should prepare for foul. Indeed, the drafters of the Treaties included several provisions that allow for the

[5] See Jonas Bornemann, 'Judicial Responses to Autocratic Legalism' (2022) 7 European Papers 651, 658, with further references.

[6] See Anna Carastathis, Aila Spathopoulou and Myrto Tsilimpounidi, 'Crisis, What Crisis? Immigrants, Refugees, and Invisible Struggles' (2018) 34 Refuge: Canada's Journal on Refugees 35 ff.; see, more generally, Matthew Seeger and Timothy Sellnow, *Narratives of Crisis* (Stanford University Press 2016).

[7] On this point, see Violeta Moreno-Lax, 'The "Crisification" of Migration Law' in Kevin Cope, Stella Burch Elias and Jill Goldenziel (eds), *The Oxford Handbook of Comparative Immigration Law* (OUP 2025, forthcoming) 3.

accommodation of severe crises.[8] In the context of migration policy, crisis preparedness features in both primary and secondary law. In the Treaties, several provisions enable the EU institutions to adopt measures in response to emergency situations (section 7.2.1). In secondary law, EU legislation tends to provide for latitude to adopt extraordinary measures in times of crises, especially where the latter threaten to jeopardize weighty public policy grounds (section 7.2.2).

7.2.1 Crisis competences in the Treaties

Articles 77–80 of the Treaty on the Functioning of the European Union (TFEU) lay down a comparatively broad competence for EU institutions to act in the field of migration law. Since EU law does not exhaustively govern all aspects of migration law, however, crisis governance may best be understood as a multilevel effort involving the EU institutions and Member State actors (section 7.2.1.1). Furthermore, the Treaties include several provisions that spell out emergency powers that allow the EU institutions to respond to extraordinary events (section 7.2.1.2).

7.2.1.1 Multilevel crisis governance

Based on the broad constitutional framework, EU legislation covers many aspects of migration law. This is not to say, however, that EU migration legislation has occupied all issues it might possibly deal with. For example, the regularization of illegal stay remains mostly untouched by standards of EU law, notwithstanding an abstract power to adopt legislation. From a constitutional perspective, the choice for inaction is perfectly valid, irrespective of whether one finds it politically convincing or not. The competences that the EU Treaties spell out in the field of migration law are 'shared', to the effect that Member States remain competent 'to the extent that the Union has not exercised its competence'.[9]

Where the EU has adopted legislation, the scope and degree of supranational prescriptions may vary considerably, depending on the contents of the instrument in question. Directives, for instance, are often said to provide Member States with flexibility to opt for the form of transposition that best fits the needs of the domestic legal system, whereas directly applicable regulations are considered to profess a higher level of regulatory detail. In practice, however, the theoretical juxtaposition between directives (requiring transposition) and regulations (being directly applicable) has lost significance, notwithstanding the claim by the Commission that it would bring about 'comprehensive harmonisation'[10] to replace the Asylum Procedures Directive 2013/32/EU with the Asylum Procedures Regulation (EU) 2024/1348. To say so may be a smart move from a public relations perspective, signalling that the Commission actively seeks to

[8] Prominent examples concern arts 122 and 347 TFEU.
[9] See arts 2(2), 4(2)(j) TFEU.
[10] Commission, 'Communication: Towards a reform of the Common European Asylum System' COM (2016) 197 final, 10.

overcome discrepancies on the ground. Yet, the practical effects will be limited. The content thereof is more important than the choice of instrument.

By way of example, the Asylum Procedures Regulation, adopted in 2024 and applicable from mid 2026 onwards, foresees an obligation to set time limits to lodge appeals 'between a minimum of two weeks and a maximum of one month'.[11] This is stricter than the vague prescription of 'reasonable time limits' in the previous directive,[12] but stays far behind the claim about 'comprehensive harmonisation'. Conversely, directives will not give Member States leeway in all cases. Exclusion from refugee status of Palestinians receiving the support of the United Nations Relief and Works Agency (UNRWA), for instance, is fully harmonized, despite being laid down in a directive.[13] Regulations, on the contrary, may require implementation, for instance regarding the meaning of 'risk of absconding' in Article 2(p) and (q) of the Asylum and Migration Management Regulation (EU) 2024/1351. The abstract distinction between directives and regulations therefore gives way to gradual variations.

Crisis governance is not limited to the EU institutions. On the contrary, it is dispersed across different levels and, for that reason, assigns a crucial role to national actors.[14] Member States' responsibilities relate, first of all, to the obligation to 'adopt all measures ... necessary to implement legally binding Union acts'.[15] It follows from the model of decentralized enforcement, prevalent in migration policy, that EU legislation is usually being applied to individuals by national authorities. To be sure, the migration agencies have been strengthened substantially, as we shall see. This does not, however, change the primary responsibility of national authorities to implement migration law.

7.2.1.2 Emergency powers in the Treaties

The Treaty framework vests the EU legislature with explicit emergency powers. Article 78(3) TFEU, for instance, provides for the reaction to an 'emergency situation' characterized by a 'sudden inflow' of third-country nationals. Owing to this provision, there was no need to revert to satellite treaties on the basis of public international law, following the example of the European Stability Mechanism (ESM) or the Fiscal Compact, for purposes of refugee relocation in September 2015. Unlike other emergency provisions in the Treaties, however, Article 78(3) TFEU does not expand the competences of the EU legislature. In contrast to Article 347 TFEU, for instance, it merely authorizes the adoption of measures that regulate aspects already encompassed by the legal basis of Article 78 TFEU.

The major difference concerns the procedure: emergency measures under Article 78(3) TFEU are adopted by the Council on a proposal of the Commission, without the

[11] art 68(7)(b), Asylum Procedures Regulation (EU) 2024/32.
[12] art 46(4), Asylum Procedures Directive 2013/32/EU.
[13] See Case C-585/16 *Alheto* [2018] EU:C:2018:584, paras 98–100.
[14] For the multitude of actors, see Daniel Thym, *European Migration Law* (OUP 2023) 173–76.
[15] Art 291(1) TFEU.

need to go through the ordinary legislative procedure involving the co-decision of the European Parliament. Majority requirements in the Council are not changed, however; it decides by qualified majority voting on regular legislation and emergency response measures. Substantively, the latter must be 'provisional', even though the Court of Justice of the European Union (CJEU) has acknowledged that two years may still qualify as provisional in light of the discretion afforded to the Council.[16]

Article 78(2)(c) TFEU comprises a power to adopt 'a common system of temporary protection for displaced persons in the event of a massive inflow'. On that basis, the Temporary Protection Directive 2001/55/EC was adopted early on—a mechanism that has been dormant until recently. As is well known, its first activation occurred during the full-scale invasion of Ukraine in 2022.[17] The reluctance to activate the Directive in relation to earlier instances of large-scale immigration has been criticized in the literature.[18] From a legal perspective, it remains the prerogative of the Council to decide whether this should be done, acting with qualified majority on a proposal from the Commission.[19] Political discretion, not legal automatism, determines whether the temporary protection regime should be activated.

Article 72 TFEU addresses the reverse scenario of crisis response at the national level, highlighting that Member States remain responsible 'with regard to the maintenance of law and order and the safeguarding of internal security'. This responsibility does not prevent EU institutions from adopting measures covering these scenarios. Rather, they should ideally include provisions in secondary legislation allowing Member States to respond to the legitimate security concerns.[20] Several judgments have highlighted that specific Articles contained in the EU migration law instruments do precisely this. A classic example is the rejecting of an application for a residence permit on public policy or security grounds.[21] When these provisions turn out to be insufficient, Member States may rely on Article 72 TFEU to justify derogations from secondary law.[22] Member States may, in other words, justify a violation of EU legislation. When doing so, they are obliged to demonstrate the necessity of their actions, subject to judicial oversight.[23] Member States have out forward such arguments on several occasions over the past ten years, but the Court has rejected all these claims. Several judgments have highlighted that the measures adopted by the EU institutions have proven sufficient.[24] Nevertheless, the option of derogation remains on the table.

[16] See Joined Cases C-643/15 and C-647/15 *Slovak Republic & Hungary v Council* [2017] EU:C:2017:631, para 96.

[17] Council Implementing Decision (EU) 2022/382.

[18] See Meltem Ineli-Ciger, 'Time to Activate the Temporary Protection Directive' (2016) 18 European Journal of Migration and Law 1.

[19] Art 5(1), Temporary Protection Directive 2011/55/EC.

[20] See Jonas Bornemann, 'Mitgliedstaatliche Gestaltungsspielräume im Schengener Grenzkodex' (2018) Integration 231 ff.

[21] See Thym, *European Migration Law* (n 14) 252–62.

[22] ECJ Joined Cases C-715/17, C-718/17, and C-719/17 *Commission v Poland, Hungary and Czech Republic* [2020] EU:C:2020:257, paras 143–45.

[23] ibid, paras 145–47, 169.

[24] See the overview by Thym, *European Migration Law* (n 14) 273–75.

7.2.2 Legislation in the limelight

Whether to make use of Treaty competences is a matter of political choice. When deciding about whether and how to act, the European Parliament is nowadays, unlike before 2009, on a par with the Council, acting as co-legislature in all areas of migration law. Ensuing debates concern the role of the Council and the Parliament, as well as of subformations therein, the changing contours of the contents of EU legislation, and the traditional aversion to implementing and delegated acts.

7.2.2.1 Consensus culture: added value and limits

Whereas some scholars had presumed that full involvement of the European Parliament would bolster a liberal regime, practices following the Treaty of Lisbon did not unequivocally live up to that expectation.[25] Especially with a view to the second generation of EU asylum legislation, which recast the different instruments of the Common European Asylum System (CEAS) in the early 2010s, the position of the European Parliament has become more closely aligned with that of the Council.[26] That tendency was reaffirmed by the contents of the third generation, adopted in the spring of 2024, in relation to which the parliamentary position was stricter than on previous occasions; even where it had adopted a more liberal standpoint, it often gave ground to the Council in the end.

Decision-making in the Council is characterized by qualified majority voting. While this mode of voting has been used on controversial files, such as future Asylum and Migration Management Regulation (EU) 2024/1351, which will replace the Dublin III Regulation (EU) No 604/2013 in mid 2026, it is a defining characteristic of rule-making that conflictual voting rarely happens. Deliberations in the Council and preparatory bodies are defined by a firmly entrenched consensus culture. Discussions do not come to a standstill just because the double majority requirement would be met if the Presidency called a formal vote. Negotiations among the Member States habitually strive to take everyone on board.[27] If need be, the content of the legislation is adapted to take on board the concerns of some Member States, as demonstrated by the small print of the temporary protection regime following the war in Ukraine, with regard to third-country nationals who had been residing in Ukraine when the war broke out.[28]

A recurring argument in the debate about controversial legislative proposals holds that the Council should abandon the search for compromise and overcome resistance by means of majority voting, as it famously did on 22 September 2015 when

[25] See Treaty of Lisbon (adopted 13 December 2007, entered into force on 1 December 2009) [2008] OJ C115/13.

[26] Ariadna Ripoll Servent and Florian Trauner, 'Do Supranational EU Institutions Make a Difference?' (2014) 21 Journal of European Public Policy 1148 ff.

[27] See Fiona Hayes-Renshaw, 'The Council of Ministers' in Dermot Hodson and John Peterson (eds), *Institutions of the European Union* (4th edn, OUP 2017), ch 4, 80–107.

[28] See Sergio Carrera and others, 'The EU Grants Temporary Protection for People Fleeing War in Ukraine' in Sergio Carrera and Meltem Ineli-Ciger (eds), *EU Responses to the Large-Scale Refugee Displacement from Ukraine* (European University Institute 2023) 18 ff.

ministers agreed on the relocation of asylum seekers out of Italy and Greece against the express will of some governments.[29] The Court rejected an action of annulment, thus confirming that the prevalent consensus culture is not legally binding.[30] This litigation draws our attention to a structural shortcoming: what happens if the reticent Member States simply refuse to abide by EU legislation adopted against their express will. Classic enforcement tools of EU law, especially the infringement procedure, apply unreservedly. Yet, principled opposition can throw into relief the limited ability of EU institutions to coerce national governments to follow suit in highly politicized contexts.[31] In the field of migration, the threat of Member States 'going rogue' is real.[32] Accordingly, the underlying logic of the consensus culture prevalent in the Council may be to ensure that EU migration law instruments have a normative basis from the outset, to the effect that compliance does not escalate into a conflict imperiling the European project at large.

This instance of concerted opposition against refugee relocation highlights the emergence of regional or interest-driven coalitions. Such coalitions are rarely formalized, although special links, common convictions, and shared problems may result in loose formations.[33] The Benelux countries, Nordic states, and, more recently, the Visegrád Group of Poland, the Czech Republic, Slovakia, and Hungary often presented similar positions, notably on asylum and border controls.[34] The influence of Franco-German cooperation has traditionally been based less on common interests than on the ability to find a compromise most Member States could support, precisely because both countries often had different preferences to start with.[35] Spain, Italy, Greece, Cyprus, and Malta have coordinated their position in light of shared geographic concerns; they even created the label 'MED5', mirroring the abbreviation 'V4' for the Visegrád countries.

One of the practical advantages of grouping up in the Council is that certain Member States may be successful in blocking reform efforts altogether. This effect features prominently in relation to the proposed overhaul of the CEAS.[36] The opposition of some Southern, Central and Eastern European Member States has proved to be a major obstacle to reform in this field.[37] As a corollary, the Commission had to

[29] See Relocation Decision (EU) 2015/1601, which was adopted against the votes of the Czech Republic, Hungary, Romania, and Slovakia, with Finland abstaining.

[30] *Slovak Republic & Hungary v Council* (n 16) paras 143–50.

[31] See Nicole Scicluna, 'Wilful Non-compliance and the Threat of Disintegration in the EU's Legal Order' (2021) 27 Swiss Political Science Review 654, 662 ff.

[32] See explicitly AG Sharpston's opinion in Joined Cases C-715/17, C-718/17 and C-719/17 [2019] EU:C:2019:917, para 141.

[33] See Georgia Papagianni, *Institutional and Policy Dynamics of EU Migration Law* (Martinus Nijhoff 2006) 204–08.

[34] See <www.visegradgroup.eu> accessed 6 November 2023.

[35] This arguably explains, *ex negativo*, why a Franco-German proposal will not usually resolve protracted disputes about migration policy nowadays, given the sheer diversity of preferences among ever-more Member States.

[36] See Natascha Zaun and Ariadna Ripoll Servent, 'Perpetuating Crisis as a Supply Strategy: The Role of (Nativist) Populist Governments in EU Policymaking on Refugee Distribution' (2023) 61 Journal of Common Market Studies 653, 659 ff.

[37] See Natascha Zaun, 'Fence-sitters No More: Southern and Central Eastern European Member States' Role in the Deadlock of the CEAS Reform' (2022) 29 Journal of European Public Policy 196, 201 ff.

withdraw and replace proposals. A 2016 reform package envisaging significant changes to the CEAS was replaced by the 'New Pact on Migration and Asylum',[38] the comprehensive reform of the CEAS which, after long debates and proposed compromises, ultimately garnered support among the co-legislatures.[39] In the context of the Schengen *acquis*, the Commission similarly put a reform on the table that was later replaced by another,[40] and ultimately equally received the support of the Council and the European Parliament.[41] While these initiatives have ultimately proved successful, the fates of these key components of EU migration law are emblematic of the long drawn-out stalemate that has characterized legislative negotiations ever since the so-called migration crisis of 2015.

7.2.2.2 Flexibilities in secondary law: boon or bane?

On the basis of the broad set of competences in the Treaties, a rich body of secondary law has emerged. Most of the rules and principles of EU migration law have been spelled out in legislation. In the interest of legal certainty, the EU legislature has largely opted for formal legislation. This is not to say, however, that EU legislation in the field of migration will be free from ambiguities or interpretative flexibility. On the contrary, the formal adoption of legislation by no means eliminates the need to interpret the existing legal framework. These ambiguities in secondary law have gained prominence in the context of crisis governance. Against the backdrop of political stalemate, provisions that engender some degree of flexibility may assume a paramount role.

Perhaps the most ostensive example of flexibility concerns the Dublin 'discretionary clause'.[42] It allows Member States to assume responsibility for an asylum application even if, under the criteria established by the Dublin III Regulation, they would not be compelled to do so. The discretionary clause owes its prominence in great part to the makeshift solutions to which it gave rise. In autumn 2015, it served as the legal basis for the decision of German immigration authorities to 'suspend' Dublin procedures for Syrian applicants, to free capacities for the process of examining in substance the large number of claims.[43] The German government had justified the sweeping refusal to transfer Syrians as a generalized application of the Dublin discretionary clause, an argument that gave rise to a heated debate, with some arguing such an interpretation would be unlawful, based on the view that it would unilaterally offset the Dublin rules.

[38] Commission, Communication, 'Towards a reform of the Common European Asylum System and Enhancing Legal avenues to Europe', 6 April 2016, COM (2016) 197 final; and Commission, 'Communication on a New Pact on Migration and Asylum', 23 September 2020, COM (2020) 609 final.

[39] The compromise texts of the individual instruments have been made available here by the Odysseus Network: https://odysseus-network.eu/wp-content/uploads/2024/02/Text-of-all-the-documents-New-Pact.pdf.

[40] Commission, 'Proposal for a Regulation amending Regulation (EU) 2016/399 as regards the rules applicable to the temporary reintroduction of border control at internal borders', 27 September 2017, COM (2017) 571 final; Commission, 'Proposal for a Regulation amending Regulation (EU) 2016/399 on a Union Code on the rules governing the movement of persons across borders', 14 December 2021, COM (2021) 891 final.

[41] For an analysis of the proposed changes, see Jonas Bornemann, 'Competing Visions and Constitutional Limits of Schengen Reform', German Law Journal (forthcoming).

[42] Nowadays, art 17(1) Dublin III Regulation (EU) No 604/2013.

[43] See Mattias Wendel, 'The Refugee Crisis and the Executive' (2016) 17 German Law Journal 1020.

Ultimately, the CJEU put an end to the debate. In *Jafari*, the Court ruled that one Member State may assume responsibility by virtue of the discretionary clause where another Member State experiences an unusually large number of third-country nationals seeking international protection. In such a situation, it may be appropriate to exercise the discretionary clause 'in a spirit of solidarity', which, in accordance with Article 80 TFEU, underlies the Dublin III Regulation.[44] Whereas the reference to the 'spirit' of solidarity and possible ramifications thereof remain opaque, the reference constitutes a relatively overt judicial endorsement of the measures taken by the German authorities.

Similarly, the Dublin discretionary clause served as a legal basis for the 2019 Malta Declaration,[45] an ad hoc solidarity instrument designed to end stalemate after Italy had unilaterally closed its ports to persons rescued at sea. This untenable situation led to a hastily summoned informal meeting of justice and home affairs ministers in Malta, during which the ministers of interior of Italy, Malta, France, and Germany adopted the said declaration; others joined them later. In this vein, they accepted 'voluntary commitments ... for a predictable temporary solidarity mechanism'. The Malta Declaration has been an emergency-driven instrument. Legally, it took the form of a non-binding joint declaration of intent.[46] Since it functions against the background of the Dublin system, it had to be operationalized, in legal terms, through the discretionary clause.

Such 'coalitions of the willing' are a double-edged sword. On the one hand, they may respond to emergency situations. On the other hand, crisis governance of that nature may call into practice the notion of legally constituted public power in EU law,[47] as such governance tends to be premised on expansive (and possibly purposive) interpretations of the existing legal framework. Based upon considerations of political expediency, such interpretations may undermine the normative force of EU law in the medium and long run.[48] Member States may, in future, feel reminded of previous crisis measures and promote a similarly far-fetched interpretation to justify actions at the margins of secondary legislation or beyond.

7.2.2.3 Traditional aversion to implementing and delegated acts

EU migration law has traditionally centred on formal legislation, adopted by the Council and the Parliament in a legislative procedure, and not on executive rule-making.[49]

[44] Case C-646/16 *Jafari* [2017] ECLI:EU:C:2017:586, para 100; further Daniel Thym, 'Judicial Maintenance of the Sputtering Dublin System on Asylum Jurisdiction: *Jafari, A.S., Mengesteab* and *Shiri*' (2018) 55 Common Market Law Review 549, 561 ff.

[45] See Council, 'Malta Declaration by the members of the European Council on the external aspects of migration' (Press release, 3 February 2017), available at https://www.consilium.europa.eu/en/press/press-releases/2017/02/03/malta-declaration accessed 1 April 2024.

[46] ibid, no 4; see, moreover, Jasper van Berckel Smit, 'Taking Onboard the Issue of Disembarkation: The Mediterranean Need for Responsibility-sharing after the Malta Declaration' (2020) 22 European Journal of Migration and Law 492, 514 ff.

[47] Similarly, see Poul Kjaer, 'European Crises of Legally-constituted Public Power' (2017) 23 European Law Journal 417, 425 ff.

[48] For this phenomenon, see Jonathan White, 'Authority after Emergency Rule' (2015) 78 Modern Law Review 585, 600.

[49] Comments hereinafter build upon Thym, *European Migration Law* (n 14) 58–59; note that, in accordance with Art 289(3) TFEU, the term 'legislation' applies to any instrument adopted on the basis of a legislative procedure, be it the ordinary or a special one.

This can be explained by the European Parliament's insistence that politically relevant questions should be determined in a legislative procedure. Members of the European Parliament (MEPs) successfully challenged an attempt by the Council to sideline co-decision for the subsequent adoption of common minimum lists of safe third countries and countries of origin under the former Asylum Procedures Directive.[50] The European Parliament succeded with an action of annulment before the Court against a first body of rules on sea-border surveillance, which had been agreed upon in a 'comitology' procedure by the Commission together with a committee of national representatives.[51] Annulment led to the adoption of today's Sea Borders Regulation (EU) No 656/2014 in the ordinary legislative procedure two years later.

This institutional background may explain why implementing and delegated acts have traditionally played a minor role in EU migration law. 'Implementing' acts allow the Commission or, exceptionally, the Council,[52] to determine the conditions for implementing legally binding EU legal acts, subject to the involvement of committees of national or private experts. 'Delegated' acts are adopted by the Commission, but its power to do so is delimited by the conditions of delegation in the 'parent' legislative act and subject to scrutiny powers of both the Council and the European Parliament.[53] The difference to legislation proper lies in the decision-making procedure, whereas the legal effects of delegated acts in domestic legal orders are the same as for any other supranational legal acts. Unlike in other policy areas, where comitology procedures are widely used (and often criticized for lack of transparency), EU migration law relies on comitology only with respect to some marginal aspects.

By way of example, implementing acts concern the details for visa stickers, whereas delegation is used for changes to visa fees or the exceptional reintroduction of visa requirements for countries refusing reciprocal visa-free travel for the nationals of all Member States.[54] Judges rejected a legal challenge by the Commission, which had sought not to be given that politically treacherous task on how to respond to the initial refusal of the United States to lift visa requirements for some countries in Central and Eastern Europe.[55] Rare examples of politically sensitive implementing acts concern conditionality in the context of the visa policy, where the EU may suspend beneficial arrangements with third states once the latter refuse to cooperate on the return of their nationals.[56] In 2019, a new mechanism was designed to sanction uncooperative third states, in the form of implementing decisions adopted by the Council. So far, this has only been used vis-á-vis Gambia.[57]

[50] See Case C-133/06 *Parliament v Council* [2008] EU:C:2008:257.

[51] Case C-355/10 *Parliament v Council* [2012] EU:C:2012:516, paras 68–85 found the rules to modify essential elements of the original Regulation (EC) No 562/2006.

[52] Case C-257/01 *Commission v Council* [2005] EU:C:2005:25 confirmed that the Council could reserve details on the visa procedure to a Council decision—a practice that was discontinued later.

[53] See arts 290 and 291 TFEU.

[54] See arts 16(9), 27(1), 29(1a) Visa Code Regulation (EC) No 810/2009, as amended by Regulation (EU) 2019/1155 [2019] OJ L188/25.

[55] Case C-88/14 *Commission v Parliament & Council* [2015] EU:C:2015:499.

[56] See Salvatore Fabio Nicolosi, 'Refashioning the EU Visa Policy' (2020) 22 European Journal of Migration and Law 467, 483–89.

[57] See Art 25a(5), (8) Visa Code Regulation; Council Implementing Decision (EU) 2021/1781.

Entry into force of the third generation of asylum legislation, which was adopted in 2024 and will apply from mid 2026 onwards, will significantly reinforce the pertinence of implementing acts in migratory matters. The reform of the Dublin system, determining the state responsible for examining an asylum application, defers the politically sensitive question of interstate solidarity to the implementing stage. The Commission and the Member States are meant to cooperate in sophisticated vulnerability assessments (as a form of crisis preparedness), the determination of migratory pressure (designating the arrival of a crisis), and interstate solidarity instruments (as a form of crisis response). Decisions during that yearly cycle will be taken by the Commission, with the support of the EU Agency for Asylum (EUAA), and by the Council, which retains the prerogative to decide on crisis response.[58] While this policy cycle sounds great on paper, it may fail to deliver in practice. We shall learn whether national governments can muster the political will and the technocratic capacity to put flesh on the procedural skeleton enshrined in the new legislation.

7.3 The Rise of Soft Law: COVID-19 and beyond

Despite the traditional focus on formal legislation, informal and non-binding instruments have assumed an increasingly important role in recent efforts to combat crises. In this respect, migration law follows a trend that equally exists in other areas of EU law, such as competition, economic policy, or state aid. In migration law, informal instruments have gained traction, inter alia as a reaction to the predicaments of crisis.[59] Informal instruments vest actors with both flexibility and swiftness—characteristics that are particularly valuable during an unfolding crisis. As a shorthand, the measures that form the basis of this mode of governance are commonly referred to as 'soft law'. Analytically, however, a clarification is warranted. In specific scenarios, non-binding measures may still engender legal effects, thereby calling into question a binary distinction between hard and soft law.[60] In addition, it is questionable whether soft law equally encompasses informal standards, such as those presented in press releases, communications, or awareness campaigns.[61] Given that such informal instruments can play a paramount role in crisis governance, they will be treated as forms of 'soft law' for the purposes of this investigation.

[58] See arts 3–15, 56 Asylum and Migration Management Regulation (EU) 2024/1351.

[59] See Jonas Bornemann, 'Of Coordinated Approaches and Fair-weather Arrangements: The EU Crisis Response to Covid-19 Mobility Restrictions' in Dominik Brodowski, Jonas Nesselhauf and Florian Weber (eds), *Pandemisches virus - nationales Handeln* (Springer VS 2023) 94 ff.

[60] See Petra L Láncos, Napoleon Xanthoulis and Luis Arroyo Jiménez (eds), *The Legal Effects of EU Soft Law* (Edward Elgar 2023).

[61] See Barbara Boschetti and Maria Daniela Poli, 'A Comparative Study on Soft Law' (2021) 23 Cambridge Yearbook of European Legal Studies 20, 22.

7.3.1 Functions of soft law as a crisis instrument

In migration law, three forms of soft law instruments have gained particular importance in the context of crisis governance: firstly, formal non-binding recommendations, adopted by the Commission or the Council; secondly, informal cooperation frameworks with third states on international cooperation; and, thirdly, Commission communications containing the legal viewpoint of the supranational executive on how to interpret secondary legislation. Such political communications carry less weight than formal recommendations, but may influence national implementation nonetheless.

These instruments can fulfil different functions.[62] On the one hand, non-binding instruments may complement existing policies as an alternative to legally binding measures. Such a substitution effect is particularly widespread in cooperation with third states, notably in the form of informal return arrangements or non-binding mobility partnerships. Going one step further, soft law can trailblaze the adoption of legislation. In this sense, it serves as a laboratory for formal and/or binding reform. By way of example, Commission recommendations served as tentative steps towards common action in the form of the Resettlement Framework Regulation (EU) 2024/1350.

On the other hand, soft law instruments seek to influence the interpretation of legislation. Measures may include profane issues of everyday application, including a summary of the case law, notably in the form of the 'Schengen Handbook' and the 'Return Handbook', which contain useful information for national officials.[63] Other initiatives go beyond codification and seek to proactively shape how national authorities, and possibly courts, handle existing rules. Such efforts to informally mould the interpretation of legislation are not legally binding but can be practically relevant nonetheless; they have been mentioned by the Court on at least one occasion, as a supplementary argument to support a specific conclusion.[64]

A prominent example of a dynamic reading endorsed through soft law instruments concerned the reintroduction of internal border control. This emerged against the backdrop of the fact that the Schengen Borders Code (EU) 2016/399 allows national governments to reintroduce such controls, subject to substantive conditions and procedural requirements. In practice, the justifications put forward have varied between terrorism, structural deficiencies of the Schengen area, secondary movements, and the COVID-19 pandemic, and have been criticized for being threadbare.[65] In this context, governments have repeatedly relied on the idea—supported by a Commission recommendation, a non-binding legal act—that new threats may justify prolonged border

[62] On the following, see Thym, *European Migration Law* (n 14) 59–60.

[63] See Commission Recommendation (EU) 2017/2338 establishing a common 'Return Handbook' [2017] OJ L339/83; and Commission Recommendation establishing a common 'Practical Handbook for Border Guards' (C (2019) 7131, 8 October 2019), which both replaced earlier versions.

[64] See Case C-635/17 *E* [2019] EU:C:2019:192, paras 63–69.

[65] See Lena Karamanidou and Bernd Kasparek, 'From Exceptional Threats to Normalized Risks' (2022) 37 Journal of Borderlands Studies 623, 631 ff.

controls on the basis of an accumulation of legal bases.[66] This view has been confirmed by the CJEU.[67]

7.3.2 Inter-crises learning and the perils of soft law crisis governance

A notorious example of soft law transforming secondary legislation was the unprecedented external travel ban for third-country nationals during the COVID-19 pandemic, emulated two years later when the Baltic states and Finland effectively closed their borders to Russians following the armed attack against Ukraine. Soft law, in this context, allowed EU institutions to design a far-reaching policy through the streamlining of administrative state practices.[68] This 'enabling function' of informal coordination marks a significant evolution in the crisis governance of the Schengen area. It permitted key actors to develop a policy that effectively barred vast groups of third-country nationals from entering the Schengen area, albeit in the absence of a formal redesign of the Schengen *acquis*. While the practice first emerged in response to the COVID-19 pandemic (section 7.3.2.1), it later inspired a similar strategy in reaction to the war in Ukraine, albeit in the absence of unequivocal support of key actors, both at national and supranational level (section 7.3.2.2).

7.3.2.1 Soft law coordination of national discretionary power: the COVID-19 travel ban

The travel ban during the pandemic aptly exemplifies the advantages and drawbacks of soft law crisis governance.[69] The main benefit was the spontaneity and flexibility with which it was designed. A first short Commission communication was written in haste and could be adapted easily by means of follow-up documents in the weeks thereafter.[70] The travel ban was somewhat formalized when the Council adopted a recommendation, updated regularly, to define countries covered by the entry ban.[71] None of these measures were legally binding, but they seem to have been reasonably successful in coordinating national practices applying the Schengen Borders Code Regulation (EU) 2016/399. Nevertheless, the downside of such reliance on soft law coordination was obvious. The most drastic travel restrictions in the history of the Schengen area were decided informally, without parliamentary involvement, and on shaky legal grounds.

[66] See Recital 2, Commission Recommendation (EU) 2017/1804.

[67] ECJ Joined Cases C-368/20 & C-369/20 *Landepolizeidirektion Steiermark* [2022] EU:C:2022:298, paras 79–80.

[68] See Jonas Bornemann, 'Informal Coordination and Inter-crises Learning – External Travel Bans during the Covid Crisis and the War in Ukraine' in Philippe De Bruycker and others (eds), *The Law of Schengen* (Elgar 2024, forthcoming).

[69] See further Daniel Thym and Jonas Bornemann, 'Schengen and Free Movement Law during the First Phase of the Covid-19 Pandemic' (2020) 5 European Papers 1143, 1155–61.

[70] See Commission, 'Communication: COVID-19. Temporary restriction on non-essential travel to the EU' COM (2020) 115 final, and follow-up documents.

[71] See Council Recommendation (EU) 2020/912 on the temporary restriction on non-essential travel into the EU [2020] OJ C208I/1, and follow-up documents.

It may be questionable, for instance, whether the existing legal framework permits a sweeping external travel ban in the first place. To start with, the entry ban was premised on the presumption that any third-country national could potentially carry and spread the virus, and may, for that reason, pose a threat to public health. Where such a threat exists, national border guards are compelled to refuse entry into the Schengen area.[72] Travel restrictions in this regard were motivated by considerations of precaution, inhibiting or at least slowing the spread of the virus. Judges confirmed this interpretation as a matter of principle, albeit without discussing the role of soft law.[73]

Going one step further, refusal of entry must be decided 'on an individual basis', as explicitly emphasized by Article 4 of the Schengen Borders Code.[74] To ensure compatibility with this requirement, the COVID-19 travel ban introduced a typecast examination assessing whether a person's travel served an 'essential function or need'.[75] The Commission identified several categories of mobility that may be viewed in such terms. While the inclusion of exceptions was imperative from a legal perspective, the informal coordination of the Commission left important questions unaddressed. Soft law failed to define, for instance, what may qualify as an 'imperative family reason', for instance with regard to non-married couples or persons attending a funeral. It should be welcomed, therefore, that the legislature decided, in 2024, to introduce the option to adopt legally binding implementing acts regarding health-related travel bans.[76] It would depend on the institutional practice whether implementing acts on this basis would contain the necessary clarity. Crucially, however, the new implementing powers are restricted to 'large-scale public health emergencies', not other, more controversial, emergency situations.

7.3.2.2 From precaution to retribution: the travel ban against Russian citizens

Bold legal engineering, like that used for the purposes of the COVID-19 external travel ban, may come at a price. Inadvertently, it may encourage actors to propose, either unilaterally or concertedly, far-reaching interpretation of EU law in other situations as well, justifying their interpretations by way of reference to previous crisis responses. This reaffirms the double-edged characteristics of extraordinary measures as instruments of political expediency which, in accordance with previous comments, may undermine the authority of law to offer guidance in critical situations.

This effect is aptly illustrated in relation to responses to the Russian full-scale invasion of Ukraine. Following these events, some Member States proposed to emulate the health-related external ban—this time by refusing entry to Russian citizens. Unlike the COVID-19 entry ban, this crisis measure was motivated by a retributive logic. Whereas the former may have been justified on public health grounds and considerations of

[72] See arts 6(1)(e) and 14, Schengen Borders Code Regulation (EU) 2016/399.
[73] See Case C-128/22 *NORDIC INFO* [2023] EU:C:2023:951, paras 124–27.
[74] See also Case C-84/12 *Koushkaki* [2013] EU:C:2013:862, para 56.
[75] Commission, 'Communication: COVID-19. Temporary restriction on non-essential travel to the EU', 2.
[76] See Art 21a, Schengen Borders Code Regulation (EU) 2016/399, as amended by Regulation (EU) 2024/1717.

precaution, a similar conclusion may not easily be drawn with a view to a nationality-based entry ban introduced in response to the Russian invasion. In the literature, it has been firmly disputed whether a sweeping travel ban of that nature could be justified, either by virtue of public order grounds or on the ground that allowing entry for Russian citizens could be viewed as a threat to the international relations of any of the Member States.[77]

Against this backdrop, the Commission quickly came to realize that some form of coordination would be inevitable. In substance, this form of coordination attempted to walk a tightrope. On the one hand, it sought to streamline national decision-making practices while ensuring, on the other hand, that the expansive interpretation of the Schengen Borders Code Regulation did not openly transgress the limits of what is permissible. With a view to the contested legality of these measures, the Commission proposed a reading of the relevant instruments of EU law that would compel national authorities to base their decisions on an individualized assessment, but which would allow them to put into practice an 'expansive approach' to determining whether a person could be considered a 'potential threat' to the international relations of a Member State.[78]

Such an interpretation significantly lowers the bar for national visa authorities to refuse entry. It is deemed sufficient that it is 'highly likely' that Russian citizens pose a threat to the international relations.[79] At the same time, the Commission calls upon national authorities to acknowledge the specificities of each individual case. Whereas Russian citizens travelling exclusively for touristic purposes may have their visa applications rejected, the motives and individual situations of other persons must be duly assessed.

Note that inter-crisis learning need not be a collective exercise. Following the war in Ukraine, soft law coordination emerged as a crisis response deemed necessary only by some Member States, while others fervently opposed it. This political opposition of key actors distinguished the entry ban against Russians from many of the steps taken in response to the COVID-19 pandemic. Unlike attempts to coordinate national decision-making practices during the first phase of the pandemic, informal coordination as a mode to respond to the war in Ukraine was markedly contested.

[77] See Daniel Thym, 'Border Closure and Visa Ban for Russians: Geopolitics Meets EU Migration Law' (*EU Immigration and Asylum Law and Policy*, 17 October 2022); Sarah Ganty, Dimitry Kochenov and Suryapratim Roy, 'Nationality-based Bans from the Schengen Zone' (2022) COMPAS Working Paper 1. https://www.compas.ox.ac.uk/wp-content/uploads/WP-2022-160-Nationality-Based-Bans-from-the-Schengen-Zone.pdf (accessed 21 October 2024).

[78] Commission, 'Providing guidelines on general visa issuance in relation to Russian applicantsfollowing Council Decision (EU) 2022/1500 of 9 September 2022 on the suspension in whole of the application of the Agreement between the European Communicty and the Russian Federation on the facilitation of the issuance of visas to the citizens of the European Union and the Russian Federation', C (2022) 6596 final; Commission, '1. Updating guidelines on general visa issuance in relation to Russian applicants following Council Decision (EU) 2022/1500 of 9 September 2022 on the suspension in whole of the application of the Agreement between the European Communicty and the Russian Federation on the facilitation of the issuance of visas to the citizens of the European Union and the Russian Federation; and 2. Providing guidelines on controls of Russian citizens at the external borders', C (2022) 7111 final.

[79] ibid, point 21.

7.3.3 Informalization in cooperation with third states

In recent years, EU migration law has seen a proliferation of informal instruments in relation to cooperation with third states. Several driving forces lie behind informalization.[80] Important benefits are speed, in the absence of lengthy ratification, and flexibility, by means of easy adaptation to changing circumstances. In that respect, informal 'gentlemen's agreements' have the same advantages as soft law in relation to the internal dimension. Moreover, an absence of legal obligations may facilitate political compromises that partner countries might not have accepted in the form of hard legal obligations. The Global Compacts and the—albeit meagre—commitments to legal pathways in mobility partnerships are a case in point. The alternative to soft law can sometimes be failure of negotiations. EU institutions generally insist on handing out financial support to third states on the basis of internal legislation, so as to preserve the flexibility to alter or stop the payment schedule. President Erdoğan, in return, might not have been willing to commit legally to a statement that reads '[a]ll new irregular migrants crossing from Turkey into Greek islands as from 20 March 2016 will be returned to Turkey.'[81] In short, informalization may be a prerequisite for political consensus precisely because it is not legally binding.

The opposite scenario might also occur. One reason for the proliferation of informal readmission arrangements was the practical failure of legally binding agreements. The EU had invested much political capital in the signature of formal readmission agreements, only to find that third states often failed to live up to them in practice.[82] Governments prefer non-binding arrangements that work rather than largely dysfunctional formal agreements. Such an outcome need not be to the disadvantage of returnees, who can invoke guarantees in the Return Directive 2008/115/EC, and human rights, nonetheless. Informalization is, however, detrimental to parliamentary prerogatives, since, unlike during the formal procedure for ratifying international agreements under Article 218 TFEU, MEPs cannot exert pressure on the EU's negotiating position through the threat of non-ratification.[83] Moreover, informal cooperation is notoriously intransparent, thus impeding public scrutiny.[84] That argument runs both ways; third states have occasionally asked for an informal measure instead of a legally binding readmission agreement whose visibility might be met with scepticism by public opinion in countries of origin and transit.[85] This evasion of political and institutional accountability mechanisms renders the informalization of the external dimension problematic, notwithstanding legitimate benefits.

[80] Comments in this section build upon Thym, *European Migration Law* (n 14) 579–81 and 537–39.

[81] 'EU–Turkey Statement' (Press Release 144/16, 18 March 2016), point 1.

[82] See Commission, 'Communication: Evaluation of EU readmission agreements' COM (2011) 76 final 3–5.

[83] See Art 218(6)(a)(v) TFEU, read in conjunction with arts 77–79 TFEU.

[84] See Paul James Cardwell, 'Rethinking Law and New Governance in the European Union' (2016) 41 European Law Review 362, 373–78.

[85] See Jean-Pierre Cassarino, 'Informalizing EU Readmission Policy' in Ariadna Ripoll Servent and Florian Trauner (eds), *The Routledge Handbook of Justice and Home Affairs Research* (Routledge 2018) 83, 90–93.

7.3.3.1 The EU–Turkey Statement

This emergence of informal cooperation left observers with the impression that EU institutions and third states were deliberately evading legal commitments and corresponding institutional safeguards.[86] One of the most ostensive examples of this effect was the EU–Turkey Statement, which took the form of a non-binding press release published by the European Council.[87] Actions for annulment were nonchalantly declared inadmissible by the CJEU. Judges qualified the statement as an informal (political) commitment of the Member States' meeting within the European Council.[88] Even if judges had attributed the statement to the EU institutions, this would not automatically have led to a decision on the substance, in light of several admissibility thresholds. Firstly, judges interpret their jurisdiction to 'review the legality of acts', under Article 263 TFEU, to include informal measures intended to produce legal effects[89]—a condition the EU–Turkey Statement might have fulfilled.[90] Secondly, claimants would have had further difficulties demonstrating that they are individually concerned, in accordance with the *Plaumann* formula. Be that as it may, the inadmissibility of the CJEU case entailed that Greek courts held responsibility for ensuring compliance with Union law. We shall see that this indirect route of decentralized adjudication proved ineffective in practice, at least until recently.

7.3.3.2 Readmission agreements

States are obliged to readmit nationals under customary international law. Nevertheless, practical collaboration is often flawed. Lack of cooperation relates to various steps of the return procedure: identity determination, acquisition of travel documents, acceptance of the transfer, and organization of the removal operation.[91] Readmission agreements address these practical deficits. Their provisions define procedures for cooperation, means of evidence regarding nationality, necessary travel documents, time limits, and modalities of transportation; supplementary implementing protocols, drawn up by Member States and the third state, designate the competent authorities and provide for practical arrangements.[92] Such technicalities are the backbone of readmission agreements.

[86] See Eva Kassoti and Narin Idriz (eds), *The Informalisation of the EU's External Action in the Field of Migration and Asylum* (Springer 2022).

[87] Available at https://www.consilium.europa.eu/de/press/press-releases/2016/03/18/eu-turkey-statement.

[88] See Joined Cases C-208–210/17 P *NF and others v European Council* [2018] EU:C:2018:705, para 16; confirming Case T-192/16 *NF v European Council* [2017] EU:T:2017:128, paras 46–75; in line with the parallel decisions in Case T-193/16 and Case T-257/16.

[89] See Case C-27/04 *Commission v Council* [2004] EU:C:2004:436, para 44.

[90] See Mauro Gatti and Andrea Ott, 'The EU–Turkey Statement' in Sergio Carrera, Juan Santos Vara and Tineke Strik (eds), *Constitutionalising the External Dimension of EU Migration Policies in Times of Crisis* (Edward Elgar 2019) 175.

[91] See Court of Auditors, 'EU Readmission Cooperation with Third Countries' (Special Report 17/2021, 13 September 2021) 38–46.

[92] See Nils Coleman, *European Readmission Policy* (Martinus Nijhoff 2008), ch 5; and, eg arts 2, 5–9, 16–17, Agreement between the European Community and the Islamic Republic of Pakistan on the readmission of persons residing without authorisation (adopted 26 October 2010, entered into force 1 December 2010) [2010] OJ L287/52.

Years of debate over supranational competences finally subsided when Article 79(3) TFEU established an express legal base in the form of a shared competence. By the end of 2009, the EU had signed thirteen readmission agreements, many of them with neighbouring European countries. Conversely, negotiations with important countries of origin or transit, such as Morocco, Turkey, or Nigeria, proved difficult. Negotiations on readmission agreements often fail in the absence of a mutually beneficial give-and-take in the field of migration or beyond. Moreover, ratification did not always translate into effective implementation either, for instance in relations with Turkey.[93] This background of protracted negotiations explains why non-binding 'standard operation procedures' or other informal arrangements have gained traction in recent years. At the time of writing, there were eighteen readmission agreements and at least six informal cooperation frameworks,[94] in addition to numerous bilateral agreements of the Member States.[95] The example of readmission agreements reiterates the benefits and pitfalls of informalization. The objective of smooth practical cooperation does not require a treaty, although informal arrangements evade institutional safeguards. The rights of migrants must be respected in any case. All returnees can rely on the Return Directive 2008/115/EC, and on human rights.

7.4 Administrative Implementation as the Achilles Heel

It is no secret that migration policy is riddled with severe compliance deficits. For the purposes of this analysis, two opposing views can be identified. On the one hand, poor compliance can be singled out as an 'internal' root cause of crisis. From such a perspective, crisis is said to result from the unwillingness or inability of migration authorities to act diligently, materializing in the ill-treatment of migrants. On the other hand, compliance deficits can be the symptom of an 'external' shock, such as large numbers of cases, time and resource constraints, and broader uncertainties. Whereas the first perspective tends to be critical of migration authorities, the second view is more empathetic of their position, locating the causes for crisis as external to the authorities, which struggle to maintain legal standards despite behaving diligently and in good faith.[96] In order to tackle the problem of insufficient administrative implementation, the EU institutions have set up, and successively strengthened, Frontex and EUAA (section 7.4.1.). In addition, the Commission has promised innovative enforcement strategies (section 7.4.2.).

[93] See Çiğdem Akın Yavuz, 'Analysis of the EU–Turkey Readmission Agreement' (2019) 21 European Journal of Migration Law 486.

[94] See Mark Provera, 'External Dimension of the Return Directive (Part III)' (European Implementation Assessment, PE 642.840, June 2020), Annexes I–III.

[95] See the useful 'Inventory of the Bilateral Agreements Linked to Readmission' coordinated by Jean-Pierre Cassarino <https://www.jeanpierrecassarino.com/datasets/ra> accessed 1 November 2022.

[96] Comments hereinafter build upon Thym, *European Migration Law* (n 14) 81–83 and 176–77.

7.4.1 Operative functions of EU migration agencies

Protracted compliance deficits are palpable in core areas of asylum, border control, and return policies. Publication of new rules in the Official Journal does not guarantee success on the ground; it would be insufficient to assume that the combination of the doctrine of direct effect and the option of preliminary references alone can guarantee respect for EU law.[97] That is why the EU institutions are well advised to consider administrative mechanisms supporting compliance. Generally speaking, there is no uniform model of EU administrative law, but variations with certain elements in common.[98] To be successful, administrative rules should reflect the distinct features of the policy field in question; it depends on contextual factors whether regulatory techniques can be transplanted from one policy field to another. If that is correct, it is essential to grasp the specificities of migration law in order to develop context-sensitive administrative measures supporting practical implementation. Arguably, a decisive element is the operational character of migration law, which one might analytically—not pejoratively—describe as an exercise of 'mass administration'.[99] The application of migration law habitually involves the application of supranational rules to numerous individuals by officials with a relatively low degree of formal education (compared with, for instance, stakeholders in competition cases).

To build an effective and accountable 'mass administration' requires a challenging mixture of administrative routine and standardization to ensure equal treatment and attention to the particularities of the individual case. The sheer number of individual files commands tremendous investment in administrative resources, organization, and training. Mutual distrust between migrants and public officials further complicates an effective fulfilment of administrative tasks. These operational challenges are particularly pronounced in the fields of border controls, asylum, and return, whereas legal migration tends to be less confrontational. EU institutions have explored different ways to support domestic authorities, for instance through financial support or databases that simplify transnational information exchange. The most tangible embodiment of EU support manifests itself in the establishment and growing operational capacity of Frontex and the EUAA.

The tasks and mandates of these two agencies have grown significantly ever since the migration crisis of 2015/16. Both Frontex and the EUAA have become veritable powerhouses, thus raising formidable political and legal questions.[100] The Frontex mandate

[97] See Daniel Thym, 'The "Refugee Crisis" as a Challenge of Legal Design and Institutional Legitimacy' (2016) 53 Common Market Law Review 1545, 1554–58.

[98] See generally Bruno de Witte, 'Institutional Variation across Policy Fields in the Evolution of European Union Law' (2013) 20 Maastricht Journal of European and Comparative Law 465; and Giandomenico Majone, *Europe as the Would-be World Power* (CUP 2009).

[99] Rainer Wahl, 'Die Aufgabenabhängigkeit von Verwaltung und Verwaltungsrecht' in Eberhard Schmidt-Aßmann und Wolfgang Hoffmann-Riem (eds), *Reform des Allgemeinen Verwaltungsrechts. Band 1* (Nomos 1993) 177, 192–96, 206–08.

[100] See further Thym, *European Migration Law* (n 14) 197–222.

has been reinforced on several occasions, thus gradually turning the Warsaw-based body into the EU agency with the largest number of personnel, as well as impressive financial and technical resources. A standing corps of supranational policepersons, to be set up during the 2020s, will be the hallmark of operational sway, to be deployed alongside national personnel in future missions. Operational powers are complemented by supervisory functions. Cooperation with third states may turn out to be dynamic in the years to come. Agency staff may be deployed in countries of origin or transit to support capacity-building, return, migration management, and operational activities. Procurement of equipment and technology-based border surveillance deserve more attention, precisely because the use of drones, for example, remains largely aloof from legal oversight.

The EUAA Regulation (EU) 2021/2303 finally became operational in 2022, thus ending several years of legal uncertainties during which the former European Asylum Support Office (EASO) had performed functions *de facto*, thus transcending the scope of its previous mandate. Involvement in domestic decision-making and the provision of reception conditions are epitomized by the 'hotspot' approach on the Greek islands, which has been widely criticized for managerial deficiencies and possible illegalities.[101] Information-gathering and practical guidance are essential functions as well. High-quality country-of-origin information, in particular, may prove a decisive tool to support the convergence of recognition rates across Europe. Monitoring of the Member States follows the model of Frontex.

7.4.2 Enforcement strategies

EU migration policy is subject to the traditional enforcement mechanisms of Union law. Still, the Commission has traditionally been hesitant to enforce standards of EU migration law. For many years, it evaded bringing Member States to Court on legally difficult or politically sensitive topics. This hesitation left observers with a sense of disappointment,[102] and, quantitatively, it stands out even if we factor in that the significance of infringement proceedings has decreased generally.[103] The period of passive supervision came to an end during the policy crisis of 2015/16, when it became apparent that administrative practices on diverse subject areas such as reception conditions and the speed or quality of asylum procedures were deficient, if not dysfunctional. Infringement proceedings for failure to effectively apply EU legislation on the ground

[101] See Catharina Ziebritzki, 'The Integrated EU Hotspot Administration and the Question of the EU's Liability' in Markus Kotzur and others (eds), *The External Dimension of EU Migration and Asylum Policies* (Nomos 2020) 253–94.

[102] See Philippe De Bruycker and Henri Labayle, 'Chronique de jurisprudence consacrée à l'Espace de liberté, de sécurité et de justice' (2014) 49 Cahiers de droit européen 719, 720.

[103] For a statistical survey, see Thym, *European Migration Law* (n 14) 81–83.

were a novelty; they provided the Commission with an opportunity to repel criticism of inertia.[104]

Hungary became a recurring 'client' of the infringement procedure when it openly refused to comply with the Council Decisions on the relocation of asylum seekers, mentioned previously, and when it introduced asylum laws in flagrant violation of EU legislation. Several of these files ended up before the Court.[105] These activities are important, yet the practical limitations of *ex post* review by a European Court are evident. A ruling on Hungarian transit zones was delivered no less than five years after the Commission's letter of formal notice, and two years after referral to the Court.[106] Notwithstanding these practical limitations, the example of Hungary illustrates why infringement proceedings are a critical instrument the Commission can—and should—use strategically whenever a government wilfully defies Union law. Intentional non-compliance by self-declared 'rebels'[107] goes beyond 'regular' breaches, which, unfortunately, are widespread across Europe in the domains of asylum and border controls. It is an act of symbolic disobedience that undermines the normative integrity of EU migration law.[108] To counter such flagrant violations is an end in itself. Having said this, strategic proceedings against 'rogue' governments have risks. The burden of proof for administrative practices on the ground rests with the Commission,[109] thus complicating, by way of example, measures against pushback allegations. Moreover, it is by no means clear whether such infringement cases will ultimately sway Member States into compliance.

Given the traditionally constrained approach of the Commission to act as an enforcer of EU migration law, decentralized enforcement through the preliminary reference procedure is paramount. Preliminary references on migration started reaching the Court in greater numbers after the Treaty of Lisbon had discontinued an earlier limitation to the highest courts. Geographically, however, the requests sent to the Court are very unevenly dispersed between Member States. Whereas a few jurisdictions account for the better part of references, the courts in some Member States have remained notably more reluctant to file preliminary references with the Court.[110] This incongruent practice implies that certain perspectives and themes do not reach the Court. A particularly notable example of judicial reluctance to file preliminary references concerns Greek courts. Until very recently,[111] not a single Greek court had consulted judges in Luxembourg on how to interpret the asylum *acquis* in the aftermath of the 2015/16 migration crisis.

[104] See Commission, 'More Responsibility in Managing the Refugee Crisis' (Press release IP/15/5699, 23 September 2015); and the follow-up action (Press release IP/15/6276, 10 December 2015; IP/17/5002, 7 December 2017).

[105] By the end of 2021, four such cases had been referred to the Court (not all had been decided): see Case C–718/17, Case C–808/18, Case C–761/19, and Case C–821/19; and <https://ec.europa.eu/atwork/applying-eu-law/infringements-proceedings/infringement_decisions/?lang_code=en> accessed 1 April 2023.

[106] See Case C–808/18 *Commission v Hungary* [2020] EU:C:2020:1029.

[107] AG Sharpston's opinion (n 31) point 141.

[108] See Evangelia (Lilian) Tsourdi, 'Relocation Blues' (2021) 58 Common Market Law Review 1819, 1839–42.

[109] See Case C–441/02 *Commission v Germany* [2006] EU:C:2006:253, paras 48–49.

[110] For a quantitative overview, see Thym, *European Migration Law* (n 14) 83–89.

[111] C-134/23 *Elliniko Symvoulio gia tous Prosfyges and Ypostirixi Prosfygon sto Aigaio* EU:C:2024:836.

Besides, the Commission has promoted alternative enforcement mechanisms. These efforts routinely centre on persuasion rather than coercion. The Commission's 'Schengen strategy' is a case in point. In 2021, the Commission announced changes in the governance structure of Schengen,[112] strengthening the Schengen evaluation mechanism—a mechanism that allows for peer-to-peer evaluations between Member States—and establishing the so-called 'Schengen Forum', a platform for biannual meetings between the Commission, MEPs, national ministers, representatives of EU agencies, and national migration authorities. From a purely legal perspective, such forms of coordination and political steering may often be overlooked, or discredited as desperate attempts to revive the principled absence of internal border controls in the Schengen area. As the experiences of the first phase of the COVID-19 pandemic illustrate, however, the effects of such coordination can be tangible. They cater to the emergence of an *esprit de corps* among key actors involved in the administration and implementation of EU migration law.[113]

7.5 Conclusion

EU migration policy has been shaped by recent crises experiences. This influence, however, does not primarily materialize in legislative changes. The third generation of asylum legislation, adopted in 2024 after years of debate, takes on board critical lessons but refrains from substantially overhauling the CEAS. In the absence of major legislative reform, crisis response has unfolded on the basis of the existing legal framework. This includes—and already included, before the latest legislative reform—mechanisms that explicitly allow for measures to be adopted in response to emergencies. Temporary protection afforded to people fleeing the war in Ukraine, and the relocation scheme for asylum seekers, are cases in point. In addition, some actors have promoted an innovative interpretation of the existing legislation to justify exceptional measures. During the so-called migration crisis of 2015/16, for instance, German authorities motivated their refusal to transfer Syrian asylum seekers to Greece through a sweeping activation of the discretionary clause in the Dublin Regulation—an argument that the CJEU ultimately accepted. Another crisis-driven instrument based on the Dublin discretionary clause was the 2019 Malta Declaration, which sought to establish an informal arrangement between a 'coalition of the willing' to voluntarily assume responsibility for examining asylum applications from persons disembarked at Italian ports.

Coalitions of the willing of that nature are a double-edged sword. On the one hand, they can pave the way towards policy reform by establishing tried-and-tested practices that inspire legislative change. On the other hand, any questionable interpretation of Union law can undermine the normative credentials of the supranational legal order in the medium term. While such measures may be expedient in times of crisis, and

[112] See Jonas Bornemann, 'Competing Visions' (n 40).
[113] See Thym and Bornemann, 'Schengen and Free Movement Law' (n 69) 1151 ff.

have been accepted by the Court on some occasions, they may call into question the authority of law to act as a guiding standard in challenging circumstances. EU institutions and Member States may justify future crisis responses with reference to previous instances of improvisation where concerted action did not materialize in formal adjustments to the legal framework, but rather in far-reaching (and possibly excessive) interpretations thereof.

In the absence of formal reforms, EU migration policy increasingly relied on informal and non-binding instruments. Both during the pandemic and the Russian war of aggression against Ukraine, external travel bans for entry into the Schengen area or selected Member States were put into practice through an informal, non-binding coordination of national administrative practices, allowing actors at EU and national level to design a far-reaching crisis measure without lengthy legislative reform. Similarly, informalization has gained traction in relation to the EU's cooperation with third states, where it may have facilitated the conclusion of legally binding agreements later-on. Internally, significant efforts have been undertaken at EU level to strengthen administrative capacities on the ground. Institutionally, this is done through the increased involvement of agencies, especially the borders agency Frontex and the European Union Asylum Agency (EUAA). The overburdening of migration administrations, especially in Member States of first entrance, may be viewed as one of the root causes for crises, regardless of whether one understands 'crisis' in terms of humanitarian hardship or rather as a state's inability to exert control over migration. Since instances of large and sudden influx are a challenge to the administrative authorities, agency support can bolster the EU's crisis preparedness.

Changes extend to the enforcement of EU migration law. While the Commission has traditionally been reluctant to initiate infringement proceedings, the blatant (and strategic) disregard of the asylum legislation by some governments has prompted more resolute enforcement practices. Likewise, the Commission is advancing alternative ways to promote conformity with EU migration rules. In the context of the Schengen *acquis*, for instance, it has strengthened peer-to-peer review mechanisms and institutionalized fora that allow for a regular exchange of views. These measures can be viewed as lessons learned from recent crises. The Commission may have come to learn that an *esprit de corps* among key actors may yield tangible effects with a view to compliance with EU law. Such an enforcement strategy is premised on persuasion rather than coercion, drawing Member State actors' attention to the adverse effect of unilateral action.

8

Foreign and Security Policy

Rule-making in Different Compartments and Times of Geopolitics

*Kolja Raube**

8.1 Introduction

This chapter focuses on rule-making in the European Union (EU)'s foreign and security-related policies in times of crisis, more specifically in the context of Russia's war on Ukraine. As such, it focuses on the changes that have emerged in procedures (procedural rules) as well as actions and tools used (substantive rules) in EU foreign and security policy. The analysis treats the war on Ukraine, which has confronted the EU with an unheard-of crisis, requiring the Union to act in a united and unprecedented way. Despite differences amongst Member States, 'it brought all member states together behind the perspective of the frontline states: Russia's neo-imperial agenda represented Europe's most serious security threat'.[1] At the same time, this crisis could be seen as 'the perfect storm',[2] which required nothing but a comprehensive response across the many different policy areas affected,[3] activating the EU's overall toolbox and, beyond it, requiring the EU to take unprecedented decisions and measures to counteract Russia's aggression to the EU's east. The EU's gradual geopoliticization[4] fostered the enactment of both procedural and substantive rules, following the understanding of crucial EU actors, including Member States and the European Commission, that geopolitics was no longer a theory but an emerging new reality[5] which eventually became a salient issue in EU politics, communication, and rule-making.

However, next to the evident overall existential geopolitical threat to Member States and the EU, the crisis confronted the EU also with the challenge of rule-making across different compartmentalized policy domains, which had so far been conducted by a

* Associate Professor for European Governance and EU External Action at KU Leuven.

[1] Mitchell Orenstein, 'The European Union's Transformation after Russia's Attack on Ukraine' (2023) 45 Journal of European Integration 333.

[2] Marianne Riddervold, Jarle Trondal and Akasemi Newsome (eds), *Palgrave Handbook on EU Crises* (Palgrave Macmillan 2021) 4.

[3] Veronica Anghel and Erik Jones, 'Is Europe Really Forged through Crisis? Pandemic EU and the Russia – Ukraine War' (2022) 30 Journal of European Public Policy 767.

[4] Sophie Meunier and Kalypso Nicolaidis, 'The Geopoliticization of European Trade and Investment Policy' (2019) 57 Journal of Common Market Studies 103–13; Heidi Maurer, Kolja Raube and Federica Bicchi, 'Shaping the EU's Identity as International Actor in the Absence of Formal Institutional Change' (2024) European Security (forthcoming).

[5] Simon Duke, *Europe as a Stronger Global Actor – Challenges and Strategic Responses.* (Palgrave 2017) 88 ff.

Kolja Raube, *Foreign and Security Policy* In: *EU Regulatory Responses to Crises*. Edited by: Diane Fromage, Adrienne Héritier, and Paul Weismann, Oxford University Press. © Kolja Raube 2025. DOI: 10.1093/9780198913825.003.0008

variety of separate rule-making procedures, actors, and objectives. Foreign policy and security-related responses to the crisis could eventually not be decided upon exclusively in the EU's Common Foreign and Security Policy (CFSP) and Common Security and Defence Policy (CSDP). A number of areas of Union action and respective rules, which increasingly became concerned with security and defence policies, were to come into the picture and form what today makes up what one may call the EU's security policy. Taking this into account, and in order to grasp the EU's rule-making in response to the crisis in Ukraine, this chapter looks at a web of rules which spans across, and touches upon, different Treaty provisions in and outside the confines of CFSP/CSDP. As will be shown in the discussion of the historical development of EU external action rule-making, 'specific rules and procedures' apply to CFSP/CSDP, according to the Treaties.

But how, then, can we best understand rule-making in the wake of the EU's response to the war on Ukraine? More specifically, how could we, under the condition of compartmentalization—a variety of separate rule-making procedures, actors, and objectives across policy domains (compartments)—expect the EU to act when confronted with the war on Ukraine, and how has decision- and rule-making evolved accordingly in the time of this crisis?

In order to guide the analysis of how the EU has decided and set rules in times of existential threats, it is argued that liberal intergovernmental or neofunctionalist accounts help give us clues to grasp how the EU has acted and may render different sets of findings in times of geopolitics and geo-politicization. The analysis of procedural and substantive rules in view of the geopolitical crisis speaks to each of these theoretical explanations.

The chapter will proceed as follows: it first lays out foreign and security policy-related EU rule-making in and at the margins of CFSP/CSDP, by taking on historical developments and theoretical approaches. Secondly, it presents CFSP/CSDP's formal and informal rule-making dimensions following the Lisbon Treaty and discusses the actual crisis response in the wake of Russia's war on Ukraine. Finally, in the conclusions, it discusses: (a) the implications of these rules in view of how we have to understand EU security policy in the future, including the set of competences and actors involved; (b) the implications of these rules for future coherent crisis responses in the field of foreign and security policy; and (c) the implication of these rules for the EU's legitimacy.

8.2 Rule-making in CFSP/CSDP in Times of Crisis—Compartmentalization and Conceptual Approaches

In order to grasp the EU's response to external shocks and crises—more specifically, its response to Russia's invasion of, and war on, Ukraine—it makes sense to see this crisis response in the context of a wider EU external action, specified in the Treaty on European Union (TEU) and the Treaty on the Functioning of the European Union

(TFEU). Indeed, it can be argued that the inception, development, and execution of EU external action has taken place in different compartments, not least in its trade, enlargement and neighbourhood policy, and its foreign and security policy.[6] These compartments were, and still are, surely interlinked with each other, but their making and development took place separately from each other, representing different integration logics and, eventually, rule-making modes.[7] While, from a historical perspective of EU integration, such a diversification may make perfect sense, it can undermine the EU's ability to react to crises or, at least, the EU's response could be scattered and inconsistent across different compartments.

8.2.1 Tracing back the EU's compartmentalization in its external action rule-making

In order to understand the EU's response to the war on Ukraine, it makes sense to trace the compartmentalization of its external action rule-making in a historical perspective. This perspective gives us an idea about the deep divide between rule-making in the so-called intergovernmental policy area of foreign policy, on the one hand, and other external relations areas, on the other.

There was no mention of foreign policy or security under the Treaty of Rome. The failure of the European Defence Community (EDC) in 1954 left open the question how the Community would relate to larger questions of foreign policy, security, and defence, especially in the context of the emerging Cold War. Interestingly enough, the European Economic Community (EEC) was able to establish an international profile in trade and development policy, but was not able to acquire a special competence in foreign policy, security, and defence. The integration of the EC Member States into the Western European Union (WEU) and North Atlantic Treaty Organization (NATO) structures was a viable alternative. By underlining the intention of avoiding duplication in the Brussels Treaty 1954, security and military cooperation was factually passed on to NATO and, with that, in essence 'Europeans also lost the opportunity to use their own military capability in pursuit of their own foreign policy choices'.[8]

Setbacks in formally advancing a foreign and security policy, such as in the case of the EDC, however, led to informal institutionalization, thanks to the need for a more active role of the EEC/EU in its external relations. Such institutionalization through the European Political Cooperation (EPC), since the 1970 Luxembourg Report,[9] was

[6] For an overview of the different compartments according to EU law, see Pieter Jan Kuijper and others (eds), *The Law of EU External Relations* (OUP 2016).

[7] Helen Wallace and Christine Reh, 'An Institutional Anatomy and Five Policy Modes' in Helen Wallace and others (eds), *Policy-Making in the European Union* (8th edn, OUP 2021) 67–107.

[8] Stephan Keukeleire and Kolja Raube, 'Common Security and Defense Policy: Development, Added Value, and Challenges' in Federinga Bindi and Irina Angelescu (eds), *The Foreign Policy of the European Union – Assessing Europe's Role in the World* (Brooking Institution Press 2012) 64.

[9] Simon Duke, *The Elusive Quest for European Security – from EPC to CFSP* (OUP 2000); Brian White, *Understanding European Foreign Policy* (Palgrave 2001) 72; ME Smith, *Europe's Foreign and Security Policy – The Institutionalization of Cooperation* (CUP 2004).

not only related to the EEC/EU's quest for a robust mandate to act, but also to the question to what degree its institutions would be involved in the formulation of external policies. When Member States of the EEC established cooperation on foreign policy-related issues in the framework of the EPC, in the 1970s, it became clear that this would not include security and defence cooperation.[10] Nevertheless, and despite the absence of security and defence, EPC proved to be an important soft tool to continue cooperating on foreign policy-related issues. EPC became gradually institutionalized in the Copenhagen Report (1973), the London Report (1981), the Stuttgart 'Solemn Declaration' (1983), and the Single European Act (SEA) (1987). Overall, the European Commission and, after the Single European Act, the European Parliament, became involved in the EPC, but the process remained largely intergovernmental in terms of consensus-based decision-making. According to the Luxembourg Report 1970, the Commission was only to be consulted if EPC was affected,[11] but over time it was associated on all levels to EPC activities (London Report, 1981) and, together with the rotating Presidency of the Council, became responsible for the consistency between EPC and other external relations, for which the Commission was also responsible. Overall, the Commission delegation network, which also developed around the world thanks to external Community competences, was also becoming gradually attached to EPC: eventually, the EEC Treaty, formalized in Title III, Article 30, point 9, underlined that both Member State embassies and EC delegations on the ground had to 'intensify cooperation', meaning that they had to consult each other and coordinate on EPC-relevant issues.

While the SEA in 1987 mentioned that 'the external policies of the European Community and the policies agreed in European Political Cooperation must be consistent' (Article 30(5) SEA), only with the Maastricht Treaty (1993) did the CFSP become an integral part of the overall integration framework and, more precisely, the European Union.[12] Obviously, the Maastricht Treaty (1993), the Amsterdam Treaty (1999), and the Nice Treaty (2003) further formalized foreign, security, and defence policy in the EU. Not only did the end of the Cold War and East–West conflict foster developments in the direction of a political Union, which for the first time fully embraced foreign policy and security as an integral part of the Union, but also several European military conflicts, including the Yugoslav wars in the 1990s, illustrated how poorly equipped the EU was to make use of tools beyond political diplomacy, including the use of military force.

From the Amsterdam to the Lisbon Treaty, the European (later 'Common') Security and Defence Policy became an integral part of CFSP: a tool that would gradually develop military and civilian crisis management, especially after the tragic non-responsiveness of the EU in the Kosovo war of 1999, as a part of the EU, following the Nice Treaty. A separate pillar indeed, CFSP and E(C)SDP, as intergovernmental

[10] White (n 9) 65.
[11] ibid 76.
[12] ibid 94.

parts of the Union, were bound to be formulated in consistent relation with other EU external policies, through the principle of coherence. At the same time though, compared with trade and development cooperation, the role of supranational actors was held back, underlining the role of Member States and the Council and, with the Lisbon Treaty, the European Council. New actors, including the High Representative (Amsterdam Treaty) and the European External Action Service (Lisbon Treaty), arrived and further tried to provide help in the vertical and horizontal coordination and coherence between Member States, on the one hand, and different policies and EU institutional actors, on the other. Eventually, the development in CFSP/CSDP provided the EU with additional tools, ranging from diplomatic cooperation to sanctions and civilian and military instruments, which prepared the Union to shape its role regionally and globally.[13] As described by Burgess, the EC, and later the EU, contained, and arguably still contains, back-to-back elements of confederal and federal structures in the areas of trade, development, diplomacy, foreign policy, and security policy, meaning that those areas of Community competence and action resemble elements of federal systems with shared sovereignty across levels of the federation, whereas the EPC and also CFSP/CSDP resemble features of a confederal system, in which decisions of the confederation need to find consensual approval by all confederate constituents; that is, the Member States.[14]

One of the reasons why this overall compartmentalization of EU external action has taken place is related to internal contestation by the EU's own Member States, which hindered the EU from becoming a fully fledged integrated EU external actor from the start of the integration process. In fact, the making of a foreign policy actor in its own right would have meant that the EC/EU would have looked similar to Member States, and that could potentially have posed a threat to Member States' sovereignty, and regarding their standing as members of the international community. Indeed, the idea that the EU could have federal-like structures not only in the areas of Community competences, but also in the area of diplomacy, foreign policy, and defence has not always been equally well-received across Member States. While certain areas have provided the EU with tools of regional and global engagement from the start, and certainly resembled federal-like structures—such as in trade and development cooperation—others were more contested and, as a consequence, competences and tools of EU rule-making took a different course in CFSP/CSDP. What evolved over time was an actor EC/EU, which became compartmentalized, and which was in a quest for a comprehensive set of tools to respond to global challenges and crises along the objectives of effectiveness, coherence, and democratic accountability.

As a consequence, the compartmentalization of the EU's external action not only finds expression in the different competences which have been lent to the areas of trade, development, and CFSP/CSDP, but also in the authority of actors in each of

[13] Stephan Keukeleire and Kolja Raube, 'The Security-Development Nexus and Securitisation in the EU's Policies towards Developing Countries' (2013) 26 Cambridge Review of International Affairs 556–72.

[14] Michael Burgess, *Federalism and European Union – The Building of Europe, 1950–2000* (Routledge 2000).

the areas and the legitimacy/legitimation of their actions. Member States have remained key sources of legitimacy in each of the different policy areas, while the degree to which supranational actors, including the European Parliament, have lent additional legitimacy to the respective decision-making modes varies across external policies to this day. As such, we also have to acknowledge gradual supranational influence in this area. In fact, already after the London Report of 1981, the European Commission had become more closely associated and involved with EPC.[15] As Nuttall writes, from a European Commission perspective 'it was hoped to bring the two machines discreetly together'.[16] However, even after the Maastricht Treaty, the elements of unanimity voting and the rather limited (yet progressively evolving) roles of the Commission, the Court of Justice, and the European Parliament (especially compared with Community areas) continued to contribute to the 'specific'—some would say, overarchingly intergovernmental—nature of CFSP, while overall it remained in the hands of the national governments to influence the direction of EPC and, later on, CFSP/CSDP.[17] Especially after the Lisbon Treaty, this overarchingly intergovernmental character of CFSP/CSDP has been increasingly questioned by scholars, which has underlined the increasingly influential role of 'Community' actors, especially the European Commission and the European Parliament.[18]

8.2.2 The effect of crises on rule-making in CFSP/CSDP and beyond

The EU has been haunted by multiple crises over the last two decades, leading to an overall multidimensional crisis[19] which threatened and/or tested: (a) the respective functioning of specific policy fields and achievements of integration; and (b) the EU's existence, legitimacy, and resilience. While the war on Ukraine is another crisis and external shock-testing the EU,[20] it does hit the EU in terms of decision- and rule-making as a compartmentalized or 'multi-faceted' actor.[21] As shown above, this multifaceted nature of the EU goes back to the underlying compartmentalization of EU external action.[22] How, then, has the war on Ukraine affected rule-making in the EU's compartmentalized external action?

[15] Simon J Nuttall, *European Foreign Policy* (OUP 2000); See also White (n 9).

[16] Nuttall (n 15) 24.

[17] John Peterson and Helene Sjursen (eds), *A Common Foreign Policy for Europe? Competing Visions of CFSP* (Routledge 1998).

[18] See also Ben Crum, 'Parliamentarization of the CFSP through Informal Institution-making? The Fifth European Parliament and the EU High Representative' (2006) 13 Journal of European Public Policy 383–40; Kolja Raube, 'The European External Action Service and the European Parliament' (2012) 7 The Hague Journal of Diplomacy 65–80; Marianne Riddervold and Guri Rosén, 'Beyond Intergovernmental Cooperation: The Influence of the European Parliament and the Commission on EU Foreign and Security Policies' (2016) 20 European Foreign Affairs Review 399–417; G Rosén and K Raube, 'Influence beyond Formal Powers. The Parliamentarisation of European Union Security Policy' (2018) 2 British Journal of Politics and International Relations 69–83.

[19] Desmond Dinan, Neil Nugent and William Paterson (eds), *The European Union in Crisis.* (Bloomsbury 2017) 2 ff.

[20] Riddervold, Trondal and Newsome (n 2) 4.

[21] Anghel and Jones (n 3) 768.

[22] Matthieu Burnay and Kolja Raube, 'Obstacles, Opportunities, and Red Lines in the European Union: Past and Future of the CAI in Times of (Geo)-Politicisation' (2023) 23(4) Journal of World Investment & Trade 675–99.

Often the EU's response to crisis, while being confronted with its own break-down, often the EU's response to crisis[23] has been seen as one of 'failing forward'[24] or 'muddling through'.[25] From a theoretical perspective of EU integration,[26] we could expect different responses and effects of EU rule-making: more potentially pro-integrative responses if Member States find ways to agree and support such measures, based on their interests and concerns (liberal intergovernmentalism), or innovative and experimental action leading to more integration thanks to the autonomy of policy entrepreneurs like the European Commission (neofunctionalism).

As such, the EU's response to its most recent crisis—the external crisis of Russia's war on Ukraine, which has evidently confronted the EU with geopolitics in Ukraine and its neighbourhood for the second time since 2014,[27] breaches of international law, and the threat of an overhaul of its values—not only teaches us lessons about how reactive the EU is, and whether this crisis has ultimately led to more integration,[28] but also about its effect on decision- and rule-making in policy areas specifically confronted by geopolitics and geopoliticization: in our case, the EU's foreign and security policy.[29]

Arguably, the overall integration and development of CFSP/CSDP and other EU external action-related policies into a compartmentalized field of different policies and rule-making, as portrayed above, sits somewhat square to the requirements of a swift and efficient regional actor which solves crisis-related problems that Member States cannot handle by themselves, especially—but not exclusively—related to insecurity related to geopolitics. In order to analyse the EU's response, we will use two specific theoretical approaches to conceptualize effects of the war in Ukraine on rule-making in EU foreign and security policy in times of geopolitics and geopoliticization.

First, rather than thinking about acute crisis response by the EU as an actor in its own right in foreign and security policy, intergovernmental thinkers have always seen European cooperation on foreign and security matters to preserve (otherwise endangered) Member States' influence, and to protect Member States' interests, at the international level.[30] In this view, Member States would remain 'obstinate'[31]and keep elements of sovereignty to themselves, to protect their interests and shape international relations. Member States would be keen to cooperate in sensitive areas, which they

[23] Riddervold, Trondal and Newsome (n 2) 6.

[24] Erik Jones, R Daniel Kelemen and Sophie Meunier, 'Failing Forward? Crises and Patterns of European Integration' (2021) 28 Journal of European Public Policy 1519–36.

[25] Riddervold, Trondal and Newsome (n 2) 9.

[26] Frank Schimmelfennig, 'Theorising Crisis in European Integration' in Dinan, Nugent and Paterson (n 19) 316–36.

[27] Anna Juncos and Karolina Pomorska, 'The Ukraine Crisis' in Riddervold, Trondal and Newsome (n 2) 553–68.

[28] See also Anghel and Jones (n 3); Tanja A Börzel, 'European Integration and the War in Ukraine: Just Another Crisis? (2023) 61 Journal of Common Market Studies 14–30.

[29] Heidi Maurer, Richard G Whitman and Nicholas Wright, 'The EU and the Invasion of Ukraine: A Collective Responsibility to Act?' (2023) 99(1) International Affairs 219–38; Daniel Fiott, 'Is Every Crisis an Opportunity? European Union Integration in Defence and the War on Ukraine' (2023) 45 Journal of European Integration 447–62.

[30] Andrew Moravscik, *The Choice for Europe: Social Purpose and State Power from Messina to Maastricht* (Cornell University Press 1998).

[31] S Hoffmann,'Obstinate or Obsolete? The Fate of the Nation-State and the Case of Western Europe' 1966 (95) Daedalus 862–915.

consider 'high' politics, but their sovereignties were also dear to them. In other words, not only would we see decisions and rule-making in CFSP/CSDP, in response to the crisis in Ukraine, being dependent on the specific interests of Member States, but also further integration steps in the field of CFSP/CSDP would hardly be possible without the support of all twenty-seven Member States. Moreover, in terms of compartmentalization, we would expect a continuous separation of non-intergovernmental and supranationional Union action, without the need to overcome the intergovernmental character of CFSP/CSDP vis-à-vis other external policies. However, in view of geopolitics and geopoliticization, we could expect Member States to be increasingly willing to opt for new measures and ways to formulate and use CFSP/CSDP rules, given the perceived threats emerging with the war on Ukraine. Alternatively, however, in the event that Member States instead come to different threat perceptions in relation to the crisis, they could potentially be split, and rather indifferent on the level of the EU, on taking common action.

Second, neofunctionalist and supranational theories, however, would foresee the uploading of competences to the European level as rooted in the ability of European institutions to act autonomously, and in a shift of loyalty of transnational actors towards the European level,[32] with the twofold consequence that supranational institutions 'defend' transnational preferences, both by shaping EU external relations and, more specifically, by protecting the EU against external shocks and crisis.

The effect of such changes could be that rule-making, even with a link to EU foreign and security domains, would also take place in non-CFSP/CSDP areas. There would be a gradual shift of rule-making to supranational areas and actors. In terms of compartmentalization, this would mean that, due to a lack of rule-making capacity on the intergovernmental end of EU external action (CFSP/CSDP), it would be supranational Union areas that would increasingly be used to pursue EU objectives. In view of geopolitics and geopoliticization, we could expect supranational actors, especially the European Commission, to promote new rules in order to counter the geopolitical threats, especially outside CFSP/CSDP rules.

8.3 Procedural and Substantive Rules in Times of Crisis

Before turning to the actual procedural and substantive rules in times of crisis, I will give an overview of the formal procedural and substantive rules in the area of foreign and security policy. Once more, the overview underlines CFSP/CSDP as a special 'island' and the compartmentalization of EU external action overall. Against this background, I will then proceed to the actual rules in times of geopolitical crisis, in order to understand how we can best understand rule-making in the wake of the EU's response

[32] Ernst B Haas, *The Uniting of Europe: Political, Social, and Economic Forces, 1950–1957* (new edn, University of Notre Dame Press 2003); A Stone Sweet and Michael Sandholtz, 'European Integration and Supranational Governance' (1997) 4 Journal of European Public Policy 297–317.

to the war on Ukraine and, under the condition of compartmentalization, expect EU decision- and rule-making to have evolved during the time of the crisis.

8.3.1 Procedural rules

Rule-making in CFSP/CSDP is specified in the TEU: in the General Provisions on the Union's External Action in Articles 21 and 22, and, more specifically, in the Specific Provisions on the Common Foreign and Security Policy in Articles 23 ff. These are followed by the Provisions on the Common Security and Defence Policy, an integral part of CFSP, which are laid out in Articles 42 ff TEU. Hence, rule-making in CFSP/CSDP is laid out through the provisions on EU external action (Articles 21 and 22 TEU), and then more specifically in the other two sets of provisions on CFSP/CSDP. The latter provisions, situated in the TEU, are separated from other policy areas, the competences and decision-making for which are laid out in the TFEU.

Underlining the compartmentalized nature of EU external action, Article 24 TEU suggests a 'carving out' of a specific rule-making machinery of CFSP, which rests distinct from other areas of the EU. Most notably, Article 24(2) TEU states that the Foreign and Security Policy 'is subject to specific rules and procedures .... [and that] the adoption of legislative acts shall be excluded'. This means that, as opposed to other policy areas in the EU, there is legally no legislation foreseen in CFSP, and that procedures other than regular legislative law-making apply. What is more, the intergovernmental character of CFSP could not have been more underscored by the current formulation of Article 24(2) TEU: 'It shall be defined and implemented by the European Council and the Council acting unanimously, except where the Treaties provide otherwise.' As such, the 'intergovernmental method' is arguably strengthened by a twofold 'manoeuvre' of Article 24: the reduction of competences and powers of supranational collective actors and Union institutions, including the Commission, the Parliament, and the Court of Justice of the European Union (Article 24(2) TEU), and the underscoring of the role of Member States in this special policy area (Article 24(3) TEU).

Rules of decision-making in CFSP are laid down in Article 28 ff TEU, as to how the Council shall take decisions, under which conditions, in regard to which international circumstances, and how, if need be, Member States can abstain from decisions. Article 30 TEU specifies that 'any Member State, the High Representative of the Union for Foreign Affairs and Security Policy, or the High Representative with the Commission's support' can forward questions and take decision-making initiatives in the Council. In CSDP, decisions in the Council can be taken on the initiative of either the High Representative or a Member State (Article 42(4) TEU). Also, so-called 'rapid decisions' can be foreseen by means of the High Representative's own motion, or at the request of a Member State, within up to 48 hours (Article 30(2) TEU). Article 31 TEU foresees that decisions in CFSP are supposed to be taken unanimously, with exceptions provided, so that a limited number of Member States can abstain from actions in CFSP (so-called 'constructive abstention', Article 31(1) TEU). However, beyond formal unanimity as a base rule, there are four additional possibilities to establish a decision beyond unanimity with qualified majoirty voting (QMV), according to Article 31(2) TEU, under specific conditions. While QMV has hence been inscribed as an exception in the rule-making of CFSP by the Lisbon Treaty, it remains a practically never-used instrument to establish decisions in CFSP. Debates about the necessity of QMV to enhance the effectiveness of CFSP decision-making have been present for a long time,[33] and surely represent the ambition not only to provide for CFSP decisions even in the absence of support by all Member States, but also more generally to supranationalize CFSP to a certain extent.[34]

8.3.2 Procedural rules in times of crisis

It is worth noting that, with the beginning of Russia's war on Ukraine, the EU was in need of establishing decisions that would respond efficiently and swiftly to a war which, with its territorial invasion of a sovereign country in Europe, posed a geopolitical threat by questioning the territorial integrity and sovereign existence of a neighbouring country of the EU and, with that, the values Ukraine shared with the EU, grounded in international law, democratic order, the rule of law, and human rights. There were hence good reasons for the EU to establish an EU foreign policy as a response to the invasion of Ukrainian territory, which would show solidarity with the Ukrainian people and Ukraine as a sovereign state, and show its aggressor, the Russian Federation, its disapproval and contestation.[35] To this end, the EU arguably needed to take geopolitically informed decisions, and these would only be possible if all twenty-seven Member States were able to agree in the context of CFSP/CSDP.

With unanimity prevailing formally and informal consensus-making practice in the Council, differing positions or even veto positions of Member States on how to respond to the war on Ukraine emerged as a serious obstacle, given the crisis and urgency at stake. Furthermore, with QMV being rather a theoretical debate on future Treaty change, rather than a practical short-term option, given the standard intergovernmental practice in CFSP, the focus was soon on constructive abstentions, and even other ways of establishing decisions in CFSP/CSDP and other areas which needed unanimity. Article 31 TEU foresees that the Member States can abstain from actions in CFSP but has only been used twice in CFSP history, and only once in the time of the war on Ukraine: in the case of the establishment of the European Peace Facility (EPF) in February 2022, [36] when Ireland, Malta, and Austria abstained from the 'sensitive assistance'—in other words 'military equipment, and platforms, designed to deliver

[33] Karolina Pomorska and Ramses A Wessel, 'Qualified Majority Voting in CFSP: A Solution to the Wrong Problem?' (2021) 2 European Foreign Affairs Review 351–58.

[34] For example, the debates about QMV in the Convention on the Future of Europe or the Conference on the Future of Europe.

[35] Maurer, Whitman and Wright (n 29).

[36] Council Decision (CFSP) 2022/338 of 28 February 2022 [2022] OJ L60/1.

lethal force'—in the EPF.[37] While this certainly underpins the Member States' neutral position—that is, their objective to remain neutral actors when it comes to military assistance—and Council practice (and need) to establish decisions despite a variety of different preferences, it also remained a viable option to establish effective (and even vertically coherent) decisions between the Union's overall action in CFSP and (reluctant) Member States.

Along similar lines, recent discussions in the Political and Security Committee (PSC) have accentuated the viability of the consensus method in the absence of unanimity voting, and in an effort to work beyond constructive abstentions.[38] Next to the use of constructive abstention, and in its debates with the General Secretariat and the European External Action Service (EEAS), the PSC has developed the idea of 'constructive silence', which essentially underlines the need, expressed by the Strategic Compass adopted by the Council in 2022, to 'become faster and effective in its ability to decide and act'.[39] Different from the framework of 'constructive abstention', which generally frees Member States of their responsibility to implement a CFSP decision,[40] 'constructive silence' foresees the implementation of CFSP decisions by all Member States in the spirit of solidarity and loyal cooperation. To arrive at this end, and to allow for the overcoming of blockades in the Council, Member States could use statements directed at their domestic constituencies and audiences, expressing their concerns while not contradicting the EU position overall. While certainly not accurately depicted by the playbook of 'constructive silence' in CFSP and rather a matter of 'constructive absence' on other unanimity decisions, including those on the opening of an accession state status to the EU, on 15 December 2023, 'about three hours into deadlocked discussions among EU leaders on Ukraine's accession to the bloc, the German chancellor proposed to Hungarian Prime Minister Viktor Orbán: Grab a coffee outside the room, perhaps'.[41] However we term the incident, Orbán was actually leaving the room, and 'in effect abstaining from the decision after having signalled for weeks that he would block consensus to start membership talks with Kyiv'.[42] And yet, while such an informal decision-making procedure may generate short-term efficiency, and certainly the outlook of a comprehensive toolbox (see below), 'the European Union will have to deal with the hangover of the highly symbolic move, which only clears the first of the 70+ veto hurdles and came at the cost of Orbán vetoing the mid-term review of the MFF'.[43]

[37] Council of the EU, 'Extraordinary meetings of the Permanent Representatives Committee 22, 24, 27, 28 February, 1, 3 and 4 March 2022, Summary Record', Brussels, 16 March 2022 (OR. en) 7282/22.

[38] Political and Security Committee, unpublished document.

[39] Council of the EU, 'A Strategic Compass for Security and Defence – For a European Union that protects its citizens, values and interests and contributes to international peace and security', 21 March 2022, 7371/22.

[40] Exceptions are decisions with budgetary implications, and restrictive measures, which require EU-wide implementation.

[41] Politico, 'Scholz Gets Orbán out the Room to Open Ukraine's Membership Talks' (*Politico*, 15 December 2023) https://www.politico.eu/article/olaf-scholz-gets-viktor-orban-out-the-room-to-approve-ukraine-accession-talks/ (accessed 31 October 2024).

[42] Steven Blockmans, 'Editorial – Fast and Furious? A Quick Digest of a Plan for the Accelerated Integration of Candidate Countries into the EU' (2024) 29(1) European Foreign Affairs Review 5.

[43] ibid.

In light of an overarching threat to Ukraine, EU Member States, and the EU itself, decision-making can, however, best be depicted as 'negotiated coherence' which understands decisions in CFSP/CSDP in times of crisis rather as a decision-making outcome and consequence of sometimes long and difficult negotiations, bringing the different perspectives of Member States together. In the context of the war and security crisis, the existential threat urges Member States to move towards decisions which are acceptable to all Member States, and which would be best depicted as vertical coherence. Rather than leaving Member States outside the scope of decisions and their implementation, as happened with constructive abstention only once (see above), the EU was remarkably consistent and able to present consistency amongst and with its Member States, in its efforts to take decisions which would respond and bounce back against the perceived threats: this is true for the EU's restrictive measures and sanction policy, CSDP mission 'EuMAM', and the establishment of the EU's EPF, amounting to more than 12 billion euros. Furthermore, the EU was able to take decisions beyond the CFSP framework, which further speaks to the idea of a coherent EU policy response not only across Member States, but also across different compartments of the EU, including EU justice and home affairs, EU budgetary policies, EU accession policy, and EU defence procurement.[44] I will turn to these CFSP and CSDP instruments, as well as other rule-making measures, below when discussing the EU's response in view of the war.

8.3.3 Substantive rules

Decisions in CFSP are bound by a catalogue of principles, as laid out in Article 21 TEU, through which the Union 'shall define and pursue common policies and actions' and 'work for a high degree of cooperation in all fields of international relations' (Article 21(2) TEU). These frame EU external action in general, and CFSP action more specifically, in terms of, to mention a few, commitments to international law, democracy, rule of law, and human rights. Along the lines of the principles and values enshrined in primary law, the Union can further define its own strategic guidelines by means of decisions of the European Council (Article 22 TEU; Article 26(1) TEU).

Decisions in CFSP can be made based on a range of different legal instruments, leading to various instances of rule-making in CFSP. Article 25 TEU foresees that: 'The Union shall conduct the common foreign and security policy by: (a) defining the general guidelines; (b) adopting decisions defining: (i) actions to be undertaken by the Union; (ii) positions to be taken by the Union; (iii) arrangements for the implementation of the decisions referred to in points (i) and (ii); and by (c) strengthening systematic cooperation between Member States in the conduct of policy.' Again, such decisions

[44] Defence procurement is covered by the 'European Defence Industry Reinforcement through Common Procurement Act' (EDIRPA), the 'European Defence Investment Programme' (EDIP), and the 'Act in Support of Ammunition Production' (ASAP), see also: Federico Fabbrini, 'Funding the War in Ukraine: The European Peace Facility, the Macro-Financial Assistance Instrument, and the Slow Rise of an EU Fiscal Capacity' (2023) 11(4) Politics and Governance 52–61; Fiott (n 29).

and actions are to be taken either by means of strategic guidelines of the European Council (Article 26(1) TEU) or decisions by the Council (Foreign Affairs Council), presided over by the High Representative, who is, as mentioned earlier, responsible for unity, consistency, and effectiveness in CFSP (see Article 26(1) TEU). In the case of CSDP, which is an integral part of CFSP (Article 42 TEU), decisions can lead to the establishment of either EU military or civilian missions abroad (Article 42(4) TEU).

Through the general provisions on the Union's external action in Articles 21 and 22 TEU, there is an close link established between the intergovernmental CFSP and other policies, through the general principles and objectives, which are formulated and applicable to all EU external actions—CFSP/CSDP, trade, development cooperation, etc. In fact, the general provisions underline that CFSP/CSDP decisions—even if practiced under the intergovernmental method—are not to be taken in isolation, but rather in conjunction with other policy areas (and vice versa) and ideally overcoming compartmentalization. To this end, Article 21(3) TEU foresees the objective of consistency between these policies, but also other policy areas outside the external relations domain: 'The Union shall ensure consistency between the different areas of its external action and between these and its other policies.' And the provision further foresees the responsibility of two EU institutions to work to this end: 'The Council and the Commission, assisted by the High Representative of the Union for Foreign Affairs and Security Policy, shall ensure that consistency and shall cooperate to that effect.' Furthermore, as Article 18(4) TEU clarifies, it is the High Representative/Vice-President of the Commission who shall 'ensure the consistency of the Union's external action'. With the HR/VP taking the role of chair in the Foreign Affairs Council (Article 18(3) TEU), it is almost logical that, in the case of CFSP, the Treaty ultimately lays out that '[the] Council and the High Representative of the Union for Foreign Affairs and Security Policy shall ensure the unity, consistency and effectiveness of action by the Union' (Article 26(2) TEU).

Despite the distinct nature of CFSP decisions, positions, and other instruments, direct links to TFEU rule-making practice are also established. In no other area does the link between CFSP and other policy areas regulated by the TFEU materialize so clearly as in the case of restrictive measures. Restrictive measures are specified in Article 215 TFEU. Interestingly, Article 215 TFEU calls for decisions under CFSP (Chapter 2, Title V, TEU) to interrupt and reduce 'economic and financial relations' with a third country, or to use restrictive measure 'against natural or legal persons or non-State entities' (Article 215(1) and Article 215(2) TEU). As Eeckhout mentions, 'the current sanctions practice therefore continues to straddle the CFSP and the policies and acts adopted under the TFEU'.[45] While CFSP lays out the 'overall sanctions', especially by making reference to Article 29 TEU,[46] such a CSDP decision is then translated into regulations under Article 215 TFEU. While, certainly, the TFEU decisions can have a

[45] Piet Eekhout, *EU External Relations Law* (OUP 2011) 506.

[46] Art 29 TEU reads: 'The Council shall adopt decisions which shall define the approach of the Union to a particular matter of a geographical or thematic nature. Member States shall ensure that their national policies conform to the Union positions.'

different scope compared with the TFEU translations (for example, on arms sales and exports),[47] there is a practice of linking the detailed CFSP decisions to the regulations adopted under the TFEU, implying that the Foreign Affairs Council decides under the CFSP rules (see below), and the Council (in the relevant configuration) under TFEU rules. In practice then, CFSP decisions, even if formally ruled out as 'legislative acts' (Article 24(2) TEU), are acts that factually inform, word for word, the follow-up regulations. This implies not only that CFSP actions are by no means taken in complete (intergovernmental) isolation, but even more so that supranational actors (for example, the European Commission) play a key role in allowing for a smooth translation of CFSP decisions into supranational rule-making practice under the TFEU.

8.3.4 Substantive rules in times of crisis

In the aftermath of Russia's invasion into Ukrainian territory in February 2022 and the outbreak of Russia's war on the whole territory of Ukraine, the EU has come up with a set of rule-making tools which respond to the emerging crisis and, eventually, fall into the areas of CFSP/CSDP and beyond. Not only does the response by the geopolitically affected EU expose a vast set of tools falling into different rule-making compartments and policy areas, but it also shows that the EU was tested to look for new ways of dealing with this unprecedented crisis, including new qualitative levels of restrictive measures, the supply of weapons in active warfare, the development of an industrial basis for defence procurement in the context of the existing Treaties, and the recognition of Ukraine, Georgia, and Moldova as new candidates to enter the EU through a future round of enlargement.

8.3.4.1 CFSP decisions and CSDP missions

In CFSP, the EU has taken a number of measures to counter Russia's invasion of Ukraine, and to respond to the geopolitical crisis. Responding to the growing need to cover and finance CFSP/CSDP-related action in view of crisis management globally, the EPF was created in 2021. It replaced former financial off-budget instruments like the Athena mechanism, by which military components of CSDP missions had been paid, and the African Peace Facility, which until then was used to finance non-EU military missions of, for example, the African Union.[48] Escaping the budgetary oversight of the European Parliament, and embedded in intergovernmental financing arrangements, the CFSP decision reads:

> A European Peace Facility (the "Facility") is hereby established for the financing by Member States of Union actions under the Common Foreign and Security Policy (CFSP) to preserve peace, prevent conflicts and strengthen international security in

[47] Eekhout (n.45), 482–83.
[48] See also Keukeleire and Raube, 'The Security-Development Nexus' (n 13).

> accordance with point (c) of Article 21(2) of the Treaty on European Union (TEU), in cases where, pursuant to Article 41(2) TEU, the operating expenditure arising from those actions is not charged to the Union budget.[49]

After the invasion of Ukraine, the EPF quickly turned factually, however, into a 'Ukrainian Peace Facility', as many of the EU's efforts to support Ukraine militarily were financed by the EPF. Originally established with a maximum budget of approximately 5.5 billion euros, efforts to support Ukraine with non-lethal and lethal support quickly exhausted the financial arrangement and top-ups were added. The current EPF amounts to a total of 12 billion euros, following a Council decision in June 2023. With the EPF, two major novelties arose within the context of the EU.

First, the EU actively contributed to a war, not only financially, but also via its Member States' weaponry, and, as such, became actively involved in the conflict through the respective lethal and non-lethal support structures. Next to these multilateral arrangements, Member States also became bilaterally involved and contributed to Ukraine's defence efforts. Second, the EU was able to establish an overall support mechanism, which was originally intended for a larger scope of crisis interventions, but had to deal with Member State-related deteriorations. As such, Ireland, Austria, and Malta abstained from, but did not block the EU's efforts to arm Ukraine to defend itself as of 2022

One of the many ways in which the EU, over time, has established a security crisis response component has been through CSDP missions according to Article 42(4) TEU. The EU's track record is especially strong in relation to civilian crisis response and management, where most of the EU's engagement in and outside Europe has been found. However, in the case of Ukraine, and the support of Ukraine in an effort to defend itself against Russia's invasion and ongoing assault on its territory, the EU has expanded its presence in the region. The EU had already been present in Ukraine through the CSDP mission European Union Advisory Mission Ukraine, which was deployed in December 2014 'to advise state security bodies on security, police, judiciary, prosecution, anti-corruption and human rights', and whose mandate was extended in 2022 to provide 'support to law enforcement agencies to facilitate the flow of refugees from Ukraine to the neighbouring Member States and the entry of humanitarian aid into Ukraine. EUAM also supports the rule of law institutions to facilitate the investigation and prosecution of international crimes.'[50] In addition to the CSDP mission EUAM, the EU established the EU Military Assistance Mission in support of Ukraine (EUMAM Ukraine), in November 2022, for a preliminary period of two years. In the EU's own words, the mission 'is the EU's coordinated response to enhance the military capacity of the Ukrainian Armed Forces and build their long-term resilience. The aim of the mission is to tackle urgent and longer-term training needs that will strengthen

[49] Council Decision (CFSP) 2021/509 of 22 March 2021 establishing a European Peace Facility [2021] OJ L102/14, 24 March 2021.

[50] European External Action Service, 'EU Military Assistance Mission in Support of Ukraine', https://www.eeas.europa.eu/eumam-ukraine_en?s=410260 accessed 16 February 2024.

Ukraine's efforts in defending its territorial integrity and ability to effectively conduct military operations in deterrence of Russia.'[51] Established with a budget of 115 million euros, a total of 15,000 Ukrainian soldiers are to be trained at basic, specialized, and advanced levels. It is financed by the EPF. Overall, EUMAM works, according to the EU's own assessment, 'closely together with all other like-minded international partners to provide training support to the Ukrainian Armed Forces'. A total of twenty-four Member States are involved in the training being offered, which is 'supported by the provision of equipment for lethal and non-lethal purposes to the Ukrainian Armed Forces'.[52] Interestingly, the CSDP missions not only cover both civilian and military formats in Ukraine, but have also been established in two new candidate countries, Moldova and Georgia (see section 8.3.4.3 below), as well as in Armenia. As such, the EU's geopolitical moves in the region are obvious, and aim to stabilize the region in view of ever-increasing tensions and destabilization efforts by the Russian Federation and other regional actors.

8.3.4.2 EU's restrictive measures and sanction policy

The EU's sanction policy towards Russia has developed over the last two years in a remarkably rapid, qualitatively new, and consistent manner.[53] Already, before the outbreak of the war, the EU was able to experiment with new ways of using restrictive measures specifically in the area of human rights breaches, and developed what later became known as the 'EU's Magnitzky Act'.[54] In the face of the perceived need to respond to human rights abuses worldwide, but especially in the Russia and China, Council Decision (CFSP) 2020/1999 of 7 December 2020 concerning restrictive measures against serious human rights violations and abuses,[55] and Council Regulation (EU) 2020/1998 of 7 December 2020 concerning restrictive measures against serious human rights violations and abuses[56] were introduced and officially became the 'Global Human Rights Sanctions Regime' (GHRSR) of the EU.

Under this framework, for example, the EU foresees sanctions against natural persons, groups, or legal persons due to human rights abuses. In 2020, the practice of the EU has listed fifty-five natural persons and twenty entities, 'including 18 persons and 8 entities linked to the Wagner Group and other associated groups'.[57] As such, the regime has decoupled human rights atrocities from blacklisting countries, and focuses instead on a horizontal regime of sanctions against, say, individuals and companies, to

[51] ibid.

[52] European Union, EU Military Assistance Mission in support of Ukraine , (last visit on 31 October 2024).

[53] Katharina Meissner and Chiara Graziani, 'The Transformation and Design of EU Restrictive Measures against Russia' (2023) 45(3) Journal of European Integration 377–94.

[54] Steven Blockmans, 'The EU's Magnitsky Act: Obsolete in the Face of Russia's Crimes in Ukraine?' (2024) 28(2) European Foreign Affairs Review 110.

[55] Council Decision (CFSP) 2020/1999 of 7 December 2020 concerning restrictive measures against serious human rights violations and abuses [2020] OJ L410 I/13, 7 December 2020.

[56] Council Regulation (EU) 2020/1998 of 7 December 2020 concerning restrictive measures against serious human rights violations and abuses [2020] OJ L 410 I/1, 7 December 2020.

[57] Clara Portela and Kim B Olsen, 'Implementation and Monitoring of the EU Sanctions' Regimes, including Recommendations to Reinforce the EU's Capacities to Implement and Monitor Sanctions', Report, AFET Committee, European Parliament, Brussels, October 2023, 6.

the degree that critics have highlighted a potential 'depoliticization' effect by not explicitly linking violations to a specific country like Russia, but rather to country-related individuals and groups.[58] It has, however, been questioned how practicable and useful the sanction regime is in the context of Russia's atrocities in Ukraine. As Blockmans writes, 'even if the novelty of the GHRSR lies in the grave nature of the human rights abuses it covers, the targets of such violations might as well be blacklisted under (existing) vertical sanction regimes, especially if a case-centric approach is necessary'.[59] What is more, it may even be recommendable and advisable to politicize human rights abuses by clearly linking them to vertical sanctions against states as a whole, and by adding them to country-specific sanction lists.[60]

In the meantime, the EU has indeed come up with twelve rounds of country-specific sanction packages against the Russian Federation. They express a continuation of country-specific sanction policy of the EU after Russia's invasion of Crimea in 2014,[61] but the substantive rules emerging with the sanction practice, as of 2022, have been praised in the literature as remarkably new in quality and consistency.[62] This has mainly been for three reasons.

First, 'the scope of the EU's sanctions against Russia has become more comprehensive over time and the entailed costs for the entire population have expanded'.[63] In fact, the various sanctions imposed by the EU on Russia have targeted not only individuals and high-ranking leadership and politicians, including Vladimir Putin, Sergey Lavrov, and most of the members of the State Duma, as well as industrial sectors, but increasingly the wider Russian population (ibid).[64] As such, the sanction rules emerging are much more comprehensive in nature compared with previous rounds, targeting Russian citizens and aiming for an effect not only on Russia's economy, but a general declining support of the Russian people for the war on Ukraine, and for the Russian government. Second, the sanction practice has become consistent in the sense that: (a) on the one hand, fewer exceptions and derogations exist to EU-wide sanctions vis-à-vis Russia by specific Member States, including transformatory practices with regard to oil and gas imports to Bulgaria, Croatia, and the Czech Republic;[65] and (b) on the other hand, the implementation practice of the EU has altered in the sense that the Commission can now oversee implementation breaches against sanction rules centrally rather than, as used to be the case, relying on decentralized implementation. Under Article 83(1) TFEU, the violation of a sanction practice can now be seen as a 'minimal crime'.[66] (Overall, in the words of Portela, the 'crisis has accelerated' the centralization of the

[58] Blockmans, 'The EU's Magnitsky Act' (n 54).
[59] ibid 114–15.
[60] iibid.
[61] For an overview of all Russia-related sanctions, see Portela and Olsen (n 57) 5–6
[62] Meissner and Graziani (n 53); Clara Portela, 'The War over Ukraine and the Transformation of EU Governance' (2023) 8(3) European Papers 1125–30; Kolja Raube and Raquel Vega Rubio, 'Coherence at Last? Transatlantic Cooperation in Response to the Geostrategic Challenge of China' (2022) 10(2) Politics and Governance 176–85.
[63] Meissner and Graziani (n 53) 386.
[64] Ibid.
[65] ibid.
[66] Ibid.

implementation practice, including 'a whistleblowing tool allowing individuals to alert the Commission of possible violations without having to approach national authorities first'.[67] Third, the sanction rules developed by the EU have been increasingly consistent and coordinated, not only with the United Kingdom in the aftermath of Brexit, but also, and importantly, with the United States and Canada, following a more coherent practice of transatlantic coordination during the Biden administration.[68]

8.3.4.3 Non-CFSP/CSDP rules

Beyond CFSP/CSDP, a number of measures and tools have also been taken and activated in different compartments of the EU, including EU justice and home affairs, EU budgetary policies, EU accession policy, and EU defence procurement, in order to respond to Russia's invasion of Ukraine. In the EU's justice and home affairs, Eurojust's mandate, based on Article 85 TFEU, was amended in June 2022 to deal with international war crimes, more specifically the legal possibility to collect, preserve, and share evidence on war crimes. The European Commission underlined, in its statement accompanying the proposal, that 'to ensure accountability for the crimes committed in Ukraine, it is crucial to ensure safe storage of evidence outside Ukraine as well as to support the investigations and prosecutions by various European and international judicial authorities'.[69] According to Eurojust's own information, 'the Agency analyses the evidence to establish links, identify investigative gaps and advise prosecutors on the way forward. Eurojust works closely with the International Criminal Court, so that analysis can also benefit their investigation, through their cooperation with States concerned. Access to the information is subject to the approval of the country who provided it.'[70] Moreover, in her statement at the establishment of the new operationability of the International Centre for the Prosecution of the Crime of Aggression against Ukraine (ICPA) at Eurojust in the Hague, in March 2023, Commission President Von der Leyen underlined:

> I was there myself and I have witnessed the atrocities committed by Russian forces ... Torture, ill-treatment, sexual violence, and summary executions are known to have been committed by Russian forces. Not even children are being spared. Russia must be held accountable for these horrific crimes. Putin must be held accountable. ... The European Union is supportive of the role of the International Criminal Court. ... The European Union will continue to work, with our partners, to ensure that Russia pays.[71]

[67] Portela (n 61).
[68] Raube and Vega Rubio (n 62).
[69] Eurojust, 'Legal Framework', https://www.eurojust.europa.eu/about-us/organisation/eurojust-legal-framework accessed 16 February 2024.
[70] ibid.
[71] Commission, 'Statement by President von der Leyen on the establishment of the International Centre for the Prosecution of Crimes of Aggression against Ukraine, Brussels, 4 March 2023' (last accessed 16 February 2024).

In November 2023, the United States (US) announced that it would support ICPA with 1 million US dollars.[72]

The geopolitical nature of the Commission of Ursula von der Leyen, famously self-proclaimed, shows in a number of other areas which have a security and defence component beyond CFSP/CSDP, most notably in regard to the EDIRPA, EDIP, and ASAP. Such a move into security and defence had already started before von der Leyen's Commission, with what became the EDF, in an effort to 'coordinate efforts to boost integrated security and defence research in times of growing international insecurity during Juncker's political Commission'.[73] In the wake of the 2022 invasion of Ukraine, the Commission has been even more 'active' in 'its contribution to the support the effort to stop and counterbalance Russia's ongoing assault on the territorial integrity of Ukraine'. [74] The Commission's contribution to the EDIRPA and the EDIP, as well as the 500 million euro fund called ASAP, clearly underlines the Commission's ambition to step up its efforts to establish an integrated defence market. ASAP, more specifically, supports the EU's defence industry to produce up to 1 million shells capacities in ammunition and missiles, co-financed by the EU budget, the EDF, and EDIP.

The Commission's comprehensive moves in order to generate foreign and security-related policy responses further became apparent in late 2023, when, along with the European Council's decision, it became evident that the Commission was—together with the European Parliament—a driving force in the effort to grant Ukraine, Georgia, and Moldova candidate country statuses.[75] As Maurer, Raube, and Bicchi argue, it 'was even more evidence of the EU's enlargement policy being clearly related to the geopolitical ambitions and security needs promoted by the self-proclaimed 'geopolitical' Von der Leyen Commission: 'Enlargement is a vital policy for the European Union. Completing our Union is the call of history, the natural horizon of our Union. Completing our Union, also has a strong economic and geopolitical logic. Past enlargements have shown the enormous benefits both for the accession countries and the EU. We all win.''[76]

Finally, it is thanks to the same geopolitical Commission that financial assistance to Ukraine was approved in early 2024. With a total of 50 billion euros of support to be provided between 2024 and 2027, the EU has provided Ukraine with a special funding scheme in the Multi-annual Financial Framework (MFF). This was established and finally approved by the EU Member States in early 2024, shortly before the European elections, and despite the ongoing vetoing efforts of Hungary. With Hungary increasingly isolated (see, above, its 'absence' on the question of candidate statuses and the initiation of accession talks), and a shortage of US financial support due to a veto of

[72] US State Department, 'U.S. Assistance to International Investigation of the Crime of Aggression Against Ukraine', 14 November 2023, <U.S. Assistance to International Investigation of the Crime of Aggression Against Ukraine - United States Department of State> accessed 16 February 2024.
[73] Maurer, Raube and Bicchi (n 4).
[74] Ibid.
[75] Blockmans, 'Fast and Furious?' (n 42).
[76] Ursula von der Leyen, cited in Maurer, Raube and Bicchi (n 4).

Republicans in the US Congress, the EU's financial support for Ukraine was seen as of utmost importance.

8.4 Conclusion

Be it the end of the Cold War, which led to the adoption and ratification of the Maastricht Treaty; the early experiences of the Balkan wars, in the 1990s, which led to the adoption of changes in the Treaty of Amsterdam and the Treaty of Nice; the aftermath of the attacks on the World Trade Center in New York on 9 September 2001, and the Iraq War; the migration crisis of 2014/15; the terrorist attacks on EU soil; or the Russian War on Ukraine, the making and conduct of CFSP/CSDP has been reactive to such crises over time. The compartmentalized nature of CFSP/CSDP and other policy areas has not been overcome by the geopolitical crisis which the EU has evidenced since 2022. And yet, in various compartments, responses have triggered action that often would not have been imagined before the crisis. In fact, since the last Treaty reform with the Treaty of Lisbon, and with the war on Ukraine serving as an existential crisis to which the EU needed to adapt in unprecedented ways, rule-making itself has further advanced due to external shocks and internal adaptation. This chapter's analysis shows that the EU has found new ways of, more comprehensive than before. In fact, against the background of the geopolitical and geopoliticized reality of the EU, both intergovernmental and neofunctional accounts of European integration have proved to be accurate in their theoretical ways of foreseeing EU responses.

We saw, indeed, that 'negotiated coherence' of EU Member States, finally agreeing to, or at least abstaining from vetoing, EU action, served as a ground to take numerous actions in CSFP/CSDP which could not otherwise have been done: think of the execution of the EPF and the support of Ukraine through lethal weaponry and the active training of the military in Ukraine by EU Member State forces. But also take into account the often-difficult restricted measures of the EU, which were often countering intuitively important economic relations with Russia. The analysis also showed the creeping supranationalism in areas related to foreign and security policy, including defence. The 'geopolitical Commission' played and plays an important role in this regard, to be able, with the support of Member States that saw the added value, to deepen the EU's support of Ukraine, but also EU integration in areas which had not previously been developed well enough (ie defence procurement).

Eventually, this also implies that EU foreign and security policy can no longer be seen as a policy bound by the rules of CFSP/CSDP only. Which dynamics are at play, and which institutional actors increasingly get to co-decide rules, matters for how foreign and security policy may be conducted in the future. The war on Ukraine and the EU responses thereto have changed the outlook of an EU foreign and security-related policy fundamentally, as action took place across different compartments and not CFSP/CSDP alone. This may imply that the EU is increasingly living up to the Treaty objective of coherence across different policies and rule-making.

If, indeed, foreign and security policy-related crisis responses are increasingly deliberately dealt with not only in CFSP/CSDP, but also, at least indirectly, through areas of the TFEU, then there may be, overall, a more coherent EU security policy in the making. This can have an impact on the legitimacy of the EU's actions and reactions in response to crisis, in the sense that the EU will be able to present a comprehensive toolkit of policies rather than limited actions in response to crisis. While the EU may look increasingly able to live up to what is expected from her (output legitimacy), it will also be important to measure how effective and efficient the EU's overall responses to the war on Ukraine have been. With the support of the US potentially eroding, it may become even more important for the EU to consider how to sustain its policy toolbox in the future, and whether it can or should further step up its engagement in the conflict.

9

EU Regulatory Responses to Crises

Summary, Horizontal Perspective, and Conclusions

Diane Fromage[*], *Adrienne Héritier*[**], *and Paul Weismann*[***]

9.1 Introduction

At the start of this book (Chapter 1), we stated that crises normally require that decisions are taken faster and with a greater willingness to take big leaps. In the European Union (EU), crisis measures, just like non-crisis measures, have to be taken on the basis of the EU Treaties. The Treaties shape and constrain swift and effective action, essentially by means of their competence regime, and by means of procedural requirements, in particular the thresholds of political agreement they prescribe. Some of the restrictions turn out to be insurmountable; others are eventually overstepped or removed by EU institutional actors and Member State actors. It was the objective of the previous chapters to analyse, from a legal and a political science perspective, how and why these restrictions have or have not been overcome in a particular policy field, and to what effect as regards rule-making.

The aim of this final chapter is to look at the policy fields addressed so far in this book from a greater distance. Taking a transversal perspective, we intend to distil, from the policy-specific chapters as a whole, common themes of rule-making in crisis, thereby fleshing out the idiosyncrasies, or even a routine, of EU regulatory responses to crises.[1] It is not the intention of this book to scientifically prove causalities in the sense that specific crises have worked as *conditiones sine quibus non* for specific regulatory action on the part of the EU. Rather, we assume, on the basis of the assessment made in the respective policy-specific chapter, a link between a certain crisis and measures taken in this context.[2] This context is evident where the initiators of a measure have

* Professor of European Law at the University of Salzburg.
** Emerita Professor of Political Science at the European University Institute.
*** Associate Professor of European Law at the University of Salzburg.

[1] The notion of a 'routine' in the given context is inspired by Stephan Lessenich (ed), 'Routinen der Krise – Krise der Routinen. Verhandlungen des 37. Kongresses der Deutschen Gesellschaft für Soziologie in Trier 2014' (2015) <https://publikationen.soziologie.de/index.php/kongressband_2014> accessed 8 March 2024; see, in particular, the chapter 'Routinen der Krise – Krise der Routinen' by Martin Endreß, who addresses the paradoxical relationship between 'crisis' as the epitome of new circumstances which meet with our lack of experience, on the one hand, and 'routine' as a well-rehearsed way of going about certain occurrences, on the other.

[2] Attempts to make, with claim of scientific exactness, counterfactual conclusions at this scale would be frivolous. This is not to challenge the general value of counterfactual assumptions even for scholarship outside the realm of 'exact science'; see, eg Daniel Nolan, 'Why Historians (and Everyone Else) Should Care about Counterfactuals' (2013) 163 Philosophical Studies: An International Journal for Philosophy in the Analytic Tradition 317.

Diane Fromage, Adrienne Héritier, and Paul Weismann, *EU Regulatory Responses to Crises* In: *EU Regulatory Responses to Crises*. Edited by: Diane Fromage, Adrienne Héritier, and Paul Weismann, Oxford University Press. © Diane Fromage, Adrienne Héritier, and Paul Weismann 2025. DOI: 10.1093/9780198913825.003.0009

explicitly dubbed it a 'crisis measure', but it may also be plausible, for example, because the measure tackles specific ramifications of the crisis, or because it constitutes a political breakthrough which had been unsuccessfully attempted prior to the crisis.

Our initial view—half observation, half assumption or expectation—was that the EU's regulatory responses to crises encompass an unprecedented or otherwise creative use of competence clauses, an increased reliance on technocratic governance structures, the emergence of new modes of rule-making or an innovative (ie novel) use of pre-existing modes, political paradigm changes, and the reinforcement of measures by increasing coherence across different policy fields. In the following, after summarizing the main findings of the various chapters in the order in which they are included in this edited volume (section 9.2), we assess which responses can actually be observed across different policy fields (section 9.3). We end by drawing conclusions and providing a brief outlook (section 9.4).

It should not be concealed that, even in times of crisis, paradigm changes may fail, long-awaited political initiatives may falter, and innovative approaches may not be acknowledged. The general legal and political dynamics of rule-making in the EU are not suspended during crises. Whether or not an idea eventually succeeds in the process of rule-making depends on a variety of factors. Crises may very well be more conducive to the adoption of creative approaches, but even promising solutions to existing problems may eventually be dropped due to legal or political reservations. As a final note prior to delving into the proposed analysis, it ought to be underlined that this book is mainly about regulatory responses to crises which were actually adopted. Failed responses are addressed only exceptionally.

9.2 Recapitulation of Findings

9.2.1 Economic and monetary policy

The most relevant crises in the context of economic and monetary policy are the Great Financial Crisis (GFC), the COVID-19 pandemic, and the Ukraine crisis. The EU's reaction to these shocks has led to unprecedented developments regarding both prongs of Economic and Monetary Union (EMU). In the field of economic policy, these developments concern, on the one hand, the rules on fiscal discipline and, on the other, the building up of collective fiscal capacities. Faced with the euro crisis (as part of the GFC), the EU legislator adopted eight secondary law acts to reinforce and complement economic policy coordination and fiscal discipline under the Stability and Growth Pact (SGP)—the so-called 'six-pack' and 'two-pack' of legislation. In addition to that, Member States concluded the Treaty on Stability, Coordination and Governance, inter alia obliging euro-area Member States to incorporate a 'debt brake' in their respective national (constitutional) law. In terms of collective fiscal capacities, the European Stability Mechanism (ESM) and its predecessors, all effective only in the euro area, are to be mentioned. At the outset of the pandemic, the fiscal rules for

Member States were temporarily suspended in accordance with the so-called general escape clause enshrined in the SGP. As far as fiscal capacities are concerned, the short-term European instrument for temporary Support to mitigate Unemployment Risks in an Emergency (SURE) and the Recovery and Resilience Facility (RRF) are to be mentioned.

As regards monetary policy, in the wake of the GFC/euro-area crisis the European Central Bank (ECB)[3] availed itself of a number of non-standard measures, most prominently the Outright Monetary Transactions (OMT) programme (announced in 2012, but so far not implemented) and the Public Sector Purchase Programme (PSPP). These two programmes were aimed at the purchasing of state bonds of euro-area Member States on secondary markets. In reaction to the pandemic, the ECB again made use of non-standard measures, notably the Pandemic Emergency Purchase Programme (PEPP), which included the purchasing of public sector securities. One of the economic consequences resulting from the Ukraine crisis was a drastic increase in inflation. This high inflation is in stark contrast to the situations during the GFC and the pandemic, which were characterized by very low inflation rates. Thus, the ECB adapted its monetary policy. In terms of its non-standard measures, it phased out its purchase programmes and started to engage in quantitative tightening. The ECB reserves to itself the possibility to activate a new tool called the Transmission Protection Instrument (TPI), in order to ensure the orderly transmission of monetary policy. The instrument would focus on public sector securities. Also, the traditional monetary policy instrument—the adjustment of interest rates—was used, and the key interest rate was increased swiftly.

It is worth emphasizing that all of the above developments were brought about (nearly) without Treaty reform. The introduction of paragraph 3 of Article 136 TFEU, in an attempt to legalize the ESM, was the only (simplified) revision of primary law. It turned out to be, in the eyes of the Court of Justice of the European Union (CJEU), legally unnecessary. Essentially, the authors observe a twofold asymmetry of EMU, as designed in primary law. This asymmetry, on the one hand, is mirrored in the different degree of integration of economic/fiscal policy (in large parts left to the Member States; mere coordinating competence of the EU) and monetary policy in the euro area (exclusive competence of the EU). On the other hand, it comprises the existence of strict fiscal rules for (euro-area) Member States, while leaving out effective macroeconomic rules and/or fiscal capacities at the European level. The latter could even seem to be impeded by the 'no-bailout clause' (Article 125 TFEU). The authors call these *asymmetry in terms of sectoral integration* and *asymmetry regarding EMU's institutional provisions*.

This asymmetry is problematic due to the different growth models prevailing in the various Member States of the euro area. Broadly speaking, the northern countries

[3] For the European System of Central Banks and the Eurosystem, to which the ECB belongs, see art 282(1) TFEU. For convenience only, we collectively refer to these actors as the 'ECB' (as did the authors of the EMU chapter).

pursue export-led growth strategies, whereas the remaining countries rely on demand-led economic growth. The fixed exchange rate of the single currency deprives demand-led economies from devaluing against their trading partners. This fundamental difference between Member States' growth strategies leads to macroeconomic imbalances across the euro area.

Against this background, the primary law provisions on EMU are qualified by the authors as a '"good-weather" framework' whose flaws—unconcealable, in particular during various crises—were then provisionally fixed by means of secondary law and *inter se* agreements, in conjunction with an unconventional monetary policy on the part of the ECB in which it assumed the political role of a lender of last resort.

The acts taken in the field of economic/fiscal policy brought about formal and material development of this policy field, although only in an incremental manner. Apart from reforms of the SGP, the two gaps—macroeconomic rules and fiscal capacities—were addressed, but this could not fully do away with EMU's (second form of) asymmetry. The ECB stepped in and partly compensated for the shortcomings of the 'E' part of EMU. It was, in particular, the pandemic which led the EU institutions in charge to perform a paradigm change as regards fiscal capacities, thereby building on the experiences of the euro-area crisis. The RRF, even if referred to as an exceptional instrument, represents a significant EU-wide capacity, allowing in particular the Commission to influence—albeit weakly—how each Member State spends the respective RRF contributions allocated to it. Nevertheless, in comparison with the euro crisis and the financial support provided by the ESM to ailing euro-area Member States, the recipient Member States of the RRF—that is, all EU Member States—enjoy a considerable measure of national ownership as regards their respective investment priorities, and they remain, of course, free not to request RRF funding. This has strongly mitigated the divide between 'creditor countries' and 'debtor countries', at least in a political perspective.

The creation of the ESM and the resort to non-standard monetary policy instruments by the ECB led to clarifications regarding important EMU-related rules of primary law. Article 125 TFEU and its counterpart, Article 122 TFEU, as well as Article 123 TFEU—the prohibition of monetary financing—were interpreted by the CJEU cases *Pringle*, *Gauweiler*, and *Weiss*. The Court approved of these measures. Against this background, Article 122 TFEU, which had, albeit hesitantly, already been used during the GFC, turned into an important legal basis for all kinds of measures, be it for SURE, the financial support from the RRF (in conjunction with other provisions), or various EU measures taken to tackle negative economic effects of the Ukraine crisis.

9.2.2 Financial regulation and supervision

In the field of financial regulation and supervision, the crisis which was of primary relevance was the GFC (including the euro-area crisis). The authors depict three main (essentially legislative) steps which were taken in reaction to this crisis: the establishment of the European System of Financial Supervision (ESFS), the establishment of banking union, and the establishment of capital markets union.

The ESFS brings about institutional innovation, as it comprises new EU bodies in charge of financial market supervision: the European Systemic Risk Board (ESRB) and the three European Financial Market Supervisory Authorities (ESAs). The ESRB is in charge of macro-prudential supervision, and is composed of representatives of relevant bodies at the national and EU levels, including the President and Vice-President of the ECB. By means of its secretariat, the ESRB is also institutionally linked to the ECB. It acts by means of soft law.

The banking union effected institutional reforms, as well, most importantly the empowerment of the ECB as a banking supervisor, and the creation of the Single Resolution Board (SRB), a new European agency. Banking union applies to all euro-area Member States and to those other Member States which joined voluntarily. Its main aim is to facilitate the stability of the financial markets by improving the monitoring of banks. To this end, specific supervisory powers have been conferred on the ECB, thereby also ensuring a more uniform application of pertinent EU law. Another concern was to break the interrelation of banks and sovereigns. This interrelation (or banks–sovereigns doom loop) was disclosed in the wake of the GFC, when banks—often the main creditors of states—were bailed out by Member States. This aggravated the already strained public finances and contributed to a sovereign debt crisis in the euro area. The ECB and the SRB are supported by national supervisory and resolution authorities in the banking sector. The originally envisaged third prong of banking union, a European deposit insurance system for bank deposits, could not be adopted for lack of agreement among the Member States. Thus, the national deposit guarantee schemes remain in place.

The third main step taken in reaction to the GFC, the creation of the capital markets union, was aimed at tapping new financial sources for consumers, investors, and companies, thereby reducing their dependence on banks. In this context, legislative schemes for securitization and covered bonds were created, and a new Prospectus Regulation was adopted.

The authors emphasize two main challenges which the EU had to face when approaching these reforms: first, finding a compromise over competing interests and different priorities of Member States; and, second, striking a balance between depoliticizing certain financial aspects of financial regulation and supervision with sufficient accountability, not least in view of the close ties between states and their respective domestic banks. In this context, the authors observe a phenomenon which they call regulatory cycles. Specific political issues gain more attention when faced with a pertinent crisis, but the decision-makers become less and less stringent in their reform ambitions the longer the crisis is over. This may even result in the subsequent attenuation of measures taken in the wake of a crisis.

At the core of Member States' different priorities and even competing interests lies the divide between Germany and other Member States with sound fiscal positions and mostly healthy banks, on the one hand, and France, together with Member States at the periphery of the euro area, with weaker fiscal positions and several ailing banks, on the other. The second group was, for example, in favour of a common financial support mechanism which would strongly benefit their domestic banks. Similarly, the capital markets union was favoured by Member States with developed and diversified financial sectors, notably the United Kingdom, Ireland, the Netherlands, Sweden, and Luxembourg, whereas Member States with less competitive capital markets were sceptical.

Depoliticization was brought about by the creation of European agencies (ESAs, SRB) and the empowerment of the ECB (as a banking supervisor, and in the context of the ESRB). The ESAs' accountability to the European Parliament (EP) and the Council was reinforced in 2019. The authors note that, while these new accountability regimes are the result of the negotiations in the concrete legislative procedures, account is indeed taken of previous experiences.

Prior to the GFC, EU financial regulation was characterized by a harmonization of material law, which still allowed considerable leeway for Member States. The institutional coordination, however, was minimal. In reaction in particular to the GFC, the institutional involvement of EU institutions and bodies, and the coordination between EU and Member State actors, were reinforced significantly, mostly by creating new EU bodies (in particular, European agencies) or by giving new powers to existing institutions (in particular, the ECB). The empowerment of the European Securities and Markets Authority (one of the ESAs) led to Court proceedings, which resulted in an important development of the Court's old *Meroni* doctrine on the delegation of powers by EU institutions to other (EU) bodies. The legislators again had to take due account of this doctrine when establishing and empowering the SRB under the SRM, thereby deviating from the original legislative proposal to vest the Commission with the power to take resolution decisions. The introduction of the ECB as a banking supervisor required the separation of the then new supervisory branch from the ECB's traditional monetary policy branch, most importantly due to the potential conflict of (main) objectives (that is financial stability and price stability). The legislator took account of this requirement by providing for a sophisticated intra-institutional set-up, drawing a line between banking supervisory and monetary policy tasks, while allowing the ECB's Governing Council to be the final (formal) decision-maker in both cases. As a banking supervisor, the ECB is held accountable not only by the EP and the Council, but also by national parliaments.

In addition to that, material rules were adopted in new areas (eg bank resolution, securitization), with more stringency—overall the authors detect a less principle-based and more detailed approach towards rule-making—and reflecting a new trend regarding the public–private divide (eg bail-in rules for banks). Important legal bases for these developments were Article 114 TFEU, the until-then dormant Article 127(6) TFEU—the interpretation of which caused some controversy at the political level, but also at the level of courts—and an intergovernmental agreement on the transfer of contributions to a newly created EU fund for the resolution of banks (Single Resolution Fund). The authors also note instances of replacement of soft law by hard law, an increasing use of 'harder soft law' (notably by the ESAs and the ECB) and 'softer hard law' by EU actors, and a trend towards the adoption of regulations rather than directives.

9.2.3 Health policy

With regard to health policy, the COVID-19 pandemic is the most relevant crisis in the given context. The authors note at the outset that this policy field is not only affected by the TFEU's title on public health—Article 168—and by the acts based on this provision, but that Treaty provisions and acts of secondary law belonging to other policy fields may also have a strong effect on health policy. This holds true, in particular, for rules related to the internal market (notably measures based on Article 114 TFEU) and Economic and Monetary Union (EMU). The interrelation of health policy with other areas of EU activity reflects the fact that health and healthcare belong to 'the very core of the political economy'. In view of this particularity, a broader set of measures is to be taken into account when depicting the development of EU health policy.

From among the measures taken in reaction to the pandemic, the authors emphasize the creation of the Health Emergency Preparedness and Response Authority (HERA), the reinforcement of existing European agencies, an EU capacities tool called 'rescEU' (eg for purchasing vaccines), and the adoption of the EU4Health programme 2021–2027 (adopted in 'seemingly happy disregard for the limitations of Article 168 TFEU'). With regard to the institutional innovations, it is to be noted that HERA, in spite of the term 'authority' in its name, was not created as an independent body (eg a European agency) but was eventually established as new Directorate-General of the Commission. The 'massive increase in the EU's practical capacity' HERA brings about, according to the authors, may be one of the reasons why it was institutionally attached to the Commission. After all, one of the political ambitions underlying the creation of HERA was to reduce the EU's dependence on the output of the World Health Organization (WHO), and even to compete with this international organization. Furthermore, existing agencies relevant for the field of health policy, namely the European Centre for Disease Control (ECDC) and the European Medicines Agency (EMA), were vested with additional powers. For the authors, this confirms a long-lasting trend away from indirect administration ('Community method') to 'a more direct administrative form'. Apart from these institutional reforms, dedicated EU capacities (funds, helicopters, shelters, etc) were made available under the name 'rescEU', and on the primary law basis of Article 222 TFEU. This is an expression of risk-pooling and cross-subsidization. Finally, the EU4Health programme 2021–2027 is to be mentioned. It is a tool aimed at supporting Member States in improving access to healthcare.

Crisis measures adopted in other policy fields, too, may facilitate health policy. This applies, for example, to country-specific recommendations (CSRs) adopted within the framework of the European Semester. These recommendations also address Member States' health policies and the related spending. The effects of these CSRs are being reinforced by the financial support for Member States provided by the RRF. This support requires Member States to meet certain conditions, among others compliance with the respective CSRs. In this way, the Commission has gained power also in the field of health policy. As a legacy of economic policy measures taken in reaction to the GFC, the International Monetary Fund—involved in the scrutiny of conditionality, for example under the ESM—has gained increased surveillance capacity, including on national healthcare spending. This focus has also had an influence on the Commission and other fiscal surveillance bodies in the EU.

Historically speaking, Member States were concerned with shielding national health(care) systems from interference by the EU. At the same time, the authors also observe a determination on the part of the Member States to 'mainstream' health. This paradox has resulted in a 'long-standing process of competence creep' in EU health policy. Against this background, the main Treaty provision on EU (public) health, Article 168 TFEU, may have developed from a 'norm of constitutional suspicion' to a norm of 'constitutional toleration', in the course of the crisis.

In the development of EU rule-making in health policy, the authors observe instances of 'liquid authority', characterized by dynamism, informality, and institutional multiplicity. Dynamism requires institutional actors to be 'more attuned to processes of learning and creative adaptation'. In the authors' view, the open method of coordination (OMC), which has been used in health policy, is the epitome of this dynamism. Another illustration of dynamism is the flexibility the EU, hit by the pandemic, granted for the implementation of the European Structural and Investment Funds. The broadening of relevant indicators (so as to include, eg health) in economic policy (eg in the evolution of CSRs) is an example of this dynamism, too. Informality finds its expression, for example, in the coordination of Member States in the framework of the Health Security Committee—resulting in coordination beyond its legal mandate, where the Member States so wished—and institutional multiplicity has played out in overly detailed European Council Conclusions in the preparation of the NextGeneration EU (NGEU) project and the Multiannual Financial Framework 2021–2027. According to the authors, this puts maximum strain on the European Council's mandate, and in particular its exclusion from any legislative function (Article 15 TEU) is strained to the maximum.

These features of EU health policy, which had already been 'foreshadowed' in the years prior to the pandemic, but played out in full in reaction to this crisis—according to the authors—can be partially explained by the heavy reliance on scientific expertise which characterizes this policy field. This expertise often comes from international actors like the WHO or the World Medical Association. The high (factual) authority of science may outweigh the sometimes malleable authority of constitutional barriers. In the authors' assessment, the way liquid authority has played out in health policy—not liquid authority in itself—has led to a considerable tension with some of the main rule of law commitments of the EU, namely clarity, predictability, and justiciability.

An extensive use and creative interpretation of competences has allowed for the increasing inclusion of redistributive elements in health policy. The RRF has proven to be a means to influence health policy in the Member States, allowing for a rather generous, and only loosely conditioned, distribution of money. The market logics which used to be applied also in the health context—for example, in the austerity measures applied during the euro-area crisis—seem to have given way to increased solidarity and redistribution.

Against this background, the authors have also, on a broader scale, detected signs of a paradigm change from non-discrimination to solidarity: a 'moral renegotiation of the terms of integration'. They consider the EU to be at a crossroads. It must decide whether to stick to its largely efficiency-based approach or to encompass the goal of just and fair integration. The current 'in-between solution', as exemplified in the EU's reaction to the pandemic, is 'not only inherently unstable; it is a betrayal of the EU's own rule of law principles', the authors hold.

9.2.4 State aid control

State aid control has been strongly affected by the GFC, the pandemic, and the war in Ukraine. Crisis measures in this field have been characterized by the timely adoption of generally applicable so-called temporary frameworks. This was a means to provide for a regulatory scheme tailored to the requirements of the specific crisis, and a way of avoiding a case-by-case application of primary law on the part of the Commission. In these frameworks, the Commission, in the interest of efficiency (swift decision-making), set up the criteria under which it considers acceptable certain state aid measures by the Member States, thereby fleshing out its understanding of specific discretionary exceptions under Article 107(3) TFEU.

In reaction to the GFC, which severely hit the banking sector, the Commission adopted a specific framework for state aid for banks (Banking Communication 2008). Through a number of amendments, and eventually a replacement of this Communication (Banking Communication 2013), over time, the Commission has gradually increased the strictness of the scheme (eg by making burden-sharing a condition for approving state aid for banks). The pandemic also saw the adoption of a temporary framework, which was again corrected and adapted repeatedly throughout its period of application. Unlike the regime adopted in reaction to the GFC, the COVID-19 temporary framework became more flexible over time, extending the possibilities for Member States to financially support domestic undertakings. In view of the war in Ukraine and the considerable direct and indirect effects it had on Member States' economies, the Commission adopted a Temporary Crisis Framework in 2022, later revised, and eventually replaced it with its Temporary Crisis and Transition Framework, in 2023.

In terms of procedures, the authors noted an increased efficiency of state aid control, as well. This turned out to be necessary in the context of state aid for banks, which sometimes required decisions to be taken within twenty-four hours. But an increase in efficiency was also in the interest of the Commission, given the extraordinarily high number of notifications it had to examine during the various crises. Thus, the efficiency gains made during the GFC were carried over to the schemes adopted in reaction to the pandemic and the war in Ukraine. In exchange, Member States, if they wanted to avail themselves of fast-track decision-making, were required to submit complete notifications, and had to agree to communication with the Commission exclusively in English.

In view of the Commission's preoccupation with assessing, and regularly approving of, a large number of Member State notifications, some general state aid rules could not be reformed as scheduled. Thus, the reform of the *de minimis* Regulation, the General Block Exemption Regulation (GBER), and a number of Commission guidelines had to be postponed.

Whereas, at the outset of the GFC, no specific rules regarding state aid for financial institutions existed, the Commission quickly came up with a pertinent soft law scheme for banks. The temporary frameworks adopted by the Commission for the real economy also qualify as soft law. They set out the Commission's interpretation of pertinent exceptions laid down in Article 107(2) and (3) TFEU. While the use of Commission soft law in state aid control, due to a lack of pertinent legislation, let alone a revision of Articles 107 or 108 TFEU, had become a well-established tool even before the GFC, the shape of these acts changed significantly during the crises at issue here. The frequent referral to Article 107(3)(b) (second alternative) TFEU is unprecedented, too. Only rarely applied prior to the GFC, this provision became one of the core justifications for state aid granted during the GFC. During the pandemic, the Commission, quickly and more confidently than before, resorted to this provision again, in particular once the limitations of Article 107(2)(b) TFEU had become apparent. The Commission's state aid scheme adopted in reaction to the Ukraine crisis again refers to Article 107(3)(b) TFEU as one of the core justifications, thereby building on its interpretations developed during the GFC and the pandemic. The Commission's interpretation of Article 107(3)(b) TFEU during these crises, in the authors' view, seems to go beyond what is suggested by the Court's case law. After all, the Commission applied this clause even where only 'an important part' of the economy of a Member State was in jeopardy, and not 'the economy of a Member State' as a whole. It is also remarkable that the Commission, with reference to this provision, generally allowed for aid of up to 2 million euros per undertaking in various temporary frameworks, while in normal times the ceiling for *de minimis* aid is 200,000 euros.

It is worth mentioning that the Council's power to approve, by unanimous decision, state aid pursuant to Article 108(2) TFEU remained unused throughout these crises. The authors assume that this was avoided because it would have set a precedent for future crises and could have undermined the Commission's central role in state aid control. Overall, the Commission 'benefited from crisis, or at the very least consolidated its position', the authors conclude, even if in the shadow of the Council's (unused, but still effective) power under Article 108(2) TFEU. Hence, no power gains of the Council are visible in this context. Equally, the EP only 'maintained its somewhat detached involvement in matters of state aid control'.

State aid, by its very nature, is about the relationship between the EU and its Member States, but also about relationships among Member States. State aid was also introduced to avoid subsidy races among the latter. The more flexible Commission (temporary) frameworks during crises have been, the more the different spending power of Member States (at the top, notably of Germany and France) has played out. While the Commission has resisted the requests of some Member States to outright suspend state aid rules (temporarily) during crises, the crisis regimes it has adopted instead are still rather generous. This flexible approach, according to the authors, 'risks the social, territorial and economic cohesion' of the internal market, a warning which, for example, the EP has also uttered in this context. Not least against this background, financially weaker Member States, amongst others, have called for more EU aid and less state aid. The RRF is the most successful political project of this group.

The Commission's experiences during the relevant crises, as reflected in its crisis schemes, has, in places, also had an impact on legislation. The burden-sharing rules in regard to ailing banks were developed as part of the Commission's state aid schemes for banks, and eventually found their way into legislation on bank resolution. Similarly, the Regulation on Foreign Subsidies reflects relevant rules enshrined in the Commission's COVID-19 temporary framework. Here, the positive assessment by the legislator of the Commission's ideas is apparent. But if crisis measures of the Commission apply for too long, the authors warn—and, notably, the Banking Communication 2013 is still in force—important objectives may come off badly. For example, the Commission's crisis frameworks may be used to subsidize green measures, thereby bypassing the stricter environmental and climate requirements of relevant Commission guidelines.

9.2.5 Energy policy

Even though energy policy (other than nuclear energy policy, as enshrined in the Euratom Treaty) has been part of European integration ever since the establishment of the European Communities, only with the Treaty of Lisbon were EU competences in this field introduced in primary law.

The relevant steps taken in the period until the late 1980s—when the Commission started launching a number of initiatives based on internal market- and environmental policy-related competences introduced by the Single European Act (SEA) in 1987—had been marked by a limited willingness of Member States to cooperate in energy matters. The Maastricht Treaty of 1993 eventually facilitated infrastructure-related energy projects. In the subsequent decade, the Commission proposed integration measures regarding the electricity and gas sectors (resulting in a first energy package in the mid/late 1990s, and a second one in 2003), and on various sustainability-related issues in energy policy. A third energy package inter alia entailed the establishment of the Agency for the Cooperation of Energy Regulators (ACER) and an enhanced involvement of private actors in rule-making. Together with the Renewable Energy Directive, this package was adopted shortly before the Treaty of Lisbon entered into force.

With the Treaty of Lisbon, an explicit competence clause (Article 194 TFEU) was introduced, which is why the Commission and the EU legislators no longer have to rely on competence clauses in, for example, the fields of internal market or environmental policy when proposing and adopting energy policy measures. However, the authors question the sufficiency of this competence clause to address the polycrisis which has hit energy policy since the 2000s; that is, the energy supply crisis provoked by Russia since 2006 and aggravated by the annexation of Crimea in 2014 and the comprehensive war in Ukraine (starting in 2022), the climate crisis, and the COVID-19 crisis. These challenges demanded action with regard to energy security and energy sustainability. A number of measures at the EU level have been taken to tackle these crises. With regard to energy security, the authors mention the Commission's energy union initiative of 2015 and a number of sanctions packages against Russia, starting in 2014 and reinforced and complemented since 2022, involving, inter alia, an embargo on Russian coal and a partial oil embargo. In the field of energy sustainability, the 'climate emergency' declared by the EP in November 2019 has led to increasing rule-making activity, inter alia the Von der Leyen Commission's Green Deal and the REPowerEU plan aimed at phasing out fossil fuel imports from Russia, diversifying the EU's energy supply, and accelerating the clean energy transition. Overall, however, in the authors' view, the measures taken have fallen short of expectations. In particular, the war's potential to weaken the East–West divide on climate policy among Member States could not be realized. Even the EU's sanctions had only a limited impact on the energy sector.

In terms of the toolbox and the institutional set-up emerging in energy policy, the authors observe that the traditional characteristics of rule-making, using a mix of 'borrowed' Treaty competences and soft governance, agency governance, network governance, and private governance, are increasingly complemented by what they refer to as 'geoeconomics policy tools'. Whereas the 'borrowing' of competences has given way to a combination of dedicated energy policy competences with other pertinent competences (eg regarding environmental policy) after the Treaty of Lisbon, soft governance has seen partial 'hardening', in particular after Russia's annexation of Crimea. Energy governance has become the subject of regulatory networks, both public and private. The ACER itself relies on a network, namely the network of energy regulators in the Member States. However, the further empowerment of the ACER, according to the authors, is subject to a threefold restriction: the *Meroni* doctrine, even if mitigated by recent case law; the Commission's reluctance to relativize its own position in energy policy by promoting a different EU actor; and the Member States' reluctance to shift additional powers from the national level (national regulators) to the EU level. As regards private actors, the increasing role of transmission system operators and their authority in technical matters and matters related to infrastructure is to be emphasized.

The new category of geoeconomics policy measures involves political intervention which, in the words of the authors, 'seeks to proactively shape economic relations of interdependence', strives for 'power maximization', and achieves 'relative rather than absolute gains'. These measures have been exemplified by the EU's economic sanctions against Russia (since February 2022), an increasing emphasis on financial compensation (instead of regulation) as a reaction to the ensuing energy crisis, and the temporary suspension of important principles of environmental policy in order to speed up energy transition. In terms of competences, the increasing use of Article 122(1) TFEU as a legal basis for energy-related measures—which underlines the urgency of the matter—and the strong reliance on Article 107(2)(b) TFEU in the context of energy-related state aid are to be noted.

The authors observe instances of both path dependency and innovative change. Path dependency is mirrored in the way existing regimes are adapted and complemented in reaction to new challenges. This way is characterized by the far-reaching conflicts of interest between the EU and its Member States in the triangle of energy market integration, security of energy supply, and sustainability. On the contrary, innovative change can be observed in the EU's rebalancing of policy objectives, for example where it favours the establishment of renewable energy sources over the protection of wild birds, or of water quality, by relating the underlying projects to an 'overriding public interest'. For certain solar and other renewable energy projects, a significant facilitation and acceleration of the approval procedure has been provided. These measures are complemented by new, more ambitious goals as regards the share of energy from renewable sources, the creation of 'go-to areas' (for the installation of power plants producing renewable energy), and a number of further instruments to ease the administrative procedures relating to the production of renewable energy.

Two themes of the above reforms are pivotal in the eyes of the authors: speed and simplification, on the one hand, and rebalancing, on the other. An increase of speed can be perceived in the relevant EU legislative processes. Administrative decision-making procedures at the national level have also been sped up, but also simplified. Rebalancing is mirrored in the 'overriding importance' which is attached to renewable energy projects, for example at the cost of highly relevant parts of environmental regulation. Even though it is supposed to be only temporary, restricted in scope, and accompanied by reporting requirements, this rebalancing is to be carefully monitored, as, according to the authors, 'there is a hint of a rebalancing of key constitutional objects' which have been fleshed out over decades, in particular by EU courts.

9.2.6 Migration policy

In this field, three crises deserve mentioning: the so-called migration crisis of 2015/16, the pandemic, and the Russian invasion of Ukraine since 2022, which has led to a massive displacement of Ukrainians. These crises, and here in particular the migration crisis, laid bare the structural flaws of EU migration law. At the same time, strongly divergent attitudes of Member States have long barred structural reforms. The (presumed) attitude of the electorate in the Member States towards the massive influx of migrants to the EU had a strong impact on the (non-)application of EU migration law at the national level, thereby further damaging the functioning of EU migration policy.

The primary law competence regime in migration law has some peculiarities: in general, it provides for a relatively broad competence of the EU and also specifically allows for (multilevel) crisis governance. Thus, from a competence perspective, the EU has been well-equipped to prepare for, or react to, crises in the field of migration policy. However, the Member States' prerogative as regards 'the maintenance of law and order and the safeguarding of internal security' allows for autonomous action at the national level which may, in places, even violate EU legislation in this field. As regards the form this legislation takes, regulations seem, in general, to have become the preferred type of instrument—as the replacement of the Asylum Procedures Directive by a regulation illustrates—even though experience proves that the regulatory intensity of migration rules may be very similar, irrespective of whether they are contained in a regulation or a directive.

As regards specific crisis-related competences, Article 78(3) TFEU may serve as an example. It allows the EU to react in the event of a 'sudden inflow' of third-country nationals. In fact, this provision does not materially add to the EU's legislative competences in migration law, but it allows for provisional measures to be taken by the Council (on a proposal by the Commission), instead of the Council and the EP together (in the course of the ordinary legislative procedure). The Temporary Protection Directive of 2001, setting up a regime for temporary protection in the event of a massive inflow of third-country nationals, was first activated during Russia's attack on Ukraine in 2022.

Since the Treaty of Lisbon, the EP has acted as a co-legislator in all areas of migration law. In the Council, a qualified majority is required for the adoption of legislative acts. Nevertheless, the authors underline, the Council's rule-making activities in migration law have been determined by a continuous striving for consensus. The famous example of the relocation of asylum seekers out of Italy and Greece, adopted by majority voting (ie without consensus), exhibited the frailty of mere majority decisions in migration law. While the lawfulness of the decision was confirmed by the Court, single Member States outright refused to apply it. Depending on their respective political agendas, in some cases influenced by their respective geographical exposure to mass immigration, different interest groups among the Member States (eg the Visegrád Group or MED5) have strongly informed the discourse on migration policy.

EU migration law has been dominated by formal legislation. The underlying acts, however, display a number of textual ambiguities and other forms of interpretative flexibility. The 'discretionary clause' of the Dublin framework, for example, served as a basis for the partial non-application of this regime on the part of Germany, in an attempt to alleviate the situation in peripheral Member States. Considering that these countries were overburdened by asylum applications from Syrian refugees, the Court gave its blessing to this specific application of the discretionary clause 'in a spirit of solidarity', as it added. In line with the dominance of formal legislation, authorizations to adopt delegated and implementing acts have been exceptional, mostly due to resistance from the EP. The 2024 reform of asylum legislation, which, in the words of the authors, 'takes on board critical lessons but refrains from substantially overhauling the CEAS [Common European Asylum System]', breaks with this tradition. It provides for the Commission's competence to adopt implementing acts in a number of cases.. Within this framework, the Commission and the Member States ought to assess, among other things, the migratory pressure at a certain point in time and coordinate instruments of interstate solidarity, if need be.

The traditional focus on legislation has not prevented the occasional adoption of different categories of soft law by the Commission and the Council. With the incipient COVID-19 crisis, the use of soft law gained significantly in importance. It served, in particular, to coordinate Member States' restrictions on free movement of persons within the Schengen area. The apparent advantage of using soft law in cases of urgency—speediness and flexibility—is confronted by its lack of legitimacy. During the pandemic, the most far-reaching travel restrictions since the introduction of Schengen were brought about by informal rule-making, without the involvement of the EP, and on a questionable legal basis. The relative consonance of Member States as regards travel bans during the pandemic could not be achieved when it came to deciding on (the soft coordination of) travel bans against Russian nationals after the full-scale invasion of Ukraine.

The EU's relations with third countries in matters of migration policy have also intensified, and so has the use of soft instruments of cooperation, not least due to negative experiences with formal (readmission) agreements which have been concluded with a number of countries, and which are, notwithstanding their disenchantment, still being negotiated. The EU–Turkey statement, published as a press release of the European Council, is the most prominent example of a non-binding form of cooperation with a third country in this context.

Implementation and enforcement of the rules in place are of key importance in all policy fields. European agencies play a key role in coordinating and monitoring these features. In migration policy, the two agencies in charge are the European Border and Coast Guard Agency (Frontex) and the EU Agency for Asylum (EUAA), which in 2022 succeeded the European Asylum Support Office (EASO). Their respective tasks and powers, along with their respective capacities, were extended significantly in reaction to the migration crisis of 2015/16, during and after which the shortcomings of implementation and enforcement in migration policy became apparent, as was exemplified by the Relocation Decision of 2015. With regard to law enforcement, the authors point to the repeated use of Treaty infringement proceedings after 2015/16—a novelty in migration law. They stress the need for making strategic use of this instrument, irrespective of its drawbacks, in particular against 'symbolic disobedience [eg by Hungary] that undermines the normative integrity of EU migration law'. In complementation of this, the Commission also facilitated soft forms of monitoring, for example within the framework of its 'Schengen strategy'.

9.2.7 Foreign and security policy

EU external action (in particular, its trade, enlargement and neighbourhood policy and its foreign and security policy) is divided into different compartments. These compartments are interlinked, but because they represent 'different integration logics' they have largely developed in separation from each other, and apply different forms of rule-making. Russia's war on Ukraine, as the most important crisis to look at in this context, has increased the coherence of EU external action.

Foreign and defence policy has come a long way since the early days of European integration. With the failure of the European Defence Community (EDC) in 1954, the Member States' security and military cooperation was essentially limited to the Western European Union (WEU) and the North Atlantic Treaty Organization (NATO). More generally, cooperation in foreign and security policy, for lack of a legal basis in the EEC Treaty of 1958, took place on a loose and informal basis in the first decades of European integration. The (limited) institutionalization within the framework of European Political Cooperation (EPC), starting in the 1970s, did not include security and defence cooperation. This cooperation intensified gradually over the subsequent years. The end of the Cold War and the emergence of European conflicts (eg the wars in former Yugoslavia) gave the development of this policy field a new drive. It was the Treaty of Maastricht which incorporated the Common Foreign and Security Policy (CFSP) in primary law and further formalized the procedures in foreign, security, and defence policy. This formalization was continued by the subsequent reform Treaties (Amsterdam, Nice, and Lisbon), which also added provisions on what is now called the 'Common Security and Defence Policy'.

While the principle of consistency of the different fields of EU external action among themselves and with other policy fields (Article 21(3) TEU requires some degree of consideration across policy fields), the intergovernmental CFSP (including the Common Security and Defence Policy) is markedly different from supranational areas of EU external action (such as trade or development cooperation). This difference may have been nuanced in different ways over the years, but due to the Member States' fear of a loss of sovereignty at the international level, it essentially remained intact.

From a theoretical perspective, the author holds a priori that the development of rule-making in CFSP in reaction to the war in Ukraine can be expected to result in 'innovative and experimental action leading to more integration' due to the autonomy of supranational actors like the Commission (neofunctionalism), in 'pro-integrative responses' on the basis of agreement among the Member States (liberal intergovernmentalism), or in inaction due to obstruction, in particular by Eurosceptic parties at both national and EU levels (postfunctionalism).

When contrasting the regime for rule-making in CFSP as laid down in the TEU with its application in reaction to Russia's attack on Ukraine, it appears that practice differs from the rules (without violating them). The instrument of constructive abstention, for example, has been used only once in the EU's responses to the war, namely in the context of the European Peace Facility (EPF). With all the other CFSP acts, the Member States succeeded in reaching unanimity (which in practice means consensus). The drawback of constructive abstentions is that abstaining Member States are exempted from implementing the decision taken. Thus, alternative routes such as 'constructive silence', whereby the silent Member State would be obliged to implement the decision, have been considered or—in the case of the 'constructive absence' German Chancellor

Scholz proposed to Hungarian Prime Minister Orbán when the decision, inter alia, to start accession negotiations with Ukraine was at issue—even practiced. Overall, the author concludes, the EU and its Member States have managed to ensure 'vertical coherence', for example in their sanctions policy and the establishment of the EPF, but also in related policy fields such as accession policy and defence procurement.

As regards the substantive rules of CFSP, a comparison of the rules on the book and the rules in practice reveals the following: with restrictive measures pursuant to Article 215 TFEU, for example, the CFSP decision in practice predetermines the follow-up regulation 'word for word'—a result which primary law arguably allows, but does not prescribe. While only here is an intertwinement between CFSP and supranational rule-making explicitly foreseen, the EU's response to the war in Ukraine displays numerous decisions across the divide between intergovernmental and supranational rule-making. What is more, substantially far-reaching measures have been taken, including new qualitative levels for restrictive measures, the supply of weapons in active warfare by the Member States, unprecedented steps in defence procurement, and the recognition of Ukraine, Georgia, and Moldova as new candidate countries. The EPF and the European Defence Fund (EDF) have largely been used to support Ukraine. Another response to security crises has been Common Security and Defence Policy missions. Ukraine is also being supported within the framework of such (civilian and military) missions, but other neighbouring countries of Russia are also subject to EU missions.

At the other end of the scale, the EU has adopted restrictive measures against perpetrator countries, for example Russia and China, in the context of human rights violations. Here, the EU has created a horizontal regime of sanctions which addresses country-related individuals and groups rather than the countries as such. Apart from that, the EU has also adopted country-specific sanctions. Twelve packages, so far, have contained sanctions against Russia which are unprecedented in terms of comprehensiveness, the limited number of exceptions and derogations across the EU, and the implementation practice. Implementation breaches are now centrally monitored by the Commission.

Also, in supranational policy fields incisive measures have been taken in order to react to Russia's invasion of Ukraine. Among these are the expansion of Eurojust's mandate to be able to collect, preserve, and share evidence on war crimes, and a number of acts and programmes to facilitate the armament of Member States.

The mutually reinforcing measures taken both in (intergovernmental) CFSP and in related supranational policy fields have contributed significantly to the coherence of EU foreign policy and defence action. At the same time, these actions mirror a leap forward in the geopoliticization of EU external action.

9.3 Horizontal Perspective

In general, crises are heydays of rule-making. This effect, which is also mirrored in the etymology of the term 'crisis', applies to all organizations which are hit by crises

(Chapter 1). But in a complex organization like the EU, with so many different actors being involved in rule-making at different levels, the various crises at issue here have unfolded a particular dynamic. The EU, for a number of years, has been characterized by rule-making deadlock on various key issues. This is due to fundamentally diverging interests among (groups of) Member States, but also among EU institutions. The diverging ideas as to how the EU should develop overall are exacerbated by the unanimity requirement in the Council, which still applies in some important fields, such as CFSP and the EU's finances. The fact that conventional wisdom rates as very low the likelihood of a comprehensive revision of the Treaties is equally illustrative of this gridlock. In the contributions to this volume on various EU policy fields, it could be observed that the crises at issue here have, to varying extents, mitigated these divergences. They could not be resolved for good—which is also why the odds for a Treaty reform continue to be low, even in the face of numerous crises—but they were partially overcome in the form of concrete acts adopted in response to crises. Thus, it is fair to say that, in general, these crises have worked as accelerators and encouragers of EU rule-making. The process of European integration, including—over time—paradigm changes, true innovations, and unexpected agreements, is prevalent also in normal times—that is, in non-crisis times—but at a smaller scale and a slower pace. Vice versa, a crisis mode of rule-making does not necessarily involve unprecedented acts. As noted earlier (in section 9.1), it may well continue a pre-existing trend, but with an unprecedented scope or at an unprecedented speed.

In the following, we shall look at what, in a horizontal perspective, characterizes the techniques of EU rule-making in crisis situations, following up on our authors' policy-specific findings. On this basis, we will examine whether there is a peculiar crisis mode of rule-making.

Let us begin with the ever-increasing use of soft law by EU actors to engage in rule-making across different policy fields. In financial regulation and supervision, EU actors established in reaction to a crisis have adopted a very diversified body of soft law (eg on macro-prudential supervision or on national options and discretions). In order to ensure efficient state aid control, the Commission availed itself of soft law, as it did prior to the relevant crises, but this time both in more detail and with a broader scope. Bank resolution law, as a new field of EU rule-making, emerged partly from the Commission's soft law acts. The same holds true for the Foreign Subsidies Regulation adopted in 2022. That the Commission's rules gradually became stricter during the GFC but were relaxed over time during the pandemic does not affect the soft law character of these rules. Rather, it gives proof of the high adaptability of soft law acts, hence perhaps their attractiveness for EU institutions and especially the Commission. In other policy fields, soft law was used, as well, often to ensure that rules were available even where the EU or the concrete EU body did not have the competence to engage in hard rule-making. In health policy, soft coordination was applied within the open method of coordination. In EMU, we saw the CSRs as a means of influencing all kinds of national policies, including, for example, national health policy. These recommendations, with their rather broad scope, were then reinforced by other EU measures, for example by the conditionality applied in the context of funding by the RRF or the eligibility criteria set up by the ECB for its public sector securities purchases. That way, legally non-binding EU measures with a broad scope may be given more bite. Thus, the finding that the use of soft law has gained ground across policy fields may be correct but simplistic. On a more nuanced account, in places a change of the shape of soft law and the use which is made of it can be observed. Following up on the examples just mentioned, a more traditional form of 'hardening' could be observed in energy policy. Here, soft rules were made more specific and stringent for Member States, so that non-compliance became more obvious. In the field of banking regulation and supervision, the development was described as a 'proliferation of "harder" soft law and "softer" hard law'. The EU also made abundant use of soft law in migration policy, in particular in reaction to the pandemic. While the increasing popularity of soft law among EU actors is a general trend which loomed long before the series of crises at issue here, there may still be exceptions to the rule: in foreign and security policy (including defence policy), which—after ambitious projects like the EDC and the pooling of resources and knowledge to create a European nuclear bomb within the framework of Euratom were jettisoned in the 1950s—historically roots in soft forms of coordination among the Member States, the Ukraine crisis seems to have promoted the adoption of hard measures.

One of the many reasons to adopt soft law at the EU level has been the lack of a (primary law) competence to adopt hard law in the respective field or on the respective issue. This leads us to the more general question how primary law competence clauses have been applied during the crises at issue here. A number of examples illustrate an unprecedented use or interpretation and/or unprecedented combination of (competence-related) provisions of primary law. Here should be mentioned Article 127(6) TFEU, which the Member States, with a remarkable farsightedness, introduced with the Treaty of Maastricht, but could not agree on making use of for twenty years. In reaction to the GFC and the banking crisis it comprised, it served as a basis for the installation of the ECB as a banking supervisor. Article 122 TFEU, with its two very different paragraphs, one of which allows for deviations from the no-bailout principle, has developed into a workhorse during the crises of the past years, in all kinds of policy fields (EMU, which also extended, inter alia, to health policy; migration policy; energy policy).[4] That its paragraph 2 refers to 'a Member State', not a plurality of Member States, has not prevented the adoption, on this very basis, of measures benefiting all Member States. Article 122 TFEU was also used in combination with a cohesion policy provision—Article 175(3) TFEU—in order to bring about NGEU, a move which de Witte described not only as 'politically bold' but also as an act of 'creative legal engineering'.[5] The 'integration-friendly' interpretation of primary law is well illustrated by the narrow reading of the no-bailout clause, enshrined in Article 125 TFEU (and its

[4] For quantitative data on the use of art 122 TFEU (and its predecessors), see Merijn Chamon, 'The Use of Article 122 TFEU. Institutional Implications and Impact on Democratic Accountability' (EP Study 2023) 17 f, who relativizes the high numbers between 1975 and 1985.

[5] Bruno de Witte, 'The European Union's COVID-19 Recovery Plan: The Legal Engineering of an Economic Policy Shift' (2021) 58 Common Market Law Review 635, 638.

variant enshrined in Article 123 TFEU), by various actors (including the Court) in EMU; the broadening by the Commission of the state aid-related exception laid down in Article 107(3)(c) TFEU; a wide—perhaps overly wide— conception of the EU's competence in health policy, as laid down in Article 168 TFEU, which was drafted in rather restrictive terms; and also in the smooth replacement of Article 114 TFEU by the newly introduced Article 194 TFEU in the EU's legislative practice in energy policy. In EU external action, mention is deserved of the ideas on how to evade unanimity while keeping all Member States committed ('constructive silence', 'constructive absence'), on the one hand, and of the restrictive measures of an unprecedented scope which were based on Article 215 TFEU, on the other. A counter-example may be seen in migration policy, in which field the TFEU provides for a comparatively wide legislative competence of the EU. Here, the long-term stalemate in comprehensively reforming EU asylum law was caused by fundamentally opposing standpoints among the Member States, not (also) by a lack of powers. This controversy is still reflected in the 2024 reform, which was achieved on the basis of the lowest common denominator.

Furthermore, a long-term trend which can be observed over the past decades of European integration is a gradual shift from rule-making by directives to rule-making by regulations, as illustrated, in the policy fields discussed here, by the replacement by regulations of the Prospectus Directive and the Asylum Procedures Directive, respectively. This does not seem to be a genuine crisis trend, but a trend which is also visible in reaction to crises.[6]

At an institutional level, the building up or reinforcement of technocratic structures is to be mentioned. As crises often reveal deficiencies in governance, calls for new depoliticized bodies with a high degree of expertise usually follow suit. At the EU level, these calls have resulted in the gradual 'agencification' over the past thirty years,[7] but there may also be institutional innovations other than founding new agencies. In financial regulation and supervision, the creation of the three European financial market supervisory authorities and the Single Resolution Board, in the wake of the banking crisis (as part of the GFC), was seen as an attempt to depoliticize administration, but to some extent politics have kicked in, nevertheless. The European Systemic Risk Board and the Supervisory Board (which was established as an internal body of the ECB) are alternative institutional solutions, by which the legislator essentially pursued the same objectives. The reinforcement of existing agencies in health policy can clearly be linked to the pandemic. The same is true for HERA, which was originally envisaged as another agency, but was eventually established as a new Directorate-General of the Commission. Similarly, Frontex and the EUAA were strengthened in terms of tasks, powers, and capacities, in reaction to the migration crisis. In energy

[6] See Carl Fredrik Bergström, 'EU Rulemaking in the Internal Market after the Financial Crisis' in Carl Fredrik Bergström and Magnus Strand (eds), *Legal Accountability in EU Markets for Financial Instruments: The Dual Role of Investment Firms* (OUP 2021) 3, 7.

[7] The first agencies were established in 1975, but the repeated recourse to agencies started only in the early 1990s. While not all agencies can be linked to a crisis in this way—such as, eg the BSE scandal and the European Food Safety Authority or the oil spill caused by the wrecked tanker *Erika* and the European Maritime Safety Agency—these bodies have been created in order to improve public governance in specific policy fields.

policy, the creation of ACER cannot be seen as an immediate reaction to a crisis. Again, we observe that developments which have become a regular (ie non-crisis) characteristic of European integration in general are resorted to more frequently and/or more daringly in times of crisis.

Apart from the formal aspects of EU rule-making which may have changed in reaction to crises, the substance of rules has also changed. It is part and parcel of European integration that existing rules are, over time, revised and adapted to new circumstances. This process continues and even accelerates in times of crises. The main rules adopted in selected policy fields in reaction to crises were presented and discussed in the previous chapters. What ought to be reiterated now are the paradigm changes which some of these reforms represent. One of these paradigm changes is the increasing readiness, across different policy fields, to raise financial means at EU level and distribute them to Member States. There was a time when the opponents of what was called a 'transfer union' dominated political discussions. Today this group of Member States, with Germany still at its spearhead, remains powerful, but the factual necessities of crises have gradually mitigated and nuanced its resistance. The so-called 'umbrellas', set up in reaction to the euro-area crisis, were measures to preserve the stability of the euro area, with the ESM eventually being established as a permanent facility. Subject to geographical, financial, and conditionality-related restrictions, these mechanisms have had a strong thrust towards austerity, and, in remembrance of the painful reforms which were demanded from—some would say imposed on—the beneficiary Member States in exchange for the necessary financial support, nowadays suffer from a bad press. This bad reputation, in conjunction with the stigma attached to being an ESM beneficiary, is one of the reasons why euro-area Member States refused the ESM support offered during the pandemic.[8]

From a legal perspective, the clarification the Court provided with regard to Article 125 TFEU and, to some extent, also with regard to Article 122 TFEU, was a most important long-term effect of the euro-area crisis. The *Pringle* judgment opened a new door and allowed the Member States to move on. In the subsequent years, a number of attempts to pool money at the EU level for a more general purpose failed for political reasons. It was the pandemic which gave the discussion new swing. The RRF, apart from reforming cohesion policy,[9] has further paved the way for the idea of raising money (or other resources) at EU level at a considerable scale. Without intending to neglect the idiosyncrasies of each of these measures, a line can be drawn, at a very abstract level of capacity-building, from the umbrellas set up in reaction to the euro-area crisis (European Financial Stabilisation Mechanism, European Financial Stability Facility, ESM) to the Single Resolution Fund, SURE, the RRF, rescEU4health, the EPF,

[8] See Gabriele de Angelis, 'A New Role for the European Stability Mechanism in Post-COVID-19 EMU? Explaining the Failure of the Pandemic Crisis Support and Assessing Ways Forward' (2022) 51 International Journal of Political Economy 18, 26 f.

[9] See, eg Robin Huguenot-Noël, '"Cash for Reforms" in the EU after the RRF: Can Cohesion Benefit?' (Final Report, August 2023) <https://ec.europa.eu/regional_policy/sources/policy/how/future-cohesion-policy/Expertpaper_Huguenot.pdf> accessed 29 February 2024.

the EDF, etc. That the desire for further capacity-building at EU level has not yet been satisfied is proven, inter alia, by numerous proposals as to how to move on after the RRF has been exhausted,[10] and by calls for a common capacity related to the capital markets union.[11] The debate is embedded in the more general discussion on which new financial sources the EU could tap.[12]

At the same time, conditionality has, in the past decades, gained ground as a new mode of rule-making with still considerable potential. Known already prior to the crises at issue here, for example from agreements the EU concluded with third countries, or from structural fund policies, it has been refined and extended to numerous policy fields (eg rule of law and, through CSRs, to many further areas) in the past fifteen years.[13] It may also serve as an example for political learning effects. Whereas conditionality in the context of financial support for ailing euro-area Member States during the euro-area crisis resembled an imposition of reforms focused on austerity, RRF support is conditional upon reforms proposed by the respective Member States which should, to some extent at least, promote 'greening' and digitalization. This comparison illustrates the new approach taken by the EU: from 'money in exchange for strict and imposed reforms' to 'money to support largely self-chosen reforms and investments'. This is not to deny, however, that conditionality may work differently in other cases, for example rule of law cases. A variant of this conditionality may be seen in the Commission's detailed and generally applicable regulatory frameworks adopted in state aid policy. While it is the Member States' funds which are at issue, the Commission—as already stated—indicates under which conditions the granting of state aid will be approved, thereby going beyond a mere competition policy perspective, but involving considerations of energy security, financial stability, or environmental protection.

Paradigm changes do not always occur like the beat of a drum, but may also be perceptible in the course of time. In this vein, solidarity—a notion which had already been prominently addressed in the Schuman Declaration—seems to have come to the fore as a result of various crises. Used rarely and disparately in primary law, the notion has become more prevalent, for example, in health policy, migration policy, and energy policy, but also in foreign and defence policy, and has even received recognition

[10] See, eg Michele Chang, 'Euro Area Fiscal Policies and Capacity in Post-pandemic Times' (EP Study, 2021) 31–33; Philipp Heimberger and Andreas Lichtenberger, 'RRF 2.0: A Permanent EU Investment Fund in the Context of the Energy Crisis, Climate Change and EU Fiscal Rules', Policy Notes and Reports No 63, The Vienna Institute for International Economic Studies (wiiw), 2023.

[11] See János Allenbach-Ammann, 'ECB-Panetta: Capital Markets Union might require EU fiscal capacity' (2023) Euractiv <https://www.euractiv.com/section/economy-jobs/news/ecb-panetta-capital-markets-union-might-require-eu-fiscal-capacity/> accessed 29 February 2024.

[12] For the Commission's proposals, see 'Questions and Answers: Commission proposes to reinforce long-term EU budget to face most urgent challenges' (2023) <https://ec.europa.eu/commission/presscorner/detail/en/qanda_23_3346> accessed 29 February 2024.

[13] The broad material ambit of conditionality, notably under the RRF, provides the EU with a means to discipline Member States in a way which has so far been available only in the pre-accession phase, ie in the relationship between the EU and its (potential) candidate countries; see also Antonia Baraggia and Matteo Bonelli, 'Linking Money to Values: The New Rule of Law Conditionality Regulation and its Constitutional Challenges' (2022) 23 German Law Journal 131, in particular 142.

by the Court as a principle which 'underpins the entire legal system of the European Union'.[14]

Similarly, the recalibration of the public–private divide in terms of gathering financial resources seems to be a phenomenon which can be found in different policy fields.[15] It finds its most explicit expression in the creation of the Single Resolution Fund, representing a renunciation of the practice of using taxpayers' money (ie public funds) to save ailing (and mostly private) banks, and in discussions on the further development of deposit guarantee schemes or the creation of new industry-funded safeguard measures.[16] It is also apparent in the critique of state aid more generally, which has become more pronounced in the recent years of polycrisis. This critique points at the different spending power of Member States, leading to 'subsidy races' among unequal competitors and the risk for cohesion across Member States this imbalance poses. Thus, the discussion also has a solidarity dimension. The Commission's attempts to contain subsidy races through its regulatory frameworks have been only partially successful. The calls for the creation of (general or policy-specific) fiscal capacities at the EU level—a different, although related, topic– are also fed by this debate, as already highlighted.

A recalibration can also be observed in the following case: in order to facilitate energy production from renewable sources in the short term (the purpose of which has an energy security but also a climate neutrality prong), opposing environmental commitments (as laid down in particular in the Birds and Habitat Directives) have been suspended by EU legislation. While this is supposed to be an only temporary recalibration of different policy objectives, it also drastically exemplifies the general tendency: to aim at climate neutrality (as one of the objectives of this measure) while neglecting other, seemingly less pressing, problems of environmental protection.

In other areas, the political paradigm change the respective crisis called for did not meet with success; likewise a number of ambitious proposals (mostly launched by the Commission) more generally.

A recurring observation was that EU actors succeeded in increasing the coherence between different but still interrelated policy fields—a quest which, in general, can be based on Article 7 TFEU, and apparently a more general (intended) effect of rule-making in crises. One example is the ECB's recurring unconventional monetary policy measures. First used in reaction to the euro-area crisis, these have now become an established, though still contested, means of ensuring price stability as well as the stability of the euro area and financial stability (two further objectives which, according to the ECB, are astrongly related to the objective of price stability). The eligibility criteria for

[14] Case C–848/19P *Federal Republic of Germany v European Commission* ECLI:EU:C:2021:598, para 41; see also Carl Fredrik Bergström, 'EU Rulemaking in Response to Crisis: The Emergence of the Principle of Energy Solidarity and its Use' (2023) 6 Nordic Journal of European Law 100, 106–08.

[15] This is neither co-regulation nor self-regulation, which are already well-established forms of involving private actors in rule-making, including at the EU level, but could be described as (financial) self-responsibility, as requested and organized by EU legislative/executive actors; for the phenomena of co-regulation and self-regulation, see Adrienne Héritier and Sandra Eckert, 'New Modes of Governance in the Shadow of Hierarchy: Self-regulation by Industry in Europe' (2008) 28 Journal of Public Policy 113.

[16] Judith Arnal, Karel Lannoo and Rosa Lastra, 'Is CMDI what the Banking Union Needs?' (CEPS Policy Brief, 2024).

the acquisition of state bonds, for example, strongly link monetary policy to economic policy which itself has become increasingly broad and also more coherent (note, for example, the CSRs or the new focus on macroeconomic policy) conception of economic policy—of which the CSRs. This increases the effectiveness of EMU and contributes to the consistency of the unequal (policy) sisters enshrined in this policy field.

An increased degree of coherence across policy fields has also been achieved with regard to the EU's external action in its response to Russia's attack on Ukraine, which also signalled an increasingly geopolitical approach in external action, and in particular in CFSP. This is not to say that the EU ignored geopolitical considerations prior to the war in Ukraine, but the geopolitical thrust of its actions has become stronger since the beginning of the war. Unsurprisingly, in view of the strong dependence of some EU Member States on fossil energy from Russia—a problem which, for example, the Commission had pointed to long before the war[17]—an increasing sense of geopolitical and geoeconomic interrelations has also characterized the EU's energy policy since Russia's annexation of Crimea, and even more so since February 2022.

A particular case of coherence has been promoted by the climate crisis. The mitigation of climate change—due to its importance for all facets of life, and ultimately to human existence—has become an objective which is, of course by different means and to very different degrees, pursued not only in environmental policy, but also, for example, in economic policy, state aid policy, and energy policy.[18] This *viribus unitis* fight against climate change, which is sloppily referred to as 'climate mainstreaming', may also contribute to an increased coherence across policy fields.

9.4 Conclusions

At the beginning of this century, Olsen stated that 'Europe is still in a period of transition. The continent is moving towards a new form of political organization and it is experimenting with the procedures by which the political order itself is to be changed.'[19] At that time, the EU had just passed through one and a half decades of repeated Treaty change. It was expecting accession by a two-digit number of states, most of which had earlier belonged to Europe's 'Eastern bloc'. The one comprehensive Treaty change which followed was a difficult birth which resulted in the entry into force of the Treaty of Lisbon in 2009, when the EU, like the rest of the world, was struggling with the first of a series of crises which would determine EU rule-making in the years to come. Now, one and a half decades after the entry into force of the last reform Treaty, this period of transition seems to be over. The EU and its Member States have got accustomed to the new reality in which achieving political agreement on incisive reforms in the (European) Council is exceedingly difficult, and a Treaty change virtually unthinkable.

[17] Commission, 'An Energy Policy for Europe' (Communication), COM (2007) 1 final, 4.
[18] See also art 11 TFEU.
[19] Johan P Olsen, 'The Many Faces of Europeanization' (2002) 40 Journal of Common Market Studies 921, 944.

These actors had to find other ways to eventually adopt the reforms which they—or at least the necessary majority of them—deemed vital. The crises addressed in this book have facilitated this adjustment.

With 'integration by stealth' or 'covert integration', to name just two examples, scholarship has established concepts to grasp these multifaceted implicit forms of broadening the scope of EU action, which were observed long before the multi-crisis period at issue here.[20] The EU's regulatory responses to various crises differ both in quality and quantity, in particular if perceived across different policy fields. One and a half decades have seen a number of innovative measures without a single (comprehensive) Treaty reform. Some of these measures represent adaptation; that is, the adjustment to specific circumstances for a limited period of time. To this group belong, for example, the suspension of EU rules on Member States' fiscal discipline during the pandemic, and the prioritization of renewable energy over other environmental policy objectives. Other measures brought about fundamental and permanent change as compared with the *status quo ante*. This is true, for instance, for the different fiscal capacities at the EU level which were established in various policy fields, and—as a separate phenomenon which is, however, often linked with fiscal capacities—for the new forms of conditionality by means of which the EU is granted a considerable influence on policy decisions at the Member State level. It is also true for the EU's response to Russia's attack against Ukraine, which contributed greatly to the emergence of the EU (not single Member States) as a global power in foreign and security policy, in a 'world [that is] no longer *Eurocentric*'[21]—even if, so far, only with regard to sanctions. Again, other measures were envisaged as short-term measures in a state of acute crisis, but—as collateral effect—they contributed to breaking a taboo and thus paved the way for much more far-reaching reforms. Such a 'dwarf in size, but a giant in shifting a paradigm' was the short-term measure SURE, which contributed to paving the way, in particular, for NGEU.[22]

Do crises which were overcome culminate in learning effects, meaning that the regulatory responses to one crisis may serve as a legacy which is—in an adapted form—reapplied in subsequent crises, perhaps, over time, establishing a permanent kit of EU crisis management tools? First of all, it appears that during crises affecting numerous or even all Member States, their governments display a greater willingness to act together at the EU level in cooperation with the Commission and the EP. When comparing the EU's responses to various crises across policy fields, both parallels and discontinuity in the EU's crisis management are visible. In general, however, it seems that regular

[20] See Giandomenico Majone, *Dilemmas of European Integration: The Ambiguities and Pitfalls of Integration by Stealth* (OUP 2005); Adrienne Héritier, 'Covert Integration in the European Union' in Jeremy Richardson and Sonia Mazey (eds), *European Union: Power and Policy-making* (4th edn, Routledge 2015) 351.

[21] Enrico Letta, 'The European Union as a Global Power?' in Helen Wallace, Nikos Koutsiaras and George Pagoulatos (eds), *Europe's Transformations: Essays in Honour of Loukas Tsoukalis* (OUP 2021) 228 (emphasis added).

[22] See René Repasi, 'A Dwarf in Size, but a Giant in Shifting a Paradigm – The European Instrument for Temporary Support to Mitigate Unemployment Risks (SURE)' (2020) EU Law Live <https://eulawlive.com/long-read-a-dwarf-in-size-but-a-giant-in-shifting-a-paradigm-the-european-instrument-for-temporary-support-to-mitigate-unemployment-risks-sure-by-rene-repasi/#> accessed 29 February 2024.

'non-crisis' tools are simply used more frequently or in a more nuanced way. This may include, as we have seen, legislative breakthroughs which politically would not have been possible earlier. Where the Treaties contain provisions applicable (only) in crisis situations—for example, Article 78(3), Article 107(2)(b), or Article 122 TFEU—they are additionally applied. Article 352 TFEU, the so-called flexibility clause, has been used much less often after the entry into force of the Treaty of Lisbon—which broadened the room for EU activity—than before.[23] Even in the context of EU responses to crises, rather limited use was made of Article 352 TFEU. The potential for uniformity of EU rule-making tools across different policy fields—a phenomenon we referred to as 'cross-fertilization potential' in Chapter 1—has been increased significantly by the combination of EU fiscal capacities and a conditionality mechanism reaching into various fields of (national) policy. This combination allows the EU to evade restrictive competence regimes. In our view, this is one of the rule-making tools which, even if not entirely without precedent in non-crisis times, has most strongly developed during the crises of the past years.

Our assumption is that the importance of using money as a lever in the implementation of EU law will continue to increase in importance.[24] There is strong and authoritative opposition among the Member States against an EU fiscal capacity with as general a scope as the RRF, it is true, but as this tool has been applied and tested repeatedly by now, it is impossible to ban it from debates on reforms: 'die ich rief, die Geister, werd' ich nun nicht los'.[25] Even if there may be no new capacity which, in terms of size and scope, is comparable to the RRF, there may be smaller funds applying essentially the same rule-making technique. The outstanding decision on how the EU should pay back its RRF-related debt (once it is due) will be one more opportunity for Member States to discuss this issue more broadly.

[23] See, eg Walter Frenz, 'Art. 352 AEUV' in Matthias Pechstein, Carsten Nowak and Ulrich Häde (eds), *Frankfurter Kommentar zu EUV, GRC und AEUV* (2nd edn, Mohr Siebeck 2023) para 2.

[24] See, eg Fabian Amtenbrink and Menelaos Markakis, 'Never Waste a Good Crisis: On the Emergence of an EU Fiscal Capacity' in Alicia Hinarejos and Robert Schütze (eds), *EU Fiscal Federalism: Past, Present, Future* (OUP 2023) 171.

[25] This famous passage of Goethe's *Zauberlehrling (The Sorcerer's Apprentice)* we would (prosaically) translate as follows: 'I cannot get rid of (nor control) the spirits I have cited.'

Even the negative form of this tool has been tested: financial contributions from Member States in exchange for non-compliance with certain rules of EU law; see Chapter 7 on migration policy.

Index

For the benefit of digital users, indexed terms that span two pages (e.g., 52–53) may, on occasion, appear on only one of those pages.